RELIGION, DHARMA AND POLITY

About the Editor

Rakesh Kumar Jha is a senior faculty member of the Department of Political Science, University of Rajasthan, Jaipur, India. Since joining the Department in 1989, he has been actively engaged in teaching and research work. He is teaching Gandhian thought at postgraduate and M.Phil. level. He has to his credit dozens of articles published in journals of national and international repute. He is a member of the Editorial Board of *Political Science Review*, a research journal published by the Department. He had also been a member of the Editorial Board of *Rajya Shastra Samiksha* and *Rajasthan Journal of Political Science*, research journals of the Department and the Rajasthan Political Science Association respectively. Besides this, he has also authored two books titled *Gandhiya Chintan mein Sarvodaya* and *Prachin Bhartiya Chintan mein Prashasnik Niyantran ka Swarup*. He has presented a number of research papers at different national and international seminars. He has also organized some national seminars. At present he is engaged in the study of the problem of terrorism and Naxalism.

More than a dozen research scholars have been awarded the degree of Ph.D. under his supervision. Also he has guided many M.A. and M.Phil. students in writing their dissertations. He is on the panel of experts in different universities.

Religion, Dharma and Polity

Edited by

Rakesh Kumar Jha

CONCEPT PUBLISHING COMPANY PVT. LTD.
NEW DELHI-110 059

ISBN-13 : 978-81-8069-860-6

First Published 2012

Published and Printed by

Concept
Since 1974

Concept Publishing Company Pvt. Ltd.
A/15-16, Commercial Block, Mohan Garden
New Delhi-110059 (India)
T: 25351460, 25351794, *F*: 091-11-25357109
E: publishing@conceptpub.com *W*: www.conceptpub.com
Editorial Office: H-13, Bali Nagar, New Delhi-110 015, India.

Cataloging in Publication Data--*Courtesy:* D.K. Agencies (P) Ltd. <docinfo@dkagencies.com>

Religion, dharma and polity / edited by Rakesh Kumar Jha.
p. cm.
Contributed articles.
Includes bibliographical references and index.
ISBN 9788180698606

1. Political science---Philosophy. 2. Dharma. 3. Hindu law. 4. Religion and politics—India. 5. India—Politics and government—20th century. I. Jha,Rakesla Kumara.

DDC 201.72 23

Commemorative volume in the memory of the

Late Professor D.B. Mathur

Retired Professor and Head

Department of Political Science

and

Coordinator SAP

and

Former Director,

Centre for Gandhian Studies

University of Rajasthan, Jaipur

and

Former President,

Rajasthan Political Science Association

Acknowledgements

It is my immense pleasure and privilege to edit the commemorative volume in the memory of late Professor D.B. Mathur, the teacher in true sense and a devout man. I have chosen this topic to be discussed because Professor Mathur had been an expert in Indian Political Thought and had severe concern about the misconception of the concept of Religion and Dharma and their role in Politics. The distinguished contributors to the volume correspond to an extensive continuum of specialization and empathetic concentration. To bring together such eminent contributors was a rewarding experience. It was made possible because of the fraternity of Professor Mathur. First of all, I would like to give my heartiest thanks to all the eminent contributors of this volume because it would not have been possible without their valued cooperation. I feel privileged by incorporating their articles in this volume.

I am deeply indebted to Professor Ramashray Roy, eminent political theorist and former Director, Centre for the Developing Societies, Delhi, former Director, Indian Council of Social Science and Research (I.C.S.S.R.), New Delhi, for his superb guidance, valuable suggestions, constant inspiration and encouragement which culminated in the completion of the present work.

My sincere gratitude is to my elder brother, Sh. Mihir Kumar Jha for his constant encouragement in my academic work. My affectionate appreciation is also due to my son Saket Kumar Jha and daughter Aditi Jha, for their ever encouraging presence and without whose willing cooperation and support this volume would not have been published.

I am thankful to all my teachers, colleagues and friends for extending help and cooperation in completion of this collection. Last but not the least, I am thankful to Mr. A.K. Mittal, of Concept Publishing Company (P) Ltd., New Delhi, for the aesthetic printing of the present volume.

Date: 1-1-2012 **Rakesh Kumar Jha**

Introduction

Indian political thought is deeply embedded in the understanding of the reliability of the both mundane and ultra-mundane. Instead of their hierarchical placement, the intrinsic potential of their harmonization is highlighted for enriching of integral meaning of life. The acquired knowledge of balancing commitment and harmony between the mundane and ultra-mundane is well defined. This explains, for instance, the necessity of upholding and living up to the objective of *dharma, arth* and *kama* for attaining *moksha*. Each of these imperatives has often been misinterpreted to suggest an alleged self-contained role. The persistent motto of *Dharma* is to act as the guiding and binding force regulating individual, social, systemic and relational obligations and duties. *Dharma* is the essence of self-regulatory and self-elevating thinking, expression, action and existence. Confusion often arises due to equating *dharma* and religion (*panth*). Mistaken interpretation of both has led to the confusion of *dharma and religion* (*panth*).

The initial stages of Indian thought clearly upheld universal categories of *Dharma* equated with duty, compassion, honesty, moral grounds and dominance of blemishless values, awakened perception and eminent wisdom of holism of existence. This is in contradiction with religion (*panth*) which abounds in scriptural determination, appropriately organized and institutionalized faith system, hierarchy, monasticism, rituals and ceremony, confusion of theology and legends, orthodoxy of denominationalism and pretense of artificial images of life in future and deliverance. Religion (*panth*) is incompetent conformism and firmness of devotion. It leads to variety of Theo-fascistic tendencies. As a result, the confused plurality of religion is a rejection of tolerance, curiosity and the right to question and to enquire. Religion damages the autonomy to leading to firmness and fanatic loyalty. This leads to exacerbated conflict-ridden and aggressive attitude of self-proclaimed denominational superiority. *Dharma,* on the other hand, is different from theism, skepticism and it is a mission for universal civilized social survival, disregarding multiple idioms of power-fixations intrinsic to religion. The ideal of political thought in India is to uphold *Dharma* and defy *Panth.*

The major demarcation between *Dharma* and *Panth* has enabled political thought in India to distinguish mundane and ultra-mundane issues in terms of symbolic validity. The mundane, interpreted as a 'reality', calls for inspiring qualitative contented life by looking for positive and humanitarian interpersonal alternatives. Resolution of problems, challenges and controversial issues are required to conformity with *Dharma.* Theoretical and artistic contributions decisive of perceptions and activism are restricted by *Dharma.* The dominance of *Dharma* aims at to ordering matters mundane and ultra-mundane, preventing conflictual evaluation there of and accepting the autonomy of expected reassessments of the credential of both. The important contribution of Indian thought to the world is the essentiality of *Dharma.* This has been helpful in regulating and ordering the whole of life, ideas and relational ambience.

Indian thought also altered the sense of the ultra-mundane as sign of the 'ideal' consolidating into 'autonomy' to re-examine the apparent, and searching potential of expanding efficiency of the 'established'. *Dharma,* once again, enlivened the recognition of the trustworthy and the genuine without being swept away by rude egotism. No validity was granted to religious society as the basic unit of the social order. This idea is completely unfamiliar to Western experience, for long plagued by rival determination of both, sacerdotal and the temporal. Due to non-appearance of an imperative, as comprehensive as that of *Dharma,* western worldview continues to be unilinear and connected in fine stereotypes and therefore, does not evoke faith.

Critical role of the individual for maintaining harmony buttressed by the feeling of brotherhood in society is a unique thrust of the tradition of Indian thought. Worry of dignity, self-sufficiency and progressive perfectibility of individual's potential identify the meaning, purpose and essence of existence. The essence of *Dharma* contradicts assertive mandates and imperatives of accumulated experience and wisdom constitute regulatory instrumentalities. The individual, is therefore, recognized as the ethical expression of diverse nucleus of civil society. Hence, the determinants of *Dharma* supplement corresponding values to individual and society.

The Indian tradition justifies the illustrious identity of the 'political' and the 'secular' as mechanism of the ethical and the humane restricted by the priorities of *Dharma*. Scriptural enunciations, epics and philosophical treatises emphatically state the reliability of the 'politics' and the 'political' as absolute essentials inherent to *Dharma*. In contrast, contemporary statements are exhortations of power, decision-making, restricted and the like and interpret ethical and moral determinates, at best, as secondary. In the Indian thought, the identity, existence and provisions of the state is approved with the crucial difference that was neither conceived in segregation as personification of dictatorship nor detached from social liability, but fundamentally and permanently as yet another reappearance of *Dharma* in deed. This ensured transparency of relational decorum between the ruler and the ruled. The exchange between politics and virtue becomes prominent, curving from essential impactiveness of *Dharma*. Later, certainly, as the benign regulatory, position of *Dharma* got diluted, 'politics' relapsed into unpredictable change of materialistic concerns, compounded by the erosion of duty, decent behaviour, moral and humane relationship.

In the medieval period of Indian thought religion (*panth*) replaced essentials of *Dharma* as circumstance and procedures sought to legitimize political effort as alternative recourse to the priestly and the spiritual dejecting the moral essential of *Dharma*, duty, sympathy and humanity. State sovereignty, law governing institutions and procedures were flooded by dictatorial inclination concealed as 'rulers' goodwill and concern for the 'good' of the governed. The mission to damage the virtues of *Dharma* has succeeded by irresistible partiality for political supremacy. By such disparate tendencies, the tradition of Indian political thought was prejudiced.

The ongoing rivalry between *Dharma* as the summum bonum, the good and the humane and alternative priestly and the religious supremacy in the name of the divine, come out as the variation of priorities, resulting in the conversion of the medieval and the materialization of modern perspectives. Certainly, concern about nationalism became most important powerhouse of thought and action in India. There was extensively supported western analysis of nationalism in terms of territorial, ethnic, racial and autonomous in combination with material and profit-making aspirations, culminating to violent inconsistencies, hostility and aggression. Nationalism in the West develops gradually as antecedent of the organization of power and aggressive commitment to exaggerated sense of security of interest and honour. National pride which became the flag bearer of the march of history in the West was entirely devoted to declaration of goals of the pursuit political power. In contrast, political intimation and premises in India sought to reassert the priority of the eminent goals of freedom of the individual and collective cohesiveness. The clarion call in India was revival of higher virtues of decency and humanitarian concerns. This was a prerequisite exert to cancel out the mobocracy beneath in violent and materialistic nationalism. Indian thought does not emphasize the elevation of nationalism as the image of the all powerful state, but underlines humanizing conversion of nationalism by critical evaluation of the social authenticity and of what had taken roots as well thought-out trust and established practices.

The purpose of this collection is to underscore that tradition forms the framework of political thought in India. Its evidences continuity and change, adaptive of new situations and search for unending potentialities for sustaining purposive sovereignty. Indifferent and unresponsive thinking in intellectual analyses and indifference to even minor impartiality of appreciation of diverse aspects of human achievement deceive self-satisfied distinctiveness of colonial mind-set and stereotypes. This needs to be resolved.

In this volume, eminent scholars have contributed to the resolution of the above-discussed dilemma. Ramashray Roy, in his article entitled, "*Purshartha* and its Contemporary Relevance" explains, that it is clear that when the soul of the individual gets attuned to the divine ground of being he seeks identity with it to be actively engaged in such an endeavour, for his salvation, *moksha*. In addition, it is *moksha,* again, that enables one to acquire a *dharmic* perspective. He argues that the pursuit *kama* and *artha* can be beneficial on it when is subjected to the rule of *dharma*.

It is against this background that we can appreciate the significance of the Sanskrit saying *'yamadhikritya purushah pravartate'*, that is, all duties emanating from the man's relationship with the divine deep in his being and the phenomenal world in accordance with the principles derived from this relationship go into the definition of what *purusharthas* are. And is not only regulating appropriate but also essential for a person to perform all the duties, understood as *purusharthas,* involved with this two-fold relationship. Without the performance of all the *purusharthas,* the crisis of modern civilization will persist.

B.N. Pande in his paper entitled "Quest for Synthesis in Indian Religious and Cultural Tradition" argues that all the great living religions are of Asiatic origin. The personal, domestic and social life of the Hindu is largely governed by the rules of what he considers as his religion. So is that of the Muslims, so of the Jew, so was, and to a considerable extent still is that of Christians belonging to the Roman Catholic form of Christianity. Such also is the case with followers of other religions, known as the Zoroastrian, the Buddhist, the Jain, and the Sikh. The study of all these religions makes it clear that there is a basic similarity not only in the form but also in the essence. The essential is that truth is universal and not the monopoly of any race or teacher, while non-essentials vary with time, place and circumstances. The same fundamental truths have been revealed in different scriptures, in different languages through different persons in different nations. *Ekam sadviprah vahudha vadanti.*

Ramjee Singh in his article entitled "Indian Fundamentalism and Its Way Out" clearly mentions that religion is not an 'ism', not a bundle of creeds, beliefs, rites and rituals but, it is the inner nature of man and our whole life. It is that which holds together or upholds the integrity of individual, of society, of cosmos. It is useless to give a particular label like Hindu, Muslim or Christian. It is "Eternal" (*Sanatan*) and "Universal"; it is "Ethical" and "Spiritual".

Sureshwar Jha in his article entitled "The Political Thought of Yājñavalkya" concludes that *Yājñavalkya's* intelligence and originality lie in social and legal spheres as a social reformer, lawgiver and jurist. He is consistently progressive, and a true revolutionary. Even the present-day society in Mithila in particular and the whole country in general is based, by and large, on the structure of legal and ethical rules and political obligations, designed and framed by Yājñavalkya.

P.D. Kaushik in his paper "Kautilya on Dharma and Politics: A Study of Arthashastra" analyses that Kautilya was well-versed in *Dharmashastras*, but he was a political thinker who wrote about Dharma only as far as it was relevant to his concept of state. He talks of *Rajdharma* and enjoins upon the king to uphold *Dharma* and social order. He approves Brahmanical mode of life in so far as it is in consonance with maintenance of *Varnashrama dharma* but rejects religious practices which come in the way of the expansion of state. He performs a distinct service to the cause of the political theory by excluding priests from organs of the state. He not only separates political thinking from *Dharmashastra* but also gives a badly wanted corrective to other worldly bias of Indian temperament and character. Kautilya for the first time gave *Arthashastra* an exalted position in the realm of political literature in ancient India and to that extent he may be credited with raising it to an independent status.

Ram Singh Solanki in his paper of V.D. Savarkar "Concept of Hindutva and Indian Nationalism" argues that the concept of Hindutva is the child of Savarkar's keen and original mind. He explains in detail that Savarkar saw that Hindutva is one which has kept India united through the ages. He was ready to accept Mohammedans as Hindus if they proclaimed their commitment to their fatherland that is India and its cultural heritage.

Mahesh Chandra Sharma in his article entitled, *"Dharma,* Religious Denomination and Politics: Reflection of Pt. Deen Dayal Upadhayaya" notes that Upadhyaya argued that the mediaeval Western history made 'Dharma' synonymous with "sect" in place of a set rule. Upadhayaya was of the opinion that it would be an error to punish *"dharma tatva"* as a punishment of this mediaeval culpability. Therefore, he accepts *Dharma* in its original form and refuses to accept it as sect as the translation of "Dharma". For worldly and heavenly advancement of life, today man has developed the concepts of "science", "constitutionalism" and "spiritualism". Upadhyaya considers 'Dharma' with these concepts, but he deems incorrect the desire to live by snapping relations to include these "concepts". He considers unnatural and a firm reaction. Perhaps this is the reason that he refused to support modern "scientists", "constitutionalists" and "spiritualists" for their acts to equate "Dharma" with "sect". However, he staunchly believes in providing a secular form to "Dharma". He does not support the idea of Dharma according to which entrance of a *Harijan* to the "Vishwanath temple" leads to loss of *Dharma*. Upadhyaya says: "*Dharma* has no relation with temple or mosque. Offering prayers may be a component of human-*Dharma*, but *Dharma* is broad. Temples and mosques also have been the effective medium of the teaching of *'dharmacharan'*, the conduct according to *Dharma*, as if we can say that a school is not 'learning', likewise a temple is different from *Dharma*". He defines it like this: "*Dharma* means conception. The components which are responsible for the concept of a thing, person or nature are known as 'Dharma'. For example, the *Dharma* of fire is heat."

K.S. Saxena in his paper entitled, "Glimpses of Swami Dayanand Saraswati" analyses Swami Dayanand's teachings which produced a sense of pride for Vedic religion, Vedic language and other old institutional ideas and values of our country. The effect of his teachings was that people became conscious of their great religion and social heritage and this was one of the most potent factors in the general awakening of the Princes and people in India. Moreover, the Arya Samaj movement opened the way for the people to think about their political rights and establishing various institutions which created conditions favourable to the successful development of revolutionary movements in India. Thus Swami Dayanand Saraswati and the Arya Samaj movement played an important role at a time when there was no ray of hope, and the morals of the people had declined considerably. In fact, Swamiji gave confidence to the people and the politically conscious about their rights and duties. Swami Dayanand wrote, "What can you expect but misery and poverty when the people of a country trade only among themselves, whilst foreigners through their international trade rule over them!" Thus the most important contribution of Swamiji was that he gave a feeling of self-respect to the citizens of the country because they traded among themselves whilst foreigners did it through their international trade ruled over them!"

Adi H. Doctor in his article entitled, "Roy's Religious Modernism, Social Reform and Political Liberalism" argues that Roy accepted religion as the basis of society but after removing it from orthodoxy and dogma. While preaching *Advaita* as the true Hinduism, Ram Mohan's religious liberalism would not permit him to claim anyone religion alone as true. He was enchanted by the writings of the Sufi Muslim philosophers whose views tallied with the Vedantic school. He admired Christ as the greatest humanist born ever. Roy's whole life was dedicated to interpreting religion, rationally and morally. This explains his rejection of many things in many religions. Roy was essentially a theist who prized above all being a moralist and a rationalist.

Rammohan claimed that since society and religion are very closely related, religious modernism must precede social reform. According to him, the motivation for religious modernism was the political advantage and social comfort it would bring into the lives of the people. He argued that such Hindu customs as idolatry, subjection of women, *sati* and caste destroyed the texture of Hindu society and led to immoral practices like the Kali and Krishna cults. He condemns the degeneration of the worship of Kali to senseless animal sacrifice, accompanied by drinking of wine.

Radha Krishan in the paper entitled "Gopal Krishan Gokhale's Spirituazation of Politics" explains that Gokhale agreed that without morality, there is no politics as Leo Strauss described "A value free politics is impossible". He agreed that service of the nation is service of God as Gandhi agreed that service of lowest man is service of God. Everybody should be ready to sacrifice all things in the interest of the nation without any attachment. To achieve this ideal, he organized *BHARAT SEWAK SAMAJ* which was meant to inculcate moral values in the human society.

The political ideas of Gokhale are based on moral and spiritual consciousness. Similarly, his personal and public life is based on moral dimension. According to Gokhale ends and means are based on cause and effect theory. Goodness of means is contributed to goodness of ends. Respect for means is the respect for ends. Gokhale's conception of the relation between means and ends is based on morality. Gokhale was one of the thinkers who emphasized the importance of means as prior to ends and building of high moral character in India. He did not believe in machiavellism. He was not in favour of the view that every deed whether moral or immoral is correct in game of politics. His whole life was dedicated to truth and morality. His politics was not driven by the purpose of getting *SATTA* and *SHAKTI* but *SEWA DHARAMA*, because Gokhale never approved the concept that everything is fair in politics. He tried to develop a type of politics which must be based on, morality and high moral character, sacrifice and purity of ends and means.

Rudranand Jha in his article entitled, "M.G. Ranade: Apostle of Indian Freedom" describes Ranade's political ideas. He treats him as creator of modern *Smriti* for our social life and there can be no difference of opinion in calling him the Parasar of modern India. Ranade said that Manu was for *Satyug*, Gautam for *Treta* and Sankhya and Likhit for *Dwapar*, whereas Parasar Smriti should be deserved for *Kaliyug* only. Manu was rigid in the imposition of *varnashram* system on the fabric of Indian social life, whereas Parasar relaxed the compulsion of *varnashram* system and advocated a change in the prevailing social system. Like Parasar, Ranade stood for a revolutionary change in our outlook which became the percept for the struggle for Indian independence.

M.R. Kazimi in his paper entitled, "The Political Philosophy of Bal Gangadhar Tilak: An Analysis of Religious Concepts and Symbols used Therein" notes that Tilak felt that the roots of nationalism must not be merely an intellectual appeal but must rest on sentiments and emotions of the people. His sole intention was to arouse nationalist sentiment by recalling past glories. He was a harbinger of new nationalism in India which was deeply rooted in the soil of the land; he was evidently religious and his ideas seem to be revivalist but are liberal in fact and secular in content. He used religious idioms to spread a message which aimed at nationalism befitting in a secular setting. Religion, if correctly understood, could be an element in nationality. Dogmatism and fanaticism did not find a place in the political philosophy of Bal Gangadhar Tilak. Tilak emphasized the fact that common people pay attention to and understand the message if it is couched in religious idioms. Religious sentiments continue to be strong in India. The Hindus and the Muslims sail in the same boat in this regard. It remained so in the days of Tilak and remains even today; religious symbols are the principal means of communicating with the common message. Today, religious sentiments are aroused to serve a narrow and parochial cause. The case was different with Tilak. He aimed at something much higher. If Tilak was responsible for the revival of Ganpati festival, which gave the message of nationalism to masses, he promised all support to the Khilafat Movement if the majority of Muslims supported it. Tilak wanted reintroduction of national festivals because, in his view, nationalism is a kind of sentiment and the historical memories of the great figures of a country play a part in restrengthening and refreshing that sentiment. Shivaji was the symbol of that resistance and resentment of the people against oppression and injustice.

Asha Kaushik and S.N. Kaushik in their article "Religion as a Political Ideology: the Separatist Crusade of Jinnah" described that, prior to the 1937 election, Mohammad Ali Jinnah did not believe in the sanctity of religion-based nationalism and the philosophy of 'two-nation' theory. He adhered to the constitutional approach to solve the political problem of the Muslim minority. However, 1937 election destroyed the foundation upon which Jinnah had built his strategy ever since his return to India from England in 1934. A shrewd tactician that he was, Jinnah launched a tirade against the Congress, and put forth a grossly exaggerated apprehension of the impending dangers for Muslims and Islam through the imposition of the so-called 'Fascist Hindu Raj' under the leadership of the Congress. Thus, in the post-1937 phase, Jinnah became the messiah of the movement for separate homeland for the Muslims of the subcontinent. Asgar Ali Engineer rightly commented that India got divided not because Hinduism and Islam were incompatible, they never were—but because the elites of two communities could not successfully evolve proper power sharing arrangements between themselves. Indeed the secular elite in both the communities while showing indifference to religion in personal life used it most cynically to realize their political ambition.

In spite of intense political indoctrination accomplished in the name of Islam, the subsequent political scenario in the Indian subcontinent, and particularly in Pakistan, persistently raises inconvenient questions about the legitimacy of religion intermingling with politics, especially when it is trigged with questionable motives.

T.K. Mathur in his article entitled "Sir Syed Ahmed Khan: Educationist, Social and Religious Thinker" describes that one is hard pressed to find another Muslim so keen and determined to preserve the honour of Islam as Sir Syed in the world of scholarship. He had in fact, a secular mind, rather one dominated by common sense, and he sought to achieve essentially secular values. He was convinced that orthodox view of Islam was a hindrance in the progress of Muslim. He was fascinating that educational progress, scientific temper, economic security, to open avenues of honest employment, removal of blemishes in social life and eradication of orthodox and bad habits were not attributed to religiousness and to love of the Muslims but to absorption in worldliness. Even such basic consideration of welfare could reduce religion to a means of worldly benefit and deprive it of spiritual content. He had insight and sincerity to pick up those issues with religious thinkers which the latter had been evading for generation.

M.R. Kazimi in his research paper entitled "Religious and Moral Education as an Important Component of Sir Syed's Educational Programme : A Critique" points out that Sir Syed was first and foremost a fighter for a modern life for the Muslims and this image of a passionate and dogged fighter is something which the learned academicians, who are prone to find faults in his works, will probably never get the better of. And it is this fighting, examine and inspiring spirit of Sir Syed Ahmed Khan which is to be emulated. An attitude to life which promotes liberalism, rationalism and humanism is to be inculcated.

M.M. Shankhdhar in his article entitled "Vivekanand's Hinduism" argues that to the ears of rigid fundamentalists and religious fanatics, Vivekanand's teachings of universality, divinity and tolerance sound utterly blasphemous. Unless *Dharma* replaces religion conflicts over gods, books, faiths would continue. *Dharma* is like an ocean, not a wave; but religion is a muddy stream that can be purified by falling into the ocean. When he addressed all kinds of religionists assembled in Chicago as "brothers and sisters", he, at once, demonstrated the hallmark of Hinduism as *Dharma* that rises above *panth*, faith and community. To equate *Dharma* with religion has been one of the most retarding and sinister errors committed by populist secularists with a view to bring down *Hindu Dharma* from its high pedestal to the level of religion. That impedes proper comprehension, for Hinduism is unique because, unlike religions, Hinduism is not mere social ethics, it is also a metaphysics, a philosophy, a mode of spiritual realization and a personal code, all rolled into one. Its excellence lies in operating both at the cosmic and the mundane levels.

R.T. Jangam in his paper entitled "Aurobindo from Revolutionary Nationalism to Spiritual Internationalism", discusses Aurobindo's revolutionary activities and achievements and note that his place in the Indian freedom struggle is great. However, his conversion to spiritual mysticism was not easy to predict in the early years. But it did come and his residency in Pondicherry revealed the mighty spiritual and mystic dimensions of his great personality. The model that he set up represents an international endeavour in the transformation of the human society into a rational and moral society. It should be noted that, as a whole time philosopher and a mystic, Aurobindo took only a limited interest in the mainstream politics of India and his involvement in politics was less than significant. However, the Pondicherry experiment had thorough widespread dissemination of his ideas and influence, has deeply touched the lives of many intellectuals and (other) educated people in India and abroad.

Ranjan Kumar Ray in his article entitled "Subhas Chandra Bose: A Pilgrim of Revolution" noted that Subhas Chandra had profound faith and respect for Indian religion and culture, but, this he did not followed blindly or dogmatically. His religion was patriotism and his culture was nationalism. In the ultimate analysis, Subhas Chandra had been an ardent nationalist revolutionary, both in thinking and in deeds. He realized that India's major national problems relating to the eradication of poverty, illiteracy and disease and scientific production and distribution could be effectively tackled only along socialist lines. Subhas Chandra underlined the need for self-preparation of the people spiritually, morally and materially. Organization should aim at providing physical, intellectual and moral training so that they may, individually and collectively, turn out to be ideal citizens of future India. In this *"Taruner Swapna"* (Dream of the Youth) he reiterated his feelings about the country's improvement.

Janardan Pandey in his paper entitled "Political Philosophy of Gandhi and Subhas: A Comparative Study" notes that both Gandhi and Subhas wanted an ideologically oriented political party as on unavoidable needs. Like Gandhi who wanted to dissolve the Congress and build up a new political party to rule the country, Subhas also wanted a party with people's power at the bottom of the power of a people's state. Both wanted national ideology on the basis of the acceptance of the Indian philosophy of synthesis and emphasized the necessity for a harmonious fusion of the values of spiritualism. They wanted to consolidate Indian freedom and reinvigorate the spirit of national integration of the Indian people for promoting harmony of various values, cultures and aspiration of the Indian people belonging to various regions, religions, races, communities and linguistic fraternities. They both were opposed to building the foundation of the national polity of India by imitating the political system of Fascism or Communism or British system of parliamentary democracy. They wanted to base the national institution of Indian polity as a *Panchayat Raj*, an age old Indian system of the rule of the *Panch*. They wanted the power of the people at the bottom and as such both of them urged for the gradual devaluation of political and economic power.

M.S. John in his research paper entitled "Gandhi: Religion, *Dharma* and the Concept of Politics" points out that traditional Indian polity was governed by the principle of *Dharma* which made the immanent order subservient to the transcendental one. *Dharma* concerned the society and not the state. It never has a compulsive character. According to Aurobindo, state arose at "an advanced stage of corruption of *Dharma* marked by the necessity of the appearance of the legislator and the formal government of the whole of life by external or written law and code or rule. Hence, confrontation with the West especially Western imperialism, led modern Indian thinkers like Gandhi to go back to Indian traditions. The notion of *Dharma* is supposed to harmonised the relationship between freedom and order, one of the perennial problems of political theory.

S.H. Patil in his paper entitled "*Manavadharma* and Pt. Nehru's Concept of Secularism" notes that Pt. Jawaharlal Nehru did not believe in any religion, yet he believed in and practiced *Manavadharma* on secular basis. He had the greatest concern for humanity and wanted to lift it from poverty, ignorance, superstition, communal passions, etc. and planned to make men and women prosperous, rational, scientific, humane, secular, etc. The means that he adopted for realizing these goals were democracy, socialism and secularism. The last one runs through the former two means. His concepts of democracy and socialism were coloured by secularism. His concept of secularism is based on enlightened *Manavadharma* and rationality is not only relevant to India but also to the whole world. Essentially it is a unifying ideological force for the whole mankind. For Nehru one world, peace, prosperity, freedom and secularism are indivisible.

D.N. Mallik in his article entitled "Rajendra Prasad and Religion, *Dharma* and Politics" argues that, it may be held in Prasad's political thinking and behaviour based on *Dharma* which was the cardinal concept and he conducted himself behaviourally as well as intellectually as an individual in relation to society within or without the ambit of politics and in relation to religion with or without reference to politics..

T.R. Sharma in his paper entitled "Acharya Narendra Deva's Ethical Dimension of Socialism" notes that Narendra Deva was convinced that the future belonged neither to capitalism nor to totalitarianism but to democratic socialism. He also stood for a greater role to the village *panchayats*. He visualized a new world order based on freedom, quality, social justice and peace. Narendra Deva wanted to reach the Marxist goal of socialist society by Gandhian techniques of non-violence. In fact, all the time Narendra Deva stressed the ethical dimension of socialism as an end and non-violent struggle as the means. He realized that real problem in India was that democracy was being introduced here in the midst of an undemocratic economic system and a hierarchical social structure.

Prakash C. Shastri in his paper entitled "The Notion of *Dharma,* Society and Polity: A Lohian Perspective" thinks that the time has come when Indian social scientists must try to look at their 'roots', if they want to find the solutions of the present day conflicts that are afflicting the 'body-politic' of India. In this regard, one must proceed to take help from the pioneering efforts of both M.K. Gandhi and his 'conscientious' follower Rammanohar Lohia who provided us with 'perspectives' to develop 'empathy' and critical appreciation regarding the basic tenets of the 'Hindu' culture.

Rakesh Kumar Jha in his article entitled "Vinoba's Concept of Religion, *Dharma* and Politics" notes that Vinoba's concept of religion has made it clear that religion and politics have outlived their utility. This is the age of science and spirituality. Vinoba is critical of the roles played by religion and power politics and wants to reconstruct them on the principles of spirituality, science and morality. Similarly, politics without spirituality, service and sense of equality is irrelevant and untenable. Without morality, it is demonic. Both religion and politics have to undergo a radical change. It must perfect itself by recognizing *"manavadharma"* as regulator.

Bijay Dhari Singh in his paper entitled "Jayaprakash Nararyan : Life, Thought and Action" argues that Jayprakash began to turn away from the basic postulates of Marxism. Because of this view J.P. says, "That ideal polity is built neither on power nor on material prosperity, rather, it is built on the spiritual re-generation of man". As J.P. says, "For many years, I have worshipped at the shrine of the Goddess dialectical materialism.... which seemed to me intellectually more satisfying than any other philosophy. But while the main quest of philosophy remains unsatisfied, it has become patent to me that materialism of any sort robs man of the means to become truly human. In a material civilization man has no rational incentive to be good. It may be that in the kingdom of dialectical materialism, fear makes men conform and the party takes the place of God. I feel convinced, therefore, that man must go beyond the material to find the incentive to goodness. As a corollary, I feel further that the task of social reconstruction cannot succeed under the inspiration of materialist philosophy." Dwelling upon the varying nature of the ideological and value commitments, J.P. says, "I am concerned only with the type of men I should like to live with in society."

S. Sri Krishna in his article entitled "Ambedkar's *Dharma*: Upliftment of Oppressed Class" notes that Dr. B.R. Ambedkar considered that, "Unless the Indian people secure political power and this political power concentrates in the hands of the socially suppressed section of the Indian society, it is not possible to completely wipe out all social legal and cultural disabilities, from which this section suffers." He further said, "Nobody can remove these unless you get political power into your hands..... we must have a government in which men in power will not be afraid to amend the social and economic code of life which dictates of the justice and expediency so urgently call for." Dr. B.R. Ambedkar is the Liberator of Downtrodden Classes in India, Hero of the oppressed masses, Saviour of the suppressed souls and the father of the Indian Constitution. He was a social revolutionary who spent his life fighting against social evils, which have weakened India and made her a slave.

The eminent contributors to this volume highlight the fact that religion is a set of beliefs. It may involve a specific philosophy, a framework of life values, forms of worship and affiliated rituals based on teachings, percepts and scriptures. A small group of people who organized in sects for a certain point of time, who are demographically and territorially widespread. Essentially all religions are equal. The tree of religion is the same, though there is not the physical equality between the branches. As Gandhi stated in *Harijan*, 30-11-1949: "They are all growing, and the person who belong to the growing branch must not gloat over it and say, 'Mine is the superior one.' None is superior and none is inferior to the other. Just as one's own country is best for oneself, similarly each religion is best for its respective adherents. In a fundamental sense, all religions converge towards the same goal. Virulence of religious fanaticism is slowly tending to disappear from the world."

Indian tradition does not suppress any religion and sect. India has shown a remarkable spirit of accommodation to the followers of various religions to sought and has given shelter to them, from time to time, to escape from being prosecuted in their own homelands. After the second destruction of the temple of Jerusalem, Jews came to India and were received here. They were given lands and homes and were allowed to live their own religion in their own way. Within a century of the death of Jesus Christ, the Syrian church of Christianity could find a place and establish itself and carry on its activities freely in south India. And when Muslims invaded Persia, the remnants of the Zoroastrian community left their homes and came to India.

They were well received and were provided with all facilities to establish their own modes of religious worship, India met the Muslim traders with hospitality and there were many happy contacts with the Muslim countries long before the actual political invasion of Muslim rulers. As a matter of fact, when Christianity and Islam first came to India, there was no hostile resistance to them. We have also examples of India offering shelter and hospitality to the Dalai Lama and his followers who came to India from Tibet. It is rightly observed that "throughout the vicissitudes of India's history she tried to give expressions to the sense of universality in religious as well as racial matters." Her outlook was acumenical rather than parochial. She provided home for each and every mode of universal tradition and did not exclude even those who had no faith in any religion.

But quite often *Dharma* is mistaken as a Hindi version of religion. To equate *Dharma* with religion has been one of the most retarding and sinister errors committed by populist secularists. *Dharma* helps the evolution of the soul to a higher level of life; *Adharma* is what obstructs its progress. *Dharma* is derived from the Sanskrit root *dhr*, which means "to hold together"; it is the innermost constitution of a thing, the law of its inner being. It is an ethical concept which includes a moral code and a whole range of man's duties and responsibilities. This *Dharma* is a part of *ṛta*, the fundamental moral law governing the whole universe and humanity consists in acting in harmony with this, moral order. It bears not only on human beings but also on all other animate or inanimate objects, so much so that it may well be attributed to the tiger, the crow, the rose, fire or water apart from human beings. Among human beings the *Dharma* of the father may not be the same as the *Dharma* of mother. It may have diverse callings on diverse individuals in diverse situations. It has to do with the intrinsic nature of a person or an object, may be with the reference to its kind or its particularities along with its resultant functional dispensation. Linked inseparably with the question of legitimacy, which has its reference to violation beyond brute force in collectively, politics concerns only with human beings dose so in specific social context of theirs—the context of governance—which however is of utmost importance of their social existence that context may involve several levels.

The three—Religion, *Dharma* and Politics—may well be perceived as linked in the human context and that perception has prevailed in the Indian political thinking right from its ancient origins. The concept religion has made it clear that religion and politics have outlived their utility. This is the age of science and spirituality. What all this amounts to saying that Indian thought is critical of the roles played by religion and power politics and wants to reconstruct them on the principles of spirituality, science and morality. Similarly, politics without spirituality, service and sense of equality is irrelevant and untenable. Without morality, it is demonic. Both religion and politics have to undergo a radical change. It must perfect itself by recognizing ***"Manavadharma"*** as regulator.

Rakesh Kumar Jha

Contents

Acknowledgements 7
Introduction 9
List of Contributors 31

1. *Purushartha* and Its Contemporary Relevance —*Ramashray Roy* 33
2. Quest for Synthesis in Indian Religious and Cultural Tradition—*B.N. Pande* 51
3. Indian Fundamentalism and Its Way out —*Ramjee Singh* 68
4. The Political Thought of Yājñavalkya—*Sureshwar Jha* 83
5. Kautilya on *Dharma* and Politics : A Study of Arthshastra—*P.D. Kaushik* 97
6. Concept of *Hindutva* and Indian Nationalism of V.D. Savarkar—*Ram Singh Solanki* 107
7. *Dharma,* Religious Denomination and Politics : Reflection of Pt. Deen Dayal Upadhyaya —*Mahesh Chandra Sharma* 124
8. Glimpses of Swami Dayanand Saraswati—*K.S. Saxena* 134
9. Roy's Religious Modernism, Social Reform and Political Liberalism—*Adi H. Doctor* 145
10. Gopal Krishan Gokhale's Spiritualization of Politics —*Radha Krishan* 160
11. M.G. Ranade : Apostle of Indian Freedom —*Rudranand Jha* 171
12. The Political Philosophy of Bal Gangadhar Tilak : An Analysis of Religious Concepts and Symbols used Therein—*M.R. Kazimi* 186
13. Religion as Political Ideology : The Separatist Crusade of Jinnah—*Asha Kaushik* and *S.N. Kaushik* 202

14. Sir Syed Ahmed Khan : Educationalist, Social and Religious Thinker—*T.K. Mathur* 213
15. Religious and Moral Education as an Important Component of Sir Syed's Educational Programme : A Critique—*M.R. Kazimi* 225
16. Vivekanand's Hinduism—*M.M. Shankhdhar* 238
17. Aurobindo from Revolutionary Nationalism to Spiritual Internationalism—*R.T. Jangam* 245
18. Subhas Chandra Bose : A Pilgrim of Revolution —*Ranjan Kumar Ray* 257
19. Political Philosophy of Gandhi and Subhas : A Comaparative Study—*Janardan Pandey* 264
20. Gandhi : Religion, *Dharma* and the Concept of Politics—*M.S. John* 278
21. *Manavadharma* and Pt. Nehru's Concept of Secularism—*S.H. Patil* 297
22. Rajendra Prasad and Religion, *Dharma* and Politics —*D.N. Mallik* 308
23. Acharya Narendra Deva's Ethical Dimension of Socialism—*T.R. Sharma* 327
24. The Notion of *Dharma*, Society and Polity : A Lohian Perspective—*Prakash C. Shastri* 337
25. Vinoba's Concept of Religion, *Dharma* and Politics —*Rakesh Kumar Jha* 345
26. Jayaprakash Narayan : Life, Thought and Action —*Bijay Dhari Singh* 363
27. Ambedkar's *Dharma* : Upliftment of Oppressed Class —*S. Sri Krishna* 383

Index 390

List of Contributors

Adi H. Doctor, Former Head, Department of Political Science, Goa University, Goa.

Asha Kaushik, Dean Social Science, University of Rajasthan, Jaipur.

B.N. Pande, Former M.P. and Vice Chairman, Gandhi Smriti and Darshan Samiti, New Delhi.

Bijay Dhari Singh, Retd. Professor of Political Science, J.N. College, Madhubani, Bihar.

D.N. Mallik, Retd. Professor and Head, Political Science, B.R.A. Bihar University, Muzaffarpur, Bihar.

Late Janardan Pandey, Retd. Professor and Head, Department of Gandhian Thought, Bhagalpur University, Bhagalpur.

K.S. Saxena, Former Director, Academic Staff College, J.N.V. University, Jodhpur.

M.M. Shankhdhar, Retd. Professor of Political Science, University of Delhi, Chairperson, International Political Science Association Study Group on "Welfare States".

M.R. Kazimi, Rtd. Professor and Head, Department of Political Science, B.R.A. Bihar University, Muzaffarpur.

M.S. John, School of Gandhian Studies and Peace Science, Mahatama Gandhi University, Kottayam, Kerala.

Mahesh Chandra Sharma, M.P. Former President, B.J.P., (Rajasthan).

P.D. Kaushik, Retd. Professor and Head, Department of Political Science, B.H.U., Varanasi.

Late Prakash Chand Shastri, Former Professor of Political Science, Director, Gandhian Study Centre, University of Rajasthan, Jaipur.

R.T. Jangam, Retd. Professor of Political Science, Dharwad, Karnataka.

Radha Krishan, Senior Lecturer, Governemnt P.G. College, Sambhar Lake, Jaipur.

Rakesh Kumar Jha, Department of Political Science, University of Rajasthan, Jaipur.

Late Ram Singh Solanki, J.N. Vyas University, Jodhpur.

Ramashray Roy, Eminent Political Philosopher and former Director, Centre for the Developing Societies, Delhi, former Director, Indian Council of Social Science and Research, New Delhi.

Ramjee Singh, Former M.P., former Vice Chancellor, Jain Vishwa Bharti Institute, former President Indian Society of Gandhian Studies, former Director Gandhian Institute of Studies, Rajghat, Varanasi.

Ranjan Kumar Ray, Professor, Department of Political Science, Presidency College, Kolkata, West Bengal.

Rudranand Jha, Retd. Professor and Head, Department of Political Science, Marwari College, L.N. Mithila University Darbhanga, Bihar.

S.H. Patil, Professor of Political Science, Karnatak University, Dharwad, Karnataka.

S.N. Kaushik, Former Director, South Asia Studies Centre, University of Rajasthan, Jaipur.

S. Sri Krishna, Professor of Political Science and Public Administration, Shri Venkateswara University, Tirupati, Andhra Pradesh.

Sureshwar Jha, L.N. Mithila University, Darbhanga, former Member Sahitya Akademi, New Delhi.

T.K. Mathur, Professor of History, M.D.S. University, Ajmer, Rajasthan.

T.R. Sharma, Professor, Department of Political Science, Panjab University, Chandigarh.

1

Purushartha and Its Contemporary Relevance

Ramashray Roy

Talking about the prevalent political order in Athens, the Polis, Werner Jaeger observes: The rise of the city-state meant that man received besides his private life a sort of second life, his bios politikos. Now every citizen belongs to two orders of existence; and there is a sharp distinction in his life between what is his own (*idion)* and what is communal (*koinon*). There is no doubt that every person's life is characterized by these two orders of existence, the private and the public (or communal, to use a much abused word these days). It is also true that there frequently exists a situation of tension and conflict between the two. As a result of the individual lives and public order, both tend to be severely affected and afflicted by disorder and directionlessness. As such, there is no denying the truth of what Jaeger has to say about the distinction, difference and conflict between the private and the public. However, he can be accused of missing the main point in two important senses. First, it is not a fact that it is only the citizen that is a participant in the two orders of existence that Jaeger refers to; it is true of man in general.

The individual and the citizen are two different conceptions. If the term "individual" refers to the totality of person's existence, the term "citizen" stands for the membership of a particular political order. The significance of the term "citizen" lies in the fact that the individual rises or should rise above his particularistic interests, and that he should not only be positively oriented to the public good but that he is or should be actively engaged in promoting and defending it. Thus the substantive significance of the term "citizen" lies in the fact that when a person is engaged in performing the role of the citizen, then the distinction and difference between the private and the public would disappear from his mental horizon. Jaeger ignores this fact completely.

Second, Jaeger also fails to take into account the fact that the distinction and difference between the two orders of existence, that is, the private and the public are not caused by the phenomenon of citizenship. On the contrary, it is caused by nature; that is, it is the characteristic feature of man endowed by nature itself. The installation and organization of a political order is symptomatic of man's effort to control and regulate the adverse consequences of the difference and the consequent collision between the private and the public. That a system of governance is needed to curb the tendency of self-aggrandizement is testimony to the fact that the interior of man is already divided and split by the difference between the private and the public. It is because of this already established division that the individual, turning away from serving public good, gives preference to the pursuit of his own self-interest. This is what *Bhisma Pitamaha* refers to in the *Shanti Parva* of the *Mahabharat* when he was initiating Yudhishthir into the knowledge of *Rajadharma*. As he told Yudhisthir, there was earlier neither King, nor Kingdom, nor still any political institutions. Every person was righteous and committed to the protection of *dharma*. But to follow the path of *dharma* proved to be an onerous task. For various reasons people became tired of following the tortuous path of righteous conduct. Cupidity increased and the distinction between right and wrong began eroding. And then a situation of *matsya nyaya* (the law of the fishes) came into being. The institution of kingship, which could keep the people on the right path with the help of *Danda* was felt to be sorely needed. What all this signifies is that when private concerns become dominant and personal aspirations and ambitions become so irresistible that they eclipse the sense of serving the public good, social order is badly shaken and tends to disintegrate. In order, therefore, to restore the social order, make it viable and vibrant, and to make inviolable the rule of *dharma*, the king and the king's *danda* become necessary.

It is thus clear that the distinction and difference between the private and the public is both logically and empirically prior to the installation of the system of governance. The establishment of a political order and the installation of a king confirm this fact. As such Jaeger's argument that the distinction and difference between the private and the public came about as a result of the emergence of the polis or the city-state is neither logical, nor supported by fact. Be that as it may, the difference and opposition between the private and the public aspects of man's existence and social disorder emanating from it is real. And if this difference and opposition cannot be fully uprooted, at least they must be controlled and restricted. This is simple for the simple reason that if social order degenerates, it also affects individual lives adversely and makes them extremely unpalatable. And, then, a vicious circle comes into being from which it becomes very difficult, both for the individual and the collectivity he belongs to, to easily escape. It is, therefore, necessary to bridge the gap between the two and find ways and means to bring about reconciliation between them and make them compatible. It is needless to say that this prôblem is not only important but also it is eternal and recurring.

What is the most difficult question in this regard is: What could be a dependable and long-enduring, if not an eternal, solution of this problem? It is not that thinking persons have either been ignorant of or indifferent to this problem. Also, a lot of discussion has taken place on this problem. Several ways of resolving this problem have also been suggested. Some of these ways and means have been adopted and tried to get the solution of this problem. And yet a long enduring, if not a permanent, solution to this problem is still eluding. Even if some solution is found, it proves to be only temporary because it loses all its attraction and efficacy after it has been tried for some time. This state of affairs gives rise to some important questions. There in no denying the fact that the problem of difference and the opposition between the private and the public arising out of this difference have taken a virulent form in modern times; their adverse effects are being felt in almost all aspects of life today. As such, the first question is: What is the factor or situation which has accentuated and exacerbated the difference and the consequent opposition between the private and the public?

Second, it is true that this difference and the consequent opposition between the private and the public cannot be totally uprooted. However, they can be controlled, regulated and reduced to a tolerable limit so that social concord is ensured and safeguarded. The question that assumes importance in this regard is: Is social discord an object which, like other objects, can be shaped and moulded and then installed in the temple of society with all fanfare and consecrated to make it a live, conscious and dynamic god who can be regularly worshipped, propitiated, and tested in times of trouble? Or, if social concord is not an object which can be created and sustained at will and then used, even abused, according to the exigencies of the time, then, what is the real significance of social concord? Where does its source lie; what is its generative factor? If social concord is not something like an object, then, it is obvious that it is an attitude, a mental state capable of reducing, to the minimum, the difference and the consequent opposition between the private and the public. By doing so, this attitude of mental state safeguards not only social harmony but also individual well-being through the creation and maintenance of an appropriate social institutional arrangement. It does not need to be emphasized that only appropriate answers to these questions can throw ample light on the modern day relevance of *purushartha* (objectives worthy of man's pursuit).

The point of departure for a discussion of the modern day relevance of *purushartha* it can be the nothing else but the substantive conception of *purushartha* is a topic that has been much discussed; its significance, its importance and ramifications have been subjected to close scrutiny; its utility has evoked wider attention. How many *purusharthas* are there, what is their sequence, what is the importance of different *purusharthas*, all these questions have been examined and analyzed from different perspectives. However, the central focus of all these discussions and explorations has at their core the question of the place and role of *purushartha* in the life of an individual. If the principal significance of *purushartha* is to define, categorize and put boundaries to different life-objectives of the individual, then, it is clear that the exploration and analysis of *purushartha* must be undertaken from a perspective that incorporates both the individual and society. Such a perspective needs to deal with two very important aspects of *purushartha*. In the first place, it is true that to accept the underlying principle of *purushartha* and to give it a practical shape concerns mainly the individual; it is the responsibility of the individual and is involved with the well-being of the individual *qua* individual. However, whatever the individual, driven mainly by the consideration of his well-being does, has, however, certain ramifications and consequence for others and for the society at large; it influences social institutions and process in several important ways. In this sense, individual persons do not have a separate existence from the social world; individual action cannot he explored, analyzed and evaluated in its isolation from the social world. As such, it means that individual actions have social consequences and ramifications.

In the second place, if individual action has social consequences and ramification, it is, then, necessary to examine these actions from the vantage point of society. This means that the main purpose of *purushartha* is only to classify and categorize all life-purposes relevant for man from this point of view. As such, *purushartha* aims simply at classifying all activities of man, all human purposes that either worthy of his manliness or compatible with his given but unrealized and realized capabilities. This is no doubt true. But it has also a practical aspect. And when *purushartha* evinces its practical aspect, then, it throws a lot of light on the inclination and activities of the individual. It is quite possible that whatever the individual does is only partial. In its partiality it may only twist and distort the totality of his personality. And it is not unlikely that society, too, will have to bear the brunt of the adverse consequences of what the individual does. This makes it essential to raise questions about the reciprocal relationship between different *purusharthas* and in a person's life, how they are coordinated and how the different claims of different *purusharthas* are reconciled to each other. Thus any discussion about *purushartha*, must concern itself with the question of the reciprocal relationship between different *purushartha*, a relationship that is maximally beneficial for both of individual and the collectivity. This question needs exploration.

To justify this close look on this relationship, it is necessary to discuss the modern worldview and its pragmatic manifestations. As is quite well known, the modern worldview is the product of the western world. This view appeared during the Renaissance in the Fourteenth century, grew and attained its maturity during the Enlightenment in the Seventeenth century. It does not need any demonstration to suggest that the era which is known as the modern era also began its fateful journey in the Seventeenth century. It was during the Enlightenment that a radical shift occurred in the extant worldview. It is the institutional and attitudinal manifestations of this revolutionary change in the worldview that are reflected today in such concepts and realities depicted by them as industrialization, modernity, development etc. The totality of all these manifestations constitutes the pivot of the common man's life and everydayness; again, it is these manifestations that are reflected in individual and social life and relations.

What was the revolutionary transformation that occurred in the life of Europeans in the Seventeenth century? To answer this question satisfactorily, it is necessary to dwell, even if only briefly, at the distinctive features of the traditional and the modern worldviews. No matter whichever traditional world-view we may take, its distinctive characteristic has been the incorporation of two distinctly different life purposes. One of the life purposes pertained to some higher objective in life, some summum bonum, an ultimate aim in life while the other was concerned with the satisfaction of ordinary, material life needs. It has always been emphasized that in so far as the higher life purpose is concerned, the pivot of man's life must be the active pursuit of some higher end, such as self-realization, self-development, better citizenship, etc. Without the pursuit of some such higher end, man's life becomes purposeless, directionless and is turned into a veritable desert. It has been felt that it is in the process of the pursuit of a higher life purpose that man rises above the level of the animal and succeeds in developing those attributes and qualities that endow him with humanity. As a result of this, the individual human being becomes capable of disciplining and regulating his life.

It is beyond doubt that the active pursuit of some higher life purpose was considered to be the pivot of man's life. It was also emphasized that it was this active pursuit of some higher life purpose which brought some discipline in man's life and made it noble and opened up the possibility of the achievement of higher virtues. It did not, however, mean that the satisfaction of ordinary life needs was considered unnecessary or ignored. Their fulfilment was considered inevitably essential inasmuch as, on the one hand, they are involved with the process of production and reproduction and, on the other, the pursuit of a higher life purpose is not simply possible without the fulfilment of ordinary life needs. The significance of the saying that "a hungry man cannot worship" can be appreciated only in this context. Thus the fulfilment of three life needs – particularly these needs that pertain to wealth, power and prestige – has been considered necessary to be sure; however, these needs are treated only as infrastructural, a necessary aid in the pursuit of a higher life-purpose. In view of this; it has been considered necessary to subject the fulfilment of these needs to the suzerainty of the higher life-purpose and control, regulate and discipline the process of their fulfilment by the requirements of the pursuit of a higher life purpose.

With the coming into prominence of the Enlightenment, the rational, questioning mind of man put a question mark on the traditional worldview. Man's questioning rationality threw doubt on the existence of any higher life purpose and argued that there was no such thing as a higher life purpose. As a result, not only the existence of a higher life purpose but also its necessity came to be questioned. Also, along with a higher life purpose, the divine ground of being as its substratum and its focal point, too, came to be questioned and declared non-essential, therefore, not relevant. It was forcefully argued that there is neither an absolute being nor any higher life-purpose associated with this being. It was asserted that the only purpose of life was the quest of felicity. Once the existence of God and a higher life purpose grounded in and associated with the divine ground of being were denied and rejected out of hand, the existence of the soul as the locus and sensorium of the divine was also negated. Mind displaced the soul and it is the mind that is supposed to be the locus of rationality. As a result of these conceptual transformations, man emerged only as a complex of desires and appetites and reason. Along with it, there also came about a radical change in the definition of felicity. According to this change, felicity now consisted in satisfying one desire after another. It is necessary to make it clear that the significance of satisfying one desire after another is that the desires that are meant to be satisfied have, in fact, to do only with the process of production and reproduction. And all of these desires are involved with ordinary life needs. These ordinary life needs, in turn, are substantively linked with the acquisition and accumulation of wealth, power and prestige.

In this changed perspective, all those life put poses which had to do with the pursuit of higher, noble values were displaced by those purposes that are related with man's earthly existence and this-worldly pursuits. And the importance of material resources necessary for giving effect to worldly concerns increased manyfold. Obviously, it is very difficult, if not impossible, to fulfil ordinary life needs in a situation where these resources are either non-existent or very scarce. It is, therefore, necessary to produce and enlarge the quantity of these resources. The unprecedented advances on the frontiers of science and the mind-boggling progress in the sphere of technology, both helped, to a very large extent, in the solution of the problem of the scarcity of resources. As a result of this, needs have become endless. And the endeavour of satisfying these endlessly proliferating needs has speeded up the process of industrialization pushing the boundary of its domain farther and farther.

At the root of all these factors is the changed perspective on man and his world and their relationship. Needless to say that there are certain ramifications and consequences of this changed prospective for both man and his external world. But before we discuss them, it is necessary to indicate that the modern worldview accepts and incorporates only two of the components – *kama* and *artha* – of the traditional idea of *purushartha*. Only these two *purusharthas* are supposed to be relevant and meaningful in modern times. It is believed that the pursuit of these *purusharthas* alone will help in the improvement of human existence. This belief rests on several underlying assumptions. It is assumed that the satisfaction of desires is not only the means of felicity, it is also the necessary ground of personality development and the progress of civilization. It is believed that it is in the process of the satisfaction of desires that potentialities slumbering in the breast of the individual get actualized. As these potentialities are progressively actualized, the chariot of civilization moves forward on the path of progress. It is also believed that it is only as consequence of the activation of this process that the course of change begins, moves forward from one stage to another; it is in this dynamic process of change that civilization moves from one level of achievements to the next higher one and thus attains new heights. It is also in this process that man is believed to acquire the capacity and develops appropriate moral values with the help of which he acquires the ability to mould himself and adopt to changing circumstances. It is only against this background that Lord Keynes' dictum: "Economic development is the possibility of development", makes sense.

It is thus obvious that the conception and the reality of the traditional idea of *purushartha* have been severely violated, even discarded. This violation endows the modern times with a particular distinction. It accepts as valid, relevant and meaningful only two components of the traditional conception of *purushartha*. It then calls for and legitimizes the attempt to refashion and elevate individual and collective life on the basis of the pursuit of only *kama* and *artha*. However, such a perspective carries several adverse consequences for both man and his external world. The modern day relevance of *purushartha* can be apprehended and appreciated only when these adverse consequences are fully explored.

It is beyond doubt that the predominance of the active pursuit of *kama* and *artha* to the neglect of, even unconcern with, other *purusharthas* is a fact that distinguishes the modern times with other past historical eras. As a result of the prominence and dominance of these two *purusharthas*, the modern identity of man has taken on a particular character. The prominence of *kama* and *artha* can be seen to be fully reflected in personal aspirations, family life, social institutional arrangement, political processes, economic life and relations, etc. And because of this, a distinctive relationship in individual and social life has developed. In addition, with the preeminence of the pursuit of *kama* and *artha*, it has become inevitably necessary to produce more and more consumption goods and services. This has necessitated the launching of the process of the transformation, manipulation and exploitation of nature with the help of continuously improving sophisticated technology. It is only on this basis that the process of industrialization begins, becomes dynamic and offers the promissory note of satisfying the unabatedly multiplying needs. However, the process of industrialization has given a new direction and content to the relationship between man and nature.

The emergence and the progressive institutionalization of the modern world view have wrought three important changes. All these changes affect not only man but also society and nature. In so far the question of the individual is concerned, the satisfaction of the progressively proliferating needs has become the pivot around which his life, activities revolve. Man's needs have become endless in two important senses. In the first place, these needs are not attached to any higher life purpose and, therefore, not controlled, regulated or disciplined by any higher value. These needs are no more required to be submitted at the bar of any higher life purposes, whether spiritual or secular, for scrutiny and judgment in terms of rightness and wrongness. They have become their own end; they are auto-legitimating.

Second, as these needs have successfully contended for and acquired auto-legitimacy, the boundaries drawn by tradition around needs and their fulfilment have disintegrated and lost their efficacy. As a result of this the process of satisfying one desire after another has become endless. It is also necessary to point out in this connection that the significance of needs becoming endless in these two senses is that the standards of determining which need to fulfil, which to postpone and which to be never fulfilled have lost their relevance and become lifeless. What is also interesting in this regard is that no other criterion for determining the appropriateness of needs has yet been found, nor it is possible to find one. After the demise of higher life purposes it has become extremely difficult to determine which needs to satisfy, which to postpone and which to suppress. One of the main reasons of this is the fact that the fulfilment of all needs is considered to be legitimate because they are not only natural but also rational. The source of man's desires is his own nature and to satisfy them is rational inasmuch as their satisfaction is the basis of felicity, realization of hidden potentialities and civilizational progress.

In addition, desires cannot be checked or prevented from arising. What is, therefore, important is to be able to judge the merits of the emergent desires and to refuse to satisfy those desires which do not conform to certain moral and normative standards. However, as desires have gained autolegitimation, it has become increasingly difficult to devise moral and normative standards or to stick to them if they are somehow formulated. In so far as the traditional way of looking at things is concerned, certain desires were treated as destructive which today are considered very necessary for good life. As such, the traditional perspective considered it necessary to suppress them in the interest of both the individual and the collectivity. However, today the distinction between desires in terms of right or wrong has almost evaporated under the blaze of self-regarding action. One contributory factor in it is the fact that all desires are considered to be equally valuable, useful, and valid. Consequently, the substantive definition of contentment has been rendered difficult, if not utterly impossible. This is so for the simple reason that the decision regarding which desires to satisfy, which to postpone and which to altogether suppress is very difficult to arrive at. Questions in respect of these issues have become very difficult to answer.

Answers to these questions can be had only when the individual feels deep down in his consciousness what is good for himself, on the one hand, and knows what consequences, both good and bad his actions will have for others, on the other. As has been pointed out earlier, after the suzerainty of the divine ground of being was thrown off, it was supposed that the reasoning capacity endowed by nature to every person would determine which desires to satisfy and which to suppress. But it must be made clear that the rationality which is bandied about these days is incompetent to do so for three very important reasons. First, the substantive meaning of rationality in modern times is expedient, calculative reasoning which makes calculations of costs and benefits of different available means that can be employed to realize a particular purpose or end. The ground for such a calculation is obviously instrumental, that is, the determination of the best (in terms of least costly) way of realizing a particular purpose. The aim here is not to judge the merits of desires in terms of their appropriateness, etc. It is also interesting to point out that it is not for reason to decide which alternative means suggested by itself to choose for realizing a given purpose; it is for the will-power to make the decision about how to go about realizing a particular purpose.

Second, the importance of reasoning in the instrumental sense also came to be gradually eclipsed. It came to be believed that the fulfilment of biological needs themselves is the realization of a higher moral aspiration. As such, it is necessary to fulfil all those needs which have their origin in the biological structure of man. And, third, it is quite obvious that instrumental rationality recorded a definite decline in pre-eminence after the rise of Romanticism. However, it can be asserted without the fear of contradiction that keeping in mind the nature of rationality, the ground of rationality is rationality itself. It does not recognize any criterion outside of itself for judging and evaluating the merit of anything. As such, rationality refuses any outside authority which can discipline and govern it. Because of all these reasons, it becomes very difficult to decide which desire, when satisfied, will prove beneficial and which will turn out to be harmful.

When the satisfaction of desires is judged to be very crucial in attaining happiness realizing potentialities and impelling civilization on the path of progress, when the fulfilment of needs is considered not only natural but also rational, then, to distinguish between beneficial and harmful desires and to determine the right path of action on this basis is difficult, it is not completely impossible. And as is clear from the preceding discussion, it is very difficult for the individual to adopt a standard of evaluation on the basis of which he can make a distinction between beneficial and harmful desires. In such a situation the ground for the satisfaction of desires can only be the self-defined notion of felicity. But once self-defined conception of felicity is allowed to have a way in the social world, the possibility of tension and conflict between individual well-being and collective well-being becomes, very strong indeed. With this possibility becoming strong, social unrest, discord and conflict pervade the social world and individual and social life becomes unbearable. As a result, society virtually becomes an arena where is continuously waged what Alasdaire MacIntyre calls "civil war carried on by other means." To escape such a situation, it becomes necessary to distinguish between beneficial and harmful desires. But this is not possible at the individual level. One alternative is for the individual to decide what to do only after he has taken into account the interest of others. But this is difficult for two reasons. To take note of other's 'interest in determining one's own action requires information about what impact one's action is likely to have on other. It is quite obvious that it is not at all possible for anybody to have such an information.

Second, it is argued that this difficulty can be overcome easily by accepting a universal principle that provides the basis of determining what is worth doing and what is not? To put it differently, the individual certainly has the intention that whatever he is or thinks of doing may have adverse consequence for other. And if, even after having this intuition, he has engaged in an action which has harmful effects for other, it is indicative not of the lapse of his understanding but of the weakness of his will (*akrasia*). And *akrasia* can be overcome only when a person adopts, consciously, knowingly, for himself a general, universally applicable rule of conduct which guides him in determining the proper course of action. The defect in this argument is that this problem is not linked with will-power, but with morally disciplined knowledge. Nobody will deny the fact that a universal principle of conduct is impractical because the context of applying this universal principle keeps on changing. As a result, it does not avail to make any general principle of action applicable in all situations. On the contrary, what is necessary is to train the conscience in such a way that it becomes possible for the individual to decide what he must do in different contexts. In so far as action is context-bound, the determination of what ought to be done does not depend upon any universal principle or even categorical imperative; it depends on morally-disciplined rationality or conscience.

For all these reasons it is not possible for the individual to take into account the interest of others in determining the course of his own action. As a result of this, the individual is forced to take note of his own interest while making a decision about what he must do. This is so for the simple reason that the modern world-view lacks standards for judging the merit of the contemplated action. In such a situation, there is no escape for the individual from being driven by the considerations of his own good in deciding a course of action. It can, however, be argued that even while the individual is a self-defined subject, he is not separated from others. He is born in a society which has a distinctive structure, a particular institutional arrangement, a particular style of working, and contains constitutive and regulative norms and principles to define and control these roles. Born in such a society, the individual certainly acquires the knowledge of its structural, functional and procedural forms and a character. Using this knowledge, he can certainly make a distinction between what is socially permissible to do and what is not in order to determine his own action plan? Needless to say that there is a lot of substance in this argument. It must, however, be pointed out that the intrinsic merit of this argument pertains to a society which retains its capacity and authority to predefine not only the purposes of individuals but also the means of their realization.

But the version of worldview that we discussed above, does not equip society with this capacity and authority. According to the modern version of the worldview the individual is a self-defined subject. He himself defines and determines his purposes. In this determination, he does not tolerate the interference of any external agency whether it is tradition, society or any other authority. From this point of view, society has already lost its authority to control and regulate individual behaviour and has come to be simply a mechanical aggregate of self-defining subjects. In addition to this, since individual purposes are treated as primary, the external world, both society and nature, is treated as potential means of realizing individual purposes. And the significance of both society and nature lies in their utility, not in their inherent significance. Since individuals now have an instrumental orientation towards the external world, social institutions, operative principles, its traditions, all come to be questioned and usually thrown overboard. Their evaluation comes to be grounded in their utility, not in their inherent worthwhileness. As a result, the social order, instead of controlling and regulating individual motivation and behaviour, becomes nothing more than the instrument of realizing individual purposes.

There is no doubt that society is reduced to an instrument of realizing individual purposes. In addition to this, society is also the playground of contending and conflicting interests. Bound together in the ties of reciprocal resistance, different individuals, groups and corporations make use of society and its different resources for safeguarding and promoting their own interests. Towards this, they endeavour to aim at gaining and retaining privileged access to and control over scarce societal resources. As a result of this, the unity of society becomes fragmented and splits into numerous contending forces because of the activation of antagonistic interest. And since society loses its constitutive and regulative authority, it becomes anonymous and faceless. Consequently, it also loses its right to impose discipline, bring about integration and install equilibrium. Its place is taken by the state which, by acquiring all kinds of power and authority, becomes a sovereign institution and emerges as a body that symbolizes the unification of separate and separated self-defining subjects.

The main reason why the state has emerged as the sovereign and the most powerful institution lies in the fact that the individual has lost auto-control in the sense of self-control. As has been indicated earlier, the satisfaction of desires is not only natural but also rational. It is very difficult, in the modern perspective, to analyze desires and judge their merits and demerits with a reference to a universal and universally acceptable principle. The individual can, therefore, do nothing else than to engage in the pursuit of his own interest. But the endeavour by one individual to satisfy his desires has certain consequences for others and society. However, the process of the fulfilment of individual needs is supposed to be such a dynamic process which ensures felicity, helps realize human potentialities and propels civilization on the path of progress. It is, therefore, considered harmful as well as wicked to restrain the process of the satisfaction of desires, to put any limits on this process. As such, one can only think of taking care of the adverse consequences of individual actions, regulate them, put limits on them. And since there is lack of a substantive concept of contentment, the responsibility of this regulation or of prescribing limits cannot be discharged by the individual himself. Society, too, is incapable of performing this role inasmuch as it is looked at only from an instrumental point of view. Consequently, the responsibility to take care of the adverse consequences of individual actions falls upon the state.

However, the state itself is such an institution which has the responsibility of safeguarding order from the ravages of aggressive pursuit of self-interest by individuals and groups, to be sure. However, for various reasons, it does not succeed in this. First, if the state is considered as the providential check on human cupidity, it also becomes a powerful weapon in the hands of the powerful who seek to keep the weak out. Second, the definition of the good life that we try to realize in our lives requires that, first, there should be equitable, if not altogether equal distribution and consumption of societal resources and, second, that efforts must be made to satisfy the ever-escalating demands for consumption goods and services. Without satisfying these two basic requirements, the realization of the good life would ever remain a dream. Failure in this will plunge society into tension and conflict. And if these requirements are sought to be met, then a different kind of trouble will raise its ugly head. Technologically induced and sustained economic growth does degrade nature. It also leads to fatal decline in social cooperation and harmony. With the erosion of social cooperation and harmony the way is paved for pervasive conflict and violence.

It is thus apparent that the condemnation by Mahatma Gandhi of the modern civilization as Satanic is rooted in the emergent pragmatic social condition and, therefore, quite justified. In the chariot of the modern civilization grounded in the modern worldview have only two wheels; they are *kama* and *artha*. It is claimed that the pursuit of these two *purusharthas* can make one righteous. And in so far as *moksha* is concerned, it has no relevance at all in modern times. In the perspective of modern times, the unabated and unlimited satisfaction of desires is supposed to pave the way for the terrestrial heaven. However, as has been pointed out earlier and as our analysis reveals, the pursuit of *kama* and *artha* itself has deepened the crisis of civilization today. Even more important in this respect is the fact that everybody is acutely aware of the civilizational crisis. However, it seems that a dependable, straight-forward way out of this crisis is beyond our grasp. In such a situation, whenever the symptoms of deep civilization malaise become manifest, ways and means are sought to be found for its treatment. This usually takes the form of changing the institutional structure, or the external aspect, of society; it is invariably forgotten that the problem is not simply social, economic, or political; the problem is spiritual or moral. As such, without apprehending the deeper factors producing the crisis of civilization or without undertaking a proper treatment even after the apprehension of these deeper factors, the civilizational crisis continues to persist and grows more serious everyday.

There is only one way out of this crisis. This is to subject the pursuit of *kama* and *artha* to the suzerainty of *dharma*. The significance of *dharma* in this connection lies in the need of becoming well-oriented to the interest of others while pursuing one's own interest, and of making this possible pragmatically. But this is possible only when the individual realizes that he is neither autonomous nor self-complete. He is an integral part of a larger order. With this realization also comes another realization; that is, the realization of one's own good depends on the realization of the good of all. Along with it, the individual also realizes that his good is limited not only to the fulfilment of material needs alone. There are also non-material needs whose fulfilment elevates his own and his society's life. In this perspective, then, the significance of *dharma* does not lie in externally imposed laws or rule of law. Its import is the cultivation of such an orientation and disposition which helps the individual to determine what is worth doing and what is not and to acquire the will-power and strength to follow the path one has chosen.

It is, then, very clear that it becomes possible only when the soul of the individual gets attuned to the divine ground of being and seeks identity with it. To be actively engaged in such an endeavour is to seek salvation (*moksha*). And it is this endeavour, again, that enables one to acquire a *dharmic* prospective. It is, then apparent that the pursuit of *kama* and *artha* can be beneficial if it is subjected to the rule of *dharma*.

It is against this background that we can appreciate the significance of the Sanskrit saying, *yamadhikritya purushah pravartate,* that is, all the duties emanating from the man's relationship with the divine deep in his being and the phenomenal world go into the definition of what *purusharthas* are. And it is not only appropriate but also essential for a person to perform all the duties, understood as *purusharthas,* involved with this two-fold relationship. Without the performance of all the *purusharthas,* the crisis of modern civilization will persist.

2

Quest for Synthesis in Indian Religious and Cultural Tradition

B.N. Pande

In this vast land of ours have dwelt, since time immemoraial, peoples of different races and into this land entered races from beyond the mountains and the seas. But the old inhabitants and the new-comers, after they had struggled and fought, eventually forgot their enmities, made peace and joined in their common endeavour. Each epoch of such a fusion was marked by an efflorescence of culture in which the different elements were so mixed as to make one whole.

This unity of spirit has ever been conveying to the different groups and communities, which form part of the whole, known as India, the fundamental realization that although the waves upon sea are many and play of winds upon its surface gives rise to varied and even contradictory phenomena like calms and storms, yet the substance of this multiplicity and variety is the unchanging sea.

The socio-cultural continuity is the distinguishing feature of Indian history. The harmony found in the many-sided cultures of the people of India stems from this source. Thus although India has many religions, many languages, many races, its fundamental attitudes towards life have persisted through centuries and millennia. It is a remarkable fact that the socio-economic structure of India, which originated in the settlements of the Aryan and their assimilation of the pre-Aryan inhabitants of India, continued without any radical change till the Nineteenth century.

This unity of her history, her ideals and of her humanity is the living spirit of India. It is greater than any of its particular manifestations in time or in type. It underlines the multiplicity of our creeds and sects, customs and institutions, and art and philosophies. It underlines our historic failures and successes, our struggles and triumphs. It abides in the midst of these changes. It is this spirit which fused the pre-Dravidian, the Dravidian and the Aryan, into that ancient social organism, which found utterance in the sublime philosophies, beautiful crafts, the stirring arts, which make-up the first chapter of our history. Rama and Krishna, Mahavira and Buddha, Chandragupta and Ashoka, Valmiki and Vyasa worthily represent the spirit of this synthesis. The monuments of Sarnath and Sanchi, the paintings of Bagh and Ajanta, the temples of Khajuraho and Bhubaneshwar, the dramas of Kalidas and Bhavabhuti constitute the living memory of this glorious age.

The close of this epoch saw the impact of new races, Arabs, Turks and Mughals. The ancient culture of India came into violent conflict with the new-comers, but even before the political struggles had ended, our construction had begun. Islam and Hinduism, which appeared at the start, so antithetical, at last intermingled, each one stirred the profoundest depth of the other and from their synthesis, grew the religion of Bhakti and Tasawwuf, the religion of love and devotion, which swept the hearts of millions following different religions and sects of India. The currents of Islamic Sufism and Hindu Bhakti combined into a mighty stream which fertilized old desolate tracts and changed the face of the country. It was in this spirit of India which achieved apparently an impossible task of reconciling the puritanical severity and awe-inspiring transcendence of Islam into the luxuriant fullness and abundance of forms and the intuitive perception of their immanent unity with Hinduism, and created those monuments of architecture and painting, music and poetry and love-inspired religion which are the heritage of Indian history during the middle ages.

The Similarity of Religion

The essentials are comman to all religions: that truth is univrsal and not the monopoly of any race or teacher, that non-essentials vary with time, place, and circumstances, that the same fundamental truths have been revealed in different scriptures, in different languages through different persons in different nations.

As Jesus the Christ said, "I came only to fulfil the law and the prophets."

And Prophet Muhammad adds the positive counsel:

Let all of us ascend towards, and meet
Together on, the common ground of those
High truths and principles which we all hold.

(Q. 11-62)

So too Veda enjoins on all :

Your heart, mind and object may all these be one.
So shall you prosper, all, and live in peace;
In Common be your food and drink and work;
God harnesses you all to the same yoke;
The sacrificial fire of spirit tend
Ye all with one intent, as spokes the nave,
Walk ye together on the path of Life,
And speak ye all with voice unanimous
And may your mind all know the self-same Truth.

So also Bible tells :

Be ye all like-minded, compassionate, loving as
brethren, tender-hearted, humble minded,
not rendering evil for evil or reviling for
reviling, but contrariwise blessing...be of
one mind, live in peace. (B. Corinthians)

Says Rumi :

By loving widom doth the soul know life.
What has it got to do with senseless strife
Of Hindu, Muslim, Christian, Arab, Turk.

The 'Bhagwat' has also laid stress on this essential unity of universal Truth :

In varying ways the sages have described.
The same unvarying and essential truths.
There is no real conflict 'twixt them all.
The knowers know the way to reconcile.
Many the words and ways in which the wise
Have tried to teach one truth to all mankind.
Each way, each word, is right in its own place.
There is no conflict 'twixt them all.
The sages see and say the same in each.

All the great living religions are of Asiatic origin. The personal, domestic, and social life of the Hindu is largely governed by the rules of what he regards as his religion. So is that of the Musalman. So of the Jew. So was, and to a considerable extent still is that of the Christian belonging to the Roman catholic form of Christianity. Such also is the case with the followers of the other religions, known as the Zoroastrian, the Buddhist, the Jaina, and the Sikh.

The study of all these religions makes it clear that there is a basic similarity not only in the form but also in the essence.

The 'Bible' says :

Every scripture inspired of God is profitable,
for teaching, for reproof, for correction,
for instruction which is in righteousness,
that the man of God may be complete, furnished
completely unto every good work.

(B.2 Timothy, 3.16-17)

The 'Quran' says :

> *We believe in what hath been revealed to us and revealed to you. Our God and your God is one and to Him are we self-surrendered.*

(Quran 29.45)

Lord Krishna says that :

> *The teaching he is giving to Arjun was given by Vivasvan to Manu, by Manu to Ikshvaku, and then by many Rishis, age after age. All is always present in the memory of God, the Omniscient, Omnipotent, Omnipresent universal self, the one Principle of all life and consciousness.*

The 'Bhagwad Gita' says:

> *The royal saints, the king-philosophers,*
> *Of ancient days, from one unto another.*
> *Did pass this Wisdom on, from age to age !*
> *That same eternal Yoga, Ancient Wisdom,*
> *Have I declared to thee this day, to strengthen*
> *Thy mind and heart for Life's perpetual strike.*

And Prophet Muhammad adds the positive counsel :

> *Let all of us ascent towards, and meet*
> *Together on, the common ground of those*
> *High truths and principles which we all hold.*

(Quran 11-62)

> *Verily, all who faithfully believe*
> *In God, and Day of judgment, and do good,*
> *Be they Jews, Christians, Sabians or Muslims.*
> *They shall have their reward from the Lord God*
> *There is no fear for them, nor shall they grieve*
> *We do believe that which has been revealed*
> *To us, and also what has been revealed*
> *To you. Your God and our God is one,*
> *For sure, and unto Him we both submit.*

(Quran 29, 49)

The 'Bhagwat' says about universal Truth :

Each way, each word, is right in its own place.
There is no conflict 'twixt them all.
The sages see and say the same in each.

If the humanity is to be brought together it is only on the basis of mutual understanding, especially in matters of fundamental belief. The philosophical understanding of the nature of ultimate reality and the practice of love irrespective of distinction of caste, creed, community and nationality, these are the basic assumptions of all living faiths.

If we make a comparative study of the scriptures, we shall notice that the basic truths presented by each are the same in every case. Some of the stories narrated therein and a good many of their expressions and passages appear so similar as to create an impression that these scriptures have proceeded from one common source. They appear an branches proceeding from one and the same trunk, each in its own place and in its own time offering cooling shade to many a weary way-farer wandering in search of truth, and also solace and peace of mind to many a sorrowful heart.

Of the six scriptures referred to above, the 'Rig Veda' is regarded as the earliest, and the 'Quran' the latest. And Yet in the chapter of the 'Quran' entitled 'light' the portion of it which from the praise of God and of his Almighty Power brings to mind parallel hymns of the 'Rig Veda' in praise of God.

Let us now see what the great founders of religions have said of their forbears and of those who would come after them. It we carefully look into their utterances, we will find that all these great men have frankly and in plain terms endorsed the truth presented by every religion.

Sri Krishna says in Gita :

In that way in
Which they worship Me, I give them Fruit
Accordingly. O Purtha; whichever path is followed,
A man ultimately comes and joins into
My path. (4.11)

Says Zoraster

We recognize the religions whichw ere delivered in the past.
They all directed men to goodness in life.

(Yesna. 16:3)

The followers of Buddhism and Jainism believe that from the very beginning a series of Buddhas and Tirthankaras (Guides) have come into the world to show but one and the same path of truth, and that similar guides will come after.

The 'Quran' says :

There must be no compulsion exercised.
In matters of religion. Unto you
Your faith be welcome, so my faith to me.

Regarding respect for all religions, the 'Quran' says :

We believe in what hath been revealed to us and revealed to you.
Our God and your God is one and to him are we self-surrendered.

Regarding basic oneness of all religions the 'Quran' states :

This that I am now uttering unto you
The Holy Quran, it is to be found
Within the ancient seers' writing too
For teachers have been sent to every race
Of human beings. No community
Is left without a warner and a guide
And aught of difference we do not make
For disagreement there is none 'twixt them,
Between these prophets. All that have been sent,
Have been so sent but one truth to proclaim
I, verily the I All-one, am God
There is no other god than I,
And I alone should be adored by all.
Teachers are sent to each race that they may
Teach it in its own tongue, so there may be
No doubt as to the meaning in its mind.
An Arabic Quran is thus revealed,

That Mecca and the cities around may learn
With ease the truth put in the words they know.
For had we made them in a foreign tongue
They surely would have made objections thus
Why have not these revelations been made clear ?

Maulana Azad states that the obvious significance of this remarkable text is that the essentials are common to all religions; that truth is universal, and not the monopoly of anyone race or teacher, that non-essentials vary with time, place, and circumstances, that the same fundamental truths have been revealed by God in different scriptures, in different languages, through different teachers, in different nations. The 'Quran' gives the positive counsel:

Let all of us ascend towards, and meet
Together on the common ground of those
High truths and principles which we all hold.
Verily, all who faithfully believe
In God, and Day of judgment, and do good,
Be they Jews, Christians, Sabians or Muslims,
They shall have their reward from the Lord God.
There is no fear for them, nor shall they grieve.
We do believe that which has been revealed
To us, and also what has been revealed
To you. Your God and our God is one,
For sure, and unto him we both submit.

According to Maulana Azad, the 'Quran' assures us that Islam is not new. God revealed it in earlier times to peoples of other countries through prophets sent to them. Hence this religion is eternal (*sanatan*) and immutable. It was declared to every people through the messengers of God, as stated in many verses of the 'Quran'. This faith is common to all the people of the world, for truth is one and ever abiding. The need for revealing it, again, through Mohammad arose because the people to whom it was previously revealed had corrupted it. They had deviated from the truth of the oneness of God, a truth which must be followed in thought, word, and deed, and not merely repeated by word of mouth.

Maulana Azad further stresses that besides this faith (*din*), the 'Quran' lays down the law (*shara*), which is the external form of the faith, and which regulates man's conduct and prescribes the standards of action. But the law is relative to time and place. It varies according to the social circumstances and the mental capability of a people. In the matter of ritual and worship, therefore, people follow different ways, and the 'Quran' recommends that there ought to be no ground for dispute regarding such matters. The 'Quran' expressly states that God has made for every group of nation a different law and standard. God wished He could have made one law for all.

In his 'Tarjuman-ul-Quran' Azad says :

> *The principle underlying faith in God.(Din-i-Ilahi) is brotherhood and unity of the human race, not difference and hatred. All the Prophets of God who appeared on earth gave the same lesson, i.e. all human beings are one people, and the Supporter of all of them is one God.*

He writes further:

> *God wishes to establish this truth in the mind of everyone, that differences in thought and action are national characteristics of the human race. These differences are present in every aspect of life, including religion. It is not, therefore, proper to consider these differences as the yardstick for truth and falsehood.*

And:

> *The way of belief is to accept the truth of all the prophets and not to deny anyone of them. The way of disbelief is to deny anyone or all of them.*

In conversations with Abdul Razzaq Malihabadi, Azad had stated:

Hadith cannot be the source of law for the whole of human society. The Quran is responsible for universal guidance, but the Quran contains only a limited number of laws. The reason is that no code of laws can apply to the entire world because of differences in times and conditions. Nor can such a code be useful. This explains why the authority to suspend the operation of the authoritative laws of the Quran has been entrusted to the Imam of the Muslims. For example, Ahl-i-Hadith amended the law of divorce and prohibited severance of the hand of a thief.

The Quran teaches that all religions are, in essence, identical however much they may have drifted from their original purity. The Muslims are required to show equal reverence to all the Prophets and the Books that came before the advent of Mohammad and the Quran. Islam brings peace to the world and not the sword. It expressly prohibits the use of force in propagating religion and does not approve disrespect to the places of worship of the non-Muslims.

The Process of Cultural Synthesis in India

The harmonious synthesis amongst votaries of various religions was rendered possible because her ancient religion and culture was comparatively free from racial and territorial jealousy. Though orthodox and exclusive in her social tendencies, India was always ready to adopt and assimilate all that was noble and life-giving in other systems of culture. India's tolerance, like her power of steady assimilation, except in the one respect of caste, was boundless, and it was this tolerance which made it possible for the Hindu and the Muslim communities to co-operate wholeheartedly in her political and economic advancement. Her people, moreover, both Hindu and Muslim, believed (whether rightly or wrongly) kingship to be a divine dispensation, and consequently without any qualms of conscience they could be loyal to any king whether Hindu or Muslim. The social sphere of life was thus freed from much of the acerbity and conflict which usually results from political revolutions. Every king no doubt had to maintain his position against ambitious claimants and rebellious nobles, but the people in general took no interest in their court competitions and conflicts, and readily offered their loyalty to the person who ascended the throne irrespective of whether he had done so through rightful power or through treachery. This social device served as a safety valve to limit the destructive results of ever-recurring political revolutions, and it permitted the widest scope for evolution of that fresh political synthesis after which the collective mind of India was aspiring and which it was trying to achieve by using the personal ambitions of able men as instrument.

Besides all this, a great merit of this theory lay in the fact that as it secured to the ruler the allegiance and loyalty of the whole mass of his subjects almost automatically, it deprived him of the motive of sowing religious or communal discord among his people. We find the kings (with unfortunate exceptions, of course) playing a high role, irrespective of caste or creed, in helping movements of cultural assimilation and social harmony. They welcomed and by their personal example encouraged that synthesis of thought and belief which the saints of both religions vere working into the life of the common people.

The Social Synthesis

While the two religions co-operated in the political field to give shape and form to the synthesis of Indian national life, their influence on social synthesis was no less remarkable. Obviously, the social organizations of the two communities are very different. The Hindu system is a collection of separate units mutually exclusive and deliberately made impervious to all foreign intrusion by a rigid denial of inter-dining and inter-marriage. The social system of Islam is the reverse, broad-based, inclusive, inspired by a feeling of brotherliness and equality. The Hindu system had its own absorbing and assimilating potentiality, but worked slowly and imperceptibly and with many limitations. The Muslims system had great powers of ready adoption and conscious expansion, though it also had its own aloofness and distinctiveness in some respects.

The age and the rigidity of the caste system of India are a marvel for the present-day world. But from all times it has been a problem of the first magnitude to all Indian thinkers and reformers. The indigenous population of India was divided into clans and tribes, before the Aryan civilization crossed its northern valleys. There is reason to believe that the early Aryan thinkers and leaders developed a scheme of social organization, in accord with the psycho-physical laws of heredity as well as spontaneous variation, by which they were able to absorb and civilize and Aryanize the tribes they subjugated as directed in the Vedas, assigning them to one or another of four Main vocational classes. In the course of time, the living elasticity of this scheme was lost, and it became ossified into a caste-system based rigidly on heredity alone, which broke up Hindu society into thousands of fragments. But the national mind continued to yearn for a higher synthesis and its yearnings at last found a powerful expression in Buddhism.

Buddha enunciated again, in a famous verse, the basic principles of the system of four-fold vocational social organization which had degenerated into the so-called caste-system. Though a profound reaction followed after twelve hundred years of Buddhism, yet the higher minds and instincts of the nation continued to move in the same direction. With these Islam was quite in tune, and its advent in India rallied them anew, so that within the Hindu fold concerned, though there was an antagonism on the surface between Islam and Hinduism, yet both were trying, the former consciously and the latter subconsciously so to say, to lead the social system in the same direction. In matters of proselytization there was a fundamental difference between Islam and Buddhism. Buddhism acted from within the social organism and Islam acted wholly from without. Buddhism tried to destroy the hold of Brahmanism, and its Bhikshus were the competitors of Brahman priests. Muslim kings almost universally recognized the special privileges of the Brahmans and there was no competition whatever between the Muslim learned and pirs and faqirs, and the Hindu religious orders—their clientele being different. Islam claimed its disciples mainly from the lowest strata of Hindu society which were practically outside the pale of orthodox Hinduism, and the Hindu religious orders and learned men, who were the custodians of its religious knowledge, could well afford to look upon its successes with indifference.

Its greatest successes were in the Punjab and Bengal where the revival movement had met with the strongest resistance and where, though Buddhism had been crushed, the old order had not been able satisfactorily to assert its authority. But this fact had not and could not have dawned upon the collective Hindu consciousness as no such consciousness existed, on account of the divison of the people into innumerable creeds, each of which was as real and as self-contained and self-assertive as Islam itself. The consciousness of a collective unity could not grow till a real and living religious synthesis had been established, and though the national mind was fast moving in that direction, it was at that period not an accomplished fact. This process of synthesis had already included Buddhism in the array of its other cults, and gave promise that when it became an accomplished fact, Islam would be as much a part of it as the other religions of India.

Comparatively free trom social and religious rancour, co-operating closely in many concerns of life, the two communities generally lived together in peace and harmony. The foreign element in the Muslim community was almost microscopic. And even those who came from other countries generally married women of the land. The Indian woman carried into the homes of those strangers her own spiritual yearnings and religious outlook and thus created a powerful link between their home-life and the life of the country. Besides she imparted into the new home all her graceful and mystic talents and social ceremonies and thus laid the first foundations for the evolution of a common culture.

Apart from this section, exceedingly small in numbers, the rest of the Muslim community consisted of Indians who had accepted Islam as their religion but had never seen any other culture of life than their own. These made a few necessary adjustments in their daily life while the whole tenure and background of that life on the cultural side remained practically unaltered. Conversions, were generally *en masse*, whole *biradaries* deciding together to accept the new religion. Consequently in the lower strata of Mulslim society the old caste organization prevails, sometimes to the exclusion of the personal law of inheritance itself. At no point, therefore, were the social contacts between the two communities ever broken and the change of religion involved no violent break with past.

In the region of politics, in mutual alliances and intrigues, in wars and treaties of peace, Hindus and Muslims acted as members of a common brotherhood. In the sphere of Art of Painting, and Architecture, and even in Music, the two grew side by side and took education, training, and inspiration from common masters. Hindu savants taught Muslim pupils and Muslim savants had Hindus as their disciples, and consequently a synthesis in the genius of two cultures was created which, in its richness and beauty, surpassed all that had been achieved in the past. The military life of the two communities was a mosaic in which Hindu and Muslim officers and Hindu and Muslim chiefs all were placed together. And there could scarcely have been a battle of any consequence in India in which the war-cries of the two communties, "Har Har Mahadeva" and "Allaho Akbar", did not both rise equally on each side of the warring hosts.

Amalgamation of the Two Cultures

The Hindus and Muslims borrowed ideas from each other in philosophy, science, astronomy, medicine, etc. in fine arts architecture, music, dancing, painting, calligraphy, illustration and illumination of manuscripts, weaving of fine clothes of cotton, linen, silk and wool, jewellery, perfumery, etc., in crafts (metal-working, weapon-making, utensil making, etc.) and in almost every conceivable department of life. And in all these lines there was a synthetic progress which enriched life and made it more beautiful than before. Especially in arts connected with gustation and fragrance did the Musalmans introduce many improvements. Many of the most favourite flowers of

India today were brought from other lands or were improved here—Gulab, Gul-i-Daudi, Gul-i-Shabbu, Gul-i-Abbas all show the country of their importation or the religion of their improvers. Many fruits were newly introduced, many indigenous ones were perfected. Along with the flora, the fauna of India also enriched. The breeds of horses, camels, and pigeons were greatly improved. In music, Khayal, Thumri, Dadra, Ghazal, all were developed during this period. The lower we descend the wider becomes the basis of this synthesis. In food and dress, wonderful interchange and additions took place in this period. While the basic articles of food remained common to Hindu and Muslim homes, such as *dal*, rice, *chapati, roti* and *sabzi*. Many new additions were made to sweets and other delicacies such as *Halwa, Qalaqand, Khurma, Balushahi, Barfi, Gulab Jamun, Imarti* etc., which were developed by the common tastes of the people. The additions to meat dishes were innumerable, as Muslims were meat-eaters and so were a very large majority of Hindus. The names of the clothes and utensils and articles of furniture used by Hindus and Musalmans alike are an inseparable mixture of Sanskrit and Persian words.

Many teachers arose, from time to time, with numerous following, within Hinduism, Kabir in the middle country, Namadeva and Tukaram in the south, Chaitanya in the east, Nanak in the north, to mention only a few, who preached the essentials of Universal Religion. They tried hard to break the unreasonable, harmful, tyrannical, and withal largely unreal and hypocritical, system of countless rigidly hereditary castes and sub-castes; to promulgate simple forms of worship; and to reconcile Hinduism and Islam, using in their teachings and preachings terms and conceptions taken from both religions.

Islam came into India at a time when reactionary conservatism had defeated Buddhism and Jainism and was trying to revive the rigidly hereditary social order and its connected ways of worship of all sorts of things. The deeper side of Buddhism naturally could not appeal to the masses of India because it was too metaphysical. No doubt, it was presented to it also in a popular form, but Mahayana, on its intellectual, emotional or mystic sides, was not substantially different from or superior to the other great cults of India. But though India gave up Buddhism in name and form it assimilated and retained within itself its metaphysics and moral consciousness, and high and wide spiritual yearnings in the shape of revived Vedanta and the Jnana-yoga, Bhakti-yoga and Karmayoga of the Gita.

Just before Islam entered into India this powerful tendency of the revival movements was finding, expression in re-emphasizing the old great conception of the Tri-murti which represented the three gods—Brahma, Vishnu, and Mahesha—as three aspects (*Sat, Chit, Ananda,* or *Wujud, Ilm, Shuhud*) of the same divinity. Shortly before or after Islam's entry into India was born the great Shankara who was one of the profoundest thinkers of his age. Shankara systematized anew the teachings of the Vedanta and gave to his nation's genius the conceptual synthesis and the spiritual principle it was struggling to reconsider. He put this synthesis on a sound philosophic basis, and reconciled and disarmed conservatism by basing it on the authority of revealed scriptures. Shankara showed that the diversity of religious beliefs and forms of worship was due to misunderstanding and misinterpretation of the scriptures, that *Sanatana Dharma* had always insisted on the worship of one God, the creator and sustainer of the Universe; that his worship was the true worship and the rest was all delusion. The burning Monotheism of Shankara had a fraternal resemblance, and there was nothing in the two systems which could repel one another.

The Saints and Sufis

No sooner the principle was discovered and put before the people in the proper form than the genius of India began to think of applying it to the practical concerns of life. India works upon her people not through economic and political motives but through moral and spiritual ideas, and consequently her approaches to life's problems are not so much intellectual as emotional. Two centuries or so after Shankara, another great teacher and preacher, Ramanuja gave a devotional turn to Shankara's Monism. The worship of the Divine Principle became the ruling passion of the Indian people. This movement found its emotional expression in the dominance of the Bhakti schools of thought with their fervour of devotion and their (at least theoretical) disregard for established ritual and caste restrictions. Islam, through Sufism, was developing its emotional side identically on the same line; and here the synthesis of the two systems became so complete that they virtually lost themselves in one another. The joy of the new-found oneness transcended all social and religious barriers, and through the emotional side India came near to the realization of that social unity which Buddhism had assayed to achieve from the intellectual side. Thousands upon thousands of hymn-singers coverd the land with their songs of divine oneness and human brotherhood. Many saints, Hindu and Muslim, wandered from place to place, propagating the same message. Many Gurus and Pirs settled down in every corner of land to whom millions of Hindu and Muslim disciples went for moral and spiritual guidance. The intellectual understanding and sympathy which after Shankara between the learned and higher existed sections of the two communities was thus carried through the emotional side to the lowest strata of Indian society.

3

Indian Fundamentalism and its Way Out

Ramjee Singh

Fundamentalism is considered merely as a reaction against the liberalizing tendencies of modern thought. It has been a reaction against something new. The term 'fundamentalism' is used to designate what is more generally called a conservative type of the thought as opposed to liberal or modernist tendencies and as a name of a specific conservative movement with its own organizations and agencies devoted to the propagation of a definite doctrinal programme.[1] Needless to say that in the past it has been used in the context of Christian thought. However, today it is being used in a wide sense including religious fundamentalism of all types—Islamic, Zionist, Hindu, Buddhist etc. It is thought to be an extreme position characterized by the belief that the Bible or the Quran, or the Vedas is verbally accurate rendering of the word of God and the writers were inspired to the smallest detail of revealed truth it adheres to traditional beliefs of any kind.[2] Thus it stands for strict adherence to traditional orthodox tenets of beliefs.[3]

Hopkins says that "India always has been a land of religions."[4] At least four religions—Buddhism, Jainism, Sikhism and different strands of Vedic-Brahmanic religion—are of indigenous origin. However, "the national form of Indian religion is Hindusism."[5] But other world religions like Christianity, Islam, Zoroastrianism have also deep roots in India. At the same time there is an underlying unity in the religious life of India.[6] Indian culture is a continuous process of synthesis. It has assimilated not only the religious beliefs and practices of the Aryans and the pre-Aryans (like the Negrits, Mongoloids, the Dravidians etc.) but also of many other races like the Sakas, the Sethians, the Hunas, the Gurjars, the Pratiharas etc. The cultural history of the Muslims also is an integral part of Indian culture. Similarly, the Pre-Islamic Indian culture is as much the heritage of the Muslims of India as of the Hindus. India's relations with the Arab world did not start with the dawn of Islam; trade between the West Coast and the Arabian Peninsula was a part of its ancient history. Arab traders and the religious men after the advent of Islam (570 A.D.) came to South India even before Muslims came as invaders starting with the conquest of Sind by Muhamad-bin-Kasim (711-713 A.D.).[7] In the 8th century Arab settlements in the South multiplied due to increase in the commercial activity. The Zamorin rulers of Calicut patronised the Arab marchants and were permitted to constuct mosques and religious institutions and follow the Islamic Personal Law. Quazis were endowed with full powers to decide disputes. Similarly, the original Christians are scattered in the Southern peninsula of India. These MarToma Christians and a later group of Christians, flowing from persecution in the Middle East arrived in India for refuge in 350 A.D. Thus, the 'Syrian Christians' are the original Christians of India. They were never persecuted by the Hindus, Buddhists, Jainas or Muslims but the zealous Christian missionaries from the occident persecuted them and burnt their literature because of their so-called deviations from European beliefs and practices.[8] St. Thomas and his disciples came to India with the gospel of Jesus[9] and founded the Christian Church in Southern India in the seventh century A.D. Jessuit missons were well received in the court of Emperor Akbar (1556-1605 A.D.) but his tolerance for all religions was disliked by the Jessuits who had already set up an inquisition Court at Goa. A mixture of motives of trade and missionary zeal led many missions of the Roman Catholics, Protestants, American Methodists and Baptists, up to Mother Teresa from Albania to work with honour and distinction in India. Even after partition of India, precisely on religious lines. India today is the second largest Muslim population in the world (150 millions) and the Constitution of India has declared India to be a Secular State, where all citizens enjoy equal rights, irrespective of caste, colour, creed, religion or sex.[10] There is complete freedom for every citizen to practise any religion[11] he or she chooses and no discrimination is made on this account.

This separation of religion and State has been a characteristic feature of the Indian political system. The Hindu rulers allowed Muslims and Christians to practice their faith with freedom. The children of Israel received hospitality in India several centuries before the beginning of the Christian era. The Zoroastrians, the first group of Pilgrim Fathers in history, fleeing from Iran before Mohammedan persecution, were hospitably received by a Hindu Prince and given land to build their temple. Neither the Jews nor the Zoroastrians have been persecuted in India. Muslim mystics, saints and sufis have always been looked with veneration by the Hindus. The medieval Indian society was influenced by the rise of the Sufism among the Muslims and the Bhakti movements among the Hindus. Among the Muslims saints, sufis and poets, the names of Mohaddis, Amir Khusro, Nizamuddin Auliya, Sharafuddin Yaha Manyari, Sh. Amars, Miyan Mir, Sah Mohibullah, Sh. Burhan Shaffari Bulle Sah, Rahim, Raskhan etc. and among the Hindu mystic saints, we have Raidas, Meera, Sankaradeva-Madhavadeva, Ramdas, Tulsi, Sura, Thyagaraj etc. who also have advocated universal humanism. Kabir and Nanak are symbols of human unity. It was a Muslim who had laid the foundation of the sanctum sanctorum of the Sikhs at Amritsar. Devotional cult is basically against all fundamentalism. Even during the modern Indian Renaissance, the voice of liberalism is always heard. Ramakrishna-Vivekanand advocated 'Universal Religion', so Tagore stood for the 'Religion of Man', Bhagawandas pleaded for the 'essential unity of all religions' and Gandhi lived and died for upholding 'Equal respect for all religions'.

This legacy of liberalism has been wisely inherited by the great Moghuls and other Muslim monarchs. Unlike the Muslim rulers in Arabia and Africa, Muslim rule in India was almost secular because propagation of Islamic religion was not their objective. Muslim rulers even offered gifts to Hindu temples and royal assistance to classical Hindu schools. From Emperor Babar (Babarnama) to Aurangzeb (Adbe Alamgiri, Rukat Alamgiri) and Ţippu Sultan, they had prohibited cow slaughter to respect the sentiments of their Hindu subjects. They did not play the role of 'defenders of faith' or 'custodians of faith' but acted as the chief of the law and order machinery. This is one of the reasons which not only allowed uninterrupted 400 years of Muslim rule in India but also provided Hindu devotional reform movement to grow without state interference. Not to speak of liberal Muslim rulers like Akbar, Darashikoh, Bahadur Shah, Tippu etc., Muslim political establishments in India with a few exceptions like Sultan Sikandar of Kashmir, Firoz Tughlaque, Sikander Lodi etc., rejected repugnant intolerance and anti-humanistic fundamentalism of some Muslim theologians and interpreters. This even led to repeated tensions between the Muslim political rulers and some of the fundamentalist Muslim theologians in India. Ziauddin Barni's *Tarikh-I-Firozshahi* (pp. 42-72) and *Fatwa-I-Jahandari* have ample evidences to show that the Muslim rulers denied the mandate of some of their theologians for making unnecessary state intereference in the religious practices of the Hindus or making their persecutions.

We can conclude that exclusiveness of thought or behaviour is alien to Indian culture. What it aims is not the monopoly of a particular religion or culture but it wants that particular groups follow particular cultures or philosophers with spirit of co-existence and harmony. Indian history does not point to any massacres, forcible mass migrations, religious bans, forced conversions. Buddhism and Jainism challenged the Vedic orthodoxy and its authority but this was done not by the sword, but by the pen. This led to cross-fertilisation of ideas and cultures. The cultural diversity of India can be explained only on the basis of its socio-cultural dynamics of tolerance of doctrinal differences and cultural forms. What is not accepted is that any such philosophy or religion should think of lording it over. Change from one such philosophy or religion is not indeed prohibited, what specifically forbidden is non-intellectual methods of persecutions or declaring any particular religion as the State Religion and treating other co-religionists as second-rate citizens. Hinduism, by its character and constitution has never been an exclusive religion. In it, there is room for worship of all prophets of the world. It is also not an evangelical or missionary religion. It has no taste for religious conversion. It tells everyone to worship God according to his own faith or *Dharma* and so it lives at peace with all religions. In short, it is not a religion of the prison-house.

There is thus, an underlying liberalism and tolerance for other views in the Indian psyche and its racial unconscious that is aware of plural truth-claims or faith in alternative standpoints and a non-absolutistic cultural frame has become the characteristic Indian way of thought and action. The Hindu doctrine of spiritual level of competence of a person (*adhikars*) advocates that the truth should be formulated in accordance with the level of understanding and competence of different persons who all differ from each other also serve to promote non-fundamentalism. Then there is also a faith that we can worship the essential formless divine being in any form of one's own choice (*Ista-devata*). This means that no one form can claim to be intrinsically more desirable than another, so that the desire to convert others or bring about uniformity in belief and worship is uncalled for. This brings so much of catholicism in thought and behaviour that even the belief in God is not adhered to. There are a good number of sceptics, agnostics, heretics, and atheists etc. in the Hindu-fold who enjoy freedom of thought. The Buddhists and the Jainas, not only denied the very existence of God but also challenged the authority of the Vedas and the Vedic priest and yet Lord Mahavira and Lord Buddha were regarded and revered as incarnations of God by the Hindus. The most ancient Indian Scripture called the Vedas (knowledge) is eclectic enough to declare : "The one Reality, the learned speak of in many ways."[12] Next to the Vedas, the most hollowed and philosophic treatises called the *Upanisads* (secret knowledge) follows the same line. "Cows are of many different colours but the milk of all is of one colour, white : so the proclaimers who proclaim the Truth, use many varying forms yet the Truth enclosed in all is one or as streaming rivers pass in the sea, abandoning all separate name and form and merges into the State Beyond."[13] Next to the Vedas and the Upanisads, the most venerated and popular work called the Gita (Song Celestial) try to elucidate the same catholic spirit : "All men approach Me, so do I accept them; men on all sides follow My path"[14]...All human beings, though they seem to walk on divergent paths are marching to One God."[15] Even as the several senses apprehend the different qualities of the same thing, so many lines of searching sciences show aspects, numerous of the One Lord".... Whatever form any devotee with faith wishes to worship, I make that faith of his steady." Echoing the Vedic spirit, the Jain heritage is even more eclectic, when Samantabhadra while paying his obesiance expresses the same spirit "In you, O Lord airse all view-points, even as rivers rise out cf the ocean and just as the ocean cannot be seen in those rivers so long they remain separate, even so, you cannot be seen in the separate view-points." The Jain philosophy of Non-absolutism (*Anekantavada*) and Conditionality of Judgement (*Syadavada*) are classic instruments of foundational basis of catholicity. According to this theory, we are not the sole possessors of truth and the rest are in the clutches of devils. Even in the monistic system of Vedanta, three different levels of reality corresponding to three levels of perspectives provide abundant scope for catholicity of thought and judgement and its doctrine of non-violence is the very anti-thesis of fundamentalism and aggressiveness. The famous scholar-poet Pushpadanta supports this spirit so beautifully : "Whatever paths the ordinary mortals, according to their varying tastes and aptitudes adopt for seeking the Lord, by each and everyone of those paths is He attainable, as the sea is to the waters of all the rivers running towards it." Like the Jaina doctrine of Non-absolutism (*Anekantavada*), the Buddhist doctrine of (*Vibhajyavada*) and the doctrine of Middle Path (*Madhyama Pratipada*) are ample proofs of methodological and ideological non-fundamentalism. The Great Emperor Ashok's Edict says : "Whoever honours his own sect and dispurges another man's does his own sect the greatest possible harm." The most renowned poet of India Kalidasa says : "All paths of realization, though manifold and different traditions. How to you only even as all streams of Ganga How into the ocean." (*Raghuvamsa*)

Hence, what has been happening in India on the religious front like the rise of fundamentalism is only an aberration and mostly politically motivated phenomena. The Indian Freedom Movement right from 1857 to 1947 has a tradition of religious harmony. The last of the Moghul, Bahadur Shah Jafar had become the hero of both Hindus and Muslims against British imperialism. During Gandhi's leadership, the Hindus zealously fought together with their Muslim brethren the battle of Khilafat. Due to the British policy of Divide and Rule, the country was divided on communal lines and its bitterness continues. Not only the country was divided but this naturally created division in the minds of men. The rise of fundamentalism is the result of hopes behind, frustrations and mistrust. However, even now after the division of the country on religious lines, Indian State is an ideal of secularism. It has the second largest Muslim population in the world living with equal rights. At least two eminent Muslims have ocupied the supreme position of the President of India. It has inducted Muslims, Christians, Sikhs on other high positions of the country without discrimination. Besides, India developed intimate relations with Afghanistan, Iraq, Iran, Indonesia and other Islamic countries. It fought most valiantly for the right of self-determination of the Palestinian people. It has maintained most cordial relations with the Egypt and the Arab world.

The very fact that India has a synthetic culture, it cannot become fundamentalist. This synthesis and growth of mixed culture is a proof against insolence, pride of a particular race or religion. There has been constant give and take between the Aryans and the Dravidians, between the Vedic Brahmanas and the Sramanas, among Hindus, Muslims and Christians. What to speak of philosophy and religion, there has been sharing together in the fields of language and literature, art and music, folklore and festivals. Notwithstanding political rivalries confined mostly to the corridors of power, people in India do not like extremism or fundamentalism.

However, there is no denying the fact that even as aberrations, both Islamic and Hindu fundamentalism have raised their ugly heads in recent past in India. Muslim fundamentalism is a world-wide phenomena whether it is in Libya or Iran, Afghanistan or Pakistan, Bosnia or Sudan. The very fact that most of the Muslim countries have adopted theocratic structure of State and they have set up organisation of Islamic Countries on the global plane and there has been growing intolerance towards freedom of expression and writing in some parts of the Islamic world, all these have its impact on the minds of Indians. The majority of the Hindus feel disillusioned with Muslim leadership as primarily under their influence, India was divided. Not only this, almost all political parties in India try to make some appeasement and use the Muslims as their vote banks. This has created a reaction in the Hindu mind and they have become more conscious of their own religious identity. But non-fundamentalism has been an article of faith with the people of India. Forcible conversion, discretion of places of worship have no approval. India is a multi-ethnic country with a distinctly pluralistic heritage. The current belligerent posture of Hindutva is a passing phase. That is why the Ram-wave has not only been halted in Indian politics but has received a setback after the Ayodhya tragedy. Fundamentalism among Muslims also has received a severe jolt and saner sections of the Muslims have asked the Babri Masjid agitation to stop. India has two kinds of identity : cultural and political. Political identity is firmly rooted in a secular and federal constitution with multi-verse all India political parties and unified administration. The question of political identity of India is thus too important to be brushed aside. It is one of the largest democracies with the finest judiciary at the apex in the world. It has shown remarkable unity against secessionism and any external threat. However, its spiritual cultural identity distinguishes itself from the West and this is a common heritage. So far its socio-cultural identity is concerned, it is based on the fellowship of diversity in unity which has the quality of creativeness and universalism. The cultural tradition and identity has always been synthetic and adaptive with values of tolerance, accommodation and co-existence. Milton Singer (The Modernisation of Religious Beliefs in Myron Weiner) (ed.

Modernisation : The Dynamics A Growth, New York; Basic Book, 1968), M.N. Srinivas (*On Living in a Revolution and Other Essays*, London : Oxford University Press, 1992), Yogendra Singh (*Modernisation of Indian Tradition : A Systematic Study of Social Change*, Delhi : Thomson, 1973) maintain that the Indian society has been adopting and assimilating itself. Narayan has shown that "tolerance and respect for other's views and feeling" has been "the hallmark of Indians over the centuries." This signifies the pluralist character of Indian cultural identity. Srinivas is perhaps realistic when he says that those who deplore various forms of sub-nationalism such as ethnicity, communalism, linguistic consciousness and regionalism are unaware that they are all parts of the package of nationalism itself when it hits a developing country and the danger that such nationalism may overwhelm nationalism is an ever present one. Hence uniformitarian model is unsuitable for multi-ethnic societies like India. To obliterate every other religion than one's own is a sort of Bolshevism in religion.[16] The Indian solution seeks the unity of religion not in a common creed but in a *common quest*. It believes in a unity of spirit and not of organisation, a unity which secures ample liberty not only for every individual, but for every type of organised life which has proved itself effective. Deeper experience of reality is no monopoly of any particular prophet or church. The world would be a much poorer place if one creed absorbed the rest. God has bestowed upon India a rich harmony and not a colourless uniformity. Ramkrishna, who had tried successively Hindu, Muslim and Christian symbols as means of *Sadhana* compared, "different religions to the *ghats* (shores) around the same tank." Hence, Vivekanand says : "There never was *my* religion or *yours*, my national religion or your national religion; there never existed many religions, there is only the one—expressing itself in its various ways.[17] The famous Rock Edict of Emperor Ashoka clearly warns to "avoid the extrolling of one's own religion to the decrying of the religion of the other or speaking lightly of it without occasion or relevance.[18] India has been a laboratory of synthesis of facts and creeds. There has been synthesis of Vishnu and Siva cults, Aryan and Non-Aryan cultures. After Ashoka's efforts to establish Universal Religion, Emperor Akbar and Saint Kabir tried to bring Hinduism and Islam together. So Vivekananda also pleaded for synthesis of Islam and Vedanta. Brahmos tried to bring together Hinduism and Christianity. Ramkrishna, Vivekananda, Tagore, Iqbal, Gandhi, Radhakrishnan and Nehru and all leading lights of modern India provided religion a cosmic dimension, all-embracing and all-inclusive, as the world or the same God. The third President of the Republic of India Dr. Zakir Hussain has said : "Providence has destined India to be the laboratory in which the greatest experiment of cultural synthesis will be undertaken and successfully completed."[19] In the Indian mind, there is no rivalry among religions for supremacy or for superiority. Indeed, a good Hindu as Gandhi used to say, would admonish the Muslim to be a better Muslim, a Christian to be a better Christian and so on.[20] Emperor Ashoka valued neither gifts nor honours so highly as that there should be a promotion of the essential elements of (High) Religion in all religions ... there should be no exaltation of one's religion and finding fault with others.[21] Indian secularism is the logical outcome of this philosophy of religious tolerance which is its natural character and its philosophical faith in alternative standpoints and *homo hurarchius*. Indian culture hates proselytization and persecution because it knows that it will be unspiritual and counter-productive. Besides, the Hindu socio-religious arrangements are so structured that spread of its dogmas by force is impossible. Hindu king was no Caliph and there was no Hindu sword to propagate religion by wars or by sanguinary persecution to force consciences.[22] *Ortho-prasix* is more central to man's life than *ortho-doxy*. Therefore, Ashoka pleaded only for "*Dharma*" or as Gandhi said : "Ethical Religion". Vivekananda says : "It is not the man who believes a certain something, but the man who does the will of the Father is heaven, who is right. On this basis being right and doing right—the whole world can unite."[23] The Indian approach to relativization of religions are not reduced to mere pragmatic and intellectual levels because true religion is of intuitive order. "Religion is not the acceptance of academic abstractions or the celebrations of the ceremonies, but a kind of experience."[24] Here there is a tolerance not at the lower intellectual, but at a higher intuitive and different levels. Popular model of interrelationship of different religions can be understood as "many rivers leading to the sea"[25] or "colours of a spectrum of light"[26] or as pluralism of langauges referring to the same reality.[27]

Conclusion

Both ideologically as well as historically, Indian culture has been secular in character except a very few minor aberrations. Perhaps, this was its genius and also its destiny. However, Indian secularism is not necessarily either anti-religious or anti-theistic. Since ancient times up to the present period, there has been disassociation of religion and politics in India. What to speak of the ancient Hindu period, even during the long regime of Moslem and Moghul Kings, this cult of secularism continued only with a few exceptions. This is one of the reasons which has allowed Hindu Bhakti movement to grow uninterruptedly. However, it is no denying the fact that the most grievous wounds to Indian secularism was inflicted by playing imperialistic game of "divide and rule" and dividing the country on Hindu-Muslim communal lines in 1947. If there would have a religious state in India at that time, it could have been only a Hindu State with more than 90 per cent Hindu population but it is interesting to observe that the idea of India being anything but a secular state was never seriously raised in the Indian Constituent Assembly, not even by the Hindu Mahasabha, a Hindu organisation. The founding fathers of the Indian Constitution guaranteed equal fundamental rights to all citizens including full religious freedom. This has been recently upheld both by the people at the mini-general election ousting substantially such forces trying to mix up politics with religion as well as in the recent full bench verdict of the apex Court of the country that secularism is the "basic structure" of the Constitution of India and any government which violates this principle is bound to be dismissed. In fact, such a faith in non-fundamentalism is both its heritage as well its sociological compulsion. There are some grounds :

1. Firstly, we know that in the field of speculative knowledge or knowledge of final truth, it is difficult to say that a particular theory is false or true. Hence any absolutistic stance is wrong. Therefore, the Indian genius has devised several ideological weapons to fight fanaticism like the philosophy of Non-absolutism (*Anekanta*), Relativity of Judgement (*Syadvada*), Levels of knowledge and Reality, all-inclusive universalism and so on. While philosophical systems represent varying stages in an ascending order, they are coordinated by a "synthetic process a sublime picture of synthesis", might emerge.
2. Secondly, the Indian mind believes in the principle of dignity of man and respect for individuals. Liberty of individual conscience is granted to the maximum. That is why there is a rich store of philosophical systems and religious schools flourishing side by side. There is no tradition of persecution or inquisitions for practicing any faith like scepticism, agnosticism, atheism, materialism and so on. There is, thus, "ideological autonomy" or "Swaraj in Ideas". This tradition of "individual freedom" has been continuing up-to-date. This is the strongest pillar of Indian secularism and catholicism.
3. The Indians are constrained to believe that in the sphere of ethics, *"there are truths but not one truth"*. "To one who has such a desire, any doctrine that the pattern of the ideal life should be the same for all is intolerable."[28] Even there is no one idea about God or Reality. Then there is not one single path of self-realization or salvation. There are paths of knowledge, action, devotion etc. all equally good. This is not cheap compromise at the cost of truth but a way of life to foster diversity in the pursuit of ideal ends.

4. It is true that majority of people are Hindus in India, hence all other religious societies are influenced by its usages and action and *vice versa*. Hinduism is not a proselytising religion. However as a reaction to Christianity, the Arya Samaj launched its *Shuddhi* (reconversion) movement to reclaim for the Hindu fold people who had been converted to Islam or Christianity. However, this has not been able to become a popular and regular feature as we find in Christianity or Islam. Recently in South India, when the entire village people of Meenakshipuram were converted to Islam, there was strong resentment in Hindu society and a Bill called "Freedom of Religion" was moved in the Indian Parliament by a Private Member so as to curb religious conversion either through "fraud, force or temptation." But great hue and cry was raised by evangelical religionists mainly Christians, and then the Bill was withdrawn with the consent of Hindus, who constituted the majority.
5. Democratic structure of the Indian State and inclusion of Articles 14, 15, 16 (Right to Equility, No Discrimination), and Articles 25 and 26 (Freedom of Conscience and right freely to profess, practice and propagate religion, and freedom to manage religious affairs including religious institutions), and Articles 29 and 30 (providing for the protection of minorities) are one of the safest guarantee against fundamentalism. No political party can afford to go against the minorities because they have the balancing vote. Indian judiciary is perhaps most impartial as well as most strong. The Election Commission is also extremely impartial and non-partisan. Over and above, there is absolute freedom of Press in India. All these provide an insurance against fundamentalism in India.

India's religious heritage is unmatched in the world. Practically all living religions of the world have found refuge in the land. She gave hospitality to Judaism, Zoroastrianism, Christianity and Islam. The geography of India points to her natural isolation, but her history reveals a record of uninterrupted contacts with the outside world. She has been engaged not only in rewriting but also reconstructing her own past history. Religion is not an 'ism', not a bundle of creeds, beliefs, rites and rituals, but it is the inner nature of man and our whole life. It is that which holds together or upholds the integrity of the individual, of society, of the cosmos. It is useless to give a particular label like Hindu, Muslim or Christian. It is "Eternal" (*Sanatan*), and "Universal", it is "Ethical" and "Spiritual".

REFERENCES

1. *Encyclopaedia Britannica,* 1964 ed., vol. IX, p. 1009.
2. *New Webster English Dictionary,* p. 384.
3. Ali, Syed, "India's Cultural Traditions : Hindu-Muslim Synthesis", *Tolerance in Indian Culture,* ed. R. Balsubramanian, Delhi : I.C.P.R., 1992, p. 71.
4. Hopkins, E.B., *The Religions of India,* New Delhi, Munshiram Manoharlal, 1970 (2nd ed.), p. 1.
5. Weber, Max, *The Religions of India,* Illinois : The Free Press, 1958, p. 4.
6. Morgan, K., *The Religion of the Hindus,* Delhi : Motilal Banarsidass, 1987, (Reprint), p. 6.
7. Ali, Syed, *Tolerance in Indian Culture,* ed. R. Balsubramanian, Delhi, I.C.P.R., 1992, pp. 72-73.
8. Mazumdar, H.T., *India's Religious Heritage,* Delhi : Allied Publishers, 1986, Vol. I, p. 148.
9. "And he said unto them. Go ye into all the world preach the gospel to the whole creation". *New Testament,* Mark 16 : 15.
10. *Constitution of India :* The Preamble to the Constitution says that India shall be a"Sovereign, Socialist, Secular Democratic Republic" which will "secure to all its citizens".
11. Art. 14 : The State shall not deny to any person Equality before the law.
    Art. 15 : Prohibits discrimination on grounds of religion, race, caste, sex or place of birth.
    Art. 16 : Prohibits discrimination against opportunity in matters of public employment.
    Arts. 25 and 26 : Freedom of conscience and right freely to profess, practice and propagate religion, and freedom to manage religious affairs including religious institutions.
    Arts. 29 and 30 : Provide for the protection of minorities.

12. *Rigveda*, I. 164, 46.
13. Quoted by Bhagavan Das from Upanisads (*Essential Unity of All Religions*), Bombay Bhartiya Vidya Bhavan, 1960 (ed.) p. 75.
14. *Bhagavad Gita*, IV. 11.
15. *Ibid*, III, 33.
16. Radhakrishnan, R.K., *The Hindu View of Life*, London, 1927, p. 42.
17. *The Gospel of Ramkrishna*, New York, 1907, p. 151.
18. Swami Vivekananda, *The Complete Works*, Vol. IV, p. 180.
19. *Edicts of Emperor Ashoka*, trans. by S. Murthy and A.N.K. Ayangar, Madras, Adyar, 1951, *Rock Edict* XIII. pp. 33-37.
20. Quoted by Dr. H.T. Mazumdar in *India's Religious Heritage*, Allied Publishers Private Limited, Bombay, 1986, p. ix.
21. *Edict of Emperor Ashoka*, quoted *Ibid.*, p. xiv.
22. Bacon spoke of 'Mohamet's sword'.
23. Swami Vivekananda, *Complete Works*, V, p. 273.
24. Radhakrishnan, S., *The Hindu View of Life*, p. 13.
25. Swami Vivekananda, *Complete Works*, Vol. I, p. 390.
26. Pannikar, K.M., *The Inter-religious Dialogue*, New York, 1978, pp. 21-22.
27. *Ibid.*, pp. XXIV-XXV.
28. Strawson, P.F., *Freedom and Resentment and other Essays, Social Morality and Individual Idea*, Methuen 1974, pp. 28-29.

4

The Political Thought of Yājñavalkya

Sureshwar Jha

In ancient India, political thought and philosophy were not formulated as independent disciplines by political thinkers, but by metaphysicians and philosophers. Political affairs were treated in the Indian tradition as a part of human behaviour and seen as inseparably intertwined as with the problem of human destiny and moral and spiritual values. In the study of the ancient political thought of our country, we have to appreciate the comprehensive and religious approach of our writers. Only with the advent of the *Arthaśāstra* literature we witness the rise of an intensive and realistic approach to the problems of politics and administration. Even this sort of literature is, however, heavily influenced by the dominant religious and philosophical concepts of the ancient tradition.

That there was a great deal of thinking and speculation in the realm of political science, law and administration of justice many centuries before Christ is evident from the *Mahābhārata* and the early *Dharmasūtras* such as those of Gautama, Baudhāyana and Āpastamba. In the *Śāntiparva,* the word *Nitiśāstra* is used several times in the sense of political science. Bṛhaspati's views on politics and allied matters are frequently quoted in the great epic : the pages of the *Mahābhārata* clearly illustrate that the author had before him an extensive treatise on *Arthaśāstra* by Bṛhaspati. The *Mahābhārata* had also before it a treatise of *Rājanīti* by Uśanas, an ancient sage. Aśvaghosh in his *Buddhacarita* (1.46) mentions the *Rājaśāstra* authored by Śukra, the son of Bhṛgu. In the *Rāmāyaṇa* also, we have a good deal of information regarding the principles of *Arthaśāstra.*

Besides the two great epics, some of the *Purāṇas* also deal with *Rājadharma* at great length. The names of the *Matsya* and the *Agni Purāṇas* may be specially mentioned in this regard.

Indian political thinkers including those of Mithila have dealt with political thought connected with *Dharma* since the time of the Vedas down to the age of digests and *Nibandhas*. *Dharmaśāstra,* besides dealing with *Ācāra* and purification also deals with *Rājadharma* (politics), *Vivāda* (law proper) and *Vyavahāra* (auxiliary or procedural law). Hindu thinkers did not consider the principles of political science, theories of state, law and jurisprudence as separate from the general rule or mode of moral conduct and behaviour of the individual vis-á-*vis* the community. The term *Dharmaśāstra* is a very comprehensive one and baffles a precise and categorical definition in Western terms. It is, however, only fair to attempt to have first a clear idea of the term *Dharma.*

"*Dharma* is one of those Sanskrit words that defy all attempts at an exact rendering in English or any other language."[1] Though used at least as many as fifty-six times in the Hymns of the *Ṛgveda,* it is not clear what the exact meaning of the word was in the Vedic language. "Right from the Vedas, the most ancient of the world's literature, down to the most modern times, this word will be found to have been used in a variety of senses expressing Diverse notion."[2]

Dharma is derived from the root *dhṛ* (धृ), 'to hold', 'to support', 'to nourish' and denotes the same idea as the word law derived from 'lago', 'to bind'. In religious ordinances and rites as in the *Ṛgveda,* I. 22.18, V. 26.6., VIII. 43.24., IX.64.1 2C. In other passages, e.g., IV.53.3., V. 63. 7., VI.701., VII.89.5, the meaning seems to be fixed principles or rules of conduct.[3] In the *Aitareya Brāhmaṇa,* the word seems to be used in an abstract sense, meaning 'the whole body of religious duties'. In the *Bṛhadāraṇyaka* and the *Chāndogya* Upaniśads, the word is used with different connotations. The former, attributed to Yājñavalkya treats *Dharma* and *Satya* as equivalent (I.14.14) while according to the latter (2.23), *Dharma* has three branches : one is constituted by sacrifice, study and charity (i.e., the stage of the householder); the second by austerities (i.e., the stage of being a hermit) and the third is for the stage of the *brahmacārin,* dwelling in his teacher's house.

The word *Dharma* has thus passed through many transitions of meaning and at long last its most prominent significance came to be "the privileges, duties and obligations of a man, his standard of conduct as a caste member and as a person in a particular stage of life."[4]

Dharma has several aspects. In ancient times, it was treated as a divine being, but generally it is alluded to as an impersonal precept. For example, sacrifice, that which is propounded by the Veda (वेद प्रतिपाद्य); the ancient *Ṛta,* the ethical duty and virtue, that which is morally proper; or good deeds; religious duty or virtue; the ideal; a universal law or principle identical with God or Absolute Truth; Divine justice; a code of custom and traditions; common or international law. According to *Smṛticandrikā, Dharma* stands for the rules laid down for the proper administration of different classes of people, such as *Varṇadharma, Jātidharma, Aśramadharma, Varṇāśramadharma, Guṇadharma, Rājdharma* and other *Dharmas.* It is also used in regard to actions and behaviour of people in this world such as *Pravritti-Dharma* and *Nivṛtti-Dharma.*

Dharma, or law, therefore, has an abstract significance and at the same time a concrete one. The term 'law' coincides thoroughly with the term *Dharma,* not in origin and derivation, neither linguistically, nor socially and scientifically, but in that the derivations as well as the connotations of the two terms are co-extensive in all respects. For, while the term 'law' is derived from a Latin root which means 'to uphold', 'to bind', *Dharma* also owes its origin to the Sanskrit root meaning 'to uphold', 'to bind'. Law and *Dharma,* therefore, in their abstract conception, have a complete and grand coincidence.

Next to the *Vedas* and the *Vedāṅgas* comes the *Dharmaśāstra* which constitutes the principle source of law, political theories and practice of jurisprudence. *Dharmaśāstra* assimilates within its scope the *Sūtras,* the *Smṛtis,* the *Nibandhas* and the digests. *Dharmaśāstra* discusses polity, statecraft and administration. It is clear from the above discussion that the modern English term 'religion' in no way conveys the content and meaning of the term *Dharma.* The latter is used encompassing a much wider scope. Religion is a set of principles and rituals propounded and established by a single person, such as the founder of Buddhism, Christianity and Islam. The word secular is used today in contrast to such religions, but not to *Dharma.*

The names of well-known works like the *Manusmṛti,* the *Yājñavalkyasmṛti,* the *Parāśarsmṛti* and *Śukranīti* show that in ancient India, authors often preferred to remain anonymous and attributed their work to divine or semi-divine or legendary persons. We need not, therefore, suppose that works on polity attributed to Brahmadeva, Manu, Śiva or Indra existed in the imagination of a Kautilya or the author of the *Mahābhārata.* Apart from the *Rājadharma* section of the *Śāntiparva, Arthaśāstra* of Kautilya and the different *Smṛtis* deal with the problems of administration in a general way.

In a limited sense, *Smṛtis* constitute that portion of the *Dharmasūtras.* The *Smṛtis* of Manu and Yājñavalkya are true pioneers in the field. The *Manusmṛti* is the oldest and was written many centuries before Christ. The other *Smṛtis* are said to be of the period between 400 A.D. and 1000 A.D. Such works are quite numerous and the Commentaries on them still more so.

Pre-eminent among the *Smṛtis* are those of Manu and Yājñavalkya. The former is supposed to be the foundation of all the schools of *Dharma;* the *Smṛti* of Yājñavalkya is practically the basis of the *Dharmaśāstra.* This is the general law of Hindu India, specially of Mithila. In point of methodical presentation of the rules, the *Smṛti* of *Yājñavalkya smṛti* consists of three parts, viz., the *Adhyāyas* while the latter presents the codes over twelve chapters. The *Vyavahāra* (civil law and rules) and the *Prāyaścitta* (penal and penance laws).

It is against this background that we have to examine briefly Yājñavalkya's contribution to political thought, administration and law.

Yājñavalkya was a scholar based in Mithila, living under the patronage of Janaka-Vaideha (Kīrti Janaka), a different Janaka from Sītā's father and Daśaratha's contemporary, who was called Siradhvaja Janaka. It is to be noted in passing that Janaka is the name of a dynasty of which fifty-four Janakas reigned over Videha or Mithila before the *Mahābhārata* period.

Apart from the *White Yajurveda* (Madhyandin Śakha), the *Śatapatha Brāhmaṇa* and the *Bṛhadāraṇyaka Upaniśad,* Yājñavalkya is also credited with the authorship of a *smṛti* called Yājñavalkyasmṛti. This *Smṛti* was composed during the golden Vedic era of Videhan monarchy. Though at that time Mithila was famous for religious and philosophical studies and deliberations, yet Yājñavalkya wrote fairly prominently about *Rājadharma* in a section of the first part of his *Smṛti* called *Ācāra* and about *Vyavahāra* in the second part.

Hindu thinkers like Yājñavalkya never saw politics and law as fields of study separated from other problems of human life. They treated the life of the human being as an individual or a member of a social or political unit, i.e., the state, in a large comprehensive way, assimilating all aspects including the political. As every individual has some moral, religious and special duties, so too a ruler or a king has certain definite obligations to be fulfilled in a particular manner, having moral and religious sactions. The *Smṛti* authors have, therefore, either included political thought in their writings or have separate treatises on *Vivāda, Vyavahāra* or *Rājanīti*. They contain rules and regulations for the guidance of society. Ancient Indian literature uses *Rājadharma,* i.e., the *Dharma* of the King, for expressing views on politics such as those referred to in the *Dharmaśāstra,* the *Mahābhārata* and the *Manu* and *Yājñavalkya Smṛtis. Rājadharma* is monarchical in its orientation. There are a number of words in ancient Sanskrit literature which we find in use in nearly the same sense, viz., the *Arthaśāstra,* the *Dandanīiti,* the *Rājaśāstra* or *Rājanīti,* or *Rājanītiśāstra,* or simply *Nītiśāstra.* Yājñavalkya uses the term *Rājanīti* (I.309 and II.1.307). The medieval *Nibandhakāra* Candeśvara has written a political treatise and named it *Rājanīti-Ratnākara.*

Yājñavalkya as a Political Thinker

Yājñavalkya is the earliest political thinker of Mithila. In the *Yajurveda,* the *Śatapatha Brāhmaṇa* and the *Bṛhadāraṇyaka* Upaniśad, he is seen more as a philosopher and a *Bṛhmajnānī* rather than as a political ideologue, though in the former two works, there are stray references to political ideas, specially regarding the ruler and his role. The *Smṛti* is Yājñavalkya's most important work as far as his political ideas are concerned. The whole of the thirteenth *Prakaraṇa* (section) of the first chapter is devoted to *Rājadharma,* i.e., the duties of the king and the theory of state, and the whole of the second *Adhyāya* to *Vyavahāra,* i.e., civil and criminal law, substantive as well as procedural.

It is believed that monarchy was not the only form of government known to ancient Mithila. Since early times, both the Oligarchic and republican forms of government flourished here. We have, however, little knowledge of the constitution of these states. It is believed that the whole state was divided into a number of small administrative units. According to Kautilya, the king is the state. It is because of the predominantly monarchical constitution in this period and owing to Kautilya's completely monarchical attitude that he attached the greatest importance to kingship.

The seven-fold factors of the state according to Yājñavalkya, who called them the *prakṛtis* of the kingdom, are the King, Ministers, People, Forts, Treasury and the Army along with Friends, or the Allied States, and hence the State composed of them is said to be seven-limbed, *Saptaṅgyam Rājyam.*[5] Yājñavalkya whose *Smṛti* is believed to have been compiled towards the beginning of the Gupta period, the value of *daṇḍa* is stressed just after the enumeration of the seven elements of the State. He says that having secured the seven elements, the King should use his authority (*daṇḍa*) to punish the wicked, for *Dharma* was created in the form of *daṇḍa* by the Brahmaṇa in ancient times.[6] Then he discusses the usefulness of coercive power.[7] The element of *daṇḍa* assumed considerable significance in Yājñavalkya's time. Manu preaches with zeal and vigour the rule of law and law's sovereignty. It is further laid down by Manu that justice should never be administered by the King alone, but with the help and advice of the *Sabhā* or the Jury and the Judge. The codes of Nārada and Bṛhaspati also record the duties and jurisdiction of the *Sabhā* in the administration of justice.

This theory was a settled principle of Hindu jurisprudence and Yājñavalkya adopted the same.[8] He propounds the same kind of law for the Crown-Prince, the King's brother, father, father-in-law or uncle as for an ordinary citizen. Nobody could be exempted from the operation of the law.[9] Yājñavalkya did not make any repressive law against the Śudra teaching, owning property and so forth.[10] Falling in with the change and the mood of the times, Yājñavalkya shows his greatness as a jurist. To quote the words of K.P. Jayasawal, "Yājñavalkya does not adopt any portion of the claim of Brahmaṇa's sovereignty".[11]

Yājñavalkya seems to be very particular regarding the virtues and attributes of a king because the whole state and its entire administration revolves round his personality and power. According to him, the king should possess various kinds of intellectual, moral and administrative qualities and should be versed in the sciences of logical philosophy, politics, diplomacy and theology. He should be great, an enthusiast, a philanthropist and serviceable to the elderly, and the humble; of high family, truthful, gifted with good qualities, of religious temperament, grateful, wise, brave, capable of keeping secrets and an adept in the art of dialogue and parleys.[12] He should employ persons of high calibre and of integrity as his ministers and *purohitas;* he should be aided in the performance of his duties by them. Yājñavalkya lays much more emphasis on the qualities and functions of the *purohitas* than does Kautilya. He stresses the importance of the secret advice of parleys with the ministers in the affairs of the State. The King should maintain strict and total secrecy at peace and war. He should reside in a fort set up in a forest and at a place surrounded with high land and water. And there he should discuss State policy matters and other affairs with superintendents, heads and other experts in different departmental activities. The king should give charities to the brahmaṇs and manage the security of his subjects. The king who is killed on the battlefield while seeking wealth and territory attains heaven.

Since time immemorial, Mithila followed the paths of peace and non-involvement in wars of aggression and expansion. It is noteworthy, however, that Yājñavalkya eulogises the act of war, expansion of territory and the death of a ruler on the battlefield. However, in keeping with the code of war in ancient India, Yājñavalkya's ideal king would not kill those who surrender to him.[13]

The *Rājadharma* in ancient Hindu political speculations mainly constituted the ruler's duty towards his subjects and his other administrative activities. The *Yājñavalkyasmṛti* enumerates the everyday duties of the king in seven verses (327-333).

In the first half of the day, the king is to give personal attention to the problems of the defence of the capital, himself as well as problems relating to revenue and expenditure. Afterwards, he is to attend to the work of the administration of justice. Only after these duties have been performed, the king is allowed to take his bath and his food. The king has to supervise treasury work, confer with his spies and the ministers regarding state administration afterwards. In the afternoon, the king should make inspection, discussions and consultations with the commander-in-chief; he must take due and adequate care of the army. Towards evening, the latest information gathered by the secret services are to be conveyed to the king and only then he should enjoy his time in entertainments like listening to music, watching a dance performance and having dinner, but also engage in the study of the scriptures. After he has performed these daily duties, the king should retire to his inner apartments for rest.

Among the everyday duties, the King had to look to local affairs with the assistance of the *Sabhyas,* i.e., the members of the *Sabhā.* V.P. Verma holds that "There is a remarkable similarity between the allotment of time-divisions of day and night to the performance of various duties in the *Artha-Śāstra* as well as in the *Yājñavalkyasmṛti."*[15]

The fundamental administrative duty of the King and the State is to protect the subjects from internal and external dangers to life and property, *"Prajānām paripālanam".* In case the King performs his duties well, he receives the sixth part of the merit earned by his subjects.[16] In the footsteps of Aśoka and Kautilya's *Arthaśāstra,* Yājñavalkya's ideal king is also expected to pursue a paternal policy towards his people.[17]

Though Yājñavalkya lays great stress on the importance of financial resources and the State treasury, yet he cannot tolerate the King taking recourse to evil or improper ways and means to enrich the State finances. The king who would oppress the people would be destroyed with his wealth and his family. The fate of Karāla Janaka, probably the last ruler of the dynasty, who lost his kingdom owing to the wrong done to his subjects, is amply justified in the *Yājñavalkyasmṛti.*

According to the Hindu theory of monarchy from the Vedic times, the monarch was a servant of the people and his title rested on a contract between the ruler and his subjects. The king was obliged under this contract to protect his people and work incessantly for their prosperity and well-being; he was to receive taxes as remuneration in return. Yājñavalkya warns the king that illegal and arbitrary action on his part would result in forfeiture of kingdom and his banishment with his whole family.[18] The acts of oppression and persecution directed against the people would result not only in the deprivation of majesty and condemnation of the dynasty, but in infliction of the highest punishment.[19] Here the great political thinker was merely translating the coronation oath taken by the Hindu king.

The coronation oath and pledge bound the king to follow the advice and guidance of his ministers and to act in keeping with the *Dharmaśāstra*. It also imposed the condition that the king must follow the law strictly, to maintain it and to regard the nation as the deity. Yājñavalkya fully canonized this ancient and time-honoured principle of constitutional monarchy. He even goes a step further when he limits the king's prerogative in a land he has conquered. The conquest gives exactly the same rights to the conquered people and imposes the same duties on the king in regard to his new subjects as the king is bound by, and the subjects enjoy in the old country. Indeed, the king should not enforce new laws there. The people of the new country should be ruled in exactly the same manner as the subjects of his own country.[20]

According to Yājñavalkya, the state administration has its roots in its policy (*mantra*). Hence the secrecy of the policy should always be well-guarded. As long as the desired objective is not attained, the royal and state secrets should not be divulged to anyone.

Yājñavalkya does not favour fatalism in political affairs. It seems that by his time the Buddhist theory of *Karma* had crept into the philosophic temper and mood of Mithila. He holds that fate cannot be realized without the human architect.[22]

During Manu's time, *gaṇas* (republics) were not considered seriously and he is definitely hostile to them. Brahmaṇs were prohibited to receive hospitality in republican countries and Brahmaṇ students were debarred from entering them.

Yājñavalkya, however, witnessed the destruction of most of them and he was not hostile to their laws being superseded by the royal courts.

Unlike Manu, Yājñavalkya does not expect the state to be puritanical and of correct morals, but "expects the King to be more practical, to reduce the vices by administrative methods rather than by a moral crusade."[24]

Yājñavalkya as a Lawgiver

The second chapter of the *Yajñavalkyasmṛti* is entitled *Vyavahārādhyaya* and comprises 307 verses. According to K.P. Jayasawal, "There are indications that the secular and municipal laws were called the *Vyavahāra* laws."[25] The *Mahābhārata* equates the authority of the *Vyavahāra* laws with that of the *Dharma* laws. According to the great epic, the *Dharma* law originates from Vedic lore whereas the *Vyavahāra* has its origin in political governance and the king, and being ordained by the creator, they are sacred. During Lord Buddhas time, the loyal judge was called a *Vyāvahārika*. According to Jayasawal, he was called as such also by Aśoka's inscriptions. Khārvela's inscription distinguishes between *Vyavahāra* and *Vidhi*. *Vyavahāra* means municipal law whereas *Vidhi* means *dharma*, although *dharma* is occasionally used to denote law generally in Buddhist literature and in Kautilya, e.g., *Dharmastha* for a judge.[26]

Yājñavalkya uses *Vyavahāra* as secular law. Etymologically, the term originates from 'vi' (different, diverse, or various) 'Ava' (doubt) and *Hara* (removal). It stands, therefore, to mean 'the proceedings by which various doubts are removed'. This then is the primary meaning of the term. It is in this primary sense that Yājñavalkya observes: "If one injured by others in a way which is a violation of the *Smṛti* laws and usages informs the king, that becomes a fit subject for a judicial proceeding."[27] Bhatta Nilakantha also uses the word in this sense when he says that "*Vyavahāra*, or political proceeding, is a transaction which facilitates the tracing of an unknown wrong to one of the disputing parties; or it is a transaction started by the plaintiff and defendants, and in which are involved evidence, possession and witnesses and which makes it possile to decide between conflicting pleadings."[28] "A very workable definition, exactly corresponding to modern jurists like Dicey, Holmes, Gray and Salmond, who define law with reference to the courts of justice, is given by Anantdeva that *Vyavahāra* comprises the rules according to which judicial proceedings are conducted."[29] It is in this conventional sense that the word appears as linked up with the ultimate purpose of the State or in relation with the functions of the State as a whole.

In the *Sutra* period, the secular laws or King's laws were quite different from *Dharma* law. Yājñavalkya's code covered the whole area of the law secular as well as law canonical. He deals with the secular law quite distinct from the *Dharma* law in the middle section of his code. He treats law proper as an independent subject in the fashion of a finished lawyer.

As a jurist, Yājñavalkya's contribution is very concrete in the sense that he bifurcated the realms of the two kinds of law. He made the royal law or *Vyavahāra* quite distinct from *Dharma* law.

According to Manu, the object of law (*Dharma*) and its administration is the maintenance of peace and order in the community (M. VII.223; 18, 20). Yājñavalkya is silent on this issue. But whereas Manu (VII.26) and Kautilya (p. 50) take the king to be agent of the administration of law and the source of justice, Yājñavalkya prefers ascetics/recluses as the prime movers of law (III.186).

The chapter on *Vyavahāra* consists of twenty-five topics, *Prakaraṇas,* such as (i) Ordinary *Vyavahāra* law, (ii) Extraordinary *Vyavahara* law, (iii) Loans, (iv) Sealed deposit, (v) Witness, (vi) Written document, (vii) Ordeal, (viii) Partition of inheritance, (ix) Settlement of disputed boundary questions, (x) Dispute between the owner and keeper of cattle, (xi) Sale without ownership, (xii) Non-delivery or resumption of gifts, (xiii) Returning a thing purchased to the seller, (xiv) Negligence of promised service, (xv) Breach of contract, (xvi) Payment of wage, (xvii) Gambling, (xviii) Defamation, (xix) Assault, (xx) Aggressive act, (xxi) Non-delivery of articles already sold, (xxii) Joint dealing, (xxiii) Theft, (xxiv) Seduction, and (xxv) Miscellaneous.

Yājñavalkya's *Vyavahāra* comprises both substantive and procedural law. The substantive section consists of both civil and criminal law. There are social laws as well as laws of contract. It deals with witnesses as well as legal defenders. It examines and analyses other problems of civil law such as lending money on interest, deposit of money, witnesses and evidence. Yājñavalkya discusses minutely the registration of various kinds of royal documents, inheritance (*Dāyabhāga*), boundary disputes, disputes between master and servant, sale of commodities, non-delivery and resumption of gifts, return of commodities brought to the seller, breach of contracts, non-payment of wages, penalties for dice-playing, slander and criminal acts, joint enterprises, theft and several other miscellaneous categories.

Yājñavalkya is a more liberal and progressive legal thinker and jurist than his celebrated predecessor, Manu. He has reduced and modified with mild and considerate sanctions Manu's fanaticism in regard to penances. He raised the position of the Śūdra in society by allowing him to observe *Cāndrāyaṇa* penance which had been open only to the twice-born in the past. The extravagant punishment prescribed by Manu for the Śūdra has been deleted or reduced by Yājñavalkya. The immunities in the legal word of the Brahmaṇs have been set aside and they have been brought under the province of the King's laws of *Vyavahāra.*

According to K.P. Jayasawal, the advancement brought about by Yājñavalkya was owing overall to the impact of the Buddhist revolution in the past. He not only made an advance over Manu, but also over Kautilya in this regard. Women's position was raised and their right to inheritance was fully admitted. The change in the social laws made in Yājñavalkya's code was received by people with such relief and enthusiasm that his code became the ruling authority not only in Mithila, but in the whole of Āryavarta. His name must be remembered ever for endowing women with the right of inheritance.[30] He adds wife and daughter to the list of heirs to a sonless deceased.[31] He served the great cause of bringing the position of women nearer that of men, if not at par with them, in the field of inheritance and the modern parity between the two sexes in this country owes itself to this great political, social and legal revolutionary. Not only this, he brought 'wife' and 'daughter' in the same position without making any discrimination as to their rights.

A special notice has been taken of the rights to property and ownership, joint and severally, by Yājñavalkya. His most eminent commentator, Vijñāniswara, the author of the *Mitākshara,* has been regarded as the leading authority; he has discussed at length the meaning of certain terms, having technical significance.

These are *Dāya* and *Svatva.* The former has been defined by him as "that property which becomes the property of another solely by reason of its relation to the owner."[32] This definition requires a further enquiry to find out an owner and the tests of ownership (*Svatva*). "It is the interpretation of these terms, namely, *Dāya* and *Svatva,* which has led to the parting of ways between the great *Dharmaśāstra* scholars, namely, the *Mitākshara* School and the *Dāyabhāga* School."[33]

Yājñavalkya has paid considerable attention to the reform of Manu's laws on the criminal side. The *Mānava* code, with its ferocious puritanism and its bloodthirsty religious zeal, remained a controversy rather than the law on the subject of crime. Yājñavalkya sat down to remedy this defect and he succeeded in giving a workable code of criminal law.[34]

K.P. Jayasawal holds that Yājñavalkya does not deserve credit for originality in this regard as he had Kautilya before him. It is a fact, however, that Yājñavalkya was quite bold and original in mitigating the injury and humiliation done to the major portion of the society. For one thing, he brought uniformity to law. He "overhauled and rearranged the social system, and saved society from becoming a furious ocean of battering interests and views and rising to the occasion, solved the problems and sowed the seeds which grew and blossomed into the majority of peace, progress and culture of the Gupta period."[35] The period that followed could not add anything new to Criminal Law and accepted Yājñavalkya *in toto*.

As a political thinker, Yājñavalkya is most precise and specific. He has discussed the *Saptāṅgya* theory of the State and the fourfold policy not in detail like his former and later counterparts. V.P. Verma rightly observes that "his treatment of political matters is more or less like a synopsis of the traditional Brahmanical wisdom rather than a systematic presentation of political theory."[36] Yājñavalkya's genius and originality lie in social and legal spheres. As a social reformer, lawgiver and jurist, he is consistently progressive, and a true revolutionary; he is superb. Even the present-day society in Mithila in particular and the whole country except Bengal in general, is based by and large, on the structure of legal and ethical rules and political obligations, designed and framed by Yājñavalkya.

REFERENCES

1. P.V. Kane; *History of Dharmaśāstra;* Vol. I; p. 1.
2. J.R. Gharpure; *Teaching of Dharmaśāstra;* p. 3.
3. P.V. Kane; *op. cit.;* pp. 1-2.
4. J.R. Gharpure; *op. cit.;* p. 3.
5. *Yājñavalkyasmṛti;* 1.353.
6. *Yajna. Smṛti;* 1.354.
7. *Ibid.,* 1.355-359.
8. *Ibid.,* 1.354-356.
9. *Ibid.,* v. 1.357-358.
10. K.P. Jayasawal; *Manu and Yājñavalkya;* p. 91.
11. *Ibid.,* p. 104.
12. *Yajna. Smṛti;* 1.309-311.
13. *Ibid.,* 1.326.
14. *Ibid.,* 1.360.
15. V.P. Verma; *Studies in Hindu Political Thought and Its Metaphysical Foundations;* p. 339.

16. *Yajna Smṛti;* 1.335.
17. Yajna. Smṛti; 1.334.
18. *Ibid.*, 1.340.
19. *Ibid.*, 1.341.
20. *Ibid.*, 1.342-343.
21. *Ibid.*, 1.344.
22. *Ibid.*, 1.350-351.
23. *Ibid.*, ; 1.360-361.
24. K.P. Jayasawal; *op. cit.*, p. 108.
25. *Ibid.*, p. 13.
26. *Ibid.*, p. 10.
27. *Yajna. Smṛti;* II.5.
28. *Vyavahāra Mayukh;* Gharpure's Translation; p. 2.
29. R.K. Gupta; *Political Thought in the Smṛti Literature;* p. 233.
30. K.P. Jayasawal; op. cit., p. 233.
31. *Yajna. Smṛti;* II.135.
32. *Mita. Text;* p. 73.
33. J.R. Gharpure; *op. cit.*, p. 85.
34. *Ibid.*, p. 87.
35. *Ibid.*, p. 145.
36. *Op. cit.*, p. 341.

5

Kautilya on *Dharma* and Politics
A Study of Arthshastra

P.D. Kaushik

'Arthshastra', composed by Kautilya or Chanakya (also known as Vishnu Gupta), the mighty Prime Minister of Mauryan Emperor Chandragupta in 4th Century B.C., is unique among the ancient classics on *'dandniti'* or the 'Science of Polity'. The work has been a subject of great admiration. To quote Bhandarkar, "The work is indeed so precious in the whole range of Sanskrit literature that it has revolutionized all our ideas about the culture and civilization of ancient India."[1]

"Arthshastra" or Politics—As an Independent Science

When Kautilya wrote *Arthshastra*, the whole field fo knowledge was divided into four branches. First was 'Anivikshaki' or philosophy which also included dialectics, Sankhya, Yoga and Lokayata. Second was *'Trayi'* or triple Vedas—*Rigveda, Samveda* and *Yajurveda*. Later on *Atharvaveda* was also included in this category. Third was *'Varta'* or economics which was concerned with agriculture, cattle-breeding and trade. Fifth was *'dandiniti'* or Politics (also known as *Arthshastra*). It was the Science of government, of enforcement of law and order. Like Aristotle "Kautilya deliberately freed politics from the influence of religion and morality. For all practical purposes he goes against moral principles like Machiavelli to achieve Political objectives."[2]

Subject Matter and Scope of Arthshastra

Arthshastra is a very comprehensive and up-to-date work. "To Kautilya *Dandniti* meant stability and welfare of *Åniviksiki, Trayi* (three *vedas*) and *Varta* (economics and commerce). These two words denoted concept of government and its moral implications."[3] Briefly speaking it is concerned with acquisition and preservation of dominion. The text of *Arthshastra* is divided into 15 books or parts and 150 chapters. Book I discusses various problems connected with Kingship. Book II gives an exhaustive picture of civil administration. Books III and IV give details of civil, criminal and personal laws of Mauryan empire. Book V discusses the duties and responsibilities of courtiers and retainers of King. Book VI deals with nature and functions of seven *Prakritis* (elements or organs) of state. Book VII to XV discuss problems connected with foregin policy, relationship with different states, warcraft, ways and means to sow seeds of dissensions among enemies. *Arthshastra* is secular in character, free from influence of *Dharamashastra*, and a monumental work on politics. As Dr. Beni Prasad says, "As a scheme of administrative organization, the *Arthshastra* is unsurpassed in Hindu literature. It is complete in the perspective, detailed in its regulations, thorough in its treatment. ... As a statement of Hindu administrative theory, it leaves hardly anything to be desired ... Kautilya's dialectical method points in the same direction ... Where possible, he states, discusses and corrects views of others and aims at perfection ... Kautilya's secular tone and freedom from any religious bias tend to show that priestly influence was not always so powerful as the *Dharamashastras* might lead us to suppose."[4]

Origin of the State (Kingship)

Like Aristotle, Kautilya takes the state to be a natural institution and only briefly touches on the origin of the state. He combines the super human origin of Kingship with that of social contract. Kautilya was a realist and had little faith in the ultimate goodness of human nature. He maintained that before the origin of the state situation of *'Matsyanayay'*[5] prevailed in which the bigger fish swallows the smaller ones. Similarly in the absence of *'Danda'* (Punishment) or organised political coercion stronger and more powerful persons and groups terrorise and exploit the weaker. Law of fish symbolises law of jungle where might is right. When people could not anymore suffer the wrongs of *'Matsyanayay'* they made Manu, the son of Sun God, their King who agreed to protect their properties, families and *'varnas'* in return of certain payments.[6]

Concept of Kingship

Though there were republics in ancient India, the dominant form of state was monarchy. Kautilya regarded Monarchy as the most suitable form of government and preferred hereditary monarchy to other forms. As R.K. Chaudhary maintains, "The *Arthshastra* essentially is a study of monarchy in relation to expansion of dominion of monarch and even importance of economic institutions is measured in terms of their contribution to war. The ideal of Kautilyan monarchy is universal sovereignty through conquest."[7] His theory of origin of state makes Kingship a semi-divine institution.

King's role is similar to that of Gods. He occupies the position of Indra (King of Gods) and Yama (God of death) on earth. He is able to grant favours like Indra and to inflict punishment like Yama. Those who insult the King are punished by the Gods.[8]

Kautilya witnessed Alexander's invasion of India. He was conscious of the need of a strong state. He extolled the state and made the King morally and legally foundation, source and embodiment of all sovereign authority. Kautilya maintains that as all other footprints vanish in the footprints of elephant, so all *Dharma* disappears into *Rajdharma*. The King enjoys all the powers of the state, but he has to act under the control of the society. To a king welfare of the people should be the paramount concern. Kautilya is of the opinion that a King has no personal likes: it is the likes of subject that should be followed by him, King's interest lies in the interest of the people and his happiness lies in the happiness of the people. To a King his own interest is not dear, what is dear to him is the interest of the people.[9]

King is the highest authority. King's edict is more authoritative than even the sacred law. He is regarded to be fountain of all justice. King is protector of the subjects, upholder of *Dharma* and protector of the Social order. King protects, *Dharma,* Social order and subjects through *Danda.* Kautilya believed "No *danda,* no state", King protects the subjects with the help of *'danda'* (rod of punishment) which is symbol of ruler's authority. It is the King's duty to see that the situation of *Matsyanayay* does not prevail in the Kingdom. With the help of *'Danda'* the King prevents mighty from oppressing the weak and enables the weak to hold their own against the strong. Through *danda* King protects the fourfold social order and ensures that the subjects perform their duties.[10] But the King should not apply *danda* improperly, as this may lead to revolt.

Organization of State : The *Saptang* Theory

According to Vijairaghvan, "Kautilya", wrote *Arthshastra* as a practical manual of statecraft and administration not only for Mauryan times but for all times and for any Kingdom."[11] He deals with the minutest details of statecraft and the organization of the government. However, here we will confine ourselves to the discussion of two of his famous theories : the *Saptang* theory and the *Mandal* theory.

The *Saptang* theory, concerns with the internal organization of the state. Kautilya and other Hindu thinkers did not view the state only as Government but regarded it to be a political organism which exercised sovereignty. This organism had *'Saptang'* or seven organs. These were :

1. King or *Swami;* 2. Minister or *Amatya;* 3. Territory or *Janapada;* 4. Fort or *Durga;* 5. Treasury or *Kosha;* 6. Military or *Danda;* and 7. Allies or *Mitra.*[12]

Out of these 7 organs or elements of the State 6 were internal and one-ally-external. The ally or *mitra* does not form part of the internal organisation of the State. Kautilya includes ally in connection with foreign relations. Organs have been analysed from practical point of administration. *Prakratis* or organs have been mentioned in accordance with their relative importance. First, and most importants in *Swami,* i.e. King or the ruler who is the Kingpin of the whole Structure. Secondly, there are *Amatya* or ministers who assist the King in his rule. Thirdly, there is *Janpad* or populated territory over which the King rules. Fourthly, there is *durg* or fortified capital from where he rules. Fifthly, there is *Kosh* or treasury that ensures stability of his rule and sixthly, there is army that ensures the safety of the Kingdom. Kautilya does not mention population or subjects directly but he assumes their existence by implication, when he refers to *Janapada* as one of the organs. Kautilya says in book XIII that there can be no *Janapada* without people living in it. "The Saptang Theory," writes Vijairaghvan, "as given by Kautilya was almost accepted as the standard definition to know the nature of the ancient Indian State."[13]

Among the organs of the state the King is the most important. Significantly, Kautilya describes the King as *Swami* which means "owner" or "Master". He gives a detailed description of the rights, duties and obligations of the King, which, as we have already seen, are very comprehensive. There was no permanent constitutional authority to check the King's authority, but *Dharamshastras, Varna-Vyavastha,* Brahmins, ministers and public opinion acted as moral and practical checks. Kautilya maintains that security of the state is of paramount importance. He unhesitatingly recommends the adoption of doctrine that ends justify means and advises the King to adopt force or fraud and other means which violate conventional morality for ensuring the safety of the kingdom. For this he is compared to Machiavelli. It is true that like Machiavelli Kautilya allows the King to adopt immoral means for the protection of the state but unlike Machiavelli he does not propound the theory of double morality. He does not defend immorality of the King as such. Indeed he regards virtue (*dharma*) and wealth (*varta*) as the two ends of existence applicable to the ruler and denounces the fragrantly unethical statecraft advocated by some of his predecessors like Bharadwaj.

Interstate Relations : Six-fold Foreign Policy and Mandal Theory

The *Saptang* theory discussed in Book VI of *Arthshastra* deals with internal organization of the State. Kautilya devotes Books VII to XV to an exhaustive discussion of interstate relations. More important aspects of this discussion are theories of *Shadguna* and *Mandal.*

The goal of the foreign policy of the King should be the expansion of the Kingdom. For this Kautilya delineates *Shadgunya* or sin types of foreign policies. An earlier scholar Vatavyadhi maintained that there are only two policies—peace and war and the other types of foreign policies arise out of these two policies or *gunas:* Kautilya criticises this and enumerates a six-fold classification of foreign policy as different situations call for different policies.

The six *gunas* or policies are as follows :

1. *Sandhi* : Policy of peace through making treaties containing terms.
2. *Vigraha* : Policy of hostility or war.
3. *Asana* : Policy of remaining quiet.
4. *Yana* : Policy of invasion.
5. *Sansraya* : Policy of taking shelter with another King or in a fort.
6. *Daidhibhav* : Double policy of peace with one king and of war with another at the same time.

Kautilya lays down certain general rules with regard to adoption of these policies. The King should adopt the policy of peace (*Sandhi*), when he is weaker than the enemy. He should follow the policy of hostility (*Vigraha*) when he is stronger than the enemy. He should adopt the policy of quiet (*Asana*) when he and his enemy are of equal strength. When the King is very strong, he may follow the policy of invasion (*Yana*), when he is too weak he should adopt the policy of taking shelter (*Sansraya*). The double policy of peace and war (*Daidhibhav*) is advisable when the King needs another's help in order to fight against his enemy. However, these rules can be set aside, if other considerations make it advisable to follow a different course.

Kautilya explains the system of interstate relations by the analogy of a circle or *Mandal.* Though Kautilya's predecessors like Usnas (Shukra) have mentioned *Mandal* theory, but it was left to Kautilya to develop it as a full-fledged explanation of the system of interstate relations. Kautilya speakes of a *mandal* or *rajmandal* (circle of Kings) consisting of twelve Kings or states. The Central figure would be aggressor or conqueror (*Vijigishu*). Besides him there are four types of states : friendly, hostile, neutral and unconcerned. The entire aggregate of these states is called the *mandal* or *rajmandal* (the circle of Kings). In front of *Vijigishu* there are five Kings who alternately function as his foes and friends but this relationship varies in degree according to the distance from the *Vijigishu* or would be conqueror. There are four Kings in the rear of *Vijigishu* alternately functioning as his foes and friends in the same fashion. Lastly, there are two neutral or unconcerned Kings.

The *mandal* of Kautilya consists of twelve Kings. They are :

1. *Vijigishu* : the would be conquerer.
2. *Ari* : the enemy whose territory is contiguous to that of *Vijigishu.*
3. *Mitra* : the *Vijigishu*'s ally whose territory lies immediately beyond that of the *ari.*
4. *Arimitra* : the enemy's ally whose territory lies beyond that of the *mitra.*
5. *Mitra mitra* : the ally of *Vijigishu*'s ally, whose territory is beyond that of the *arimitra.*
6. *Arimitramitra* : the ally of the enemy's ally, whose territory lies beyond that of the *mitramitra* (these five Kings (2-6) are in front of *Vijigishu*).
7. *Parshanigraha* (the heel catcher) the enemy in the rear (similar to *ari* in the front).
8. *Akranda* : the *Vijigishu*'s ally in the rear (similar to *mitra* in front) with his territory behind that of the enemy in the rear.

9. *Parshnigrahasara* : the ally of the *parshnigraha* behind the *akranda* (similar to the *arimitra* in the front).
10. *Akrandasara* : the ally of the *akranda* behind the *parshnigrahasara* (similar to *mitra-mitra* in the front).

In enunciating *Mandala* Theory Kautilya adopts the intellectual technique of modern writers on international relations, namely model building. "Though the concept of *Mandala* (Circle of States)", writes A. Bozeman, "occupies a prominent place in ancient Indian thought, it has been most fully developed in *'Arthashastra'* in relation to international politics. We may call it loose bi-centric international system. The international portions amount to an exposition of the principles and problems of foreign policy in a hierarchical system, each member of which determines upon action in the light of his inferior or superior states. *Mandala* indicates an abstracted system of international relations."[14]

Kautilya was well-versed in *Dharamshastras* but he was a political scientist and has written about *dharma* only so far as it was relevant to his concept of state. He talks of *Rajdharma* and enjoins upon the King to uphold *dharma* and social order. He approves Brahmanical mode of life in so far as it is in consonance with maintenance of *Varnashramadharma* but rejects religious practices which come in the way of expansion of the state. He does a distinct service to the cause of political theory by excluding priests from organs of the state. He not only separates political science from *dharamshastra* but also gives a badly wanted corrective to other worldly bias of Indian temperament and character.

Kautilya's contribution to political theory was immense. His *Arthshastra* embodies a theory of state, a theory of *Rajdharma* and *dandniti*, a theory of Kingship, a theory of statecraft or government and a theory of social order. To quote Chaudhary, "he raised *Arthshastra* to the position of a systematic, comprehensive and rational branch of knowlede. His method of treating subject is independent and he does not unnecessarily refer to vedic scriptures as authorities. It may be suggested that he, for first time, gave *Arthshastra* an exalted position in the realm of political literature in ancient India and to that extent he may be credited with having raised it to an independent status."[15]

"The position of '*Arthshastra*', writes Vijayraghavan, "in realm of literature on politics is analogous to that of Panini's *Astadhayayi* in field of grammar. Like Panini, Kautilya superseded all his predecessors, and therefore, all works of subsequent writers got eclipsed in course of time."[16] *Arthshastra* exercised tremendous influence on subsequent writers on Indian Polity. Kamandak, Bana, Dandin, Somdev Suri etc. mentioned Kautilya's name and his *Arthshastra* with great reverence and even today no study of Hindu polity is complete without a study of Kautilya. Little wonder that Kamandak in his *Nitisara* wrote "Salutations to that Vishnugupta. Who churned out the nectar of polity from the ocean of *Arthshastras*."[17]

REFERENCES

1. Dr. Bhandarkar : *Some Aspects of Ancient Hindu Polity*, Banaras, 1929, p. 35.
2. Vijairaghavan and R. Jayaram : *Political Thought*, Sterling, p. 34.
3. Radha Krishna Choudhary : *Kautilya's Political Ideas and Institutions*, Chowkhamba, Varanasi, 1971, p. 411.
4. Beni Prasad : *The State in Ancient India.*
5. अप्रणीतो मात्सयन्याय मुद्भवति।
   बलीयानबलं हि ग्रस्ते दंडधरोभवे। (अर्थशास्त्र, पुस्तक 1, अध्याय 4)
6. मात्स्यान्यायभिभूताः प्रजा मनुं वैवस्वतं।
   राजानां चक्रिरे। (अर्थशास्त्र, पुस्तक 1, अध्याय 13)
7. Chaudhary, *op. cit.*, p. 393.
8. इन्द्रयमस्थान मेतवद्राराजान प्रत्यक्ष दण्ड प्रसादाः।
   तात्रवन्यमानान्दैवोऽपिदण्ड स्पृशति।। (अर्थशास्त्र, पुस्तक 1, अध्याय 13)
9. प्रजाहिते हितं राज्ञः प्रजानां च सुखे सुखम्।
   नात्मप्रियं हितं राज्ञः, प्रजानाम् च प्रिय हितम्।।
   (अर्थशास्त्र, पुस्तक 1, अध्याय 19)
10. चतुवर्णाश्रमो लोके राजा दण्डेन फलितः।
    स्वधर्म कर्माभिरतोवर्ततेस्वेषु वर्त्यषु।। (अर्थशास्त्र, पुस्तक 14, अध्याय 1)

11. Vijairaghavan and Jayaram, *op. cit.*, p. 37.
12. स्वामात्यं जनपद दुर्ग कोष दण्ड मित्रणि प्रकृतय।। (अर्थशास्त्र, पुस्तक 6, अध्याय 1)
13. Vijairaghavan and Jayaram, *op. cit.* p. 9.
14. A. Bojeman : *Politics and Culture in Indian History*, Princeton, 1960, pp. 122-23.
15. R.K. Chaudhary, *op. cit.*, pp. 405-06.
16. Vijayraghvan and R. Jayaram, *op. cit.*, p. 35.
17. नीतिशास्त्रामृतं धीमान अर्थशास्त्र महोदधेः।
    समुहध्रे नमस्तस्मै विष्णुगुप्ताय वेधसे।
    (Kamandaka, Nitisara, Chapter 1/6).

6

Concept of *Hindutva* and Indian Nationalism of V.D. Savarkar

Ram Singh Solanki

Born heroic revolutionary, an ardent exponent of militant nationalism, great Hindu social reformer and a propounder of the concept of Hindutva and Hindu nationalism, ***Vinayak Damodar Savarkar*** (May 28, 1883—February 26, 1966) won endless fame by his volatile, seditious and revolutionary activities in the early decade of twentieth century. He founded ***Mitra Mela*** an organization in 1900. Later on in 1904, it was transformed into ***Abhinav Bharat.*** It was a secret revolutionary organization under the leadership of young Savarkar. And it was only in his leadership that on October 7, 1905, Poona got the privilege to hold the first big bonfire of foreign clothes in India.

After graduating from Bombay University in 1905, Savarkar in June 1906 left for London. As he got *Shivaji* scholarship offered by *Pandit Shyamji Krishna Verma* in 1906, he established Free India Society in London. On account of his revolutionary activities in India and England, he was arrested in London in March 1910. The Bombay special Tribunal sentenced Savarkar transportation for life on 24th December, 1910. Again the Tribunal sentenced him to transportation for life on 30th January, 1911. A sentence for two transportation and release after 50 years is a unique record in the world political history. After spending many years in *Andaman* and internment in *Ratnagiri* from 1924-1937, he was released on 10th May, 1937.

After release from jail Savarkar played active role in Indian politics in the capacity of President and leader of ***Hindu Mahasabha*** to achieve the absolute political independence of Hindustan and regeneration of the Hindus. His sacrifices and sufferings made him the legendary hero in the history of the revolutionary movement in India.[1]

Savarkar was a rationalist and he had enthusiastic and innovative mind. "He was a volcanic writer, a heroic author, a renaissance scholar, a historian in action, a dramatist, a novelist and an epic poet. His genius earned him a place among the first few greatest geniuses of our motherland."[2]

Origin of the Word Hindu

The word Hindu is not found in old Sanskrit Literature. It is derived from *vedic* appellation of *Saptasindhu* the home of *Rigvedic* Aryans which was region of seven rivers. Savarkar quoted the following Vedic mantra which indicates the region of *Saptasindhus* (Seven rivers):[3]

इमं में गंगे यमुने सरस्वति शुतुद्रि स्तोमं सचता परूष्ण्या।
असिकन्या मरूद्वृधे विस्ततयाऽऽ र्जीकाये शृणुह्या सुषोमया।।
—ऋग्वेद, 10/75/5

The modern names of seven rivers are—Ganga, Yamuna, Saraswati, Satlaz, Rabi, Chenab and Zhelum.

According to Savarkar—'The syllable स (S) in Sanskrit is at times changed into ह (H) in some of the *Prakrit* languages........ For example, the word *sapta* (सप्त) has become *hapta* (हफ्त), *saraswati* (सरस्वति) becomes *harhwati* (हरहवती) and *asur* (असुर) becomes ahur (अहुर) in Persian. And then we actually find that the Vedic name of our nation *saptsindhu* (सप्तसिंधु) had been mentioned as *hapthindu* (हप्तहिन्दु) in the *Avesta* by the ancient people. *Bhavishyapuran* (भविष्यपुराण) clearly cites this fact and says[4]

जानुस्थाने जैन शब्दः सप्तसिन्धुस्तथैव च।
हप्तहिन्दुर्यावनी च पुनर्ज्ञेया गुरूण्डिका।।

(प्रतिसर्ग पर्व अ. 5)

Hence the origin of the word Hindu is in accordance with the laws of Linguistics. In the words of Savarkar—"We can safely conclude that most of the remoting nations that flourished must have applied the same epithet Hindu to our land and people as the ancient Persians did."[5] Savarkar's logical argument on the basis of Linguistics is—The word Hindu is of Vedic origin. It is not a denomination which the foreigners applied to us in concept otherwise but is derived from our Vedic appellation of *Saptasindhus*."[6]

Since beginning of the 11th century *Hindusthan* has faced the cultural, political and military attack by the Muslim foreign invaders and the conflict of life and death began between Hindus and Muslim aggressors. This is the reason that Savarkar wrote—"In this prolonged furious conflict our people became intensely conscious of ourselves as Hindus and were welded into a nation to an extent unknown in our history.... The enemies hated us as Hindus and the whole family of peoples and races of sects and creeds that flourished from Attak (अटक) to Kattak (कटक) was suddenly individualized into a single Being.... This one word *Hindutva* ran like a vital spinal cord through our whole political body. *Our bards bewailed the fall of Hindus,* our seers roused the feelings of Hindus, our heroes fought the battles of Hindus, our saints blessed the efforts of Hindus, our statesman molded the fate of Hindus, and our mothers wept over the wounds and gloried over the triumphs of Hindus."[7]

Of all the works written in the Hindi language, old and new, the great epic *Prithwiraj Raso* (पृथ्वीराज रासो) by Chand Bardai is the most ancient. He uses the words *hindı, hindu, hindwan, hind,* so often and so naturally which prove that aforesaid words were quite common and accepted terms as far back as the eleventh century. In this context Savarkar quotes so many verses used in medieval Hindi literature. For example:

अटल ठाट महिपाट, अटल तारागढथानं।
अटल नग्र अजमेर, अटल हिंदव अस्थानं।।

आज भाग चहुआन घर, आज भाग हिंदवान।
इन जीवित दिल्लीश्वर, गंज न सके आन।।
निर्लज्ज म्लेच्छ लजै नहीं। हम हिंदु लजवान।[8]

Speaking of things that Shivaji achieved, Bhushan the Hindi poet says[9]:

राखी हिंदुवानी, हिंदुवान के तिलक राख्यो,
स्मृति और पुराण राख्यो, वेद विधि सुनि में।

Guru Teg Bahadur, the hero and the Champion of Hindu *Dharma* says—'How can I disgrace the Hindu *Dharma* – So dear to me' in the following verse[10]

'तिन ते सुन श्री तेगबहादुर, धर्म निवाहन विषे बहादुर।
उत्तर भनयों धर्म हम हिन्दू, अति प्रियको किमकरे निकट।'

—सूर्य प्रकाश

His illustrious son Guru Govind Singh, the poet, the prophet and the warrior of our Hindu race and culture exclaims in a moment of inspiration[11]:

सकल जगत में खालसा पंथ गाजे।
जगे धर्म हिन्दु सकल भंड भाजे।।

—गुरू गोविन्दसिंह रचित विभिन्न नाटक में

Hence, according to Savarkar the word Hindu dates its origin not from the Mohammedanised Persian but from the ancient language of Iran, the Zend. Arabians learnt it from the ancient Iranians, Jews, and other peoples. It has no contemptuous expression. It could not have been applied to us because we were black literally, for the simple reason that the ancient *saptasindhus,* i.e. Hindus in Avestic period were as fair as the Iranians. The Northern Vernacular literature refers to the words *Hind, Hindu,* and *Hindusthan* in terms of full pride and patriotic fervour.[12]

According to Savarkar, "We should not forget that the ancient Jews used the term Hindu to denote strength or vigour."[13] In fact the word Hindu has no defamatory meaning. In Arabian language Indian Arithmetic is called hindus (हिंदस) *sasamsire hind* (शमशीरे हिन्द) in Persian language (Indian Sword) is used as a weapon which strikes bravely and deeply.

The oldest source or derivative of the word Hindu goes back to 486 B.C.

According to Encyclopaedia of religion and Ethics—"The name of Hindu appears in the form of Hindus in 486 B.C. in the inscription on the monument of the Darivs Hystaspes (522-486 B.C.) near Persepolis."[14] Hence the history of the word Hindu proves that it was not coined or invented by the Arabians or Muslim invaders.

Savarkar's whole superstructure of the mission and ideology rests on the correct definition of the word Hindu. He defined the term Hindu in the following couplet:

आसिन्धुसिंधुपर्यन्ता यस्य भारत भूमिका।
पितृ भूः पुण्य भूश्चैव स वै हिन्दुरिति स्मृत।।[15]

"Everyone who regards and claims this *Bharat bhoomi* from the Indus to the seas as his fatherland and holy land is a Hindu."[16]

Savarkar's definition of Hindu is more comprehensive and broad based. It is neither communal nor religious. In fact cultural nationalism *Hindutva* is the derivative word from Hindu. The implications of the definition of the word Hindu denote the following essential characteristics of *Hindutva.*

Common Nation

The first implication of the word Hindu is geographical. In the words of Radha Krishnan—"The term Hindu had originally a territorial and not credal significance. It implies residence in a well defined geographical area. Original tribes, savage and half civilized people, the cultured Dravidians and the Vedic Aryans were all Hindus as they were the sons of the same mother."[17]

According to Savarkar—"Hindus than has come to mean the whole continental country from the *Sindhu* to *Sindhu*, from the Indus to the seas... A Hindu is primarily a citizen either in himself or through his forefathers of *Hindusthan* and claims the land as his motherland. In America as well as France the word Hindu is generally understood exactly in the sense of an Indian without any religious or cultural implication."[18]

As a matter of fact, from historical point of view the word Hindu does not convey aforesaid primary significance only. Muslims and Christians cannot be recognized as Hindus because their holy lands are outside of the India.

Savarkar wrote: "Although the root meaning of the word Hindu like the sister nickname Hindi may mean only an Indian, yet as it is, we would be strain the usage of words too much, we fear to the point of breaking—if we call a Mohammedan a Hindu because of his being a resident of India."[19]

Savarkar does not include Muslims or Christians within the Hindu fold on the basis of their different cultural and religious faiths and aggressive ego. He wrote—"It may be possible that at some future time the word Hindu may come to indicate a citizen of Hindustan and nothing else; that day can only rise when all cultural and religious prejudice has disbanded its forces pledged to aggressive egoism and religions cease to be 'isms' and become merely the common fund of eternal principles that lie at the root of all, that are common foundation on which the Human State majestically and firmly rests."[20] Hence the term Hindu cannot be synonymous with *Bhartiya* or Hindi and an Indian only. In short, a Hindu is he, who feels attachments to the land that extends from *Sindhu* to Seas as the land of his forefathers as his fatherland.

Savarkar says—"Although the first requisite of *Hindutva* is that, be a citizen of *Hindusthan* either by himself or through his forefathers; yet it is not the only necessary qualification of it, because the term Hindu has come to mean much more than its geographical significance."[21]

Bond of Common Blood (Racial Unity)

The second essential characteristic of Hindutva is the racial unity of the Hindus. Although the principle of racial unity is absolutely unscientific, yet Savarkar uses the term common race from different point of view. In context of bond of common blood Savarkar asks many questions: "Are the English a race? Is there anything as English blood, the French blood, the German blood or the Chinese blood in this world?"

According to Savarkar, the caste system of the Hindus proves the common flow of blood into the race. He wrote, "Nay, is not the very presence of these castes a standing testimony to a common flow of blood from a Brahmin to a Chandal? Even a cursory glance at any of our *smritis* (स्मृतियां) would conclusively prove that the *Anuloma* (अनुलोम) and *Pratiloma* (प्रतिलोम) marriage institutions were the order of the day and have given birth to the majority of the castes that obtain amongst us."[22]

Social development of the Hindu Dom and existence of different castes give a full expression to the racial units of the Hindu people. From historical and social point of view Savarkar wrote—"Some of us are Brahmins and some Namshudras (or Panchams) but Brahmins or Chandals are all Hindus and own a common blood. Some of us are *Dakshinavya* (दाक्षिणाव्य) some *Gaurs* (गौड़) but *Gaurs* or *Saraswatas* (सारस्वत) are all Hindus and own a common blood."[23] Savarkar emphasizes that the monists, pantheists, theist and atheists are all Hindus and own a common blood.[24]

A Hindu cannot be deprived of Hindutva irrespective of his belief in any theoretical, philosophical or social system, orthodox or heterodox.[25] Savarkar writes—"A Hindu may lose his caste and sect but not his Hindutva (his Hinduness)—because the most important essential which determines it is the inheritance of the Hindu blood."[26]

Savarkar concludes that—"All those who love the land that stretches from Indus to seas (सिंधु से सिंधु) as their fatherland consequently claim to inherit the blood of the race that has evolved by incorporation and adoption from ancient

Sapt-sindhus can be said to possess two of the most essential requisites of Hindutva."[27]

Common Culture

The third essential of Hindutva is common culture which is pre-eminently implied by the word holy land (*Punya Bhoo*). Savarkar used the term common culture in a broader perspective. It includes civilization, history, literature, laws, rites, rituals etc.

According to Savarkar, there are two qualifications of a common fatherland and therefore of a common blood cannot exhaust all the requisites of *Hindutva*. The majority of the Indian *Mohamedans* and *Christians* accept Hindustan as their fatherland and they inherit Hindu blood in their veins. But they cannot be called Hindus because their holy land is far off in Arabia or Palestine. They are followers of different cultures, religious faiths, beliefs etc.[28]

Savarkar said—"We Hindus are bound together not only by the tie of the love, we bear to common fatherland and by the common blood ... but also by the tie of a common homage we pay to our great civilization—our Hindu culture, which could not be better rendered than by the word *Sanskriti*. We are one because we are a nation, a race and own a common culture."[29]

In the words of Savarkar—"Civilization is the expression of the mind of man. The story of the civilization of a nation is the story of its thoughts, its action and its achievement. Literature and art describe us its thoughts; history and social institutions of its actions and achievement."[30]

Common History

It is absolutely ignorant weep that the Hindus have no history. Savarkar writes—"Hindus are the only people who have succeeded in preserving their history. It begins with their Vedas which are the first extant chapter of the story of our race. Some of us worship Rama as an incarnation, some admire him as hero and warrior, and all love him as the most illustrious representative monarch of our race. Maruti and Bheemsen are the never failing source of strength and physical perfection to the Hindu youths. Savitri and Damayanti, are the never failing ideals of constancy and chastity of the Hindu. The story of *Ramayan* and *Mahabharat* alone would bring us together and join into a race even if we be scattered to all the four winds like a handful of sand."[31]

In an inspiring tone Savarkar writes—"The fall of Prithvi Raj is to be wailed in Bengal; the martyred sons of Govind Singh in Maharashtra. An Arya Samajist historian in the extreme North feels the Harihar and Bukka of the extreme South fought for him, and a *Sanatanist* historian in the extreme South feels that Guru Tegbahadur died for him. We had kings in common. We had kingdoms in common. We had stability in common. We had triumphs in common and disasters in common. The names of Ashoka, Bhaskaracharya, Panini, and Kapil leave us all electrified with a sense of personal elevation."[32] In this context Savarkar's concluding remark is—"If the Hindus do not possess a common history then none in the world does."[33]

Common Literatures

Our literature and Sanskrit are inseparable part of our common culture. In the words of Savarkar—"Sanskrit is our mother tongue which has given birth to all our other present tongues to millions. It is still the language of their gods; to others it is the language of their ancestors; to all it is the language of par excellence; a common inheritance, a common treasure, that enriches all the family of our sister languages."[34]

Besides Sanskrit language, the literature of Hindu race is also common. Explaining the fundamental unity of Hindu literature Savarkar writes—"The Vedas do not constitute an authority for all Jains. But the Vedas as the most ancient work and the history of their race belong to Jains as much as to any of us. *Adipuran* was not written by a Sanatani, yet the *Adipuran* is the common inheritance of the Sanatanis and Jains. The *Basava Puran* is the Bible of the Lingayats ; but it belongs to both Lingayat and non-Lingayat. Hindus alike, as one of the foremost and historical Kannada work extant, *Vichitra Natak* of guru Govind Singh is as truly the property of a Hindu in Bengal as the *Chaitanya Charitramrit* (चैतन्य चरित्रमृत) is of a Sikh. Kalidas and Bhavabhuti, Charak and Sushruta (सुश्रुत), Aryabhatt and Varahamihir (वराह मिहिर), Bhas (भास) and Aswaghosh (अश्वघोष), Jaidev and Jagannath wrote for us all, appeal to us all, are the cherished possession of us all."[35] According to Savarkar in comparison to the works of Kambha (कंब) and Rabindranath with the works Hafiz and Shakespeare, any Hindu would instinctively say—Kambha and Rabindra are mine.[36] Savarkar says, "The works of art and architecture are also a common inheritance of our race, whether they be representative of Vedic or non-Vedic school of thought."[37]

Common Laws and rites

As regard to common laws, Savarkar says—"Common institutions and a common law that sanctions and sanctifies them, however, they may differ in details are nevertheless both the cause and the effect of the basic unity of our race. The Hindu Law with the underlying principles of Hindu Jurisprudence is too organic a growth to lose its individuality by the manifold changes wrought by times and climes."[38]

The other aspect of common culture is common fairs and festivals. In this context Savarker writes, "We have common feast and festivals. We have common rites and rituals. The Dashehara (दशहरा) and Diwali (दिवाली), the Rakhi and Holi are welcomed wherever a Hindu breathes, Sikhs and Jains, Brahmins and Panchams (पंचम) alike. The Rathyatra festivals at Jagannath, the Vaishakhi (वैशाखी) at Amritsar, the Kumbh and the Ardhakumbh (अर्द्ध कुम्भ) all these great gatherings had been the real and living congress of our people throughout our body politic."[39]

The concept of *Hindutva* is based on the definition of—who is a Hindu. Savarkar defines a Hindu in a following couplet :

आसिंधुसिंधुपर्यन्ता यस्य भारत भूमिका।
पितृ भूः पुण्यभूश्चैव स वै हिंदुरिति स्मृतः ।।

In the words of Savarkar, "A Hindu is who looks upon the land that extends from Sindhu to Sindhu, from the Indus to seas, as the land of his forefathers, his *pitri bhu* (पितृ भूः), who inherits the blood of that race whose first discernible source could be traced to the Vedic *Saptsindhus* and which on its onward march, assimilating much that was incorporated and ennobling much that was assimilated, has come to known as the Hindu people, who has inherited and claims as he own the culture of that race, as expressed mainly in their common classic language the Sanskrit and represented by a common history, a common literature, art and architecture, laws and jurisprudence, rites and rituals, ceremonies and sacraments, fairs and festivals ; and who above all addresses this land, this Sindhusthan, as his *Punyabhu* (पुण्यभूः), as his Holyland—the land of his prophets and seers, of his god men and *gurus*, the land of piety and pilgrimage. These are essentials of *Hindutva*—a common nation, a common race, and a common culture. For the first two essentials of *Hindutva*—nation and race are clearly denoted by the word *pitribhu* (पितृभूः), while the third essential of culture is implied by the work Punyabhu (पुण्यभूः)."[40]

The logical conclusion of Savarkar's definition of a Hindu is that our Mohammedan and Christian Countermen cannot claim as Hindus. Although their common Father-land is India and they inherit the Hindu blood, yet India is not their holy land. Hindustan is not the primary source of their religious system.

In the words of Savarkar—'Christian and Mohammedan communities, who were but very recently Hindus, claim though they might have a common fatherland, and an almost pure Hindu blood and parentage with us, cannot be recognized as Hindus; because their adoption to the new cult had ceased to own Hindu culture *(sanskriti)* as a whole. Their heroes and hero-worship, their fairs and festivals, their ideals and outlook of life, have now ceased to be common with ours. Their holy land is far off in Arabia or Palestine. Their mythology and god men, ideas and heroes are not the offspring of this soil. Consequently their names and outlook are clout of foreign origin. Their devotion is divided."[41]

Savarkar's concept of *Hindutva* is based on the ground realities of socio-cultural and political history of India. That is why he wrote—"Mohammedan or Christian communities possess all the essential qualification of *Hindutva* but they do not look upon India as their Holyland.

The words *Hindutva* and Hinduism both have been derived from the word Hindu. According to Savarkar a Hindu is he, who regards and claims this Bharat bhoomi from Indus to the Seas as his Fatherland and holy land. Essentials of *Hindutva* are logical implications of the definition—who is a Hindu. There is a basic difference between *Hindutva* and Hinduism. Essentials of *Hindutva* are a common country, a common race and a common culture. Hence *Hindutva* is a political concept and it is synonymous with the concept of culture nationalism. All the followers of Vedic (Sanatani and Aryasamaji Hindu) and non-Vedic (Jains, Buddha, Sikhs, Deosamaji etc.) religious systems are inseparable constituents of *Hindutva*. It is neither communal nor religious concept. In fact, it is a conceptual framework of Hindu *Sanghatan* movement. Hinduism is religious and theological system. In the words of Savarkar, 'Hinduism means the 'ism' of the Hindu; and as the word Hindu has been derived from the word *Sindhu*, the Indus, meaning primarily all the people who reside on the land that extends from *Sindhu* to *Sindhu*. "Hinduism must necessarily mean the religion or the religious that are peculiar and native to this land and his people... Hinduism is a set of systems consistent with, even if conflicting with, each other."[42]

The nature of Hindu *Dharma* (Hinduism) is federal. It is the religion of religions. Etymologically Hindu *Dharma* with all its sects and systems is the *dharma* (there is basic difference between the concept of *dharma* and religion) of all the Hindus whether they are Vedic or non-Vedic; because their holy land is Hindustan.

According to Savarkar Hindu *Dharma* is neither Vedic nor non-Vedic. Truth is its goal. Realization is its method.[43] Explaining the federal nature of Hindu *Dharma* Savarker states that "Hinduism is a word that properly speaking should be applied to all the religious belief that the different communities of the Hindu people hold... This is Hindu *Dharma*—the conclusion arrived by harmonizing the detailed experience of all the schools of religions whether Vedic, Sanatani, Jain, Baudha, Sikh or Devsamaji. Each one and everyone of those systems or sects which are the direct descendents and developments of the religious beliefs, Vedic and non-Vedic, that obtained in the land of the Saptsindhus, belongs to and is a post integral of Hindu *Dharma*... Therefore, the Vedic or the Sanatan *Dharma* itself is merely a sect of Hinduism or Hindu *Dharma*."[44]

Generally it is applied that Hinduism is that system of religion which the majority of Hindu people follow. It is the wrong use of the word Hinduism. Savarkar's emphasis is—"To avoid the loose and harmful misuse of the word Hindu. The serious mistake of using such expression as 'Hindu and Sikhs', 'Hindus and Jains' denoting thereby unconsciously that the Vaidiks or the Sanatanis only are Hindus and thus quite unawares inculcate the deadly virus of separation in the minds of the different constituents of our religious brotherhood, defeating our own eager desire to consolidate them all into a harmonious and organic whole."[45]

The definition of *Sanatan Dharma* framed by Lokmanya Tilak is as under:

प्रामाण्य बुद्धिर्वेदेषु साधनानामनेकता।
उपास्यानाम नियम एतद्धर्मस्य लक्षणम्।।

In the words of Savarkar—"In fact, it is not a definition of Hindu *Dharma*, much less of *Hindutva* but of *Sanatan Dharma* the Shrutismriti Puronokt (श्रुतिस्मृति पुरोणोक्त) sect, which being the most popular of all sects of Hindu *Dharma* was naturally but loosely mistaken for Hindu *Dharma* itself."[46]

The whole political ideology of Hindu Nationalism, as propounded by Savarkar, is based on his concept of *Hindutva*. Its essentials are a common country, a common race and a common culture possessed by the Hindus.

Savarkar does not recognize Mohammedan as Hindus, because their holy land is outside of India and they cherish extra-territorial allegiance.[47] In this context Dr. B.R. Ambedkar raised a question—"Are there any common historical antecedents which the Hindus and Muslims can be said to share together matters of pride or as matters of sorrow?"[48] Theory of two nations propounded by M.A. Jinnah in March 1940 proves that Savarkar was right in his approach pertaining to the Muslims of India.

On the basis of the profound knowledge of Indian history and cultural heritage Savarkar arrived at the conclusion that the Hindus are all one and a nation and they own a common culture in spite of much diversity. His thoughts have been supported by the noted historians. Vincent Smith observes—"India beyond all doubt possesses a deep underlying fundamental unity, for more profound than that produced either by geographical isolation or by political superiority. That unity transcends the innumerable diversities of blood, colour, language, dress, manners and sect."[49] J. Ramsay Macdonald writes—"India and Hinduism are organically related as body and soul."[50]

Savarkar's concept of *Hindutva* is neither communal nor religious. Its essence is cultural nationalism. Its nature is comprehensive. It recognizes Hindus as the followers of Vedic, non-Vedic religious systems and other sects, whose roots are in India and consider it as their holy land.

Thus Savarkar developed the concept of *Hindutva* on the basis of socio-political history of India and its cultural heritage.

Savarkar's thought regarding Hindu and Hinduism can also be seen in the judgment pronounced by the Honorable Supreme Court in 1966. And in the 52nd para of this decision it is clearly mentioned that development of Hinduism through the ages has made it apparent that whenever *'sant'* and the reformer tried to reform the drawbacks in Hinduism has every time led to the origination of new religion (*panth*) which is administered by their own thought.

Originally their own thought regarding Hinduism and Hindu philosophy are interrelated. It has been never explained that such a religion (*panth*) is far-off from Hindu brotherhood.[51]

Supreme Court again confirmed its previous judgment on July 2, 1995—"In a significant judgment, the Supreme Court held that the Ramkrishna Mission was not a separate religion, but only a denomination of Hinduism."[52] The Court gave the ruling, while setting aside the verdict of a single judge of the Calcutta High Court, holding that the Ramkrishna religion, being distinct and separate from the Hindu religion was a minority and was entitled to protection under Article 30 (1) of the Constitution.[53] In this way Savarkar's profound logical arguments have been supported directly or indirectly by the Supreme Court that Hinduism has cultural and organic solidarity.

Credit goes to Savarkar who developed the concept of *Hindutva* and separated it from Hinduism. In the words of V.P. Verma—"From the political theory point of view the distinction made between Hinduism and *Hindutva* by Savarkar is remarkable."[54]

It was Savarkar who explained the federal nature of Hinduism (Hindu *Dharma*) while comparing it with *Hindutva* and he accepted the difference between *Dharma* and Religion. Hinduism is not a religion. According to J.N. Sircar it is a synthesis of religions, a followship of faiths, and a federation of philosophies. Swami Nirvedanand remarks that it was a marvellous multifaceted of a vast number of creeds tied essentially surrounding a magnificent pivot of essential unity. Romain Rolland thinks that "Hinduism is a symphony of a variety of creeds and a bouquet of variable flowers."[55]

The concept of *Hindutva* is the child of Savarkar's keen and original mind. He explained in detail that *Hindutva* is one which has kept India united through the ages. He is ready to accept Mohammedans as Hindus if they proclaim their commitment to their fatherland that is India and its cultural heritage.

REFERENCES

1. Dhananjay Keer, *Veer Savarkar;* Popular Prakashan, Bombay, 1966.
2. *Ibid.*, pp. 207-208.
3. *Essentials of Hinutva in Samagra Savarkar Wangmaya,* Volume VI (Maharashtra Prantik Hindusabha, Poona, 1964), p. 4.
4. *Ibid.*, pp. 4-5.
5. *Ibid.*, p. 5.
6. *Hindu Rashtra Darshan in Samagra Savarkar Wangmaya,* Volume VI (Poona, 1964), p. 282.
7. Note 3, pp. 28-29.
8. *Ibid.*, pp. 29-31.
9. *Ibid.*, p. 33.
10. *Ibid.*, p. 35.
11. *Ibid.*, p. 36.
12. *Ibid.*, pp. 47, 46, 29.
13. Note : 3, p. 48.
14. *Encyclopaedia of Religion and Ethics,* Volume VI, (New York, 1955), p. 686.
15. Note : 6, p. 280.
16. *Ibid.*, p. 280.
17. S. Radhakrishnan, *The Hindu View of Life* (Bombay, George Allen & Unwin, India, 1976), p. 12.
18. Note : 3, p. 53.
19. *Ibid.*, p. 54.
20. *Ibid.*, p. 54.
21. *Ibid.*, p. 54.
22. *Ibid.*, p. 55.
23. *Ibid.*, p. 57.
24. *Ibid.*, pp. 57-58.
25. *Ibid.*, p. 58.
26. *Ibid.*, p. 58.
27. *Ibid.*, p. 58.
28. *Ibid.*, p. 59.
29. *Ibid.*, p. 59.
30. *Ibid.*, pp. 59-60.
31. *Ibid.*, pp. 60-61.
32. *Ibid.*, p. 61.
33. *Ibid.*, p. 61.
34. *Ibid.*, pp. 61-62.
35. *Ibid.*, p. 62.
36. *Ibid.*, p. 62.
37. *Ibid.*, p. 62.
38. *Ibid.*, pp. 62-63.

39. *Ibid.*, pp. 63-64.
40. *Ibid.*, p. 74.
41. *Ibid.*, pp. 65, 73.
42. *Ibid.*, 67.
43. *Ibid.*, p. 70.
44. *Ibid.*, pp. 68, 70.
45. Note : 6, p. 281.
46. Note : 3, p. 70.
47. Note : 6, p. 287.
48. B.R. Ambedkar, *Pakistan or Partition of India* (Education Department, Govt. of Maharashtra, 1990), p. 35.
49. Vincent Smith, *The Oxford History of India* (Delhi, Oxford University Press, 1976), p. 7.
50. Radha Kumud Mookerji, *The Fundamental Unity of India*, Foreword by MacDonold (Bhartiya Vidya Bhawan, Bombay, 1970).
51. *All India Reporter*, 1966, Volume 53, Supreme Court Section (Nagpur, The All India Reporter Limited, 1966), p. 1134.
52. *Ibid.*, p. 1131.
53. *Times of India* (New Delhi), July 3, 1995.
54. V.P. Verma, *Modern Indian Political Thought* (Lakshmi Narain Agarwal, Agra, 1978), p. 391.
55. 'What is Hinduism' in Hindu Vishwa Vishesank (Vishwa Hindu Praishad, Prayag Sammelan, January 1966), p. 53.

7

Dharma, Religious Denomination and Politics

Reflection of Pt. Deen Dayal Upadhyaya

Mahesh Chandra Sharma

Due to the Western influence in the study of Indian politics, the agenda of *Dharma* and sect is too much complicated. Pt. Deen Dayal Upadhyaya has been a notable thinker of the Indianness oriented thinking of 'Unified Humanism' (*Akatm Manavvad*). He has not only been the Secretary-General and President of the political party, namely 'Bhartiya Jansangh' but also has been a thinker and scholar of post-independence India. His thoughts create the possibility of a relevant dialogue in this context.

'Dharma'[1] has been considered a special feature of Indian culture. It is said that it has got no synonym in other languages of the world. Its interpretation has also been considered to be difficult. In each interpretation some or the other fault of 'non-involvement' or 'too much of involvement' is noticed. Hence the term 'dharma' assumes a new meaning according to the situation.

Grammatically the term 'dharma' is formed by inserting the suffix "mana" in "dhri dharane". Its derivation can be made in three ways:

1. ध्रियते लोकोऽनेन इति धर्मः, i.e. that which bears the world is known as 'dharma'.

2. धरति धारयति वा लोकमिति धर्मः, i.e. that which bears the world is known as 'dharma'.
3. ध्रियते यः स धर्मः, i.e. that which is borne by others is 'dharma'.

In the *Mahābhārata* the feature of 'dharma' has been described as follows :

धारणाद्धर्ममित्याहुधर्मो धारयते प्रजाः।
यत् स्याद्धारण संयुक्तं स धर्म इति निश्चयः।।

वर्णपर्व 069/58।

On account of bearing people call it 'dharma'. 'Dharma' bears the people and those who lives with the bearer is certainly 'dharma'. In *Nirukta,* the meaning of the term 'dharma' is said to be 'rule'. With the combination of these two concept, the real meaning of 'dharma' is: 'The rule which has borne this world is 'dharma'. According to Maharhsi Kanad, the writer of *Vaisheshik Darshan* "यतोऽभ्युदयनिः श्रेयससिद्धिः स धर्मः, i.e. that which provides worldly progress and heavenly welfare (Salvation) is 'dharma'.

Maharshi Manu says:

वेदोऽयिलो धर्ममूलं स्मृतिशीले च तदविदाम्।
आचारश्चैव साधूनां आत्मनस्तुष्टिरेव च।।

(2/6)

that is all the *Vedas* (*Rig, Yajur, Sama and Atharva*) are the root of 'dharma'. The character of the scholar of *Shruti-Smriti* is 'dharma'. The character of saint is 'dharma'. It is meant to say that all that satisfies is 'dharma'.

According to *Daishik Shastra,*[2] the concept of equilibrium of direct reciprocal qualities of man and nearby man bears many "rival qualities" either by human nature or due to close competitiveness. And to maintain their equilibrium is called 'dharma'. Ordinary character of human become rivals, e.g. discretion and greed.

From all the above description, the concept of topic is not quite evident. "The rule which bears the subject is 'dharma'". Then, this question always exists that what are these rules? Who is their regulator? What are those yardsticks which provide worldly and heavenly progress? Definitely, the answer to this "What" cannot be undisputable. Differences of opinion will ever be noticed in it. Are the thoughts mentioned in four books, namely Vedas are deciding factors of the final form of 'dharma'. Vedas are the books or the infinite means of acquiring knowledge? In India and the remaining world whatever opinions were expressed about the concept of 'dharma' by various great men to revive the sleepy concept of human beings, those opinions or sects were known as 'dharma', e.g. *Vedic dharma,* Buddhism, Jainism etc. Thus, Christians, Muslims and Jews are known as 'dharma'. When 'dharma' was interwoven in sects, it became itself *'Adharma'*. It banned the research of 'dharma' of rivals or those who opposed the thoughts.

Yogiraj Sri Aurobindo has analysed it clearly. We should cast our glance on the root of the evil. Its root is not pure and true *dharma,* but its root impose something illusory due to which it considering *dharma* and specific opinion, sect, religious society or church-temple the common thing and manipulates it. The tendency of this confusion of man is so strong that even the ancient tolerant idol-worshipper Paganism murdered Socrates under the pretext of *dharma* and good conduct. It tortured the opinion of Isis gave gradual suffering to anti-national *dharma* like *Mithra.* It considered the religion of the initial Christians as destructive and anti-social and vehemently tortured it. Not only this, originally more tolerant Hindu opinion religion gave birth to mutual hatred and on occasions ran riots with *Buddhists, Jains, Shaivas* and *Vaishnavas.* Temples, churches and opinion of sects brought too much hindrance in the way of Philosophy and science. Due to this tendency Gordano Bruno was burnt to death and Galileo was made a captive... Philosophy and science to get an open area and in self-defence attacked *dharma* and destroyed it.[3] According to Sri Aurobindo," The aim of *dharma* is such an inspirational tendency and law system, which is evidently to reach God." According to him, when religious opinion and sect functions with 'sect feeling' in place of 'feeling of *dharma*', automatically it becomes its own enemy.

In the past time whatever work was done by science and philosophy, was the work of the continuity of 'dharma' which unfortunately stood against 'dharma' as it was necessary to eliminate superstitions of the institutionalised *dharma*. Fortunately in India the feeling of such type of sectarian orthodox has been comparatively in less degree. Here, in the research field of *'dharma tatva'* the justice 'वादे वादे जायते तत्त्वबोध:' normally went on. Therefore, here philosophy and science developed not as a rival to *dharma* but as a component of *dharma*. Pt. Deen Dayal Upadhyaya accepted 'dharma' with its original prestigious position, not as flexible sectarian prejudice.

The mediaeval western history made 'dharma' synonymous of "sect" in place of continuous research apparatus of "rules of conception". Upadhyaya was of the opinion that it would be a fault to punish *"dharma tatva"* as a punishment of this mediaeval culpability. Therefore, he accepts *dharma* in its original form in place of accepting it as a translation of "dharma" as sect. For worldly and heavenly advancement of life, today man has developed the concepts of "science", "constitutionalism" and "spiritualism". Upadhyaya accepts 'dharma' with these concepts, but he considers incorrect the desire to live by snapping relations with these "concepts"; he considers it unnatural and created from reaction. Perhaps this is the reason that, he is not ready to support modern "scientists", "constitutionalists" and "spiritualists" for their acts of deliberately dragging "dharma" into the cage of "sect". However, he is a staunch advocate of providing secular form to "dharma". He is not the supporter of such concept of *dharma* according to which entrance of a *Harijan* to the *"Vishwanath* Temple" leads to loss of *dharma*.[4] Upadhyaya says: "*dharma* has no relation to temple mosque. Offering prayers may be a component of human-*dharma*, but *dharma* is widespread. Temples and mosques have also been the effective medium of the teaching of *'dharmacharan'* (the conduct of *dharma*) but as if we can say that a school is not 'learning', likewise a temple is different from *dharma*."[5]

He defines it like this: "*dharma* means conception. The components which are responsible for the concept of a thing, person or nature are known as 'dharma'. For example, the *dharma* of fire is heat."[6]

Sustaining principles are liable to change in conformity with the time, place and circumstances, for example Preservation of body is being *dharma*, the principles of sustenance in cold is heat, and when it is summer, cold things are to be consumed.[7] Such a conception of '*dharma*' is speciality to Indian life. Due to this longevity of India is maintained. On account of religious system in the society a well managed life continues. Therefore, he strongly opposed to declaring India as "religiously secular."[7]

Conceptually, Upadhyaya is a votary of "Secular State", yet he refutes to translating a "Secular society" or the term "Secular" or as secularity as "Religious Secularism". He states that *dharma* of the state is only "Worldly", however, the concept of the society never obtains merely on being of emerged as a revolt "worldly" or "materially". The society needs both types of advancement—physical and spiritual. Therefore, the society cannot be simply 'materialistic' or 'secular'. 'Secular State', i.e. 'Worldly State' should contribute to spiritual advancement of the society. Only then, in a wide sense, the 'dharma' of the 'society' could be followed.[8]

What meaning would then have to be assigned to the term of 'secular'? Normally for 'secular' the terms physical, *dharma* less, without *dharma*, religiously secular, unreligious, non-religious etc. are used. All these terms are not synonymous to each other. In the West, the concept 'secular state' was understood in the sense of the against 'Church State'. But, in India, actually under the hypothesis of a state, there is only the concept of a 'worldly state'. Here, *Dharmaguru* never got the place of a king. Today, the Indian leaders want to build future of India by adopting the Western ideals. In their opinion, in the context of the Western world, the meaning of "secular state" may be taken as "Worldly State". But, the Indian people are keen to "Religious State" or "Utopian State" and they cannot be satisfied by merely worldly advancement. Consequently, 'worldly state' will not be accepted even on being total synonymous to 'secular state'. In our country, without *dharma* we cannot imagine any feeling of its existence. Therefore, we understood that our state cannot neglect *dharma*. Therefore, the terms non-religious, religiously secular, without *dharma, dharma* less, diverted from religion etc. neither express the ideal of our state nor can be total synonymous to 'secular state'. Upadhyaya offers a solution for this. The word 'non-secular' does not denote the exact ideal of 'state' but the term 'secular' is quite near to the western applied meaning. Except Russia no other country abolished religion (opinion) and today even Russia has accepted the freedom of worship. However, the state will not provide any facility to anyone. In the remaining states, all the sects have spiritual and physical freedom as per their opinion. Except the king of England; all other states, have no partiality towards sect. Hence, those states may be considered worldly against the holy Roman Empire, but to call them non-communal will be more justifiable. By the term 'non-communal' the conception of our leaders becomes more evident because today, the term 'secular' is used to show difference from Pakistan which has declared itself 'Islamic State'. Due to above reason the term 'non-communal' is the nearest version to the term 'secular' and it should be used.

Despite 'non-communal state' being proper version of 'secular state' does not provide a competent expression of the ideal of a state. Therefore, Upadhyaya is a staunch supporter of 'non-communal' 'dharma Rajya'. Conceptually, the 'dharma Rajya' of Upadhyaya is the only democratic constitutional rule. But, as a translation of 'theocratic state' he rejects the version *'religious state'*. *'Religious state'* is the original and legislative hypothesis of India; it has reached this stage by imagining 'state of law' of the West. Therefore, when the West has accepted the 'religious state' in comparison to 'sectarian state' or 'personal state', then we imitate the West leaving our original concept, Mr. Deen Dayal does not think it proper. In his 'principle and policy' document declaring the hypothesis of ideal state of Bhartiya Jansangh party as 'Dharma Rajya', he writes:

"The ideal of Indian State is *'dharma Rajya'*. It is a non-communal state. The feeling of tolerance and equal respect for all sects and ways of offering prayers is an essential characteristic of Indian state. *Dharma Rajya* does not consider any person or institution full of sovereign powers. All are bound to rules and duties. The right of Executive, legislature and public, all are subject to *Dharma*. Arbitrariness is nowhere allowed. The English term 'Rule of Law' (rule according to law) is the nearest term expressing the hypothesis of *Dharma Rajya*. Only *'Dharma Rajya'* is capable of checking uncontrolled and dictatorial trend and saving democracy from being mutilated in arbitrariness."[9]

Pt. Deen Dayal in his speech in Bombay propounds with urge and at large that 'Dharma Rajya' does not mean 'Theocratic State'. 'Theocratic state' means the rule of any sectarian *guru*. In such state the people of one sect have all rights and others have no existence or survive as a slave of citizen or as second grade citizen. The Roman empire existed on this basis. This was the hypothesis of 'Khilafat' that there is no need to link State with religion. It does not add to the capability of man of offering prayers to God. Yes, the states are diverted from the fulfilment of their duties. It does not happen in *'Dharma Rajya'* i.e. each citizen has full liberty to follow their sect.[10] However, Upadhayaa has been an enthusiastic supporter of democracy. But, in favour of 'dharma' that he has described the 'sovereignty of *Dharma Rajya'* in such a way that some doubt arises whether Deen Dayal Upadhyaya is supporting 'Constitutional Monarchy'.

The concept of *Dharma Rajya* is different from today's concept of democracy. The king despite performing the duty to establish the welfare of the subject is originally controlled by *dharma*. The subject is also controlled by *dharma*. Just as the king has no right to punish the religious minded subject, likewise the subject has no right to remove *Dharma*-protector king. Democracy, considering the permanent rivalry between the interests of the king and the subject and constantly keeping the king under the control of the subject, as a rival party, hangs the sword of constantly growing revolt on the head of the king. This democracy is not conducive to human development and probably it has been born of the dual Christian thought of God and Devil. The subject can remove the king if he acts against *Dharma*. It is not the duty of the subject to remove the king, but it is the duty to follow *dharma* in the true spirit. When the king becomes a hurdle in the way of following the *dharma*, it is a *dharma* to remove him.[11] Upadhyaya calls such people as 'religious people' who revolt against the king whose activity is non-religious and acts against norms of *Dharma*. Those who are responsible for bringing about changes in ruling system mention the names of great men like Lord Ram, Lord Krishna, Chanakya, Vidyaranya Swami and Ram Das and say: "They had no lust for power, but they were the 'founders of *dharma*'".[12]

Thus, Upadhyaya affirms the *dharma* as the sovereignty to enthrone or dethrone the king. Though, he never recites anywhere the decisive system of '*Dharma*' and '*Adharma*'. Is revolt the only way of change of power? Does he really mean that the bearer of '*dharma-danda*' (the scepter of *Dharma*) should be a priest? He states "State in our country, the authority of the rules of *dharma* and the authority of following the rules of *dharma* and the right of interpretation was never given to the king. Then, the question arises so as to who will enjoy sovereignty in social life? In our country, the ruler has been termed as 'an incarnation of Lord Vishnu' the subject all the more are held to be popular regality. The king is the sole person; "the king can do no wrong". We did not believe in such things. According to our recognition and system, at the time of crowning ceremony, the king declares thrice: "अदण्डयोऽस्मि". But, at the same time the 'state-priest' says, by touching and hitting his waist with a 'palash sceptre' *(palash-danda)*. "*Dharma* is a punishment for you "धर्मदण्ड्योऽसि", i.e. sovereignty is *dharma*; *dharma* will rule over the king. Today, it is said that sovereignty lies in people but, in our country, the public was not given this power properly. The sovereignty of people is accepted when the king shows some laxity in his duties. Today, inherent right to revolt with the people has not been given in India. We have no recognition like this sovereignty.[13] Sovereignty inherent neither in king nor in people but always in *dharma*.

Upadhyaya did not consider even 'majority' as the regulator of '*dharma*'. He tries to prove it by presenting many illustrations in various ways. General de-Gaulle of France never approved the surrender of majority before Hitler, in the struggle for freedom, the majority did not fight against the British. Lincoln did not accept wrong plebiscite (referendum). He neither accepted the slavery system nor division, but he accepted civil war. On this basis, he considers it wrong to talk about referendum in Kashmir, Goa etc. The reason is: "National Unity is our *dharma*". Lastly, he propounds: "People should understand it well that '*dharma*' does not lie in majority of people. '*Dharma*' is eternal. Therefore, in the interpretation of democracy, the rule of public is not sufficient, this rule should be in the interest of the people. Only *dharma* can take the decision about the interest of the people. Therefore, for 'rule of people', 'rule of *dharma*' is also necessary. True democracy lies only there where both liberty and *dharma* exist. In 'the rule of *dharma*' all these concepts endorsed *dharma rajya*.[14]

In the complete discussion of the concept of '*Dharma Rajya*', it seems proper to call 'state of law' as 'rule of *dharma*' (*dharma rajya*) that runs according to the fundamental law of the constitution in context of natural and social laws. Likewise, in the absence of socialization and codification of rules of nature, revolt at the time of disobedience, revolution or *satyagraha* seems justifiable under the definition of '*dharma*'. Whatever encouraging support has been given by Upadhyaya to ancient Indian '*dharma-tatva*' seems to cross the limit of logic at some places. If the regulator of '*dharma*' is neither king, nor people, not even institution ascertained by them, then who is the real regulator of '*dharma*'? Upadhyaya does not give answer to this question. Thus, who will be the bearer of the sceptre of *dharma* (*dharma-danda*) to control power? Will it be the priest of the state? Probably, it is not the mentality of Upadhyaya because it does not confirm to the discussion of Upadhyaya as he has discussed democracy, public awareness and polished referendum in a justifiable and argumentable manner. Philosophically, people may accept the state of *dharma* on the concept of *Dharma Rajya* of Upadhyaya, but, some people may doubt that behind all this Philosophical conception, he has a mind set-up to induce dominance of Hindu *Dharma* in the country through imagination of *Dharma Rajya*. Due to this doubt Pt. Deen Dayal Upadhyaya became a subject to the criticism of the people.

REFERENCES

1. Govind Narainji Asopa : "Dharma" Shabda ka Lakshan aur Rahasya, *Kalyan Masik*, Geeta Press, Gorakhpur, Hindu Sanskriti Visheshank, p. 369.
2. Badrishah Duldharia : *Daishik Shastra*, Gauri Shankar Kailash, Almora (U.P.), Viradadhyay, Dvitiya Anhika, Varnashram Vibhag. p. 87.
3. Yogiraj Aurobindo : "*Dharma ki Simayen*" (Limitations of *Dharma*) as the Law of Life.
4. Dilli Sangh Shiksha Varga, Bauddhik Varga, 9-6, 1958, Deen Dayal Upadhyaya, Bauddhik Varga Panjika, Sangh Karyalaya, Jhandewala, p. 11.
5. Deen Dayal Upadhyaya, Guruji, Thengariji, Ekatma Darshan,Deen Dayal Shodh Sansthan, New Delhi, "*Vyashti-Samashti mein Samarasata*", pp. 41-42.
6. Rajasthan, Bauddhik Varge, 7-6-1995, Deen Dayal Upadhyaya, Bauddhik Varga Panjika, Sangh Shiksha Varga.
7. Deen Dayal Upadhyaya : *Rashtra Jeevan Ki Disha*, Rashtra *Dharma* Pustak Prakashan, Lucknow, Adhyay-6 "Secular: Artha-Anartha", pp. 67-68.
8. Deen Dayal Upadhyaya : *Bauddhik Varga Panjika*, Deen Dayal Shodh Sansthan, (Place and date not mentioned).
9. Ref. No. 5, p. 7.
10. Ref. No. 5, Chapter 3 : *Vyasthi-Samashti mein Samarasata*, pp. 48-49.
11. Deen Dayal Upadyay : *Rashtra Chintan*, Rashtra *Dharma* Pustak Prakashan, Lucknow.
12. Bauddhik Varga, 11 June, 1960, Serial No. 4, p. 87.
13. Ref. No. 8, Chapter 18; *Saransh* (Jivan Darshan), p. 200.
14. Ref. No. 5, Chapter 3; *Vyashti-Samashti mein Samarasata*, pp. 52-53.

8

Glimpses of Swami Dayanand Saraswati

K.S. Saxena

Dayanand's life history is scanty. He was reluctant to give information about his early life. Therefore his birth place and his parentage long remained a matter of uncertainty. A short autobiography covering the period from 1824 to 1860 was published in "The Theosophist"—a monthly journal of Bombay. Earlier to it, he himself had given some information about his early life, during his stay at Poona in 1875 to his audience. However, now it has been established that he was born in 1824 A.D. in the state of Morvi in Kathiawar (Gujarat). (His original name was Mool Shanker Dayal ji or Dayaram) in a Brahman family and his father Karasamlal ji was a devotee of Lord Shiva. At the age of five, Mool Shanker tried to learn the Devnagari Slokas and Mantras. Later, he became a Vedic scholar, a great social reformer and exponent of Hindu revivalism. Romain Rolland observes "...how great an uplifter of the people he was—in fact the most vigorous force of the immediate and present action in India as the moment of the rebirth and reawakening of the national consciousness. His Arya Samaj, whether he wished it or not, prepared the way in 1905 for the revolt of Bengal. He was one of the most ardent prophets of reconstruction and of national organization."[1]

He moved from place to place inquiring about the scholars of renowned, men of wisdom and ascetics (*Sadhus*) of great religious merit. "His search was for spiritual salvation and inner truth."[2] In 1855, he visited for the first time the Kumbh Mela at Haridwar, which gave him an opportunity to have a face to face talk with the people. He extensively toured Gujarat, Rajasthan, Haridwar, Himalayas, Bengal, Bihar, the Vindhya Range, Punjab and the banks of Narmada river. He was against the out-dated age old conventions and superstitions. He was shocked to witness the sorry state of the Hindus and realized that his dear 'Aryavarta' was full of darkness. He was severely pained to see all this and resolved to work for the reformation and regeneration of Aryavarta. Swamiji proclaimed, "The world is fettered by the chains forged by superstitions and ignorance. I have come to snap as under that chain and to set slaves at liberty". In June 1875, Swamiji published *'Satyarth Prakash'* at Banaras and founded Arya Samaj at Bombay on April 10, 1875.[3] Later, Arya Samaj was established in Lahore, Roorkee, Delhi, Meerut *et cetera* and by the time of his death the total number of Samaj had risen to 79. In fact by this time, the Arya Samaj had acquired a momentum of its own.

Arya Samaj was a movement which was started to raise the patriotic feelings of the citizens and to remove the prevailing social evils from the Hindu-society. In Rajasthan, branches of Arya Samaj were founded in almost all the important towns between 1880 and 1890. Vedic Yantralaya, a printing press, was also started by Swami Dayanand Saraswati at Allahabad for the publication of the Arya Samaj literature. Later, the Press was shifted to Ajmer and was put under the supervision of Shyamaji Krishna Varma, a revolutionary of his times. Another social institution, namely 'Paropkarini Sabha' was also established by Swamiji on February 27, 1883 at Udaipur for the propagation of Vedic religion, the headquarters of which was also shifted to Ajmer later.

This Sabha came in form of Swamiji's will. Dayanand Saraswati wrote, "I Dayanand Saraswati, entrust these twenty-three persons the sole in-charge of my clothes, books, money, yantralaya and write this 'Swikar Patra' to use the same for altruistic purposes."[4] This body of twenty-three persons consisted of some prominent personalities like His Highness of Shahpura, Shyamaji Krishna Verma, Mahadeva Govind

Ranade and so on with Maharana Sajjan Singh of Udaipur, as its President.

Now Swamiji turned towards Rajputana. He was not satisfied by the popularity of his views among the masses only. He believed unless the cooperation of Princes was achieved, it would be difficult to obtain the ultimate goal of 'Swarajya'. Dayanad, therefore, wished that the rulers of the States should be brought into contact with enlightened members of the Sabha.[5] He also wished to engage the Princes of Rajasthan in public welfare by improving their character and by making them more conscious of their duties towards their subjects. Accordingly, in June 1865, the first time, Dayanand visited Rajasthan and stayed at Karauli as a guest of His Highness the Maharaja of Karauli. In October 1865, Swamiji visited Jaipur where Thakur Ranjeet Singh of Achrol became his disciple.[6] During his visit to Ajmer in March 1866, Swami Dayanand requested the Agent to the Governor General in Rajasthan to stop cow slaughter. The agitation to stop cow slaughter in Rajasthan became violent and the bungalow of Col. Tod in Udaipur was badly damaged. On November 1, 1866, Swamiji attended the Darbar of Lord Lawrence at Agra and then proceeded to Bharatpur, Jaipur, Ajmer and Churu. On the invitation of Raja Govind Singh he visited Banera. Therefrom he went to Chittor where a Darbar was organized by Lord Ripon to confer the title of G.C.S.I. on the Maharana of Udaipur. Here Maharana Sajjan Singh of Udaipur met him and requested him to come to Udaipur. Sawamiji visited Udaipur on August 11, 1882 where he emphasized over the need of adopting Indian culture instead of cultivating the Western outlook. Maharana was highly impressed by Swamiji's teachings and implemented them in practice too. Swamiji instructed Maharana on statecraft, princely duties and obligations and on moral conduct. Swamiji's lessons were based on seventh, eighth, and ninth chapters of Manusmiriti and those parts of Vanparva of *Mahābhārat* which deals with politics and development of man's character. Here Swamiji also founded the 'Paropkarini Sabha' which later became the trustees after the Swami's death. On March 1, 1883, Swamiji left for Shahpura and from there he reached Jodhpur on May 31, 1883 on the invitation of Maharaja Jaswant Singh.[7] The younger brother of Maharaja Jaswant Singh, Sir Pratap was very much influenced by the speeches of Swami Dayanand. He remarked, "...to my mind it was a fortunate thing for India that Swami came to awaken her from her slumber of lethargy."[8] During his stay at Jodhpur, he instrumented Maharaja Jaswant Singh on statecraft, Princely duties and moral conduct. Maharaja was very much influenced by Swamiji's teachings and issued orders to prohibit post-funeral dinners, alcoholic drinks and so forth but did not change his personal lifestyle. Swamiji's outspokenness annoyed a number of people in Jodhpur and in the meantime, it is believed, poison was given to Swami Dayanand by a courtesan at Jodhpur. On October 16, Swamiji left Jodhpur in a critical condition for Abu and than for Ajmer reaching there on October 26, where he took the last breath on October 30, 1883 saying, "Oh Merciful and all powerful Lord, this is your will, let it be fulfilled, you have performed a good *lila*."

II

Swami Dayanand Saraswati was a revolutionary reformer who worked untiringly for the reformation and regeneration of India. The greatest mission of his life was the liberation of the spiritual soul of India. He knew that spirituality is the very essence of Hinduism and therefore, the salvation of India depended on moral and spiritual uplift. To achieve this object, it was essential to eradicate the evils prevailing in the social and religious life and by generating a pride in the past, the Vedic past which alone is the true heritage. Swamiji, thus, stood for reforms and revival. The watchword of Swami Dayanand become, "back to Vedas". He visualized that "both Christianity and Islam were making fatal in-roads upon Hinduism. He realized that unless this process of conversion to Christianity and Islam of Hindus was stopped, India would cease in course of time to be the land of Hindus, the main body of the people being divided into Muslims and Christians, Muslims in upper India and Christians in the South. Christianity and Islam must, therefore, be fought with their own weapons and Hinduism must find this weapon in the Vedas, proclaimed as an exclusive revelation without which there is and can be no salvation for men, whatever may be his country."[9]

Swamiji interpreted the Vedas in a way that expresses his own original ideas on religion. His ideas on the universal God, Soul (*Atma*), Maya, Brahma, Truth, Morality are all based on Vedas. Dayanand took upon himself the task of rescuing the Vedas from its wrong interpretation and misconception. He held that the Vedas are the true and divine knowledge and all the religious dogmas and unjust social practices and beliefs of existing Hinduism were unVedic. He gave the Vedas, its true and real meaning. In fact, "never since Shankaracharya had such a prophet of Vedisim appeared."[10] It was the remarkable attempt by Swami Dayanand Saraswati, to re-establish the Vedas as a living religious scripture. Himself a great Sanskrit Scholar, he handled his material with remarkable power and independence. As it has been observed, "the genius of the race looking through the eyes of Dayanand pierced behind the error of many countries and received again the intention of a timeless revelation and a divine truth given to humanity."[11] For him, Vedas alone were the supreme authority. To Dayanand the key to India's full regeneration lay in the Vedas, and he was deeply convinced that knowledge of the Vedas would inevitably lead the Aryans back to their ancient glory. Swamiji took pains to prove that the prevalent form of Hinduism with such features as idol worship, animal sacrifices, polytheism, rituals and superstitions were in fact based on the Purans and not on the Vedas. The Purans, according to Swamiji were the very anti-thesis of the Vedas and of much latter period. Swamiji, therefore, appealed to the people to reject Purans and to accept the true interpretation of the Vedas. For Dayanand, God is all pervading, and all powerful. God never born or die and is free from fear, disease and decay. God is omnipresent, omnipotent and omniscience. Dayanand tried to rationalize the concept of God in such a way that while it satisfies the need or urge of man for God, it also makes it possible for him to believe in its existence in spite of the growing advances in science and human knowledge. "God is not a person whose existence we can deny or refuse to accept but it is a power which even those who do not believe in him can accept as the law of nature."[12] Swamiji, in fact, rationalized and simplified the religion. According to him God is *Nirākār* and hence there should be no idol worshipping. The mode of worship of this supreme being should be *Sandhyā Upāsanā, Havan,* prayer or *Ishwaropāsanā.* These are the only means of salvation and, therefore, there is no need to go to temples and worship idols.

III

Swamiji was also a social reformer. He relentlessly carried on his crusade against the social evils and injustices present in contemporary Hindu society. Swamiji started a dynamic revolutionary reform movement to eradicate social evils which were leading Hindu society towards dissolution and fall. Dayanand strongly condemned child marriage and advocated widow-remarriage. According to him reform in the Hindu society was essential to face the challenge and criticism of alien faith and culture. His reform movement was thus a crusading and reforming movement from within as well as a defensive organization for protection against external attacks.[13] The most important characteristics that marked the decadence of the Hindu society were the degrading and deplorable condition of women and the untouchables. Swamiji's reforms were directed towards the eradication of these evils and the improvement of the condition of women and the untouchables. He worked to restore Indian women to the position of respect and glory, which they held during the Vedic times. Swamiji accepted the *Varṇa Vyavasthā* based on merit and strongly condemned the caste system. Swamiji adopted a broader and comprehensive meaning of education. For him it was not confined to bookish knowledge but meant mental, social and spiritual development. It was a means of character-building and development of the various faculties of human being. It would help in removing ignorance, superstition, fear social inequality, exploitation and inhumanity. Swamiji emphasized education of women as well as to the *Sūdras*. Swami Dayanand's ideas on education are realistic, nationalistic, revolutionary and progressive. He gives a detailed outline of the subjects to be studied in *Gurukulas* and the duration required for the study of each subject. He insisted on *Swa-Bhāsa*.

Swamiji expressed his views on the form of government, functions and powers of the head of the State, the Assemblies, the mode of election of the *Rāja* as well as the role and the participation of people in the day to day function of the government. He was a staunched supporter of a democratic form of government based on Vedic scriptures. Swamiji also gives importance to the proper system of justice. He insists over the importance and independence of judiciary. Its aim is not only to deliver justice but also to promote the welfare and happiness of all. He believed in enlightened democracy, self-sufficient village administration, modification of the absolution of *ahinsā* and the supremacy of divine law.[14]

IV

Dayanand was not a political philosopher in the strict sense. He was influenced by the political ideas of *Manusmirti*. He was a staunch nationalist and an aggressive exponent of Hindu revivalism. Swami Dayanand mainly emphasized upon four factors, viz., *Swadharma, Swarājya, Swadeshi and Swabhāsa*. He was of the view that a nation cannot make progress unless it follows its own language, religion, and is ruled by its own Government and is otherwise generally self-reliant. He denounced the salt tax even in 1875 which was opposed by Mahatma Gandhi in 1930. He stressed that a foreign Government, whatever be its merits, cannot make the people happy.

In the first decade of the twentieth century in some parts of the country, notably Bengal, the cult of *Swadeshī* spread fast. Swami Dayanand was perhaps the first prominent leader who supported the cause of *Swadeshī* clothes. The Maharaja of Jodhpur was the first ruler in Rajputana who accepted his advice and issued the orders to wear *Khādī*. H.B. Sarda observes, "Everyone in the service of that (Jodhpur) State, from *Mahārāja* down to peons, and the elite of Jodhpur, adopted the *Khādī* produced in Marwar. Thus long before the cult of *Swadeshī* spread through Bengal, Marwar had appeared clothed in *Khādī*."[15] Swamiji appreciated the Europeans who, though living in India for hundred years, did not give up putting on their own style of dress. In his own words, "They (Europeans) have not changed the fashion of their country, but many among you have copied their dress. This shows that you are foolish, while they are wise."[16] He himself refused to take off his turban to enter in an ancient fortress guarded by British officers and abstained from sight-seeing.

For the first time Swami Dayanand used the term 'Swarājya' in 1875, and added that after the attainment of *Swarājya*, India would become rich again.[17] According to Mrs. Anie Besant it was Dayanand who first raised the slogan, "India is for Indians."[18] Swamiji knew that the Princely states of India were, more or less, dependent on the paramount power, and he deplored the condition of the states and their Chiefs. To put in his own words, "Whatsoever rule is lest to them (Aryas), is being crushed under the heel of the foreigner.... When a country falls upon evil days, the natives have to bear in told misery and suffereings."[19] He stressed over the unity of the people and expressed the view that, "Indian rulers should create a common national sentiment and a common faith in their states." Dayanand wanted to write to the various Princes who were scattered and had no unity. In his own words, "I wish to bring the Rajas and the Maharajas into the right path and want to unite the Arya race into one whole." Accordingly, he taught the Maharana Udaipur, the *Manusmriti* and the relevant portions of *Mahābhārat* which treats of politics and the development of man's character. Dayanand's conception of *Swarājya* was free from all sorts of casteism. He recognized only two communities—Arya and Anarya. Swamiji, accordingly, ask the foreigners 'not to live here as rulers' thus raising the slogan 'Quit India' which Mahatma Gandhi raised long after.

Swami Dayanand also emphasized over the adoption of Hindi as national language. To Swamiji's mind no reform was possible without having one religion and one language. He says, "it is extremely difficult to do with differences in language, religion, education, customs and manners, but without doing that the people can never fully effect mutual good and accomplish their object." Swami Dayanand advised the Maharaja of Jodhpur to teach Devnagari to his son. He also encouraged the people to support the cause of Hindi before Mr. Hunter, the Chairman of Education Commission, appointed by the Government of India.

V

The teachings of Swami Dayanand not only influenced the people of Rajasthan but virtually the whole country. The Arya Samaj in the North-West furnished the necessary corrective to the spirit of heterodoxy and even hereby which the Western learning brought with it. The Arya Samaj movement was aggressive in its patriotic zeal and while holding fast to the cult of infallibility of the Vedas and the superiority of the Vedic culture, was at the same time not inimical to broad social reforms. The movement fought some of the prevailing social evils and religious superstitions in Hinduism. The movement was not only a religious or social one but a national movement. Charles C. Heimsath[20] observed: "In all India sense the Arya Samaj's influence was unobtrusive, particularly in the main centres of modern Indian life during the 19th century...the ground work was being laid, however, for the most successful unification of religious and social reforms with nationalism that was to be found in pre-Gandhian India."

Thus Swami Dayanand Saraswati and the Arya Samaj movement played an important role at the time when there was no ray of hope, and the morals of the people had declined considerably. In fact Swamiji gave confidence to the people who made the people politically conscious about their rights and duties. Swami Dayanand wrote, "What can you expect but misery and poverty when the people of a country trade only among themselves whilst foreigners through their international trade rule over them!"[21] Thus the most important contribution of Swamiji was that he gave a feeling of self-respect to the citizens of the country.

As Shyamaji Krishna Varma, a prominent revolutionary and a disciple of Swami Dayanand, said that "of all movements in India for political regeneration of the country none is so potent as proclaimed by its founder as an absolute, free and independent form of national Government." The influence of the movement over the masses was so imminent that it was treated as "serious threat to the British power in India."[22] The movement preached equal rights to the people which helped in the emergence of political consciousness and awakening among the people to set themselves free from the foreign yoke. Swami Dayanand's teachings produced a teaching of pride for Vedic religion, Vedic language and other old institutional ideas and values of our country. The effect of his teachings was that people became conscious of their great religion and social heritage and this one of the most potent factors in the general awakening of the Princes and people. Moreover, the Arya Samaj movement opened a way to the people to think about their political rights and to establish various organizations which created conditions favourable to the successful development of revolutionary movements in India.

REFERENCES

1. Rolland, R. : *The Life of Ram Krishna*, pp. 157-58.
2. Rai, Lala Lajpat : *History of Arya Samaj*, pp. 7-16.
3. Lekh Ram, P. : *Life of Mahrishi Dayanand* (Urdu) pp. 234-35 quoted in Saxena, K.S. : *The Political Movements and Awakening in Rajasthan*, p. 108.
4. *Dayanand Saraswati : Swikar Patra*, a pamphlet.
5. Vachaspati; Indra Vidya : *Arya Samaj ka Itihas*, Pt. I, p. 133.
6. Sarda, H.B. : *Life of Dayanand Saraswati*, p. 43.
7. Hakikat Bhai : No. 31, p. 333, Rajasthan State Archives, Bikaner Quoted in Saxena, K.S. *Op. cit.* p. 109.
8. Vanwart, R.B. : *The life of Lt.-Gen. H.H. Sir Pratap Singh*, pp. 193-94.
9. Pal, B.C. : *Memories of My Life and Times*, p. 36.
10. Rolland, R. : Ref. 1, p. 150.
11. Dayanand Commemoration volume : *The Secret of Vedas*—Aurobindo Birth Centenary, p. 88.
12. Vabu, D. : *The Arya Samaj*, p. 40.

13. Nehru, J.L. : *Discovery of India*, p. 337.
14. Dayanand Saraswati : *Satyartha Prakash*, p. 114.
15. Sarda, H.B. : Ref. 6, p. 235.
16. *Ibid.*, p. 323.
17. Chamupati, N.A. : *Glimpses of Dayanand*, p. 88.
18. Besant, A.: *India : A Nation*, p. 79.
19. Dayanand Saraswati : *Satyartha Prakash*, p. 185.
20. Heimsath, Charles, C. : *Nationalism and Hindu Social Reform*, p. 130.
21. Sarda, H.B. : Ref. 6, p. 197.
22. Chirol, V. : *Indian Unrest*, p. 110.

9

Roy's Religious Modernism, Social Reform and Political Liberalism

Adi H. Doctor

A Pioneer of Religious Modernism

Rammohan Roy, born of Brahmin parents, had from early days an insatiable interest in religious matters. Oddly, the religion in which Rammohan first received systematic instruction was Islam. He went to Patna at the early age of nine or ten to learn Persian and Urdu, the language of the North Indian Court and feudal elite, and, thereafter to Benares to study Sanskrit. His biographers state that these places were selected because there were no competent treachers of Persian, Arabic or Sanskrit nearer to home. It was at Patna, while under Arabic-Persian-Islamic influence that he became convinced of the futility of idol worship which was, in those days performed with great pomp in Bengal. Thus, much before learning English, Rammohan's contact with Islam had already helped him to develop ideas of religious reform. It was under the influence of Koranic concept of "Tauhid" (Unity of God) that Rammohan first repudiated polytheistic ideas. It was again at Patna that Rammohan got acquainted with the *Advaita* doctrine, which preached the notion of a unitary Brahma and did not involve image worship. A.K. Majumdar speculates that Rammohan's Persian teacher must have acquainted him with Dara Shikoh's translation of the Upanishads and explained its Unitarian principles to him. The Patna education and background explains why Rammohan wanted to visit Benaras to study Sanskrit. Benares was after all the stronghold of the "Advaitavadins" ever since Shankaracharya preached the doctrine in the ninth century.

But though Islam may have influenced Roy with regard to the idea of "One God" and turned him against idolatory, he was not swept off his feet by Islam and, in fact, published a book the *"Tuhfat-ul Muwahhiddin"* (Gift to Deists), written in Persian with an Arabic Preface, in 1803-04, wherein he boldly questioned the doctrine of prophethood, as also exposed the fallacy of dogmatism. He argued for weighing every religious dogma on the scale of reason and traced the roots of ethical systems projected by all religions to the needs of particular societies and not to any supernatural authority. It is worth noting that Rammohan wrote all this, much before he learnt English and became acquainted with Western rationalist and Liberal thought.

Rammohan studied Christianity much after his acquaintance with Islam. He started learning English after he became the private munshi of John Digby in 1805. After settling in Calcutta in 1815 he came in intimate contact with Christian missionaries and even learnt Hebrew, Greek and Latin in order to gain access to the original sources of Christianity. In the introduction he wrote to his book, *"The Precepts of Jesus"* (1820), he confesses that what attracted him to Christianity was its ability "to render our existence agreeable to ourselves and profitable to the rest of mankind." Rammohan was profoundly impressed by Christ's, ethical teachings. Thus, he admits, "I found the doctrines of Christ more conducive to moral principles and better adopted for the use of rational beings than any other which have come to my knowledge."

But Roy's modern, rational mind was unwilling to accept Christian dogma and superstition. He once wrote to Rev. Henry Ware of Cambridge (USA) how he considered the doctrines that the missionaries preach as being less conformable with reason than those professed by Muslims. In fact, in several respects, Roy argued, Christian propaganda and beliefs were as absurd as popular Hindu beliefs and creed. Rammohan's criticism of Christianity are contained in his book *"The Precepts of Jesus*" which he wrote as a reply to the missionary claims and propaganda and in his satirical play written three years later (1823), "*A Dialogue Between a Missionary and Three Chinese Converts*". In these works, Rammohan rejects the doctrine of Christ's divinity and the doctrine of Trinity. The latter doctrine Roy claimed contradicted the notion of a unitary, single, all pervasive God or Brahma (of Advaita philosophy). Regarding Christ's divinity, Rammohan's argument (made in a letter he wrote to Rev. R. Tytler) was that if we are to admit of the manifestation of God in flesh, we must do so without any restriction regarding dark or fair complexion, large or small structure, long or short hair. In other words, what Rammohan was trying to convey to the reverend was that if Jesus could be divine, so could Ram.

Roy also criticised the Christian belief that Christ died for the atonement of men's sins. According to him the only way to attain victory over sin was through sincere repentance and solemn meditation. Another cannot atone for one's sins; nor can they be wiped away by bribes and sacrifices. Rammohan compared the Christian doctrine of atonement to the Hindu belief that the wife has to atone for the sins of the husband by committing *sati* (self-immolation on her husband's pyre). Thus Roy who praised Christianity for its social values, also did not hesitate to criticise its dogmas, superstitions, and unacceptable doctrines.

Raja Rammohan Roy's real contribution however lay in his exposure of the "Vices of Hinduism" and his attempt at reinterpreting and purifying Hinduism. In a letter written to Silk Buckingham dated 18th January, 1828, while Rammohan expressed agreement with Buckingham's view that in point of vices the Hindus are not worse than the generality of Christians in Europe and America; he nevertheless reiterated his earlier view that the present system of religion adhered to by the Hindus was not well calculated to promote their political interest. According to Rammohan, the caste system which divided the Hindus into innumerable divisions and sub-divisions, together with the multitude of religious rites and ceremonies, and the laws of purification, had deprived the

Hindus of patriotic feeling and disqualified them from undertaking any difficult eterprise. Unless some change took place in their religion, argued Rammohan, the Hindus would be at a political disadvantage and incapable of enjoying social comfort.

In the "*Tuhfat-ul-Muwahhiddin*", Rammohan exposes some of the corrupt and irrational beliefs and practices of the Hindus, like belief in revelations, prophets and miracles; bathing in rivers or worshipping trees; purchasing forgiveness for crimes from priests. Many Brahmin priests are perfectly aware of the absurdity of idolatory, Roy wrote, but since these rites, ceremonies and festivals of idolatory provided the priests with their comforts and fortune, they encouraged the same and sought to keep the true knowledge of the scriptures (*advaita*) away from the masses. Roy was convinced that for the emancipation of the masses, the monopoly of the orthodox Brahmins over the sacred texts, had to be undermined. Accordingly, he himself set about to convey the message of the Vedas by translating and interpreting them in the vernacular (Hindi and Bengali).

Rammohan claimed that since society and religion are very closely interrelated, religious modernism must precede social reform. According to him, the motivation for religious modernism was the political advantage and social comfort, it would bring into the lives of the people. He argued that such Hindu customs as idolatory, subjection of women, *sati* and caste destroyed the texture of Hindu society and lead to immoral practices like the Kali and Krishna cults. Not only is Krishna pictured as the embodiment of the principle of free love, but his devotees often imitate him and practice shameful indecencies in the name of religion. Similarly, Roy condemns the degeneration of the worship of Kali to senseless animal sacrifice, accompanied by drinking of wine.

Rejecting the superstitions and unethical practices that had crept into popular Hinduism, Rammohan sought to restate and reinterpret Hinduism as the Ethical Monoism of the Upanishads. In a sense Raja Rammohan Roy perceived himself to be another Luther, a leading light of the Protestant religious reformation in Europe. An ardent student of European history, Rammohan was aware of the rise and progress of Christianity in apostolic times and its corruption in succeeding ages and how the Protestant Reformation Movement had sought to cleanse Christianity of these corruptions. Roy sincerely believed that similar results would follow in India from a reformation of popular idolatory. Rammohan was in the line of Kabir and Nanak who had earlier in the 15th and 16th centuries sought to purge Hinduism of "evil" practices while incorporating the best that could be taken from the spirit of Islam. Rammohan preached ethical monoism as a rejoinder to the Missionaries who had equated Hinduism only with idolatory. An English educated Hindu, argued Rammohan,who was revolted by the worship of graven images, need not embrace Christianity, he could adopt the ethical monoism (or the idea of God as the impersonal absolute, preached by the Upanishads). Rammohan strongly felt that monotheism/monism supported one universal moral order for humanity, while polytheism justified sectarian moralities. Although Raja Rammohan Roy did not carefully distinguish between monoism and monotheism, the distinction between the two must be borne in mind. Chrisitianity swears by monotheism the idea of one God, but man as separate from God; while *Advaita* speaks of monoism, the idea of one impersonal absolute with which the enlightened soul merges. In the *Advaita* philosophy there is only "Brahma" and nothing else, the soul that has attained "*moksha*" becomes part of Brahma and ceases to experience any kind of duality, not even between man and God. This is the meaning of the *Advaita* dictum "That Thou Art" (You Are That God).

Rammohan accepted religion as the basis of society but after freeing it from orthodoxy and dogma. While preaching *Advaita* as the true Hinduism, Rommohan's religious liberalism, would not permit him to claim anyone religion alone as true. He was enchanted by the writings of the Sufi Muslim philosophers whose views tallied with the Vedantic school. He admired Christ as the greatest Humanist ever. Roy's whole life was dedicated to interpreting religion rationally and morally. This explains his rejection of many things from many religions. Roy was essentially a theist who prized above all being a moralist and a rationalist.

In 1815, Rammohan established the Atmiya Sabha (Circle of Friends) to discuss theological subjects, recite scriptures and chant theistic hymns. These discussions made him the prime target of the orthodox who even dragged him to Court for his heterodoxy, compelling him to discontinue the meetings of the Atmiya Sabha. Though Rammohan was convinced that we have a lot to learn from the West in the fields of mechanical arts and the sciences, he did not at the same time hesitate to proclaim that we had a philosophy of our own of which even the West could be proud.

Roy as a Social Reformer

Rammohan was not only a religious but also a social reformer. In fact the two were intertwined since many social practices among the Hindus had religious sanction. There was a pattern in the Indian awakening under British impact, viz. religious awakening being followed by social and political enlightenment. But the three aspects were not separately represented by different reformers. Thus Rammohan was not only a pioneer in religious reform, but also the initiator of social and political progress. The early Indian Liberals were concerned with freedom for the individual in the total sense (not just with the question of alien rule). They were first and foremost committed to create a new Indian society based on Social Equality, Rationalism and Humanism. While discussing the role of the Liberals in modern Indian Political Thought, we are in fact discussing, in the broadest sense, the role of the intellectuals in the modernization of society.

The greater part of his life and energies, Rammohan devoted to fighting the practice of idolatory and *Sati*. *Sati* seems to have been a fairly ancient practice peculiar to the military aristocracy of India. The Greeks found it was practised in Punjab. Muslim rulers also make reference to it. Sikandar forbade it in Kashmir, but his son Zain-ul Abdin re-permitted it. In Delhi, Akbar and his son Jehangir forbade it, but could not abolish it beyond the suburbs of Delhi.

This practice was widely prevalent in Bengal at the time of British rule is clear from several stories. One story mentions that Job Charnak, the founder of Calcutta, forcibly saved a woman from being dragged to the fire by her relatives, by taking her to his residence and subsequently marrying her. Then, in 1772, a Captain Tomyn of Tripetty on hearing that a widow was about to be sacrificed, went straight to the place and led her away to safety.

Officially the British administration was hesitant to interfere. After the annexation of the Peshwa's Kingdom, the Bombay Government, even passed a resolution that self-immolation, known as *sati,* was not murder. In 1789, when the Collector of Shahabad sought permission to halt a *sati,* the Governor General approving his stand, nevertheless advised him not to use coercive means since that may prove counter-productive and increase rather than diminish its veneration. It was only in 1812 and 1817, that the British administration sent positive instructions enjoining preventive measures based on "giving least offence to the natives". In no case, it said, should a woman be dragged to the pyre against her will. In 1821, the British brought out a Blue Book in which the history of the practice and efforts made to abolish it were narrated. As per the statistics given in the book, *sati* practice was rapidly increasing and within four years had doubled and even tripled in some divisions of the Bengal province.

It was at this time (1810-1825) that Raja Rammohan Roy came out powerfully to the rescue of women. When some subjects made two petitions to the Governor General for the repeal of the orders issued in 1812, 1815 and 1817, which enjoined preventive measures like not allowing women to be forcibly dragged, or made to do *sati* when pregnant etc., Rammohan made a strong counter petition in August 1818, narrating the gruesome practices associated with *sati* and condemning it as murder. In his petition, Rammohan mentioned how women were often induced to commit *sati* by the persuasion of their next heirs; how some women would rashly express the desire to perform *sati* in the first moments of grief, but later hesitated or developed fright, but were nevertheless "forced upon the pyre and bound down with ropes and pressed with green bamboos until consumed with the flames." All these instances, Rammohan observed in his petition, "Your petitioners humbly submit, are committing murders according to every Sastra, as well as the commonsense of all nations."

Rammohan wrote several tracts and pamphlets in Bengali (some translated into English) against *sati.* On 30th November, 1918, he issued a tract wherein there takes place "a conference" between an advocate and an opponent of *sati.* In February 1920, he brought out another tract, wherein a second conference takes place between an advocate and an opponent. The second tract Rammohan dedicated to the wife of the Governor General, Lady Hastings, describing it as "an appeal to reason in behalf of humanity."

The arguments Roy makes in these tracts can be summed up as follows: In the first place, argues Rammohan, even if *Sati* (Concremation or post-cremation) means that the woman "enjoys heaven for a considerable time", it must be remembered that Hindu authorities describe such acts performed for gratification in this world or next as being of an inferior order of merit. In truly meritorious acts, one seeks no fruit or gratification (in this or next life) but instead seeks to be free from all *karma* and its fruits. Learned men, according to Roy, should not persuade the ignorant to perform rites for the sake of fruition. Secondly, Rammohan cites authorities like Manu and Yājñavalkya who say that a widow must live voluntarily on pure flowers, roots and fruits, not pronouncing the name of another man, to argue that these authorities expected the widow to live and not commit *sati.* Rammohan also cites a statement from the Yājñavalkya to the effect that a widow must live under care of father, son, brother, father-in-law etc. to claim that a widow was not expected by Yājñavalkya to commit *sati.*

In the Tracts, the advocate of *sati* levied various charges against women, which the opponent of *sati* successfully repudiates. Thus the advocate of *sati* argues that woman is of inferior understanding, without resolution, unworthy of trust, subject to passions and devoid of virtuous knowledge. The opponent of *sati* refutes these charges by arguing "As you keep women generally void of education you cannot, therefore, in justice, pronounce on their inferiority". He gives the examples of women like Lilavati, Bhanumati, wife of Kalidasa, who were celebrated for their knowledge of the Sastras. Regarding the charge of being untrustworthy, the opponent of *sati* gives examples to show that men are less trustworthy than women since men are less loyal and faithful to their wives, with most men marrying more than once while the Hindu woman marries only once and stays devoted the whole life to her husband. Regarding the charges that women are passionate, lacking in resolution and virtue, the opponent of *sati* shows how facts prove just the contrary. The fact that the Hindu woman lives a cloisterd and isolated life, suffering silently the many indignities heaped on her by her husband and male in-laws, and the fact that she slogs and suffers for the men-folk in the household, clearly shows how resolute and virtuous the woman is.

Raja Rammohan Roy's relentless campaign for the emancipation of the Indian woman, finally bore fruit. Lord William Bentinck sent an emissary to him seeking his help in suppressing the pernicious practice. Rammohan reportedly declined to see the Governor General on the grounds that he had now given up "all worldly advocations". Thereupon Bentinck sent the message that not the Governor but Mr. William Bentinck would like to see him. Rammohan could not now refuse. But surprisingly Raja Rammohan Roy advised Lord Bentinck against legislation and expressed the preference for the practice being suppressed quietly and unobservedly by increasing the difficulties and by the indirect agency of the police. However, on 4th December, 1829, Lord Bentinck declared the practice illegal and punishable as a criminal offence. The Preamable to the Regulation clearly shows the influence of Raja Rammohan Roy. Thus it says, *sati* "is nowhere enjoined by the religion of the Hindus as an imperative duty; on the contrary, a life of purity and retirement on the part of the widow is more specially and preferably inculcated."

Orthodox Hindus, as expected, reacted to this reform by submitting a Memorandum signed by 800 citizens urging annulment of the Regulation. Rammohan, though old in years, was roused by this to organize a counter-force and submitted a Memorandum on 16th June, 1830 signed by 300 Hindus including himself. The Petitioners said they would be guilty of insincerity and ingratitude if they remained "negligently silent" when called by their feelings and conscience to express their gratitude. Equally effective and forceful was the Governor General's response, which *inter alia* observed, "I feel sincere pleasure in thinking that the Hindus will thereby be exalted in the estimation of mankind."

Though the greater part of his life Raja Rammohan Roy devoted to the cause of abolition of *sati*, he did not neglect other areas of women's emancipation, such as women's rights of inheritance and polygamy. In 1822, Rammohan published a Tract with the longish title, "Modern Encroachments on the Ancient Rights of Females According to The Hindu Law of Inheritance." In this tract, Rammohan gave instances of how ancient legislators took interest and care in the promotion of the comfort and well-being of women, and contrasts these with the subsequent laws of female inheritance which resulted in the complete deprivation of the rights of women. The ancient law givers had awarded the mother an equal share with her son in the property left by her deceased husband so that she may be able to live independently off her children. Likewise, Yājñavalkya, Narad, Vyasa all allowed a portion of the ancestral property, roughly a fourth part, to the daughter. Rammohan laments that these injunctions of the ancient law-givers are forgotten today and attributed the present plight and poverty of women due to the subsequent laws and customs which deny women property rights.

Rammohan's condemnation of polygamy (*kulinism*) was equally forthright. He cited Yājñavalkya who permitted a second wife only on specific grounds (like incurable sickness, barrenness, only female off-spring etc.) to argue that the ancient law-givers did not approve of polygamy as a normal practice. The spirit of Hindu Law, argued Rammohan clearly does not permit a Hindu male to marry more than one wife at will, but allows a second wife only with the consent of the first and on specific grounds. According to Rammohan, polygamy was responsible for many evils in Hindu society such as *sati* and the denial of women her legitimate inheritance under law.

Rammohan also condemned several other shameful practices associated with the treatment of women. Thus he wrote extensively against the custom of fathers selling their daughters to prospective husbands due to some pecuniary interests. He quoted from Manu and Kashyap to show that the custom was contrary to the dictates of sacred laws.

The study of Roy's social reform strategy shows that as a typical liberal, he trusted education and preaching to bring about reform and change of heart. He refused to believe that violent revolution could bring about genuine change based on conviction. Secondly, he worked for reform "from within" in the sense that he always quoted a respected Indian authority when he wanted a point to sink in.

Roy's Political Liberalism

Raja Rammohan Roy has been hailed as the founder of political liberalism. Basic to Roy's liberalism is his belief in the liberating, uplifting and benevolent nature of British rule. He firmly believed that the wisdom and liberality of the British government were necessary to improve the conditions of the Indians. Hence he prayed that "it may continue its beneficient operation for centuries to come". In the first place, said Roy, the people of India irrespective of religion were granted civil rights and such privileges as their forefathers never expected to attain even under Hindu rulers. He particularly contrasted British rule with the preceding Muslim rule in Bengal when civil and religious rights were trampled upon and property looted and blood freely shed. Rammohan perceived the British as Liberators who delivered India from "the long continued tyranny of its former rulers." The English, according to Rammohan, were a nation who, not only were themselves blessed with the enjoyment of civil and political liberty, but also sought to promote liberty and social happiness, as well as free enquiry into literary and religious subjects, among those nations to which their influence extended.

Secondly, Rammohan was convinced that liberal ideas could be best imbibed by the Indian mind by studying English. This explains his keenness in establishing English medium educational institutions for the spread of modern knowledge and science. He did not consider ancient Sanskrit learning and texts as relevant. What improvement can arise, he wondered from studying such Vedantic speculations as, in what manner is the soul absorbed in the Deity, or, what relation does it bear to the Divine Essence? How will our youth benefit, he wondered, from studying Vedantic doctrines which teach them to believe that our physical world has no real existence, but is an illustion (*maya*). Similarly, he felt that no benefit can be derived from the study of *Mimāmsā*, from knowing what it is that makes a killer of a goat, sinless, by pronouncing certain passages of the Vedas; or, from such speculations, as contained in the *Nyāya Shāshtra*, on the relation of the soul to the body, the eye to the ear etc. Rammohan dismissed much of the ancient learning as "imaginary". Such imaginary science and knowledge, says Rammohan, was also characteristic of medieval Europe, before the age of empirical science. Rammohan wanted instructions to be imparted in useful, contemporary sciences mathematics, chemistry, anatomy, natural philosophy and opposed the "sanskritists" who wanted to load the young minds with grammatical complexities and speculative knowledge. In 1816-17, Rammohan founded the first English school in Calcutta financed completely by Indians. Under his inspiration in 1822-23, the Hindu College was established.

Thirdly, odd as it may sound, Roy was a champion of liberty and freedom, though he welcomed British/Foreign rule. Rammohan was an uncompromising champion of the freedom of the creative spirit; and he believed that British rule would lay the foundation for such a freedom by freeing Indians from old world superstitions and thraldom, from the rigidities of a soul destroying caste system. Roy as we saw above sought active intervention by the British Government to liberate and emancipate women and low castes. Roy was a liberal who championed the cause of social and intellectual emancipation, though he may not exactly have been the prophet of *swarāj*.

Roy was one of the earliest champions of the freedom of the press. Along with other eminent citizens (Dwarkanath Tagore etc.) he submitted a petition to the Supreme Court in 1823 urging full freedom for the press. When this was rejected, an appeal was made to the King-in-Council. The Appeal addressed to his Majesty observed that a free press has never caused a revolution in any part of the world, because when men can easily represent their grievances arising from the conduct of local authorities to the supreme government and thus get them redressed, the grounds of discontent that excite revolution are removed. Further, Rammohan argued, restrictions on freedom of the press would mean stopping the diffusion of knowledge. It would prevent educated Indians from communicating to their fellowmen knowledge of the system of government. Rammohan, we must remember, pioneered Journalism in India. Rammohan was the first to believe in the publicization of knowledge, and use it for reformist political activity.

Finally, Rammohan urged reforms and corrections in the Indian judicial system in keeping with political liberalism. He urged before the Select Committee of the House of Commons, the separation of the judicial and administrative functions of the magistrates serving in India. Rammohan published a pamphlet entitled "An exposition of the Revenue and Judicial System of India", in which he argued for the Courts having jurisdiction over Europeans and for codification of laws. Rammohan opposed the Jury Act of 1827 according to which Hindus and Muslims could not sit on the jury when a Christian was being tried. He signed (along with others) a petition against the Act. He also wrote a letter to Mr. J. Crawford in this regard, wherein he stated that the Act has caused much alarm among political liberals. He specifically referred to the discrimination in the Act which permitted a Christian to be a Juror when Hindus or Muslims were tried and condemned it as degrading and unprincipled. Rammohan favoured the formation of an Indian Code of Criminal Law based on the common principles of all communities. He also suggested the minimum age limit of twenty-two years be observed in appointing civil servants so that immature persons were not appointed magistrates.

As a Liberal, Raja Rammohan Roy did strive all his life for the liberation of the Indian masses from restrictive and illiberal practices of caste and from ignorance and popular superstition which were at the root of the oppression of women and low castes. Rammohan believed that true, creative freedom can come only by the spread of correct knowledge and perceived English education in particular to be a God-send in this regard. It was in this sense that he has been hailed as the founder of modern Indian Liberalism. To Rammohan must also be given the credit for generating among educated Indians a new political consciousness and a new sense of Indian nationality, based on equality and rule of law. However, one obvious weakness in Roy's liberalism was his inability to comprehend fully the magnitude of India's poverty and how British rule was aggravating it. This was left for another eminent liberal, Dadabhai Naoroji, to highlight.

REFERENCES AND SELECT READINGS

1. Appadorai, A., *Documents on Political Thought in Modern India*, Oxford, Delhi, 1981.
2. Bali, D.R., *Modern Indian Political Thought, From Roy to J.P. Narain*, Sterling Publishers, New Delhi, 1988, Ch. 1.
3. Buch, M.A., *Rise and Growth of Liberalism in India*, Baroda, 1938.
4. Ghose Shankar, *Renaissance to Militant Nationalism in India*. Allied Publishers, Bombay, 1969, Ch. 1.
5. Grover, Verindra (Ed.), *Political Thinkrs of Modern India*, Vol. I, Deep and Deep, Delhi, 1990.
6. Heimsath, Charles A., *Indian Nationalism and Hindu Social Reform*, Princeton University Press, 1964.
7. Iqbal Singh, *Rommohan Roy : A Biographical Enquiry Into the Making of Modern India*, Asia Publishing House, Vols. 1-3, 1987.
8. Joshi, V.C., (Ed.), *Rammohan Roy and the Process of Modernization in India*, Vikas, Delhi, 1975.
9. Kotnala, N.C., *Rammohan Roy and the Indian Awakening*, Gitanjali Prakashan, New Delhi, 1957.
10. Majumdar, A.K., "The Religion of Rammohan Roy", in book Joshi V.C., (Ed.), *Rammohan Roy and the Process of Modernization in India*, Vikas, Delhi, 1975.
11. Pantham, Thomas and K. Deutsch, *Political thought of Modern India*, Sage Publications, New Delhi, 1986.

12. Rolland, Romain, *Prophets of Modern India*, London, 1930.
13. *Roy, Raja Rammohan : His Life, Writings and Speeches* (edited by K. Nag and D. Burman), G.A. Natesan and Co., Madras.
14. Roy, Rammohan, *Tuhafat-ul Muwahhiddin* (Gift to Deists), Edited and Translated by Maulvi Ubaidullah Ubaide, Calcutta, 1949 (Reprint).
15. *Roy, Raja Rammohan The English Works of* ......Vol. 1, Calcutta, 1929.
16. Sarma, G.N. and Shakir Moin., *Politics and Society : Rammohan Roy to Nehru*, Parimal Prakashan, Aurangabad, 1978, ch. 2.

10

Gopal Krishan Gokhale's Spiritualization of Politics

Radha Krishan

In ancient period, there was a unique combination of Politics and *Dharma*. *Dharma* was the basis of all state activities. The position of *dharma* was supreme and sovereign. *Dharma* was a fundamental guideline of state as well as politics. Spirituality, morality, services and happiness of mankind were basic assumptions of *dharma*. In Vedic period, king must perform his duty according to *dharma*. In *Brihadaranyaka* upnishad, *dharma* 'क्षत्रस्य क्षत्रमं अर्थात् शासकों का शासक (*Dharma* is a ruler of rulers). At the time of crowning ceremony, king has to take oath for maintaining *Dharma* in society and act according to *Dharma* 'धर्मो रक्षाति रक्षितः' (Those who defend *Dharma*, *Dharma* defend them). Politics without *Dharma* is immoral, valueless, conspiracy and struggle for power. Manu clearly states that king is subject to Law (*Dharma*). The king should decide all issues on the basis of *Dharma*. Manu could not separate politics from socio-religious practices of the time. The foundation of the state in *Valmiki Ramayana is Dharma,* which is the prime object and basis of truth. Dharma is used in different senses in different contexts. Sometimes with the meaning of right and justice and sometimes right order. Dharma is also necessary to create order in society. The main concern of Vyas in *Mahabharata* is for the establishment of righteousness (*Dharma*) in society. Politics is important because without it righteousness is not possible. Right (*Dharma*) is the activity which maintains balance and harmony amongst all other activities. Like many ancient authors Sukra too considered that 'politics' as an aspect of ethics. He called it moral science (*Nitishastra*) which he considered as the basis of virtue, wealth, enjoyment and salvation. In Indian political thought, king was subordinate to *Dharma*. In fact, the entire ancient Indian political scenario was highly influenced by *dharma*.

Dharma is an Indian concept. *Dharma* is inner emotion and feelir.g of human soul. *Dharma* cannot be detached from human society. *Dharma* is "the basis of the all societal activities". Religion is a Western concept. Religion is the outer surface of Human. Religion is a ritual activity, having its own institution and organisation. In Western philosophy, specially Christian ideology, total politics moved around church and church was supreme. Modern Western political thinkers adopted relative utilitarian approach towards religion. Religion should play its role to strengthen the state.

In the 19th century, socio-religious movements were launched by various groups of society. These movements developed a fertile land for political patriotism and spread a feeling of nationalism and unification of India. Even their spirit of revivalism and reformism positively contributed to the awakening of political and economic nationalism.

The first generation of Indian leaders or representatives namely Raja Rammohan Roy, Devendranath Thakur were highly impressed by Western culture and science. These people got impetus from English literature. They thought of reconstruction of social relations on Western style. English medium of education enabled the educated Indians to meet with each other and discuss their common problems. They began together sentimentally. For them, British connection with India was a divine dispensation for the benefit of her people. They strived for social and political development and believed that social reform was necessary for political and economic development.

The second generation Indian leaders, namely Mahadev Govind Ranade, Dada Bhai Naoroji, Fhirozshah Mehta,

Surendra Nath Banarjee, Gopal Krishan Gokhale and others were also impressed by english style of working. Ranade is known as 'the spiritual father of liberalism in India'. Naoroji is famous for his drain theory economic exploitation of India by Britishers. Mehta stood for permanency of the British empire in India. Banarjee wanted India's moral regeneration before her political freedom. Gokhale was the most prominent among them. He was a constructive politician.

Gokhale was championed for reason, Public opinion, Freedom, Justice and Tolerance. He considered that a good ends cannot be achieved from evil means, he did not advocated extreme means. He was opposed to violence and coercion as a means to social and moral awakening. He condemned coercion as an evil. Therefore, he was opposed to violent agitational method. He pleased for an empire of moral force. He believed that the British rulers practise the ideals of liberty, justice and generosity. He demanded Judicial reforms and civil rights based on the liberal concept of West. His mission as a public leader was spiritualization of politics.

The political ideas of Gokhale are based on moral and spiritual consciousness. Similarly his personal and public life is based on moral measurement. According to Gokhale ends and means are based on cause and effect theory. Goodness of means is responsible to goodness of ends. Respectiveness of means are the respectiveness of ends. Gokhale's relation between means and ends is based on morality. Gokhale was one of the thinkers who emphasized on the importance of means than ends and building of high moral character in India. He did not believe in Machiavellism. In the Machiavellism, respect to all means for getting of independence and progress of country. His whole life was full of truth and moral phenomenon. Purpose of his politics is not getting SATTA and SHAKTI but SEWA DHARAM, because Gokhale was conscious about the evils of politics. He was not ready to consider that Politics is Politics, everything is fair in politics. He tried to develop a such type of politics which should be based on *Dharma,* Morality and high moral character, sacrifice and purity of ends and means.

Gokhale's philosophy of ends and means deserves our serious attention, he emphasized on the purity of means. The means may be likened to a seed, the ends to a tree and there is just the same inviolable connection between the means and the ends as there is between seed and tree. To him the moral discipline of the individual is the most important means of social reconstruction. He believed that proper social and political regeneration can be brought by leading a good moral life.

Gokhale was also conscious of the glorious achievements of the Indian civilization, the spiritual creativism, a moral approach to life and a wholesome awareness of the primacy of the obligation to community that had made India great in the past. In the speech on "England's duty to India" at the National Liberal Club, London he stated, "because we came under the rule of the foreigners, it does not mean that we are like some savage or semi-civilized people whom you have subjugated. The people of India are an ancient race who has attained a high degree of civilization long before the ancestors of European nations understood what civilization was. India has been the birth-place of great religions. She was also the cradle and for long the home of literature and philosophy of science and arts. But God does not give everything to every people, and India in the past was not known for that love to liberty and that appreciation of free institutions which one finds to be so tricking a characteristic of the West."[1]

He was a spiritualist and a convinced idealist and lived on an elevated moral plane. His mission as a public leader has been spiritualization of politics—an ideal that was also sought by Mahatma Gandhi. Gokhale would not sanction an evil means to achieve a good ends. He believed in the nobility of human nature. He had won the affection of British statesmen and public figures. The latter recongnized his qualities as an extraordinary gifted leader of men. He was compared to Gladstone and Asquith. He won the confidence of Morley although the latter was doubtful of Gokhale's abilities in the art of political management. Through his noble life of self-abnegation, consciousness and purposefulness, Gokhale has encouraged the pursuit of the moral approach to political questions and public obligations. But Gokhale although as an idealist, was not a Platonic or Utopian idealist. He accepted the concepts of negotiations, moderation and compromise. Like Gandhi, he believed in scrupulous justice and exacting rectitude even to the opponents. In his speeches and actions he would not advocate extreme measures. He would like to work out a synthesis between idealism and the realistic demands of the situation. Hence Gokhale clung to the constitutional methods of agitation. He emphatically declared his faith in the unlimited potentialities of India.[2]

Gokhale's approach to contemporary problems was dictated by two key propositions. Firstly, he believed in Ranade's theory that the British empire in India was in the scheme of divine dispensation and was meant to be the immense benefit to India. Secondly, he believed in creating the strong foundations of nationalism through hard working and sacrifice. He believed in national consolidation. Therefore, he accepted the necessity of increasing the social efficiency and enhancing the moral character of the people as prerequisites for national growth because nationalism demands a consecrated spirit.

In order to give his work of morally-oriented national consolidation a permanent shape, on July 12, 1905, Gokhale established the Servants of India Society. The constitution of the society reveals the deep and noble idealism of the founder whose life was a record of suffering, sweat and sorrow. He wanted the concretization of the ideal of the united, strengthened and renovated India whose super structure will be founded upon sacrifices, devotion and sustained work. These ideals were meant to assimilate spiritual values in politics. He emphasized more on building of high moral character than *swarajya* and independence. He believed that India can be lead to independence through practising moral value.

The preamble of the Society's constitution clearly stated that an essential condition for the success in our work was that a sufficient number of Indians must come forward "to devote themselves to the cause in the spirit in which religious work is undertaken. Public work must be spiritualized, love of country must so fill the heart that all else shall appear as little moment by its side", the object of the society was "training national missionaries for the service of India" the principal objects to which the members of the society to direct their attention were: creating by example and precept intense love of country among the people, and promoting goodwill and cooperation between different communities.[3]

The Servants of India Society has been established to set in some measure these requirements of the situation. Its members frankly accepted the British connection, as ordained in the inscrutable dispensation of providence for India's good self-government on the lines of English colonies was their goal. These goals could not be attained without years of earnest and patient work and sacrifice worthy of cause. One essential condition of success was the involvement of the sufficient number of our countryman. We must now come forward to devote themselves to that cause in the spirit in which religious work is undertaken public life must be spiritualized. A fervent patriotism which rejoices at every opportunity of sacrifice for the motherland, a dauntless heart which refuses to be turned back from its object by difficulty or danger, a deep faith in the purpose of providence that nothing can shake. Equipped with these, the worker must start on his mission and reverently seek the joy which come to spending one self in the service of one's country.[4]

The Servants of India Society will train men prepared to devote their lives to the cause of the country in a religious spirit and will seek to promote by all constitutional means the national interest of the Indian people. Its members will direct their efforts principally towards:

1. Creating among the people, by example and by precept, a deep and passionate love of the motherland, seeking its highest fulfilment in service and sacrifice.
2. Organizing the work of political education and agitation, basing it on a careful study of public questions, and strengthening generally of the public life of the country.

3. Promoting relations of cordial goodwill and cooperation among the different communities.
4. Assisting educational movements, especially those for the education of women, the education of backward classes and industrial and scientific education.
5. Helping forward the industrial development of the country.
6. The elevation of the depressed classes.

Contact with the modern world of science and organization, as also with the political values of freedom and a national state was indispensable for a national movement of regeneration of India.[5]

He considered that after all, India's willing acceptance of the British connection can only be based on reason or enlightened self-interest. He went on to assert that, they want their country to be a prosperous, self-governing integral part of the empire, like the colonies and not a mere poverty-stricken, bureaucratically held possession of that empire. It was after this claim to freedom and prosperity on behalf of his countrymen that Gokhale uttered his grave warning to the British people.[6]

Gokhale was influenced by the writings of eminent British philosophers and statesmen, of whom John Stuart Mill and Edmund Burke appeared to have been most favoured. Many of Gokhale's ideas which lay at the root of his appreciations and suggestions concerning the current problems were derived from such classes as Mill's essays 'On Liberty' and Representative government. He had firm faith in the dignity of individual and existence of God and progress of society. He tried to spiritualization of public life. Because Gokhale was influenced with Bekan's Essays and Burke's writing "reflection on the Franch revolution", Herbert spenser, Robert Browning.[7] His clear understanding of the process of constitutional change, and in particular appreciation of healthy and lasting results of gradual reforms was the contribution of Burke. Gokhale was also influenced with the ideas, writing and style of Dada Bhai Naoroji, who considered that constitutional means should be applied for the service of country.[8]

An agnostic in his earlier years, Gokhale, surely was not laying down a metaphysical proposition but he was merely seeking to apply the spirit of religion, its spirit of devotion and renunciation, to a secular purpose. The crowning success of his endeavours in this field is reflected by the examples of a few national leaders and statesmen of outstanding repute as V.S. Srinivas Sastri, H.N. Kunzru, R.P. Paranjpye, N.M. Joshi and others who have reflected many excellences in contemporary public life but what, perhaps is far more important than these excellences, a fact which would appear to have a great relevance in current political life. India is an unfailing standard of character which has remained unrivalled in contemporary public life. Many of the problems that Gokhale grappled with in his own time may have lost their interest in the context of current conditions, but his national, secular and scientific approach to Indian politics and economics, would appear to have acquired a new and fresh significance in the context of contemporary politics during the post-independence era.[9]

Gokhale as a great saint and soldier of national righteousness, advocated racial equality in India and elsewhere in the British empire, throughout his life. He continued to take a lively and a serious interest in the Indianization of the public services, which he considered to be essential politically, economically and culturally. The most significant part of this manifesto, which is said to have been drawn up by Ranade himself, runs as follows:

"The spirit of liberalism implies a freedom from race and creed prejudices and a steady devotion to all that seeks to do justice between man and man, giving to the rulers the loyalty that is due to the law they are bound to administer, but securing at the same time to the ruled the equality which is their right under the law."[10]

Gokhale was a firm believer in communal harmony, co-operation and tolerance. He criticized the organisation of Muslim League because it was starting of both side counter-alignment. He considered all these things are hinder in the development of nationalism in India.[11]

He believed that Hindu-Muslim co-operation, unity and harmony is pre-condition for the development of nationalism.

He said that the future of country depends upon the co-operation and harmony between Hindus and Muslims. A complete separation is impossible of both these communities. Both communities have to stand for each other. Therefore, both communities should develop a common feeling of nationalism and reconstruction of country.[12]

The purpose of politics was economic, social and moral upliftment of the people. The basic problem of politics is the problem of morality, problems of value as described by Arnold Brakht "scientific value relativism". If we separate human values from the politics, what will be remain. The politics will become a struggle for power. Therefore, we cannot separate human values (morality) from politics. Therefore, the spiritualization of politics has been necessary for the future of the mankind. An ideal political system may be carried on through morally and spiritually educated persons. Gokhale's politics was based on love, sacrifice and human service for the re-construction of nation. He wanted the transformation of society by organizing BHARAT SEWAK SAMAJ and abolition of unjustice, exploitation, unequality from the society through constitutional and peaceful means. Gokhale tried to introduce NITI (morality, spirituality) in RAJNITI so that politics may work for the welfare of public.

He believed in human value—the spiritual value. He desired to impart training to man in ethical values. Therefore, he insisted on going beyond materialism. He considered that man must go beyond the materialism to find the incentive in goodness. He was also of the view that the task of social reconstruction cannot succeed under the inspiration of a materialist philosophy. He was against making man subordinate to machine. To him, science and spirituality complement each other and need one another. Our ethical life needs a great revolution. We have been neglecting the natural and divine principles of ethical life. Hence our social life is miserable. Ethical principles such as Truth, Ahimsa, Fellowship, Friendliness, Honesty, Goodwill, Sincerity, Forgiveness, Non-anger and social service should be revived and practised by every man, woman, child.

On 19 February 1915 at the time of his death, Tilak commented that Gokhale was a diamond of India, Superman of the Maharashtra. He tried to awake all *satyagarhi*. We should follow them.[13]

Gokhale has an important place in the history of Indian political thought. His politics was based on moral value. He tried spiritualization of politics. In this sense, he thought of a forerunner of Gandhi. For this Gandhi accepted him as a POLITICAL GURU. Gokhale's politics was not a SATTA NITI. He thought politics as a means of public service. He considered that without morality, there is no politics as Leo Strouss described "A value free politics is impossible". He considered that service of nation is a service of God as Gandhi described that service of lowest man is service of God. Everybody should be ready to sacrifice all things in the interest of nation without any attachment. To achieve this ideal, he organized BHARAT SEWAK SAMAJ which was meant to inculcate of moral values in the human society.

Present perception of politics in India as well as the entire world is very anxious and alarming. The whole humanity is suffering and facing emerging tendency of crime and corruption. Special reference in India, Political leaders have forgotten their ethics—*Raj Dharam,* ideals, principles and moral standard of forerunners. Present situation of society is resembling Hobbasian state of nature in which—glory, diffidence and competition—three factors were dominant. Everywhere there is struggle, crime, tension. There is no safety, no security of man. Politics has been based on Machiavellism and Darwinism. What a astonishment ! It is difficult question to intellectual class of society. How to get rid of these circumstances? For service of mankind, politics should be spiritualized-Moralization for the sake of goodness of humanity. Politics should be based on *Raj Dharam.*

We should have to establish correlation between means and ends. We have to change our mindset and preferences. Many criminals are actively participating in political process. We should check them for sustaining humanity and survival of *Raj Dharam.* Gopal Krishan Gokhale lit a lamp of purification of politics through spiritualization of politics. The next coming generations will be grateful and pay attribute to G.K. Gokhale for his benevolent legacy.

REFERENCES

1. *Speech of Gokhale* : Madras, G.A. Natesan & Co., 1920, 3rd ed. p. 925.
2. V.P. Verma : *Modern Indian Political Thought*, published by Lakshmi Narain Agarwal, Agra-3, 1986, p. 200.
3. Varinder Grover (ed.): *Political Thinkers of Modern India*, Vol. 2, Deep & Deep Publications, Delhi, 1990, p. 679.
4. V.P. Verma : *Modern Indian Political Though*, published by Lakshmi Narain Agarwal, Agra-3, 1986, p. 192.
5. D.G. Karve (ed.): *Speech and Writings of Gopal Krishna Gokhale*, Bombay, 1966, Introduction, pp. XX-XXI.
6. Note 5 : Introduction, pp. XXII-XXIII.
7. D.B. Mathur: *Gokhale: A Political Biography* (Thesis-Ph.D.) p. 149.
8. *Ibid.*, p. 153.
9. Note 2, p. 649.
10. Note 5, Introduction, pp. XIV.
11. Quoted by D.B. Mathur, p. 464.
12. *Ibid.*, p. 466.
13. O.P. Goyal, *Political Thought of Gokhale*, Kitab Mahal, Allahabad, 1965, p. 71.

11

M.G. Ranade

Apostle of Indian Freedom

Rudranand Jha

The sacred land of Maharashtra has always contributed immensely to the Indian History. The arrival of versatile scholars like Dada Bhai Naoroji, Jyotiba Phule, Bal Gangadhar Tilak, Gopal Krishna Gokhle, R.J. Bhandarkar, M.G. Ranade at one time proves the dictum of the 'Bhagvad Gita'—"when the demon rules the earth God has to come for the emancipation of mankind." Of them M.G. Ranade was different in many respects. He was a renowned jurist, a religious preacher, a social reformer, well-known name in journalism, an authority on Indian economics, and a political thinker. This great son of India was born on the 18th January, 1842, at Nasik and died at the age cf fifty-nine on the 16th January, 1901, in Bombay. In such a short span of time he was accepted as a political teacher of many of his contemporaries. A.O. Hume, the founder of the Indian National Congress, accepted him as his political Guru.[1] After his death Tilak wrote in *'Kesari'* : "Ranade can be compared with Himadri and Madhavacharya of recent times." Tilak accepted him as the first man in British India who 'imagined freedom for India'.[2] He remained source of inspiration even after his death for Indian leaders and social reformers. Ranade has an open mind on all social, political, religious and economic thinking of his time. He was a great scholar who read extensively, systematised them and examined them critically.

His conclusions on different problems were well planned and thus acceptable to a long chain of his followers.

To draw a clear picture of his thoughts it is essential to decide his writings, speeches and articles under four broad heads:

(a) Ranade : A Religious Preacher,
(b) Ranade : A Social Reformer,
(c) Ranade : A Political Thinker,
(d) Ranade : An Indian Economist.

Ranade : A Religious Preacher

He was a great scholar of Indian religion, Bhagvad *Dharma* and Smritis. He joined 'Prarthana Samaj' which was founded by Keshava Chandra Sen in Bombay. There were two important persons who remained associated with this institution, R.G. Bhandarkar and M.G. Ranade. Prarthana Samaj was founded to interpret religion in its correct perceptive and to fight against the perversion which cropped up in the long history of Indian religion. Keshava Chandra Sen was himself a theist. Ranade believed in God and accepted Him as the creator who dominates every moment of this creation. He is the cause of rise and fall of man and various phenomena. Ranade accepted religion as a vital force which steered history of a land. Unlike Jyotiba Phule and Raja Rammohan Roy, he believed that the 'Smritis', 'Vedas' and other sacred scriptures of India have every answer for all problems and evils prevalent in the Indian society. Like Dayanand and Swami Vivekanand he searched the path of emancipation of soul in Bhagwad Dharma and Vedant philosophy.

While Raja Rammohan Roy was searching for his source of inspiration in the western soil, mainly from British people, Ranade was a great admirer of Sant Tukaram, Tulsidas, Dayanand and Vivekanand. This does not mean that he had no admiration for European thinkers. He was definitely inspired by St. Augustine and Gregory who advocated tolerance in Christianity. The religious tolerance is even today the need of the time when fundamentalism is instigating the world order to throw the earth on the mouth of valcano. Religious tolerance is the basic feature of Arya Samaj and for Vivekanand the whole philosophy centred round this thesis of religious tolerance of Hinduism.

When Ranade was preaching and advocating religion, a simple sublimation to God, without pomp and show, without a dogma, on the soil of Maharashtra through his Prarthna Samaj another Great son of India, Swami Vivekanand was hypnotising the audience of the huge Galleries of Art Institute of Chicago, where four thousand men and women represeting the best culture of the U.S.A. were sitting in pin-drop silence. Representatives of all organised religions—'Buddhism, Christianity, Confucianism, Hinduism, Jainism, Judaism, Mohammadism, Shitoism, Theism, Brahmo Samaj and Zoroastrianism—were there'.[3] Vivekanand's marathon speech centred round only on one code of ethics of Hindu religious philosophy of tolerance—he told that religious gathering—"As the different streams having their sources in different places all mingle their water in the sea, Lord, the different paths which men take through different tendencies, various though they appear, crooked or straights, all lead to Thee." Ranade disagreed with the basic concept of 'Vedanta' "the creation and the creator is the same, nothing beyond Him nothing outside Him". He refuted Shankar's philosophy of 'Aham Brahamasmi'. In his opinion, God and his creation have separate entity. God regulated man and his deeds. He gives some liberty to man to attain his spirituality in totality. In his opinion material factors are guided by spiritual orders. To achieve the best of spirituality is the goal of human life. This achievement is the real concept of '*Moksha*'. He refused to accept the theory of 'Incarnation' and denouncing the world. The world is created by God for man. A man will have to perform his duties taking his soul in his confidence. No external direction is needed when one behaves with the command of one's inner soul. In this way he refused to obey the religious command without logical base. The world, for him, is a place where innumerable competitions are going on and among them man has to stand and search for his desired path with the consultation of his soul. The achievement of worldly gains and prizes must be accepted by those persons who receive them.

Like J.S. Mill, he believed in being a 'human being dissatisfied than a pig satisfied'. Man is the supreme creation of the Almighty and he must behave rationally, for that, he refused to obey religious orders. He never agreed to the concept of God as the Judge who punishes the sinner. In important religions of the world God is depicted as imposer of punishment. In Hinduism God is a father, a mother, a brother and a friend. He accepted that Hindu religion is basically more logical, rational and liberal but some sort of misrepresentation was made from time to time which needs correction and reinterpretation. Religion is meant for self-purification and loyalty to God. These are the basic values for purification of character. A characterless man is a curse for society. He who has no character cannot lead people for other attainments and developments.

This basic concept of religion was the fundamental base of Gandhian thought. Self-purification was the supreme thought of '*Satyagrah*' of Mahatma Gandhi, which later on became the foundation of non-violence in the struggle for freedom. Some of the critics of Ranade remark that the shackles of slavery are also the gift of God for Indian people. Ranade did not oppose them and accepted that the downfall of this great land was also the will of God. This country cannot attain its desired goal unless the Almighty wishes as such. Social and political upliftment is the fruit of religious revolution. Religion moves the wheel of history, and directs social renaissance.

Ranade : A Social Reformer

In this way social reformation and religious upliftment are complementary to each other. Ranade remained associated with different types of institutions and associations which were founded for divergent approaches. Prarthana Samaj was mainly concerned with the religious attainments of man and his approach towards God and one of its important aims was to eradicate evils, which were prevalent in the name of religion. 'Brahmo Samaj' was against '*Sati Pratha*', 'child marriage' and untouchability. To some extent 'Prarthana Samaj' was nearer to this approach. The basic difference between the two was that Raja Rammohan Roy, who was the founder of 'Brahmo Samaj', was Western in his outlook while Ranade was out and out a true Hindu in his approach. He inspired social reformation through the dictum of Smritis, Vedas and Upanishads. Actually, Arya Samaj or other progressive institutions those days carried a programme of social reformation through basic tenets of Hindu thought.

At that time Jyotiba Phule was fighting for the down-trodden on the soil of Maharashtra. Gradually his war took a turn against Brahminical despotism. This struggle was creating a gap between the society of haves and have-nots. This was not acceptable to M.G. Ranade. He could understand the nerve of the time. Unity was primarily important for India. He could foresee unity in diversity. While Phule's method was creating a gap, Ranade aspired for a social unity. He participated in the activities of different institutions like Industrial conference, the General library or female High school with the sole end to steer up a social transformation through united social activities having divergent curricula. The development of science and technology is basically important for the development of social upliftment. Though, India was socially, culturally and politically the most ancient civilisation of the world, we lagged behind the development of science and technology. Thus, for a social change, the development of science and technology is a must. India, a country of farmers, has many challenging tasks before it. Ranade's leadership inspired the farmers of Maharashtra to fight the famine of Maharashtra themselves. He encouraged them for a *swadeshi* movement to struggle against these ordeals themselves. This helped them to come out safely from the great famine of Maharashtra and not to die like ants as it happened in the famine of Bengal. This *Swadeshi* movement started vigorously on the soil of Maharashtra as early as in 1905. Ranade accepted social revolution as the forerunner of political consciousness. For social revolution, social justice and social equality are basic needs—widow-marraige, education for all and equal status for womanhood were the primary things for social change. On these points he was nearer to Raja Rammohan Roy and teachings of Maharshi Dayanand. He advocated for introduction of law to encourage female education as well as stopping child-marriage.

In his book *'Rise of Maratha Power'* he projected Shivaji as a symbol of national unity. Indirectly he symbolised Shivaji as a man for social unity, and as a brave fighter against foreign rule and thus he was in search of a national leader for the emancipation of India. Those days the religious orders discouraged Indians for going abroad and keeping any relation with external world. The prejudices of caste and creed were at their apex. Evil customs and bad social orders were being tolerated without a resistance. Ranade gave a clarion call against all these evils. He accepted that the ancient social order which encouraged slavery for women, untouchability and social inequality, led to encouragement of disrespect to human values.[4] He challenged the religious orders of the middle age for modern social values. Redundant and old social orders have no place in modern concept of society because they were unable to stop social degeneration. He asked for courage and tolerance for eradication of social perversions. He reinterpreted the Vedas, Smritis and religious books to bring about a change in Indian Social system. For this he took help of R.J. Bhandarkar who remained a great scholar of Sanskrit language. He further advocated for the help of State machineries and laws for a purposeful social change. Tilak did not go to this extent. He opposed social change through state order. Tilak came forward with his arguments but Ranade pleaded that the help of the state for a social reformation is not a submission before the foreigners. In his opinion wild foreign aggression was the result of our social intolerance and perverted loyalty to traditional systems. He proved his thesis of eternal liberty and freedom for all to our old valued religious social structure which steered a cultural expansion from China to Indonesia, from Ceylon to Japan and from near to distant places. In those days the social systems were more logically and intellectually based on rational value. In his opinion society needs spiritual and moral base. It is our collective responsibility to encourage a democratic social and political order where freedom and equality for all should be a basic factor. Society has the responsibility of creating a man, a free man full of optimism, just and pious, who can contribute to the attainment of rightful place for India in the community of free nations. He aspired for a value-based national character. This was not new. At that time these all leading reformers were aspiring and preaching similar views. Swami Vivekanand, while on way to Brindavan, met a cobbler. He asked for meals to be served at his house and there were yet other occasions when this great Swami launched with some Muslim devotees and Harijans. This indicates that contemporary thinkers likeVivekanand and Shivanand were free from caste and creed. They believed in universal brotherhood and equality for all.[5]

Ranade's views on social upliftment was clearly open-minded. If on the one hand he was impressed with Swami Dayanand, Vivekanand, Tukaram and Tulsidas, on the other hand he also openly accepted the ideas of Western thinkers like St. Augustine, Gregory, Stuart Mill and many others. To conclude about his ideas of social reformation in short we can say that he advocated religious tolerance, social equality, emancipation of woman, opposed untouchability and child-marriage and finally steered a *Swadeshi* movement to struggle against religious fundamentalism. The greatest contribution of Ranade was that he saved Maharashtra from Christian expansionism which raided largely the Tamil land.

Ranade : A Political Thinker

During the period when the Britishers set their foot on the Indian soil with a vow to capture the central power, the whole of the Indian subcontinent was divided into many fractions and parts. The absence of a strong rule for long had been inviting the foreign traders to seek their fortune even as rulers. From the middle of the seventeenth century India saw neck to neck competition among these foreign traders for taking the rule of the country into their hands. The Portugese, the French, the Danes and finally, the English all were trying to set their foot-holds not with a temptation of getting monopoly over business and trades but with an ambition to become the ruler or the master of the land. And as the country was divided into so many small powers and they too were also fighting among themselves, it was not very difficult for them to fulfil their unholy desire. In this race the English, the most farsighted among all of them, got the strongest foothold by whatsoever means they could adopt. They made their occupation first in Bengal and brought it under the East India Company's rule from Clive to Viscount Canning, the period noticed nothing but acquiring of more and more powers and making the Company richer by hook or by crook. Even during the period of British domain, the main policy of the administrative servants was to corrupt the character of the Indian people who were finally defeated.[6] Even the British historians like Duguit, Torren, Malcolm and Sir Thomas Mungo were honest enough who wrote that about fifty per cent of the population of British India were not having food to save their lives.[7] This plight of Indian people pressed Dada Bhai Naoroji 'The great old grandfather' of Indian political life to write in his book 'Poverty and un-British Rule in India'—that the root cause of Indian poverty is 'Cruel and senseless' misuse of Indian economic life. In his opinion the economic sources of India were heartlessly plundered.[8] We have no systematic history of our own. We never believed in history, whatever we have it is in the shape of poetry and philosophy.[9] If we have a systematic history we could have proved the plight of the people during British rule and the period before them.

Anyway before Dada Bhai Naoroji a host of religious preachers and social reformers appeared on Indian scene who tried their level best to encourage a social renaissance. But a systematic political consciousness grew after the arrival of Dada Bhai Naoroji who was followed by M.G. Ranade. They encouraged national awakening. There were other factors too like some religious and social reformers who came forward with a liberal approach to Hindu religious philosophy. This background helped the Indian thinkers to lead the country towards a political renaissance. They were called Moderates in Indian politics. After Dada Bhai Naoroji, Ranade was second in the hierarchy. These Moderates had to work under certain constraints. Before them there was the history of Indian War of Independence of 1857 which failed miserably, so they picked up the policy of co-operation with the rulers and derived the possible benefit slowly and gradually. There were some other factors also who helped them come forward to ask for some liberty. The big British empire had a limitation of manpower. So it recruited natives who could help the Britishers to rule and remain loyal to them. And the other side of the coin is that the whole of India from the Himalayas to Cape of Comorin was now brought under one government and the Indian people had started booming with a sense of political unity. The common subjugation gave rise to the unity of common Nationalism. Another most important thing was that the strong current of nationalist ideas which passed over the whole of Europe had also stimulated the growth of nationalism in India. All these factors accumulated together gave a better hand to Indian moderates to come forward and lead the country to a political upliftment.

M.G. Ranade was the most prominent among the Moderates, who was somehow a bit exception among all of them. Most Moderates at that time were influenced by Western civilisation and culture. Raja Rammjohan Roy advocated a change in the Indian life-style with the yardstick of Western way of life. Even Dada Bhai in the primary stage of his political life was of the opinion that the British rule in India had come as an emancipator and they would behave with India as if they were auspicious gift for the Indians. Surendra Nath Banerjee accepted that the history of England and their general features had given him light for survival. Ranade, though a Moderate, was inspired mostly by Indian thinkers and Hindu life-style. He was the first among the modern Indian thinkers who said—"I believe in two fundamental principles of our religion—one, this country is truly selected as a model by God and the other our fortune is guided by the Almighty."[10] But he has an open mind about Westerns of whom J.S. Mill inspired him most. Like other Moderates he was loyal to British monarchy with a limitation by declaring that "liberty and freedom means enactment of law, taxation and punishment and to recruit officers. The real difference between a free country and a slave one is that in a free country the punishment is imposed after the enactment of law, and before taxation the people are consulted as a whole, whereas in a slave country it is not."[11] He advocated the rule of law and parliamentry form of government for a real freedom. As a jurist he believed that an independent judiciary is the basic need for freedom. He hated the Imeprialistic ego of the Britishers as well as their backbone, the Anglo Indian Bureaucrats. For that he favoured the freedom of press which is collectively responsible to the comity of people. He said that "the unsympathetic and despising attitude of the victorious against the victor must be condemned, with all strength." Perhaps this was the reason that his loyalty to the British empire was doubted and he was never elevated to the celebrated post of the Vice-Chancellor of Bombay University. He encouraged all social assemblies and himself participated in their activities with a determination of uniting the people as a whole. Tilak was right when he said after the death of Ranade that in British India Ranade was the first man who used all his might for the amelioration of his people.[12] Actually when Tilak was the first modern political Indian revolutionary, Ranade was the first who imagined a free India. When all the Moderates were believing in the sense of justice of the British administrators, he was challenging the despotic ego of the rulers. He believed in gradual reforms and, like other thinkers of his time, advocated for a better understanding with British in the interest of India and simultaneously gave a call for the redemption of lost rights through continuous struggle.

He never took the Britishers as the supreme judge of Indian way of life. He favoured a self-government for the betterment of Indian people.

There are many more criticisms against the principles of Moderates that they believed that the interest of the Indians and the Britishers is the same and hence there should be a full faith in British administration. But all these criticisms cannot be made against Ranade as he had many reservations of these issues. His struggle for independence was definitely indirect, whereas the Moderates never saw a clash of interest between the two countries. Beyond all these Ranade did a great amount of spade work for national unity and political awakening. He, for the first time, aspired for the character-building of a nation and its leadership. Later on Mahatma Gandhi fought the war of independence on the concept of truth and introspection. His theory of '*Satyagrah*' was actually the view of Ranade. Ranade wedded 'God' with politics which became the main thesis of Gandhism in due course. For the betterment of farmers of Maharashtra he gave the slogan of '*Swadeshi* movement' which inspired the successive generation of leaders of Indian national movement. He favoured an individualistic theory of liberty and the rule of law and, at the same time, he advocated for the state interference for the spread of education and social reformation.

To sum up he instilled national consciousness in a section of Indian people to feel as Indians. He imagined an independent India, asked for liberty to rule themselves and thus he was the first man in modern Indian politics whose advocacy for national unity was based on the principle of universal equality, fraternity and freedom for all.

Ranade : An Indian Economist

Ranade came when Industrial capitalism was at its peak. Indian soil was a grazing ground for foreign rulers and the main sufferer, were Indian agriculturists. India is basically an agricultural country, where agriculturists had no say in the intellegentsia of the land. The condition of agricultural people was miserable beyond imagination. To win over the poverty of Indian man, which is predominantly agricultural, with eighty per cent of its population contributing a major part to its national income must be assigned the highest priority in the economic policy of the country. But at the time of Ranade, average Indian farmers were knee-deep in the mire of poverty. Generally, urban British administrators were of conviction that the poverty of farmers will compel them to produce more and more to meet their fixed obligation of rent, interest on loans and their livelihood. That compelled Dada Bhai Naoroji to say that till the Indians are not allowed to utilise their natural resources their own way, there was no chance of its materialistic revival. Dada Bhai demanded natural rights for the betterment of economic conditions of the Indian people.[13] In this back-drop Ranade came with his economic thesis and refused to accept that the laws of economics are always the same. He favoured dynamic and positive solution for Indian economic problems. He refused to accept that all the ideas of Adam Smith, Ricardo and Malthus are not acceptable in the context of Indian economics.[14] In his opinion, an economic policy must represent the time and circumstances, needs and values of the place where it is to be carried. His speech on Indian economic problems in Deccan College, Poona in the year 1892 was supposed to be very important for economic betterment of this country.[15] He favoured a sociological method to study the economic problems of Indian people who were predominantly agricultural. He decried that dictum of British administrators that the farmers would produce more and more to meet their obligation if they are compelled to remain always in deficit. This attitude of the Britishers brought repeated famines on the Indian soil which were less nature imposed.

At that time the concept of an 'Economic Man' and the thesis of Adam Smith that man needs absolute freedom in respect of his economic projects was not acceptable to Ranade. He advocated a principle of 'common welfare' because of Indian life-style, where a man sacrifices all his needs at the cost of performing social obligation and rituals. Indian social structure is specially designed to serve its people whereas it is different in the Industrially developed countries. The Indian concept of 'Tiny Republic' which is almost self-sufficient to serve the economic needs of its members and the society as a whole cannot work with a policy framed under the industrial back-drop. Here a barbar or a blacksmith serves his market still on the principle of give and take which is, to some extent, a 'Barter system'. A big chunk of economic needs is still guided not by the principle of 'supply and demand', but by the principle of 'social obligation'.

Ranade could feel that if industry is to thrive or play its rightful role in the economic structure of this country, it must depend upon agriculture and agricultural products and thus economic policies should be framed in a way which is congenial to its infrastructure of social life. He could foresee that only in this way the part of our rural masses is bound to give a tremendous boost to the entire economic growth. Later on cottage industries, the ideas of *Sarvodaya* and agriculture-based economy became the base of Gandhian thought. There cannot be denying this fact that Ranade was the first and foremost economist of India who talked of Indianisation of Indian economics. He was the man who compelled the British masters to re-evaluate their economic policies. At least principal solution to the welfare problem of the lowest-income Indian farmers 'lies in the development of better part-time and full-time non-agricultural rural employment opportunities.'[16]

He searched out six important reasons of the cause of poverty of Indian mass, i.e. dependence on only one source of agriculture as the way of capital production; non-availability of capital to invest in other industry mainly on iron, old system of capital borrowings; problem of population explosion in some part of India; absence of risk taking-habits in agricultural people; old and redundant social customs and absence of a dynamic economic management.[17] The upliftment of the country lies in a balanced and harmonious development of trade, industry and agriculture. He favoured state oriented industrialisation to some important industry. At least the Government should finance on liberal terms in iron, coal, paper, glass, sugar and oil industries. Savings and Commercial banks should come forward for financing for the industrialisation of the country.[18] All these prescriptions are nothing new. The whole economic system is borrowed from Kautilya who advocated complete participation of the state in major important industries, allowing private participation in other industries and state protection against exploitation of man by man in respect of production, distribution and consumption.[19]

Britishers in India were guided by the motive to keep India as the production centre of raw materials as well as a monopolised trade market, for their manufactured goods. There are ample evidence under which they forced the Indian farmers for the cultivation of commercial crops. The freedom struggle of Champaran in Bihar was led by Mahatma Gandhi primarily against the British exploiting and compellng the farmers for the cultivation of *'Neel'*. At the time of Ranade, the farmers of Maharashtra were compelled to grow cotton which was the back-bone of booming industry of cloth production in England. All these raw materials were being exported to England. "Thus the British administrators followed the trade policy under which the raw materials were sent to England and finished goods were sent back to the Indian people for consumption. In a planned manner they destroyed handicrafts and cottage industries of India. At least there remained no scope of finished cloth in handicrafts sector of India. Other indigenous production also died slowly. The Indian people even became dependent on British production of small agricultural instrument and tools. In the old Indian system which showed a fine harmony between agriculture and industry crumbled down under the weight of the British interests.... This resulted in the stagnation and growing poverty in the Indian Economy."[20]

In this way we owe innumerable obligations for the betterment of Indian economy to M.G. Ranade who, for the first time, looked into the defects of economic policies of India, gave a call for a separate dynamic Indian economic policy. He is the man who is still relevant in the context of Indian economy. The latest call of Indianisation of Indian economy was the call of Ranade. Basically, the Gandhian concept of reorientation of cottage industries and protection to the handicrafts and basic laws of protection of farmers from exploitation of money-lenders, laws for the systems of land revenues etc. were all first envisaged by Ranade.

Thus, he favoured liberty and freedom in all aspects of human life. He revolted against the perverted form of fundamentalism.

He is creator of modern *Smriti* for our social life and there can be no difference of opinion in calling him the Parasar of modern India, who said that Manu was for *Satyug*, Gautam for

Treta and Sankhya and Likhit for *Dwapar,* whereas Parasar Smriti should be referred to for *Kaliyug* only.[21] Manu was rigid in the imposition of *Varnashram* system in fabric of Indian social life, whereas Parasar relaxed the compulsion of *Varnashram* system and advocated a change in the prevailing social system.[22] Like Parasar, Ranade stood for a revolutionary change in our outlook which became the precept for the struggle for Indian independence. He is still relevant in the formulation of present economic policies so far as Indianisation of Indian economic policies are concerned.

Thus Ranade is a multi-dimensional genius.

REFERENCES

1. Verma, V.P., *Adhunik Bhartiya Rajnitik Chintan,* p. 178.
2. *Ibid.,* p. 179.
3. *Vivekanand* : Chicago Addresses, pp. 15-16.
4. Ranade, M.G., *Indian Social Reform,* Vol. 2, p. 91.
5. K.P. Shiv Kumar, *Incidents from the life of Swami Vivekanand,* p. 26.
6. Lal, Pt. Sunder, *Bharat Me Angrejee Rajya,* Vol. I, p. 394.
7. *Ibid.,* p. 390.
8. Naoroji, Dada Bhai, *Poverty and un-British Rule in India,* p. 203.
9. Lohia, Ram Manohar, *Bharatmata, Dharti Mata,* p. 172.
10. Verma, V.P., *Adhunik Bhartiya Rajnitik Chintan,* p. 175.
11. *Ibid.,* p. 195.
12. *Ibid.,* p. 8.
13. Naoroji, Dada Bhai, *Poverty and un-British Rule in India,* p. 203.
14. Verma, V.P., *Adhunik Bhartiya Rajnitik Chintan,* p. 188.
15. *Ibid.,* p. 189.
16. E.C.P. Prabhakar; *Indian Journal of Public Administration,* Vol. X, No. 4, October-December 1964, New Delhi-1, p. 676.
17. Verma, V.P., *Adhunik Bhartiya Rajnitik Chintan,* pp. 191-192.
18. Ranade, M.G., Easays in Indian Economics, pp. 103-104.
19. Pandey, Shayam Lal; *Kautilya Ki Rajyavyavastha* (quoted by Jain & Phadia in his book *Rajnitik Vicharak*), p. 100.
20. Dhingra, I.C., *Agricultural Economy of India,* p. 2.
21. Vachaspati, Shree Basudeo, *Parasar Smriti,* p. 5.
22. Sharma, Shree Ram, *Bis Smritian,* Vol. II, *Parasarsmriti,* p. 114.

12

The Political Philosophy of Bal Gangadhar Tilak*
An Analysis of Religious Concepts and Symbols used Therein

M.R. Kazimi

The political philosophy of the liberals, who dominated the early phase of the Indian National Congress, soon found itself out of tune with the aims and aspirations of the common people. The events had taken a course which belied the fond hope that the British rule in India would usher in a period of peace and tranquillity. Instead, the alien rule had turned into a curse. The people groaned in pain and anguish under the exploitative and repressive rule.

During the last decade of the nineteenth century, the people suffered terribly. Famine, pestilence, earthquake, war and repression were let loose on the country. Between 1860-1900, there were ten big famines in India. All these added to the woes of the people and multiplied their misery. It brought in focus the incompetence as well as unresponsiveness of the bureaucracy.[1] Increase in revenue added more to the travails,

* Bal Gangadhar Tilak (1856-1920) popularly called Lokmanya Tilak, a prominent Indian leader, scholar and writer who authored *The Orion* and *The Arctic Home in the Vedas* and *Gita Rahasya.* He was founder of the *Kesari* and the *Mahratta* in which he wrote profusely. The collections of his speeches and writings are also available including one entitled *Bal Gangadhar Tilak, His Writings and Speeches.*

which led to widespread dissatisfaction and occasional outbursts of defiance. In retaliation, repression went unchecked and those who raised the voice in protest were put to all sorts of indignities and humiliations. Physical torture was the rule of the day.The outbreak of plague in 1896 multiplied the plight manifold. The administration of Lord Curzon proved the proverbial last straw on the camel's back. In his two ill-fated terms of office, he inflicted upon the country in almost breathless succession one contentious measure after the another to which people took the strong exception.[2]

The cumulative result of the economic distress of the people and the resultant demoralization had been a sense of desperation which led people to think seriously for finding ways and means which would make them free of the helpless and unhappy period of their subjection by means other than adopted thus far. The people sought refuge in extreme measure arising out of radical and revolutionary ideology which, being already in the air[3], was only further strengthened and developed by leaders like Bal Gangadhar Tilak, Bipin Chandra Pal and Lala Lajpat Rai and also, Aurobindo Ghose.

Sources of Influence and Inspiration

The leaders of this new school were influenced and inspired by the Hindu rivalrist movements of Arya Samaj, Theosophical Society and, above all, by *Neo-Vendantism* of Ram Krishna and Vivekanand. In particular, this *Neo-Vendantism* of Vivekananda had placed the Hindu religion on a very high pedestal among the religions of the world. He had become the apostle of a new revolution. His clarion call to the people to eschew fear and timidity and to inculcate the spirit of *Shakti* stirred and enthused the hearts of Indians, and infused new hopes and aspirations and placed the service to the nation on a high spiritual level. Tilak, in particular, had also been influenced by the writings of Max Muller on India and Hinduism. As such, the three were pioneers of "new-nationalism" who drew inspiration from the old religion of the Hindus. They expounded the doctrines of *Vedas* and *Gita* in which they found way to salvation of man and liberation of the nation. They identified *dharma* with nationalism and revived Hindu pride in the old epics and classical literature.[4]

It is said that Bal Gangadhar Tilak was a changed man from 1892. He was not the same Tilak who would like to walk on the trodden path of liberalism. Above all, his agnosticism gave way to orthodoxy and love for Hindu religion. He developed a faith that Hinduism was capable of becoming a powerful force of regeneration and union. Tilak and his associates, also called "orthodox nationalists" wanted to rebuild India not in the image of an alien system of values but to recreate her on the foundations of her own greatness. On the basis of the Indian philosophy of life, they constructed an Indian philosophy of politics which was to guide and inspire the national movement.[5]

Advaita Vedanta of the Hindus was starting point of the philosophy of the extremists, Tilak included. According to *Vedanta* the multiplicity of the various objects in the world is not a true multiplicity. The substance is one though expressed through many forms and the reality is not material but essentially spiritual. It was a distorted view which sought to realise the essential unity between God and man through meta-physical abstractions, by a negation of social and civil life. There was more emphasis on subjective and universal to the neglect of objective and particular.[6] The extremists live Vivekananda sought to combine the spiritual culture of India with the secular culture of Europe and America and stressed the importance of social freedom for the uplift of the toiling starving millions of the country.[7]

Tilak held a firm belief in the excellence of the Indian culture he held that the Indian culture was based on the wisest of the spiritual principles on which alone special harmony and well being could be approached in the world.[8] Erudite scholar that Tilak was, he had made piercing study of the ancient scriptures and brought out commentaries of great value.[9] He took special fancy for *Gita*. He had come to the conclusion that *Gita* was not a book of cold philosophy but a guide to everybody, to all human beings, a treatise on the science and the art of *Karmayoga*.[10] Whenever, a man was confounded as what was his primary duty and a lesser duty and when predicaments of such character fermented his mind, the *Gita* was a sure guide.[11] As has been explained by Tilak in his preface to *Geeta-Rahasya*, he was first introduced to *Gita* during the last illness of his father when he was just sixteen. Almost from his very first perusal of Lord's song, a doubt haunted his mind. The *Shankaracharya* had prounced that *Gita* had preached *Jnan*, unqualified by *Karma*. Tilak thought otherwise. He viewed the doctrinal teachings of *Gita* as having the sole purpose of energizing Arjun into action, of enabling him to face the problems of life in manly ways and to perform his duties as warrior.

Tilak on Concept of *Karma*

An such, no analysis of Tilak's stand on issues of political ramifications can be made without reference to his theory of *Karma*, developed through his interpretation of *Gita*. Whereas, others believed that *Bhakti* or *Jnan* had been the supreme message of *Gita*, Tilak thought that it was *Karma*. Through this interpretation, he built up a bridge between politics and religion and it can be said safely that it was Tilak who first moulded religion into the channel of worldly action. The credit goes to him that he tried to base politics upon the highest principles of spiritualism as enunciated in the *Bhagvad Gita*. His stress on *Karma*, as the real message of *Gita* inspired those millions who were fighting for the cause of the nation. Tilak maintained that *Gita* advocates *Karma* in this world even after the actor has achieved the highest union with the Diety by *Jnan* or *Bhakti*.[12] This action must be done to keep the world going by the right path of evolution which the creator has destined the world to follow. In order that action may not bind the actor, it must be done with the aim of helping his purpose and without attachment to the coming result.

According to Tilak, the *Gita* enjoins action even after the perfection in *Jnan* and *Bhakti* is attained and the deity is reached through this media. He underlines fundamental unity between *logos*, man and world. The world is in existence because *logos* willed it so. It is his will which holds its together. Man will not cease to do any action because he has attained the supreme goal—the union with Almighty.[13] Shri Krishna himself says that there is nothing in the three worlds that he needs to acquire and still he acts. He acts because if he does not, he shall be failing in his duty. If a man seeks unity with the Almighty, he must necessarily seek unity with the world also and must work for it.[14]

The *Gita,* while prescribing the way to the realisation of the highest spirit of the consciousness, it does never negate the importance of action in the world. It is the philosophy of *Niskama Karma Yoga* which establishes the synthesis between knowledge, devotion and action. Action is a necessity both for the seeker of knowledge and for those who have already attained it. *Karmayoga,* according to Tilak, is an adequate and complete philosophy of life, ethics and religion. It was Arjun who had understood the message of *Gita* correctly as he readily agreed to perform duties as warrior as one's highest *Swadharma.* Arjun did not lack spiritual vision. He was perfect in divine attributes still he preferred to perform his duties which involved fighting his own kith and kin. According to *Gita,* as interpreted by Tilak, *Karma* is such as cannot be avoided. It is essential that man should perform his duties with a sense of detachment. Duty or action performed in a spirit of detachment and perfect disinterestedness is the highest endeavour.

The *Gita* is emphatic in its inculcation that duly disinterested action founded upon supreme spiritual knowledge leads to redemption. It puts emphasis on the performance of allotted functions even by wisemen. *Gita* talks of performance of action in spirit of detachment produced by knowledge.[15] Tilak interprets the *Vendanta Sutra* to mean that *Sanyas* and *Karmayoga* are the two alternative paths of living after the attainment of knowledge. In brief, *Gita* stressed the renunciation of the desire to get results.

Tilak's Concept of *Dharma*

As stated earlier, Tilak held firm belief in *Advaita* philosophy. The concept of the highest absolute which is referred to in the

Nasadiya hymn of the *Rigveda* and is elaborately discorded in the Vedantic philosophy of the *Upanishads,* the *Vedanta Sutras* and the *Bhagwad Gita,* profoundly appealed to him.[16] He, however, accepted the notion of a personal God. He said in course of a speech: "Religion in the true sense of the term means and include the knowledge of the nature of God and soul and of the ways and means by which the human soul can attain saluation."

He had a very comprehensive conception of *Dharma* which, according to Tilak, implies the moral and sacred tie between the individual soul and the cosmic soul and the social tie between the various members of the human kind. "It provides a man's imperative duties towards God and his necessary obligations towards his fellowmen."[17] Hindu *Dharma,* thus, provides a moral as well as a social tie. Tilak lamented that during the Vedic times, India was a self-contained country and was "united as a great nation." The unity has disappeared thereby causing political degradation. It was the duty of the leaders "to revive that Union."[18] Tilak wanted that various sections of the Hindu should unite into a mighty Hindu nation. He maintained: "Hindu religion as a whole is made up of different parts related to each other as so sons and daughters of one great religion. If this idea is kept in view and if we try to unite the various sections, it will be consolidated in a mighty force...Religion is an element in nationality." He gave the call: "Let the stream of Hindu religion flow through our channel with mighty consolidated and concentrated force." Not dismayed by the fact that religion had never been a uniting factor, Tilak did in his hopes on integrating aspects for the future political evolution of Hinduism as well as of Indian political system.[19] He wanted to inculcate sentiments of unity and integration rather than division and discord for the maintenance and development of a religio-political system.

Tilak on Natural Rights and Freedom

Again, Tilak's concept of natural rights and freedom may be understood in terms of his firm belief in *Vedanta* philosophy.

Because spirit is the supreme reality and because all men are portions or aspects of that absolute essence, hence all have the same spiritual potentiality which calls for spiritual autonomy. Freedom is the basic urge of human nature. "Freedom is the very life of the individual soul which *Vedanta* declares to be not separate from God but identical with Him. The freedom was a principle which could never perish."[20] This freedom, to Tilak, was a divine attribute, without which no moral or spiritual life was possible. Denial of freedom kills the soul of the nation and this explains Tilak's urge for national freedom. It may further be added that Tilak's views on nationalism and freedom carried the influence also of the Western theories of national independence and self-determination. If fact, Tilak's philosophy of nationalism was a synthesis of *Vedantic* ideal of the spirit as supreme freedom and Western conceptions of Mazzini, Burke, Mill and later on of Wilson.[21]

Tilak's concept of nationalism had some revivalist tinge in it. He wanted to enthuse the nation by reminding it of the ancient wisdom, coming out of *Vedas* and *Gita*, which once brought glory to the nation. He wanted revival of old healthy and vibrant traditions. "A true nationalist desires to build on old foundations. Reforms based on utter disrespect for old does not appeal to him as constructive work."[22] Tilak always maintained that the Hinduism was capable of becoming a powerful force of regeneration and union. He thought of giving a deep rooted cultural basis to the political movement. In the words of Aurobindo Ghose, "He aimed at developing a language and spirit and wanted to Indianise the movement and carry it to the masses."[23] It was this intention that he instituted two festivals *Ganpati Mahotsava* and *Shivaji Utsav*. He wanted to cannalise the religions fervour and allow the Hindus to meet at a place and seek inspiration from the age old religion. He wanted to use such occasions for the preparation of ideas about freedom and nationalism. "Why should not we strengthen our feeling of nationalism on the basis of religious faith", he asked? The Ganesh festival turned out to be a kind of series of extension lectures on a variety of topics and an opportunity for the study or revision of their study of the Hindu religious books like the

Vedas, the *Brahamanas,* the *Upanishads,* the *Ramayana,* the *Mahabharata* and the works of the saints and saviours of the people.[24] In fact, this Ganesh festival could successfully be used as a means of political propaganda and the message of *Swadeshi* and *Swarajya* could be given wide circulation.

Tilak, like Carlyle, believed that heroes of the world are the creators of the world. He hit upon the idea of projecting Shivaji as a national hero who stood for *Swarajya* and for national honour. "Hero worship is a thing deeply implanted in human nature and our political aspirations need all the strength which the worship of a *Swadeshi* hero is lively to inspire into our minds. For this purpose, Shivaji is the only hero to be found in the history of modern times", he wrote in an article in 1906.[25] Though through such festivals, Tilak wanted to arouse peoples interest in political and secular matters, critics have not shared him for fanning Hindu communalism. Tilak's tactics are conveniently taken to be counter-productive in the sense that, in reaction, it nurtured Muslim Communalism. Leaving aside Chirol (*India Unrest*) even sober and secular writer like Abid Hussain calls Tilak "the most prominant protagonist of the conservative Hinduism" who gave Hindu nationalism a decidedly religious and slightly revivalist bias."[26] But the fact remains that Tilak was preaching secular ideas by using religious idioms which people would easily understand. Hiren Mukherjee, refers to a Soviet scholar who maintains: "Religion had a tremendous place in India, which was just embarking on the capitalist road. It was perfectly natural that Indian nationalist should have used the religious prejudices of the masses as a means of arousing and bringing them into the struggle against colonialism."[27] Tilak himself rebutted the allegation that he was arousing anti-Muslim sentiments by eulogising Shivaji. "Shivaji festival is not celebrated to alienate or even to irritate the Mohammedans. Times are changed and... the Mohammedans and the Hindus are in the same boat or stand on the same platform, so far as the political condition of the people is concerned. Can we not both of us derive inspiration from the life of Shivaji under these circumstances? His life clearly shows that Indian races do not so soon lose the vitality which gives them able leaders at critical times. That is the lesson which the Mahommedans and the Hindus have to learn from the history of great Maharatta chief and the Shivaji festival is intended to emphasize the same lesson."[28] As stated above, he just used religious symbols to reinvigorate nationalist sentiments of the common people.

Tilak's Concept of *Swarajya*

Because of his spiritual approach, Tilak regarded that *Swarajya* was not only a right but *Dharma*.[29] He granted a spiritual and moral meaning to *Swarajya*. Politically it could mean home-rule but morally, its connotation was much wider. It could be taken to mean the attainment of the perfection of self-control which is essential for performing one's duty. It had its own spiritual significance because it also meant the realization of spiritual inner freedom and contemplative delight. Tilak explained the term thus: "It is a life centred in self and dependent upon self. There is *Swarajya* in this world as well as in the world hereafter. ... It is my conviction, it is my thesis that *Swarajya* in the life to come cannot be reward of a people who have not enjoyed it in this world."[30] As such, Tilak stood for political freedom as well as for spiritual freedom.

Swarajya, according to Tilak, is at once the self-rule of the individual and self-rule of the political community.[31] For the individual, *Swarajya* meant the exercise of his freedom lawfully. Unless he enjoyed *Swarajya*, an individual could not live in his true nature, could not fulfil the purpose of life. Similarly unless there was *Swarajya*, the conscious lawful living under *Dharmarajya*, the right ordering of the community could never be attained and the purpose fulfilled for which a political community existed. The political community existed only to preserve and promote *Dharma* and without *Swarajya*, this was not possible. As such, *Swarajya* was a moral imperative both for an individual and the community. Tilak held that our life and our *Dharma* are in vain in the absence of *Swarajya*.[32]

According to Tilak: "The restoration of *Swarajya* was moral imperative. The laws, the institutions of government, the use of power and the ordering of the political community could only be moral when there was *Dharmarajya* and *Dharma* could only rule if the people had *Swarajya*. Unless the people enjoyed self rule to legislate and enforce the reforms, the reforms were not only without meaning and merit but undemocratic and devoid of moral sanction."[33]

As such, Tilak favoured democracy. He wanted democratic *Swarajya* both for the individual and the community. It held key to all-round development and progress of the nation. He stated: "If we do not get *Swarajya*, there will be no industrial progress, if we do not get *Swarajya* there will be no possibility of having any kind of education useful to the nation, either primary or higher. If we do get *Swarajya*, it is not merely to advance female education or to secure industrial reform or social reform. All these are parts of *Swarajya*. Power is wanted first."[34]

Tilak's concept of *Swarajya* postulated complete change in the theory of government. It involved the reapplication of the classical Indian theory of the state. It meant a revolutionary recasting of those forms to accord with the Indian civilization's value system: it meant the remaining of the state so that it would fulfil the purpose and become the embodiment of *Swarajya* as it was in the Indian civilization. *Swarajya* was the restoration of the political order so that it would accord with the cosmic order and so that the individual lives might be assisted in attaining the purpose of life. To him, *Swarajya* was the foundation.

Tilak held that *Swarajya* consisted in the natural consequence of diligent performance of duty. Tilak's ideas of *Swarajya* found expression in the Home-Rule movement and stated thus: "I said that it was our right to have Home-Rule but that it was a historical and European may of putting it. I go further and say that it is our 'Dharma'. You cannot separate Home-Rule from us; as you cannot separate heat from fire; both are inseparably bound up."[35]

Tilak on Passive Resistance

Though Tilak, also Pal and Lal, chalked out on three-fold programme to bring about *Swarajya*, it was maintained that violence should be avoided always and passive resistance adhered to. Tilak stood for boycott and *Swadeshi* but asked for courage and sacrifice. He found the basis of passive resistance in *Gita*, "There is always penalties prescribed for the breach of every law. But when a law itself is immoral and is sought to be enforced by the Government authority, it becomes necessary to test our faith in truth, justice and *Dharma* and defy the immoral law... But faith and devotion to truth and justice have got to be of such a high degree or fervour that no other consideration but performance of duty must enter the mind of the devotee and the faithful. Owing duty in spite of everything is only sentiment that must take its complete possession. ... The value is not attainable by learning and scholarship ... This is spiritual power. ... This is the thing of the *Upnishads*. Although this spiritual power cannot be attained by learning or the intellect, a determined man can attain it by practice or penance according to *Gita*."[36] He asked the people: "If you have not even power of active resistance, have you not the power of self-denial and self-abstinence in such a way as not to assist the foreign government to rule over you?"[37] In short, by passive resistance, he meant 'reaching the goal by making all sorts of sacrifices'.

Tilak on Individual's Happiness

Tilak always maintained that stress should be on the moralization and rationalization of man's intention and not on the external results attained by a certain course of action. He maintains: "We cannot arrive at a correct decision as to whether a particular act is good or bad, just or unjust or moral or immoral by considering merely its external result or effect, that is by considering whether or not that will produce the greatest good of the great number. One has also necessarily to consider at the same time the reason, the desire, or the motive of the doer of the act."[38] He believed in spiritual pleasure. Happiness that is to be found in the extremely noble activities and in the purest state of mind and of the reason is that highest or the most ideal happiness of mankind.[39] Highest happiness consists in rational discrimination and spiritual vision. This kind of inner happiness is superior to both organic happiness and material happiness. *Dharma* is eternal, while pleasure and pain are temporary.

A fleeting glance over a few of concepts developed and interpreted by Tilak, leaves no one in doubt that he was a strong champion of freedom and democracy. But Tilak's insistence on freedom and democracy arose primarily out of his spiritual worldview. He believed in the essentially divine nature of the human soul. He stressed the elements of dignity and sanctity in human personality. This belief in the sanctity of personality made him an indomitable champion of freedom. At the same time, his moral viewpoint led him to put stress on duties also. To him, all human beings are bound to each other by the bonds of morality. Man is a member of a moral community and he has obligations to discharge to himself and to society. But this obligation enhances his freedom and does not militate against the state because obligation is his *Swadharma*. It is consistent with his nature and with the quality most developed in him. No obligation can be forced upon a man. Individual must be independent who can be relied upon to discharge the responsibilities sustained by moral and spiritual considerations. It is for this reason that the concept of *Swarajya* find a place of pride in Tilak's political thinking. To Tilak, *Swarajya* was a great moral imperative, completely self-justifying goal. It was the foundation upon which fulfilment of values of *Dharma* depended. The such ideas of *Dharma* could not be achieved in the absence of *Swarajya*. It is for this reason that he fought relentlessly for *Swarajya*, above and beyond any other goal. Undoubtedly, Tilak drew inspiration from ancient sacred texts of the Hindu religion and quoted extensively from those sources. In course of formulating his political idea, he preferred to fall back upon the concepts given in the *Vedas* and *Gita* for he found them to be of confirmed value and relevance which could give grit and determination to Indians to meet the challenges coming from the alien rule. He held that the high ideas, set out by the seers in the ancient India were beyond and above time and space, they represented eternal truth. India's salvation lay in reverting back to those ideals, capsuled in the concept of *Dharma*, which was all comprehensive and all embracing a term, not confirmed to the ritual and practices of any particular religion. It had no sectarian connotation at all. It epitomised highest of morality and spirituality which went much beyond the narrow confines of religions, which are outward manifestations of the misperceptions and misinterpretations of one single eternal truth. Languages are different, message is the same. Tilak's *Dharma* addressed itself to humanity.

Indeed, Tilak wanted to bring to the front the message of the *Vedas* and the *Gita* but only in order to provide spiritual energy and moral enthusiasm to the nation. His commitment was only to nationalism, reinvigorated and rejuvenated. It is most unfair to say, as some critics do, that Tilak was nationalist, whose vision was narrow and circumspect, who believed in reviving old Hindu traditions and customs and wanted to make the religion base of politics in India. It is alleged in the same vein, that Tilak and thinkers of his ilk were responsible for giving a fill-up to Muslim communalism which grew in strength to strength in proportion to and in retaliation to Hindu revivalism.[40] But such accusation smack of prejudice and lack of will to analyse and interpet Tilak in the correct perspective. The fact remains that Tilak used religious idioms and took help of Hindu symbols and images to buttress his concept of nationalism and to enthuse and inspire the people with a dynamic sense of nationalism but he had no option left. Common people pay attention to and understand the message if ccuched in religious idioms. Religious sentiments continue to be strong in India. The Hindus and the Muslims sail in the same boat in this regard. It remained so in the days of Tilak and remains even today, the principle means of communicating with the common message. Today, religious sentiments are aroused to serve a cause narrow and parochial. The case was different with Tilak. He aimed at something much higher. If Tilak was responsible for revival of Ganpati festival, which gave the message of nationalism to masses, he promised all support to the Khilafat movement provided the majority of the Muslims supported it. Tilak wanted reintroduction of national festivals because in his view, nationalism is a kind of sentiment and the historical memories of the great figures of a country play a part in restrengthening thing and refreshing that sentiment. Shivaji was the symbol of that resistance and resentment of the people against oppression and injustice.[41] He felt that the roots of nationalism must be not merely in the intellectual appeals but must rest on sentiments and emotions of the people. His sole intention was to arouse nationalist sentiments by recalling past glories. Tilak was harbinger of new nationalism in India which was deeply rooted in the soil of the land, was evidently religious and revivalist in appearance but was liberal composite and secular in content. Tilak talked in terms of religious idioms but to spread a message which aimed at nationalism borm and brought up in a secular setting. Religion, if correctly understood, could be an element in nationality. Dogmatism and fanaticism did not find favour in the political philosophy of Bal Gangadhar Tilak.

REFERENCES

1. The six famines which occurred between 1877 and 1900 wiped out fifteen millions of people, a population which was equal to the half of England during those days. The famine of 1896 was most serious one and it came due to grave failure of rains affecting 2,25,000 square miles in British India and a population of 62 million. See, *Cambridge History of India*, Vol. VI, p. 300.
2. Curzon's costly Durbars among devastating famines, his Indian Universities Act of 1904, his attack on the elected members of the Calcutta Corporation, his expedition to Tibet at the cost of Indian revenue, his address to the convocation of the Calcutta University in 1905 and above, partition of Bengal had caused indignation throughout the length and breadth of the country.
3. Some international events, too, fanned the smouldering fire into flames. The defeat of Italy at the hands of Abyssinia in 1894, resistance offered by two South African Republics to the British and, at the top of all, the defeat of Russia by Japan exploded the myth of invincibility of the Europeans and encouraged and inspired the extremists in India to chalk out a new line of action.
4. In case of Tilak, Vishnu Shastri Chiplunkar, described as friend and philosopher of Tilak, deserves mention. Known for his *Nivandh Mala* written in 1874, Chiplunkar extorted people to feel proud of themselves and their cultural heritage. He had inspired Tilak and Agarkar to dedicate their lives for the cause of the nation.

5. J.N. Vajpayee, *The Extremist Movement in India* (Allahabad, 1974), p. 69.
6. S.N. Dubey, *Modern Indian Political Thinkers* (Delhi) pp. 53-54.
7. *Ibid.*
8. P.D. Kaushik, *The Congress Ideology and Programme, 1920-47,* pp. 5-6.
9. The *Mahabharata* and *Rigveda* were subjects of Tilak's constant medication. *The Orion* and *The Arctic Home in the Vedas* established his reputation as a scholar and author in the Western world. These books are not mere compilations. They strike a new line of thought and research. In *The Arctic Home in the Vedas,* for instance, Tilak has given quite new and convincing interpretations of nearly eight intricate spots in the *Rigveda,* besides throwing light on more than twice the number. See, T.V. Parvate, *Bal Gangadhar Tilak* (Navajivan, 1956), p. 300.
10. *Ibid.*, p. 301.
11. *Ibid.*
12. V.P. Verma, *Modern Indian Political Thought* (Agra, 1985), p. 263.
13. *Ibid.*
14. *Ibid.*, p. 264.
15. *Gita Rahasya*, p. 506.
16. V.P. Verma, *Op. cit.*, p. 207.
17. *Ibid.*, p. 208.
18. *Speeches and Writings of Tilak* (1918), p. 36.
19. Verma, p. 209. According to Tilak, "Common allegiance to Vedas" and other sacred scriptures provide a "common heritage".
20. *Speeches and Writings of Tilak*, p. 354.
21. Verma, *Op. cit.*, p. 225.
22. B.G. Tilak, Letters to *Mahratta*, 13 December, 1919.
23. Quoted in Vajpayi, *Op. cit.*, p. 69.
24. Parvate, *Op. cit.*, p. 116.
25. *Maharatta*, 24 June, 1906.
26. S. Abid Hussain, *The National Culture of India*, (National Book Trust, 1978), p. 136. He writes: "Tilak's literary activities were directed towards bringing Hindus in contact wtih their glorious part ... had a great influence on the minds of a large section of educated Hindus and gave Hindu nationalism a decidedly religious and slightly revivalist lines."
27. Hiren Mukherjee, *Recalling India's Struggle for Freedom* (Delhi, 1983), p. 106.
28. Note 25.
29. B.G. Tilak, *Writings and Speeches*, p. 256.
30. Parvate, *Op. cit.*, pp. 292-93.
31. *Ibid.*, p. 276.

32. Note 29, p. 333.
33. Aurobindo Ghose, in his introductory appreciations to Tilak's writings and speeches stated the position thus "Let us first have liberty and the organised control of the life of the nation, afterwards we can see how we use it in social matters."
34. Note 29, p. 256.
35. *Ibid.*
36. *Ibid.*, pp. 237-38.
37. *Ibid.*, p. 64.
38. For details see, *Gita Rahasya*, Vol. I, pp. 114-25.
39. *Ibid.* See also *Appadorai, Indian Political Thinking in the Twentieth Century : An Introductory Survey* (New Delhi, 1987), p. 106.
40. Those who allege anti-Muslim bias in Tilak tend to forget his role in bringing about Congress League pact of Lucknow in 1916. Not only that M.A. Jinnah remained attached to Tilak, Ali Brothers too, reposed supreme confidence and faith in Tilak. Hasrat Mohani, noted Urdu poet and a militant nationalist, composed poems in honour of Tilak.
41. See, in the writings of Tilak in *Kesari* of 1st September, 1896 and 8th September 1896. See also his articles in *Kesari* of 9th April, 1901 and *Maharatta* 24 June, 1906.

13

Religion as Political Ideology
The Separatist Crusade of Jinnah

Asha Kaushik and S.N. Kaushik

The root meaning of religion is 'that which binds'. As Gandhi said 'when morality incarnates itself in a living man, it becomes religion'.[1] That is the signification of religion in its 'pure', universal form, as an ideal and a vision. In practice, it assumes the form of a complex socio-psychological phenomenon, varying with changing historical conditions. When interpreted in ideological terms, religion is accorded a specific system of ideas, icons, rituals, rites and also a network of institutions feeding mainly on the emotive aspects of its followers. When employed for political objectives, religious ideology acquires the form of political ideology.

True, no religion in its pure form comprises a political programme prescribing an attitude to its followers to be followed on political issues arising in different situations. However, there is ample historical evidence of religion—its norms and categories being used by contending groups to promote warring political and ideological ends. There are instances when even within one country, the same religion has been known to justify and serve as a foundation for opposite political programmes.Thus, the concordant essence of religion also seen as a humanistic aspiration, is subverted by political ambitions, when religion is employed as ideology.

Encountering religion in the framework of politics implies several things. First of all, the fact that religion is a form of social consciousness, makes it an active factor in political life, principally due to its prominent influence on the majority of the masses. The frame of mind, psyche, aspirations, social behaviour and political action of the followers/worshippers are actively mediated by the appeal of the divine dispensation. The ideological function of religion gets stronger with the increasing space for illusions and dreams of miracles. This explains why the political arena more often than not, is fraught with the ever-ensuing disputes between the adherents of secular ideals and denominational professions, even in contemporary context, remarkable scientific and technological progress, notwithstanding. Secondly, politicians find religion as a pliable tool and use its organizational network, dogma and moral precepts for political objectives. Sometimes, they use the same to reshape political movements, to suit their own expediency. Exploitation of religious sentiments and moods, at times, acquires subtle and dangerous form and results in religious bigotry on the one hand and in aggressive politics, on the other. Thirdly, religion begins to acquire ominous political overtones when it is used by political leaders and their followers to justify their political actions, in the form of an ideology that would express their interests, hopes and aspirations. It would warrant, therefore, to approach the question of the intermingling of religion and politics in a realistic vein, that is, to refrain from underestimating the role of religion in collective life, particularly, when ambitious, calculative political designs are in operation.

There could be no better testimony to the employment of religion in the service of politics, in all the above-stated senses, than the story of the partition of India in 1947 on religious pretext. The separatist political crusade, culminating in the demand for a separate homeland for the Muslims, carried out by Muslim intellectuals, the Muslim League and above all by Mohammad Ali Jinnah and blessed (for their own political interests) by the colonial masters, succeeded in creating the myth, however, exploded within two and a half decades and reopened the controversial question of the legitimacy/illegitimacy of substituting political categories for ill-emphasized religio-ideological categories.

The separatist political crusade, later on, termed as the Pakistan movement, was a political movement in religious guise from its very inception to its ultimate culmination in the partition, with M.A. Jinnah playing the decisive role and accomplishing the goal.

It is relevant to recall that ever since the disintegration of the Mughal Empire after Aurangzeb, Muslims in India had been urged to rally more than once. In order to acquire power, in the name of rehabilitating Islam, Shah Waliullah had gone as far as to invite Ahmed Shah Abdali to rid India of the scourge of Marathas. There had been the movement of the *Mujahideen* led by Syed Ahmed Barelvi dedicated to the establishment of an ideal Muslim state in the North-West Frontier. In Bengal the *Faraizi* Movement led by Haji Shariatullah had similar objectives.

It was with the armed rebellion of 1857 that the contours of a 'Muslim' identity were distinctly sharpened. Two major factors were responsible for this: *first,* given, the sources and pattern of rebellion, those who bore the brunt of British vengeance happened to be Muslims; *second,* influential Muslim leaders like Syed Ahmed Khan, in the wake of the rebellion, made conscious and persistent efforts to denigrate its methods and propagated arguments for its futility. They advocated, instead, a closing of the Muslim ranks and total loyalty to the British.[2] The persecution which the Muslims of North India suffered after the Mutiny as a punishment for their involvement in the holy war against the British, transformed Syed Ahmad Khan (1817-98), a *Munsif* in the East India Company's service, into a political leader committed to the Mission of turning the political tide in favour of his community by adoption of new methods. It is remarkable that he was too wise to dream of *revanche,* too practical to generate illusory aspirations of restoring Muslim rule in India, and too discreet to blame the persecutors on whose generosity he decided to depend for a prosperous and durable future for his co-religionists. Profession of unconditional and unlimited loyalty to British rule became the basis of a new political philosophy which Syed Ahmad preached for over four decades to ensure the dignity of the Muslims, as he perceived the notion.

After Syed Ahmad's demise[3], there was no Muslim political leader of stature for some time. His followers split into two groups : Nawab Mohsin-ul-Mulk (1837-1907) assumed the leadership of conservative 'Aligarh group', and, the progressive elements followed Badruddin Tyabji (1844-1906). The former persisted with anti-Congress and pro-British perspectives, whereas the latter supported the nationalist movement led by the Congress. The British rulers, not unexpectedly, persisted with their policy of wooing the Aligarh group's separatist machinations.

In October 1905, Bengal was partitioned at the behest of Lord Curzon, who had statutorily formulated and established the dormant official connivance to forge and legitimise regional identity of the Muslim community. Soon after the partition of Bengal, Nawab Mohsin-ul-Mulk persuaded the British government to create a separate political party for the Muslims of India as a parallel organisation to the Congress. On December 30, 1906, the All-India Muslim League was formed at Dhaka. Though, the Muslim League formally adopted the two-nation theory as its political ideology in the 1940s, it was born to foster the religio-communal approach for seeking political concessions and privileges for the Muslim minority.

Muslim League's demand for separate electorate was conceded by the British government under the Act of 1909. The political situation after the revocation of the partition of Bengal (1911), forced the League to take into consideration possibilities of cooperation with the Congress and to explore avenues of common struggle for the establishment of self-government in India. Under Mohammed Ali Jinnah's stewardship a temporary phase of unity between the League and the Congress was initiated.

In 1919, to Jinnah's displeasure, Gandhi took up the issue of Khilafat. The religious fervour aroused by the Khilafat Movement (1919-1924) weakened the hold of Jinnah on the League. Prominent Ulama, like Maulana Mohammad Ali and Maulana Shaukat Ali revived 'Pan-Islamic' sentiments of the Indian Muslims for the cause of the Khalifa of Turkey. However, the Khilafat agitation received a severe setback with the liberation of Turkey by Mustafa Kemal Pasha in March 1924. Consequently, the Ulama leadership of the Muslim League was relegated to inconsequential position. Also, Hindu-Muslim rivalry became more acute during the post-Khilafat agitation phase.

Mohammad Iqbal further strengthened the notion of two-nation in the subcontinent. In his opinion the crux of the problem of India was that the Hindu-Muslim conflict was a much deeper ideological cleavage, Islam *versus* nationalism. For him, the formulation of a polity on national lines meant a displacement of the Islamic principle of solidarity, and hence was unthinkable. In lending support to the 'two-nation' thereby, Iqbal was mainly concerned with the consolidation of the Muslims in the North-West of India where they were in a predominant majority. Iqbal projected the view that Muslims were not prepared to accept the notion of the Congress in respect of nationality as it could only mean submerging them under Hindu majority. In the later phase of his life, Iqbal rejected the territorial concept of nationalism as propagated by the Western thinkers. In his opinion, Muslim nationalism was based on religion and not on territorial nationality and racial prejudices.

Iqbal was not a professional politician, but his impact continued and increased in subsequent years in galvanising the two-nation theory and paved the way for the future struggle of the Muslims under Jinnah's leadership. It is notable that initially both Iqbal and Jinnah advocated one Indian nationality but while Iqbal changed his political trajectory almost as early as 1909, it took Jinnah about three decades to reach the same destination.[4] Indeed, Jinnah's long political career spans the extremes of an 'ambassador of Hindu-Muslim Unity' and a 'rank communalist'. As late as 1931, Jinnah asserted:

'I am an Indian first and a Muslim afterwards.'

True prior to the 1937 elections, Mohammad Ali Jinnah (1876-1948) did not believe in the sanctity of religion-based nationalism and the philosophy of the 'two-nation' theory. He adhered to the constitutional approach to solve political problems of the Muslim minority. He did not approve of the mass agitational tactics both of the Congress and the League during the Khilafat Movement. When Choudhry Rahmat Ali, a Bengali student of the Cambridge University, met Jinnah in 1933 at London's Waldorf Hotel with a scheme of partition, Jinnah rejected the scheme as 'an impossible dream'. For him the 'two-nation' theory was only an instrument to gain carve out a new State of which he would be the sovereign authority. Jinnah's appeal to religion was always ambiguous. Certainly it was not characteristic of his political style before 1937 and his use of the communal factor was a political tactic, not an ideological commitment.

The election of 1937 destroyed the foundations upon which Jinnah had built his strategy ever since his return to India from England in 1934. A shrewd tactician that he was, Jinnah launched a tirade against the Congress, and put forth a grossly exaggerated apprehension of the impending dangers for Muslims and Islam through the imposition of the alleged 'Fascist Hindu Raj' under the leadership of the Congress. Thus, in the post-1937 phase, Jinnah became the messiah of the movement for a separate homeland for the Muslims of the subcontinent.

When the Congress ministers resigned their offices in October 1939, on the plea that India had been dragged into the Second World War, without consulting Indian leaders, it seems Jinnah was waiting for such an opportunity. Jinnah called upon Muslims of India to celebrate the exit of Congress ministries as, what he called, the "Deliverance Day", on 22 December, 1939. Jinnah exploited the situation by brazenly distorting facts: "I wish the Mussalmans all over India to observe Friday, the 22nd December as the Day of Deliverance...That the Congress ministry both in the discharge of their duties of administration and in the legislatures flout the Muslim opinion, to destroy Muslim culture... Supported and advanced the cause of the Hindus...."

By 1940, the Muslim League perspectives had hardened and the notion of Pakistan had come to be its major political priority and preoccupation. Pakistan became a "gospel, the very soul of the Muslim League, the faith for which Muslims were asked to die."[7]

In his presidential address at the Lahore session of the Muslim League (March 22, 1940), Jinnah left no doubt about his 'two-nation' perception. He stated : 'The problem in India is not of an inter-communal character but manifestly of an international one... If the British government are really in earnest and sincere to secure peace and happiness for the people of the subcontinent, the only course open to us is to allow the major nations separate homelands by dividing India into autonomous national states... It is extremely difficult to appreciate why our Hindu friends fail to understand the real nature of Islam and Hinduism. They are not religions in the strict sense of the word, but are, in fact, different and distinct social orders, and it is a dream that the Hindus and Muslims can ever evolve a common nationality... To yoke together two such nations under a single state, one as a numerical minority and the other as a majority, must lead to growing discontent and final destruction of any fabric that may be built up for the government of such a state... Mussalmans are a nation according to any definition of a nation and they must have their homeland, their territory and their states."[8]

Jinnah was emboldened to propound the thesis that India was not a 'country' but a 'subcontinent', that it was inhabited by many peoples among whom the chief were the Hindus and the Muslims, who constituted two distinct nations, in conformity with alleged indices of classical notions in this regard. Consequently, the Muslim nation in India was entitled to the right of self-determination. In expoundng the 'two-nation' theory Jinnah had, in fact, transformed Iqbal's theory of Muslim communalism into what may be called Muslim nationalism. Jinnah's call to the Muslims was to come forward "as servants of Islam, organize the people economically, socially, educationally and politically and I am sure that you will be a power that will be accepted by everybody."[9]

On 23 March, 1940, the All-India Muslim League at Lahore in its twenty-seventh Annual Session adopted the Resolution, subsequently identified as "Pakistan Resolution". The Resolution in part read : "... this session of the All-India Muslim League emphatically reiterates that the scheme of Federation embodied in the Government of India Act, 1935, is totally unsuited to and unworkable in the peculiar conditions of this country, and is altogether unacceptable to Muslim India... Resolved that it is the considered view of this session of the All-India Muslim League that no constitutional plan would be workable in this country or acceptable to Muslims unless it is designed on the following basic principle, namely that geographically contiguous units are demarcated into regions which should be so constituted with such territorial readjustments as may be necessary, that the areas in which the Muslims are numerically in a majority, as in the North-Western and Eastern zones of India, should be grouped to constitute 'independent States' in which the constituent units shall be autonomous and sovereign... that adequate, effective and mandatory safeguards should be provided in the constitution for minorities in these units in the regions for the protection of their religious, cultural, economic, poltical, administrative and other rights."[10]

After the passage of the "Pakistan Resolution", Jinnah adopted an uncompromisng stance towards the Congress. He asserted that the Congress was not a national organisation but a "Fascist Grand Council". In his speech at the Muslim University Union, Aligarh (March 10, 1941), Jinnah categorically said : "As a matter of fact, Pakistan has been there for centuries, it is there today, and it will remain till the end of the world. It was taken away from us; we have only to take it back. What is the title of the Hindus to it? How can we be prevented from claiming what is our own? Pakistan is not only a practical goal but the only goal, if you want to save Islam from complete annihilation in this country. We have yet to go a long way, Pakistan is there."[11]

At the Madras session (April 1941) of the Muslim League, the two-nation theory was formally inducted in the Constitution, declaring it as the 'official ideology' of the party.

During the period 1940-47, Jinnah acquried a decisive place in the Muslim League. He was accepted as a messiah by and large. During this period, Jinnah's contradictions became apparent. On the one hand, he reverted to taking recourse to political and constitutional devices for realisation of the objective of Pakistan, and on the other, he did oppose the British government's involvement in the parleys that preceded the partition of India. And yet, he had no qualms about exploiting the religious susceptibilities of the Muslims in pursuance of what was basically a political objective. He realised that it was more convenient to sway the Muslims by giving a call which was expressively religious, since he was convinced that it was beyond the commonman's comprehension to discern the complicated strands of constitutional sophistication.

After the Lahore (Pakistan) Resolution, the League chose to follow an ambivalent strategy. It stubbornly stuck to its stand of rejecting any plan or proposals mutilating the basic spirit of the Lahore Resolution, and on the other hand, it agreed to negotiate with the Congress in the context of various British proposals. The expedient decision to join the Constituent Assembly (June 1946), however, amounted to hindering and obstructing the very purpose of the institution on the sole pretext of irreversibility of the demand for Pakistan.

Ironically, religion based parties such as the *Jamaat-i-Islami, The Khaksar Party* and the *Ahrar Party* condemned Jinnah's two-nation theory and openly denounced the demand of Pakistan. These religious parties had little faith in the leadership of Jinnah, perceived by them as a thoroughly westernised barrister and a politician[12] with a wavering record of affiliations. It was openly stated that Jinnah knew little about the Islamic way of life and value postulates enshrined in the Holy Quran. Instead of accepting Jinnah as 'Quaid-i-Azam,' the religious parties called him 'Kafir-i-Azam.' Punjab's Unionist Party, Bengal's Krishak Praja Party and the dominant Muslim Party in Sind spurned the relgious slogans of the League, rebuffed Jinnah's initiatives and stressed that India's Muslims had deep roots in Indian society and were natural inhabitants of an Indian world. The activitism of the Jamiyat-al-Ulama, the Momin Conference, Khudai Khidmatgars and the Shia Political Conference, disproves the generally accepted notion that the Pakistan movement was unified and ideologically cohesive or that its progress was unimpeded by the overwhelming enthusiasm of the Muslim masses and the intelligentsia alike. Maulana Hussain Ahmed Madani, in particular, advocated full Muslim participation in the freedom struggle and advanced the concept of territorial nation-hood for India, an idea sharply rebutted by Iqbal.[13]

Ultimately, however, a separate state of Pakistan was carved out of the Indian subcontinent. The Muslim League under Jinnah's stewardship raised the bogey of 'Islam in danger' and appealed to religious susceptibilities of Muslims who, in any case, were oblivious of the consequences of transfer of populations across the border and were successfully kept in the dark about the nature of the envisaged socio-econo-political system in the 'land of pure', Pakistan.

Asghar Ali Engineer has rightly commented that India got divided not because Hinduism and Islam were incompatible, they never were—but because the elites of the two communities could not successfully evolve proper power-sharing arrangements between themselves. Indeed, the secular elite in both the communities while showing indifference to religion in personal life, used it most cynically to realise their political ambitions.[14]

In summing up, it could be stated that the Pakistan political movement waged under a religious guise, substituted political categories by religio-ideological ones. Consequently, the disparity between the movement's religio-ideological shell and the genuine interests of the followers were crudely disregarded. The exaggerated jurisdiction assumed for themselves by master strategists, like Mohammad Ali Jinnah, personalized the movement to an overwhelming extent and throttled growth of spontaneous initiatives. In spite of intense political programming accomplished in the name of Islam, the subsequent political scenario in the Indian subcontinent, and particularly in Pakistan, persistently raises the inconvenient issue of the true legitimacy of religion intermingling with politics, with questionable motives. Lenin warned against pushing religion to the forefront, in the political sphere, where it certainly did not belong. Gandhi fought against the divisive consequences of the 'jehadic' religio-ideological crusade. Both have been betrayed, yet proved right by the subsequent course of events.

REFERENCES

1. See, *Harijan*, January 26, 1934.
2. See Abbas Rashid, "Pakistan : The Ideological Dimension", in Mohammad Asghar Khan (ed.), *The Pakistan Experience : State and Religion* (Lahore, Vanguard, 1985), pp. 72-73.
3. Sir Syed Ahmad Khan's contemporary, Saiyid Jamal-ul-din-al Afghani (1838-1897), had insisted that destiny of the Muslims of Central Asia was to form a state with Afghanistan and the Muslim majority area of north-western India.
4. Saleem M.M. Qureshi, *The Politics of Jinnah* (Karachi, Royal Books, 1988), pp. 1-23.
5. Rahmat Ali presented a scheme of partition in 1933 demanding a federation of three Muslim States—'Pakistan' (Punjab, Kashmir, NWFP, Sind and Baluchistan), 'Bangladesh' and 'Osmanistan'. In 1920, Muhammad Abdul Qadir had suggested the division of the subcontinent between the 'Hindus' and 'Muslims'. Lala Laj Pat Rai, one of the founders of the Hindu Mahasabha, had also suggested the partition of India between two regions—the 'Hindu' and the 'Muslim' regions.
6. Ayesha Jalal, *The Sole Spokesman : Jinnah, The Muslim League and the Demand for Pakistan*, (Cambridge, Cambridge University Press, 1985), p. 5.
7. Wayne A.Wilcox : *Pakistan : The Consolidation of a Nation*, (New York, Columbia University Press, 1968), p. 27.
8. For details see : Syed Shameem Hussain Kadri : *Creation of Pakistan*, (Lahore, Wajidalis, 1982), pp. 182-189.
9. *Ibid.*, p. 188.
10. *Ibid.*, pp. 191-192.
11. *Ibid.*, pp. 214-215.
12. For Jinnah's biographical details see : Stanley Wolpert, *Jinnah of Pakistan*, (New Delhi, Oxford, 1985).
13. See for details Mushirul Hasan (ed.), *India Partitioned : The Other Face of Freedom*, two volumes, (New Delhi, Roli Books, 1995).
14. Asghar Ali Engineer, "Gandhiji, Religion and Communal Harmony", *Towards Secular India*, (Vol. 1, January-March 1995), pp. 90-91.

14

Sir Syed Ahmed Khan
Educationalist, Social and Religious Thinker

T.K. Mathur

It is seldom in the history of human affairs that men have left their imprint in the sands of time and influenced generations of their countrymen and inspired countless number of his co-religionists to benefit from the fruits of higher education as Sir Syed Ahmed Khan did in the last quarter of the nineteenth century. Since the death of Sir Salar Jang, Sir Syed Ahmed became the foremost Mohammedan in India as regards force of character, influence over his fellow-men and literary ability. He traced his ancestry to noble families in Herat who later migrated to Hindustan and took service under the Moghuls. Sir Syed's father, Syed Mohammed Takki was a recluse—a man of deep religious feeling—and, on his father's death declined all titles from the Emperor, though offered those of his father. Early in his life Sir Syed came under the increasing influence of his maternal grandfather, Khawaja Fariduddin who became the Prime Minister of Mughal Emperor Akbar-II when the Moghul empire had virtually ceased to exist and was only there in name.[1] Around the same time Sir Syed also came in contact with Major General Sir David Ochterlony, who was British Resident at Delhi and noted for his administrative acumen. In 1836, Sir Syed lost his father and succeeded to the family titles at the hands of the last Moghul ruler, Bahadur Shah. He was also made Master of War though the only time he saw action was during the uprising of 1857 and in that he performed very creditably.

In January 1837, he entered the service of the British as *Shiristehdar* of the Criminal Department in the Sadr Amin's office at Delhi. He was soon elevated to the post of Munsif or Judge in 1841.[2] Around the same time Sir Syed took up literary pursuits and published his "Transcript and Analysis of the Regulations" in 1846. But he was really noticed when in the following year he published his "Archaeological History of the Ruins of Delhi."[3] After posting in Rohtak till 1850, Sir Syed was posted as Sub-judge at Bijnore where he remained till hostilities broke out in 1857.

During the 1857 uprising Sir Syed remained steadfastly loyal to the British. He helped to save the lives of Europeans stranded in Bijnore and was made administrator of the district. The events of 1857 sickened Sir Syed considerably and the ruin of his favourite city of Delhi left him utterly desolate. The sufferings of his family, especially his mother, who subsisted on horses' grain and nearly no water for nearly a week, made Sir Syed a very bitter but determined man. Hindus and Muslims alike suffered great repression but in Delhi and Rohilkhand it was the courtly and landed Muslim elite to whom the punishment came with a specially heavy hand.

Growth of Ideas on Education

Sir Syed's loyalty to the British during the events of 1857 was not the outcome of desire for furtherance in career advancement. He was of the firm conviction that the British regime was a vast improvement on the 'earlier more directly predatory monarchies'. He deplored the Machiavellian motives of self-seeking leaders of the 1857 uprising who sought to make use of the lack of understanding between the new rulers and the ruled. His speech at the Scientific Society Institute in Aligarh on May 10, 1866 reflected his views and deep insight into history and the view on the era gone by. He said:

> "Gentlemen, if we look back upon that period of India's history which was passed by her under a despotic government we find kings or rajahs possessed of unlimited power and authority over their subject-millions, and we

know that their governments, instead of being guided by laws of reason and justice, were carried on according to their arbitrary will, their caprices, or by their passions. The title 'Disposer of people's lives' and other similar titles which were adopted by kings and emperors of India, was meant to express their power over their people for good or evil, though I am afraid that, were the balance to be struck between the two, the later would be found to have outweighed the former, and the title in most cases to have been thus synonymous with vice, tyranny and self-seeking. The ancestors of your fellow-countrymen now present experienced this despotism, to numbers of them perhaps the sources of high position, of wealth, or of excitement; and it is, therefore, perhaps but natural that their descendants, many of them, should thirst after that Government which was so favourable to the indulgence of the passions of their forefathers. If, however, they will but calmly and deliberately reflect—if they will but review those times, those reigns of their former kings according to the principles of justice and morality—they will be convinced that the manifold evils which such Governments were to source to the country at large, were dearly paid for by the benefits wrought upon the fortunes of the few. The rule of these former emperors and rajahs were neither in accordance with the Hindu nor the Mohammedan religion. It was based upon nothing but tyranny and oppression : the law of might was that of right; the voice of the people was not listened to; the strong and the turbulent oppressed the feeble and the poor, and usurped all their privileges with impunity for their own selfish ends. It is only, therefore, by such usurpers and turbulent spirits that a despotism such as flourished in Hindustan for many long centuries is at all to be desired."[4]

Sir Syed longed to redress the indignities heaped upon his community but instead of sympathy he sought to make them self-reliant, take pride in their history, cultural achievements and contribution to national life. To keep them in the national mainstream he saw the benefits of modern education as the proper catylist.

In 1859, he made a beginning, on an experimental basis, by the foundation of a Persian madrasa in Murshidabad where English, modern history, Urdu and Persian were the main subjects to be taught. Sir Syed then shocked the establishment by his endorsement of English language as the medium of instruction in place of Urdu thus positioning himself against the official policy as advocated in the famous dispatch of Sir Charles Wood which prescribed "vernacular" education for the schools. His advocacy for preference for the English langauge steemed from the fact that their did not exist sufficient textbooks in Urdu nor could a person acquire a sharp intellect, sound mind, orginality of thought and ability to reason clearly and logically without the aid of English. The establishment of Translation Society at Ghazipur (later renamed as Scientific Society and shifted to Aligarh) was the next step in the quest for academic growth by Sir Syed.[5]

The Society embarked upon the task of translating many classics of foreign langauges into Urdu. Sir Syed also advocated to the Viceroy that either a Vernacular University be founded or alternatively an Urdu Faculty be setup in Calcutta University. Later Sir Syed backtracked on the proposal for a Vernacular University as he himself had criticized this concept earlier.

In 1869, Sir Syed embarked on a journey to England along with his son Syed Mohmud who had been awarded a Government scholarship. Sir Syed hoped to analyse the factors which contributed so substantially to the growth of civilization in England and Europe. His *Safarnama* (travel diary) makes very illuminating reading and reveals his keenness for details. His visit overseas revolutionized his outlook. His letter to the Secretary, Scientific Society, dated 15th October, 1869 reflected his changed outlook. He observed :

> "I am happy that the Bengalis and Parsis have acquired modern culture but our brother Hindus and unfortunate Muslims are still living in a primitive state. The Muslims dwell on the glorious achievements of their forefathers and consider themselves superior to all other races. They

are blind to the beauties of the modern garden of gay flowers blooming before them."[6]

It was while in England that Sir Syed finalized his plans for founding a modern college at Aligarh. His return to India in 1870 was greeted with hostility by members of his community which viewed his emphasis on English education as the first step to conversion to Christianity. But Sir Syed was undeterred by such reactions and went ahead with his plans. He formed many Committees, the premier being *Khazinat-ul-Biza 'at li Tasis-i Madrasat-ul-Musalmanan* (Contributory Fund for the Foundation of the Muslim College) and launched his scheme. To counter the malacious propoganda launched against him by the fundamentalist element in his community, Sir Syed took recourse to journalism and published strong rejoinders in *Tahzib ul Aehlaf.* Resigning from Government services in 1876, Sir Syed shifted permanently to Aligarh and got Lord Lytton, the Viceroy, to lay the foundation-stone of M.A.O. College on January 10, 1877. From the start the theologicians and the *Ulema* started issuing *Fatwas* against him and accused him of heresay because he dared to identify the laws of Nature with the laws of God. To them he was not a true believer but a *Nechari* (believer in nature). Sir Syed won many adherents from non-Muslims also. The ruling families of Viziyanagaram and Patiala were his patrons. Among the Britishers Sir William Muir, Lieutenant Governor of U.P. and W.W. Hunter, the author of *Imperial Gazetteer* series were liberal donors to the new college.

Though his primary aim was to encourage modern education amongst the Muslims yet he kept the doors of his college open for members of other communities as well. He often reiterated his position :

"... in matters of admissions and education at the college, there is absolutely no distinction between the two (Hindus and Muslims)."[7]

The Management Committee bore a secular character with the induction of six Hindus into it. Sir Syed was able to attract some of the finest educational administrators to his college.

The most distinguished of them was Theodore Beck, a prominent graduate of Trinity College, Cambridge, who succeeded H.G.I. Siddims (the first Principal of the College) in 1883. Beck soon became the dominant voice on the campus. He also became the subject of many a witty phrase. As Tufail Ahmed, an old boy, was to recall :

> "Qaum khuda ki, College Sir Syed Ka, hukum Beck Bahadur ka" (The community belongs to God, College to Sir Syed, authority to Mr. Beck.)

Beck tried to keep the students of M.A.O. away from the Indian National Congress on the grounds that it was a Hindu Organization. Sir Syed himself condemned the Indian National Congress in Lucknow during a speech in 1887, attacking it for fostering the aspirations of the lower classes and encouraging the principle of elections. This unusual stance was aimed at winning the support of the landed gentry. The bestowing of the Knighthood was probably more as a tribute to his loyalty to the British rather than his contribution to the cause of education.

Views on Society and Religion

Sir Syed's contribution to the cause of education amongst his co-religionists also displayed another aspect of his multi-faceted personality—his sense of duty towards true religion. Thus on one hand we observe Sir Syed taking up issues with his close friend Sir William Muir over the latter's views expressed in *Life of Mohammed* and on the other hand his repudiation of charges levied against him of heresy by theologians and the *Ulema.* One view which was gaining increasing acceptance in the late nineteenth century was the belief in the necessity of fitting contemporary life into the traditional framework. Sir Syed saw too much of life, and was too acutely conscious of its demands to agree, wholeheartedly with this view. He did not receive a formal education in religion as was recognized in those days nor did he lead a religious life according to the norms set in those days. In his boyhood he did study of Persian and Arabic but it seems he did it without much application or commitment. Nor is evidence forthcoming of his association with religious minded people. His attitude towards learning and knowledge was more out of an inner urge to accomplish self-imposed tasks. Thus it was subjects like mathematics, astronomy and medicine which attracted him most rather than courses in religious instructions. But whatever his academic pursuits he went about them with single-minded dedication and commitment for perfection. Thus he proposed to compile a commentary on the *Bible* with the aim of proving that there was no disagreement between it and the *Quran* and towards this end he learnt Hebrew, set up a printing-press, with Hebrew, English and Urdu types. Unfortunately, he could complete only a part of this work though the effort put into this was enormous.[8]

Sir Syed's early life and his upbringing was no pointer to the shape of things to come. He preferred service under the British to high sounding titles under the Moghuls. The strength of character and the stiffening of the moral fibre came only after he witnessed the carnage in the aftermath of the events of 1857-58. It was only then that he decided to become a leader of men and a reformer in society.

In the technical sense, as mentioned earlier Sir Syed does not merit consideration as a very serious religious thinker of his age. But his sincere convictions as a sensitive Muslim were always in evidence. In 1870, he published *'A series of Essays on the Life of Mohammed, and subjects susidiary thereto'* in English. The object appeared to be to put before the average Englishmen to true to learn nature of Islam. At the same time he took up issues with Sir William Muir over the later's *Life of Mohammed* in which the author had accused *'Mohammedanism'* as a religion of the sword. Sir Syed's rejoinder was :

> "The remark that, 'the sword is the inevitable penalty for the denial of Islam', is one of the charges falsely imputed to this faith by the professors of other religions, and arises from the utter ignorance of those who make the accusation. Islam inculcates and demands a hearty and sincere belief in all that it teaches; and that genuine faith which proceeds from a person's heart cannot be obtained by force or

violence. Judicious readers will not fail to observe that the above-quoted remark is entirely contrary to the fundamental principles of the Muslim faith, wherein it is inculcated in the clearest language possible. Let there be no forcing in religion; the right way has been made clearly distinguishable from the wrong one" (Chap. X : 98). And also: "If the Lord had pleased, all who are on the earth would have believed together; and wilt thou force men to be believers? No man can believe but by the permission of God, and he will pour out His indignation on those who will not under stood" (Chap. 11: 257). The principle upon which Moses was allowed to use the sword to extirpate all idolators and infidels, without exception of one single individual, is by no means applicable to Islam. Mohammedanism grasped the sword, not to destroy all infidels and pagans, not to force men to become Muslims at the sword's point, but only to proclaim that eternal truth, the unity of the godhead, throughout the whole extant of the then known globe. According to Islam, the best and the most meritorious act is the preaching and making generally known the existence of one invisible god. It could hardly be expected that, in the infidel countness, there could be sufficient personal security for such Muslims who might choose to inculcate by precept, exhort by preaching and practise openly the worship of the unity of God, and therefore, appeal was made at once to the sword in order to establish the superiority of the Moslem power, and to ensure security and tranquillity for such Mohammedans as might choose to preach the wholesome doctrine of their faith, and to live in peace in those countries so that their habits, conduct, and manner of living might serve as an example for the unbelievers."[9]

One is hard pressed to find another Muslim so keen and determined to preserve the honour of Islam as Sir Syed in the world of scholarship. Sir Syed had, in fact, a secular mind, or rather one dominated by common sense, and he sought to achieve essentially secular values. He was deeply concerned about the decline in the status and honour of Muslims in India.

He was convinced that the traditional view of Islam was a hindrance in the progress of Muslims. Sir Syed was intrigued that eductional progress, scientific temper, economic security, to open avenues of honest employment, removal of blemishes in social life and eradication of evil customs and bad habits were not attributed to religiousness and to love of the Muslims but to absorption in worldliness. Even such basic considerations of welfare could reduce religion to a means of worldly benefit and deprive it of spiritual content. Sir Syed had the insight and sincerity to pick up those issues with religious thinkers which the latter had been evading for generation. Take the question of a *mujtabid* (a scholar entitled to give his own opinion in matters of land and correct practice). The *Ahl-i-Sunnah W'al-Jamaah* and (concept of a united community) of the later ages had evolved the erroneous concept, thus ran the argument, that the principle of *ijtihad* (relying on one's own judgement or opinion where no known act or opinion of the Prophet could serve as a relevant precedent) was no longer to be acted upon and nobody could then become a *mujtabid.* But the *Ulema* hold the view that every age should have its *mujtahid.* But Sir Syed argued, this error in thinking rendered great harm to the Islamic community. As circumstances kept changing daily and new problems arose continuously, then a *mujhabid* was essential to resolve these issues. Sir Syed himself laid no claims to be styled a *mujtahid* but the views put forward by him entitled him to be ranked as one. He declared that the doctrines of Islam are fundamental in two ways, some are based clearly on the Quran and authentic *Hadiths* and are fundamental in themselves. They constitute the basis of Islam, and are in accordance with the laws of nature. Other doctrines, which may or may not be in accordance with the laws of nature, are to be regarded as fundamental because they follow logically from those of the first type, and both support and supplement each other. In practice, both have equal validity and belief in both is equally obligatory. To emphasize this point Sir Syed quoted for instance the fundamental doctrine in regard to *namaz* (prayer) is concentration of thought on God; other doctrines related to this, such as *wudu* (ablutions) standing sitting etc. support and establish this doctrine. That is why, in case of illness or inability, these can be given up, but concentration of thought on God always remains obligatory. This was *ijtihad* with a vengeance.[10]

Sir Syed applied the criterion of 'nature' to doctrines about the person and attributes of God and held that statements in regard to them in the *Quran* and *Hadith* were to be considered allegorical or metaphorical, and not to be taken literally. Thus for Sir Syed, statements with regard to Day of Judgement, Heaven and Hell, Angels should be considered as personified powers of nature. The *jinhs* should be equated with wild tribes of the deserts and mountains. *Satan* was not a being but the personification of man's lower self, the argument continued. But thinkers like Sir Syed (styled *Necharis*) were questioned by the orthodox school led by Maulwi Nadhir Ahmed which expressed surprise that men like Sir Syed believed in God but were surprised at or disbelieved any of the abovementioned things. Maulwi Nadhir Ahmed often advised the sensible and God fearing Muslim thus :

> "Don't let your faith be shaken....Just as we do not strain our eyes to see the dark, we must not strain our minds to discover the deep secrets of God's wisdom."

More important and more specific was Sir Syed's stand on the issue of slavery and polygamy. Time and again he drove the point home that the institution of slavery was against nature and the will of God. No human could own or be owned by another human. Sir Syed also quoted the clear and final injunction of the *Quran* which explicitly laid down that prisoners of war should either be set free or ransomed. In this, he enjoyed the support of the *ulema* as well. Scholars of that age were aghast that the injunctions of the holy *Quran* were set aside in the pursuit of worldly interests. However, slavery in the time of Sir Syed was no longer a recognized institution. Other issues on which Sir Syed lent his views were polygamy, usuary and mode of dress. On polygamy he was of the view that polygamy could only be held permissible if the husband could do equal justice to his wives. Usuary was prohibited but not interest on Government Promissory notes and loans. There was nothing which prohibited a Muslim from dressing and eating like a non-Muslim. Sir Syed often clinched his arguments by stating that side by side with love based on community of faith (*hubb-i-imani*), there could be love based on common humanity (*hubb-i-insani*).[12]

Sir Syed was either immensely admired or intensely disliked. Even amongst his admirers even those closest to him did not agree with him wholeheartedly. From mid-eighteen seventees onwards, he was increasingly pre-occupied with his newly founded school which was soon elevated to the status of a college. To get his new institution acceptance and respectability Sir Syed was willing to strike a bargain with his co-religionists. The syllabus framed for theology omitted the new ideas on Islam as propagated by Sir Syed and his friends. This compromise was not to the liking of some of his admirers who accused him of abandoning all the moral values and capacity for sustained speculation on a higher plane on religious subjects. He was also accused of sacrificing the reconstruction of the social and economic life of whole community to secure recruitment in the lower grades of Government service for the sons of a few hundred Muslim families.[13]

Sir Syed went far beyond any religious thinker before him in giving concrete form to the concept of *amal-i-salih*, good works. But his moralizing met with limited success as neither the truly religious nor those who adhered to the traditional view that a Muslim should be guided by principles that would assure his salvation, were impressed by his emphasis on success in this world. But if Sir Syed lay exposed to charges of self-interest and worldliness, his opponents and critics lacked the moral and spiritual fibre to offer an alternative leadership.

Sir Syed's views led the community to a cross-road where it was forced to choose an alternative. The dilemma laid bare was what constituted the ideal of the good life and could it be achieved. One viewpoint laid stress upon an independent and uninhibited study of the *Quran* and the *Hadith* with a view to finding out what constituted the good life. The other viewpoint stressed upon living what healthy instinct, intuition and spiritual vision indicated to them as being the good life, and regarding the *Quran* and the *Hadith* as sources of strength and inspiration. Without healthy instinct, intuition and spiritual vision, the study of holy *Quran* and *Hadith* will produce only the type of *Ulama* who were far removed from all contemporary cultural and political movements and changes. The good Muslim was thus enjoined upon to discover for himself what constitued the good life and through his work accept the social and political responsibilities and become a moral person.

Sir Syed Ahmed strode like a giant among men in the nineteenth century and in an age when the intellectual life in the country was in a ferment, he had the courage of conviction to stand by his assertions.

REFERENCES

1. Lt. Colonel G.F.I. Graham, *The Life and Work of* Syed *Ahmed Khan*, p. 2. Idarah-i-Adabiyat-l, New Delhi, Reprit, 1974.
2. *Ibid.*, p. 7.
3. *Ibid.*, pp. 9-18.
4. *Ibid.*, pp. 72-78.
5. See Prof. Iqbal Hussain, 'Aligarh : The Founder and his work' in *AMU, NEWS & VIEWS, Special Number. On Occasion of Indian History Congress* dt. 15 December, 1994.
6. *Ibid.*
7. *Ibid.*
8. M. Mujeeb, *The Indian Muslims.* Liverpool, England, 1967, pp. 458-59.
9. Lt. Col. Grahm, pp. 106-10.
10. Altaf Hussain Hate *Hayat-i-Jawed* Agra, 1903, Pt. II, pp. 215-16, *Op. cit.*, M. Mujeeb, p. 450, Hali was Sir Syed's biographer.
11. M. Mujeeb, *op. cit.*, p. 211.
12. *Ibid.*, p. 451.
13. Ram Gopal, *The Indian Muslims,* Bombay, 1959, p. 58.

15

Religious and Moral Education as an Important Component of Sir Syed's Educational Programme
A Critique

M.R. Kazimi

Philosophy will be in our right hand and natural science in our left and the *Kalimah* will crown our head.

—*Sir Syed Ahmed Khan*

The events of 1857 had left the Muslims badly bruised. All their dreams and aspirations had come to an end. They lay utterly dejected and depressed. The future did not hold out any promise. Worse still, the Muslims had been made special target of represssion. Hundreds had been done to death. Thousands had been uprooted.[1] There was darkness all-round. There was a dreary blankness in their minds, a vacuum which sought for something to fill it.[2] At this critical juncture emerged Syed Ahmed Khan (1817-1898) who has been described as 'the spokesman of the inchoate aspirations of the ruined Muslims.[3]

It may be recalled that Syed Ahmed Khan, who was in the thick of affairs during Mutiny, thought that 'British sovereignty could never be eliminated from India'. Earlier, the eminent poet, Ghalib, had advised him to examine the English mind. Syed Ahmed took the advice with a dedication which was characteristics of him.[4] Again, the first edition of his celebrated work *Aasar-e-Sanadid* contained a full chapter on Maulana Syed

Ahmed Saheed in which Syed Ahmed waxed eloquent but preferred to delete it when the second edition appeared in 1854, three years before Mutiny.[5] Even before the Mutiny of 1857, Syed Ahmed Khan had been convinced that the Britishers were destined to rule India for good. The events of 1857 simply confined him in his belief. Invincibility of the British Empire appeared to the only reality. Syed Ahmed cannot be faulted if he held the opinion in the post-1857 era.

Syed Ahmed Khan (affectionately called Sir Syed) took upon himself the responsibility to bring about a rapprochement between the ruling Britishers and the Muslims, the ruled. His first attempt was to get the Muslims exonerated of the allegation that they had been prime movers in the rebellion for which they had been made to suffer all sorts of indignities and humiliations. Sir Syed through his works, *Risala Asbab-i-Bhagawat-i-Hind* and *Risala Khairkhwahan Mussalman* (in three parts), aimed at reconciling the British rulers to their Muslim subjects. "It is my heartfelt desire and prayer to God that our Government and the people of India be so connected together as to be of one accord", Sir Syed is reported to have said in 1859.[6] Sir Syed had been pained to find that the Muslims preferred to remain in their shells, avoided modern education and lived in day-dreams of the restoration of the old order. The community had reached its *nadir*, averred Sir Syed, because it avoided modern Western education. The Hindus had marched ahead but the Muslims did not follow suit.[7] As such, the primary concern of Sir Syed had been to impart a liberal education of the best type of the Muslim youth who continued to languish in backwardness, compared to Hindus of the time. Gradually 'after much debate and difficulty',[8] Sir Syed could turn the minds of Muslims towards Western education. But Sir Syed could not make much headway in this regard, he had to cope with the widespread anti-British feelings among the Muslims which had by then, became synonymous with their religious belief.[9] As is well known, Sir Syed adoptd a two-pronged policy. He concentrated his attention on spreading Western education among the Muslims and also worked for the cultivation of friendly feelings in them towards the British.

Sir Syed knew that unless the Muslims were made free of their orthodox traditional beliefs and faiths, he would not succeed in bringing about conciliations between the Christians and the Muslims. He wanted to draw the Cross and the Crescent together and wanted a review of Islamic laws which enabled the Muslims to take a favourable view of the Christians. It is alleged, all this was done with a view to establishing satisfactory relationship between the Muslim subjects and the Christian ruler. It was with this end in view that Sir Syed prepared a commentary on the *Bible* (*Tabyinal-Kalam*) which sought to show closeness between Islam and Christianity. Similarities were focused : dissimilarities explained away.[10] In order to give a new touch to teachings of Islam, Sir Syed came out with a new version of *Ilmul Kalam*.[11]

It may be mentioned in the passing that Sir Syed had taken up this onerous responsibility of giving modern interpretation to Islam at a time when all the world over Islam had been made the principal object of attack. The decadence in Muslim world in Asia and Africa had given a new lease to the critics who maintained that Islam had lost its relevance in the fast changing world scenario. It was alleged that the new discoveries and the new dimensions of knowledge unleashed in the West by the spread of science made many fundamental postulates of the Islam redundant and indefensible Sir Syed sought to prove that such insinuations were far fetched and based on ignorance of the true spirit and meaning of Islam.[12]

Among the forces which helped Sir Syed in formulating his theological views, the principal had been his 'leaning towards *Wahabism*'. He held Shah Abdul Aziz in high esteem. Following that tradition, he decried the ever widening gap between the basic tenets of Islam, as given by the Prophet and the state of Islamic practice in India. Sir Syed had been highly critical of innovations. Hunter's uncharitable remarks against *Wahabism* had pained Sir Syed greatly. He rebuted the allegations made by Hunter and proved Hunter wrong in his understanding of the basic postulates. Sir Syed explained *Wahabism* as a system which reduces the religion of Mohammad to a pure theism—to what Islam was in the days of

Mohammad.[13] However, the Wahabi uprising in 1831 and its end in fiasco had disillusioned and depressed Sir Syed and since then, he remained committed to the belief that the British were invincible.

Sir Syed had been alarmed over the new thrust in the activities of the Christian missionaries. Not only that the missionaries had taken up the task of converting Hindus and Muslims to their faith, some of them challenged the basic tenets of Islam by calling them outdated and redundant. In particular, Henry Martyn, Rev. Joseph Wolff and, above all, Carl Gottlieb Pfander were prominent among the missionaries to intensify and sharpen the controversy between Christianity and Islam.[14] William Muir, a friend of Sir Syed himself, had taken liberty to make fun of Mussalman's "ignorance of history". Piqued over such outrageous criticism, Sir Syed had brought out a number of memoranda to defend Islam against missionary criticism.

It appears Sir Syed had been very much impressed by the reformist movements among Hindus, especially by Raja Rammohan Roy. Raja had a successful attempt to bring about a compromise between Hindu faith and modern conditions. As the Muslims were facing the same situation, Sir Syed decided to launch a movement on the same line. Much common ground between the thought of Raja Rammohan Roy and that of Sir Syed may be discerned.[15] While Sir Syed responded warmly to Raja's efforts, he was appalled at the efforts of Dayanand Saraswati, whose 'Arya Samaj' made spectacular advances in 1880s and 1890s. The message of Dayanand combined sharp criticism of many existing Hindu practices with an extremely aggressive assertion of the superiority over all other faiths. It believed in purified Hinduism based on *Vedic* infallibility. It aimed at pan-Hindu revivalism. Sir Syed could not remain indifferent to the attacks mounted on Islam in India from different corners.

It should not be supposed, however, that Sir Syed developed his theological quest only in the post-1857 phase. The importance of the events of 1857 should not be allowed to obscure the fact that his theological mind had begun forming much earlier. A perusal of his seven works done before 1857 would reveal that the upbringing and early education in his remarkable family and later on his personal religious studies in his intellectually vivid atmosphere of pre-1857 Delhi contributed to a genuine concern for the purity and strength of Islamic belief and practice in India. This led to his active participation in contemporary religious debate, and the endeavour to reform. His later works in the field of theology were, therefore, not produced for want of other, more effective means to achieve his (allegedly) secular aims. They grew out of a long-existing commitment to, and an ever-widening knowledge of the theological tradition of Islam.[16] Even in his earlier writings, Sir Syed made endeavour to bring Prophet back into the mainstream of religious life of individual and society, and his desire to unmask all innovations in the lines of Indian Muslims which could be attributed to their non-Muslim environment. He desired total conformity to *Sunnat*, avoiding innovations in any sphere of life.

It is another fallacy to maintain that Sir Syed remained only marginally concerned with theological issues. Troll rejects it and holds, instead, that a genuinely religious concern played a central role in his life and that his was a sustained effort to reformulate important sections of Islamic theology according to a set of principles which he worked out over a period of several decades.[17] Sir Syed had stated unambiguously that it was his objective to vindicate *Tauhid* in the context of his contemporary situation not by merely adjusting the Islamic creed to the new discoveries of European scholarship and science, but by restating its convincingly on the basis of a coherent set of formulated principles analogous to similar efforts made earlier in Islamic history.

Hali, in his celebrated work, *Hayat-e-Jawaid* (1901) refers to Sir Syed as the inaugurator of a new modernised Islam whose all other activities were directed towards one basic desire—to restore Islam in India to its pristine dignity and prestige. Hali recalls that Sir Syed knew it well that Muslims always considered the religion the guide in all matters whether spiritual or temporal. They would not accept anything if the religion did not permit them. For this reason, Sir Syed remained constantly engaged in religious discussion. Hali has drawn attention to the vital difference between earlier reformers and Sir Syed. While others stood for particular reforms, stressing the need for a reformation only of certain items or aspects of Islamic teaching. Sir Syed went for a comprehensive reform of Islamic teaching.[18] This is not to say that Sir Syed stood for something redically different. In fact, says Hali, "the sole aim of his reformation was simply to remove the obstacles in the way of this 'worldly' progress of Muslims and to reject the criticism of the Christian notions that Islam cannot go together with progress and moral refinement."[19]

Sir Syed himself claimed that his religious thought proceeded on rational lines as opposed to a blind following of traditions and belief. He just wanted to re-establish "pure Islam" (*thet* Islam), shunning subsequent accretions. Sir Syed accepted the challenging job of freeing Islam from irrationalities, which had corroded the spirit of the religion. His interpretation of Islam stressed the validity of free enquiry (*Ijtehad*) and he rejected, with contempt, blind following (*Taglid*). "I share it unambiguously, Sir Syed said, "if people do not break with *taglid* and do not seek that light which is gained from *Quran* and *Hadith* and if they are going to prove unable to confront religion with present-day scholarship and science, then Islam will disappear from India."[20]

As stated earlier, Sir Syed had come down heavily on innovations in Islam in India. He wanted to see all *Shariat* law personified life in the life and practice of Mohammad and an attempt to practice it as an expression of deep faith in him. "Whatever gracious gift (*Nemat*) there is, it is in the *Sunnat* of the Prophet, by God, in nothing else, in nothing else, in nothing else."[21] Thus, the sanctity lies in complete dedication to the enactment of the *Sunnat*. This conformity should be total, comprehending all aspects of life and involving the entire being of the believer. Total compliance with the Prophet's Sunnat implied avoidance of innovation in any sphere of life.

Inspired by rationalism, Sir Syed believed that the true justification of Islam lay in its conformity to the nature and laws of science. Sir Syed held the firm view that Islam was the religion of nature and reason. Nothing which conflicted with the laws of nature could be justified in Islam. Nothing could be valid in Islam which did not appeal to reason. Sir Syed expressed his views on miracles fearlessly. Legends and miracles had been rejected by Muir as "credulous beyond belief" for "an utter want of the faculty of historical criticism".[22] While Sir Syed rejected Muir's arguments against *Hadiths* and proved most of them, if not all, to be true and reliable, and laid down principles to test the validity of *Hadiths,* he appealed his brothers in faith to make critical review of *Hadiths* and to find out if they conformed to the criterion of "nature", meaning to exclude thereby possible occurrence of any strictly supernatural event. His concept of law of nature implied the denial of miracles. Sir Syed explained that miracles could be of two kinds : an unusual and unexplained event remaining within the confines of the law of nature or something supernatural that lies outside the competence of the law of nature. Sir Syed denied only the second category—miracles of purely supernatural character.[23] In fact, Sir Syed viewed all created reality as organised into a uniform system or chain of laws of nature, impervious to any truly supernatural or superrational agency.[24]

To put it in brief, Sir Syed was willing to reject all that failed to conform to modern life and to accept all those which helped in the pursuit of the same. He sincerely wanted to make a reassessment of Islam to enable it to stand up to the forces of modernization. For the reason, he remained critical of the traditional, orthodox philosophical and religious thought and held contempt for those who refused to free Islam of the shackles of taboos and rituals. He felt that traditional view of Islam remained a real hindrance to progress.[25] He always put full faith in the *Quran* and could not tolerate any challenge to its authority but desired that the injunctions[26] were to be appreciated in the light of reason. He wanted to go beyond mere formalism and legalism. He desired advocating instead, a new and critical appreciation of the sources and principles of Islam with an openness to modern science and philosophy[27], to take Islam liberal and modern.

But the fact remains that for his revolutionary views on Islam, by the then standard, Sir Syed could not be a *persona grata* to the big segment of his community. He was held as a heretic because of the heterodoxy of his aggressive rationalism in interpreting the Quran and his militant opposition to popular superstitions believed in by the bulk of the orthodox and to shaking customs consecrated by time, though wholly unauthorised by Islam.[28] Realising that if he persisted in foisting his religious views on the Muslim community, he would be jeopardizing the prospects of the College, which was destined to be the principal source of modern education to the Muslims, he preferred to main low profile in this regard. Sir Syed was found willing to make any compromise to make the institution a success. He succumbed to the demands of expediency and handed over the teaching of religion to a Committee of Orthodox Muslims.[29] Finding that he could not establish his College against the opposition of the Orthodox among the Muslims, he was forced to discard many of his liberal ideas which largely nullified his attempts to inculcate among the Muslims a modern scientific outlook.[30] Forced by the circumstances, Sir Syed planned an institution where the Muslims could get modern education without prejudice to their religion.[31] Prof. Mujeeb laments that Sir Syed preferred college to social and religious reforms of the Muslims. It appeared as if he had made a bargain and asked his community to accept his college where "new" education was offered on condition that new ideas of Islam were not offered as part of the education. The higher value was discarded for the lower.[32]

It must have pained Sir Syed that he could not carry the community with him in his sincere and dedicated mission to make Islam modern and liberal. He suffered from certain limitation. First of all, his motive had been suspect. His avowed objective to bring about an understanding between Christianity and Islam, had raised doubts that in his anxiety to please his British lords, he had put Islam on the defensive. His complementary references to the Bible aroused suspicion that he had subordinated his religious thought to his political purposes. As such, Sir Syed could not inspire confidence in his community as regard his *bona fide*. Excessive reliance on Western outlook and approach distanced him from the majority and proved his undoing.

Sir Syed also felt isolated. Not only that many had risen in revolt against him and had issued *fatwas*, declaring him a *Kafir* at times[33], even his close allies deserted him at crucial juncture. Shibli Noamani, who once shared views of Sir Syed that *Shariat* was never opposed to the demands of the times and that new conditions warranted rethinking, later withdrew himself and set up, instead, an institution at Nadwa. Notwithstanding Sir Syed's entreaties, Deoband Dar-ul-Ulum was founded in 1867 by two theologians of repute—Mohammad Qasim Navawtawi and Rashid Ahmed Gangohi—who were rigidly orthodox, and were hostile to Sir Syed for his theological innovations and political loyalism alive. Even Mohsin-ul-Mulk, a close associate otherwise, fell out with Sir Syed at times and remained critical in particular of his exegetical methods.[34] Only Chirag Ali, it appears, stood by Sir Syed and his writings carry distinct stamp of Sir Syed's teachings.[35] In view of his desertion by his colleagues, Sir Syed was left with no option but to refrain from improving his own views.

Again, Sir Syed had been aware of one basic limitation. His contact with the new sciences and the Western philosophy had been at best "coarse and superficial".[36] He was aware that he lacked authority to state his views on issues relating to science with authority. He had not heard last word on science and knew it well that the scientific knowledge lacked and still lacks finality. A gap in Sir Syed's writings came out of the fact that he did not clearly define terms like 'nature' and 'reason', so fundamental to his thought. This lack of precision marred Sir Syed's writings to an extent.

Nearly a century has passed since Sir Syed died and it is quite natural that what he fought for and what he achieved will be examined in the light of vastly changed social, religious and political scenario. His lasting material contribution will be the establishment of M.A.O. College, which later developed into an University and continues to be the most powerful stimulating centre of learning, particularly for the Islamic world.

But since Sir Syed was a sort of radical thinker and he asserted the role of reason even in religious sphere, his admirers as well as detractors find that he stopped short of the great heights which he made his Muslim brethren look up to though he failed or did not care to take them to that height. No person, howsoever great, has ever realised all his dreams in his life time. But if he succeeds in articulating his dreams, more than half of the task is done. That Sir Syed did—he liberated the orthodox Muslim mind from the fetters of blind faith and illogical interpretations and made it interpret the religious texts against the touchstone of rational enquiry. It is unfortunate that Sir Syed, made prisoner of circumstances, could not accomplish the task which remains incomplete even this day. The search is still on for one who could carry the task unfinished by Sir Syed. He had the rare combination of enlightened religious faith and a passion for transmitting the enlightened faith, as opposed to orthodox one, and this rare combination makes him, even after the lapse of nearly century, as a major reference point for all those who have the betterment of their community at heart. Sir Syed was first and foremost a fighter for a modern life for the Muslims and this image of passionate and dogged fighter is something which the learned academicians, who are prone to find faults in his works, well probably never get the better off. And it is this fighting, examine and inspiring spirit of Sir Syed Ahmed Khan which is to be emulated. An attitude to life which promotes liberalism, rationalism and humanism is to be inculcated.

REFERENCES

1. While the Hindus were allowed to re-enter the city of Delhi in October 1857, the Muslims could enter only in August 1959, by which time the best properties had been resettled. In Delhi alone, 3306 persons were put on trial; 2025 were convicted. Of these, 392 were hanged.
2. Jawaharlal Nehru, *The Discovery of India* (OUP, 1982), p. 343.
3. Moin Shakir, *Secularization of Muslim Behaviour*, 1973, p. 3.
4. M.J. Akber, *Nehru* (Viking, 1988), p. 16.
5. K.A. Nizami, *Sir Syed Aur Aligarh Tehrikh* (Urdu), 1982, p. 36.

6. Quoted in Raj Mohan Gandhi, *Understanding the Muslim Mind*, (1986), p. 24.
7. The Director of Public Instructions, Bombay wrote in 1871 that the Mohammadans availed themselves of schools but did not rise to higher schools and villages and that in the list of University graduates, there were one Mussalman M.A. and two B.As. Out of 176 scholarships awarded at English schools, only one was won by a Mohammadan, See, Lal Bahadur, *Struggle for Pakistan* (1988), p. 10.
8. *Jawaharlal Nehru*, n. 2.
9. K.M. Ashraf, quoted in Zafar Imam (ed.), *Muslims in India* (Orient Longmans, 1975), p. 25.
10. *Tabyin-al-Kalam*, in Three Volumes, published in 1862, 1865 and 1887 respectively.
    Sir Syed did not believe that the holy scriptures, the Bible included, had been totally corrupted and had, therefore, to be totally rejected. On the contrary, he believed that the Bible still contained 'revealed' passages and it continues to be relevant if it is read critically, that is uninfluenced by the distortions of the erroneous Christian interpretation and in the light of the clear *Quranic* message of *tauhid*. See, C.W. Troll, *Saiyad Ahmed Khan* (Vikas, 1978), p. 99. Troll compares views of Sir Syed with those of Rahmat Ullah, who dismissed the Bible as totally misleading.
    In all, Sir Syed authored seventeen books on matters, religious. For the list and other details, see K.A. Nizami, n. 5, pp. 241-42. Three works, however, matter most : *Tabiyan-al-Kalam, Khutubat-e-Ahmedhiya* and *Tafsir-ul-Quran* in 7 volumes.
11. Ilmul Kalam is a rational interpretation of religious faith, practice and experience. Troll describes it a new Muslim apologetic theory which Sir Syed developed when confronted with the challenges of modern age. See also Shiblis works, *Ilmul Kalam* and *Al Kalam*.
12. For a list of those then engaged in giving new interpretations to teachings of Islam in different Muslim countries, see K.A. Nizami, n. 5, p. 31. Prof. Nizami presents contrasts between the views of Sir Syed Ahmed Khan and Syed Jamal Uddin Afghani, who made a violent attack on Sir Syed in a *Refutation of the Materialists* (1882). It appears that this founder of modern Pan-Islamism, had been critical of Sir Syed for his subserviency towards the British, otherwise his own theological ideas were at least as heterodox as Sir Syed's. For details, see *ibid*, Chapter III.
13. This refers to W.W. Hunter's work entitled "Our Indian Mussalman : Are they bound in conscience to rebel against the Queen". For details, see G.F.I. Graham, *The Life and Work of Syed Ahmed Khan* (Reprint, 1974), Chapter XII, pp. 205-244.
14. Troll, *op. cit.*, pp. 60-61.

15. Troll, however, remarks : "The parallel between the ideas and working methods of the two men could be mere coincidence or the effect of a common historical situation or perhaps the result of Sir Syed being directly influenced by Rammohan Roy and his Brahmo Samaj", *ibid.*, p. 60. See also J.N. Farquhar, *Modern Religious Movements in India* (1929).
16. Troll, *op. cit.*, p. 56.
17. *Ibid.*, p. 223.
18. Hali maintains, however, that there were "very few singular reforms of Sir Syed, the roots of which could not be found in the writings of former critical scholars of Islam." *Haiyat-e-Jawaid* (Lahore, 1966), p. 513. Hali enumerated forty one points in the teachings of Sir Syed where one could cite some traditional authority in support and only ten were the points without precedence in earlier Islamic tradition. See also, Atique Ahmed Siddique, *Selections From Writings of Sir Syed* (Urdu) (Lucknow, 1983), pp. 23-26; for how Sir Syed differentiated between traditional thinking on religion and the modern line of thinking on the same.
19. *Hayat-e-Jawaid, ibid.*
20. *Maktubat-i-Sir Syed* (Lahore, 1959), p. 130.
21. *Maqabat-e-Sir Syed,* Vol. V, p. 273.
22. William Muir's *The Life of Mohammat and the History of Islam to the Era of Hegira* in 4 Volumes (London, 1861) had left Sir Syed in a restless and agitated state of mind. Muir had accused the Muslim authors of failure to discriminate the grains of truth from the masses of fabricated traditions. He even accused Mohammad of "pretended inspiration". Provoked by such outrageous accusation, Sir Syed journeyed to London and consulted libraries there. The lectures are to be found in *Khutubat-e-Ahmadiyah* (1870). Sir Syed found that the *Quran* is arranged in an ordered manner, without any contradiction or mutual abrogation and is the full account of all that Mohammad ever uttered as revealed to him word by word by God. Troll calls it 'dogmatic outlook'.
23. Sir Syed explained Mohammad's birth in the state of having been circumscribed in terms of an accidental variation in the law of nature. The splitting open of the chest of Muhammad was described as a part of dream of his nightly journey which Sir Syed held, did not violate the law of nature. He, however, questioned the validity of the belief that Prophet had one night been physically carried from Mecca to Jerusalem and subsequent to *Arsh* and argued that it referred to a dream. The Muslims call it *Meraj*.
24. Sir Syed's ideas on angels, Satan and Jinus fit into his scheme of one uniform universe. As regards Jinu, for example, he explains that Jinu means bedovins and other uncivilized people and not the supernatural beings as generally believed.

25. M. Mujeeb, *Indian Muslims* (Allen & Unwin), p. 448.
26. The explicitly revealed injunctions, held Sir Syed could be divided into three categories : fundamental precepts which fully accorded with the law of nature, precepts for the safeguarding and maintaining of the fundamental precepts and, finally, precepts built on the imperfect evidence of ambiguous verses. Sir Syed further held that "deterministic" verses of the *Quran* were fortyone in number.
27. Troll, *op. cit.*, 229.
28. Maulana Mohammad Ali in course of his Presidential address at Annual Conference of the Muslim League.
29. See in particular Md. Saud Alam Qasim, "AMU The Dinneyat Ki Talim or Tanzim", *Tahzibul Akhlaq*, April 1991 (Urdu). This paper recalls, in particular, the role of Maulana Abdula Ansari who joined the College in 1893.
30. M.R.A. Baig, *Muslim Dilemma in India* (Vikas, 1974), p. 50.
31. Shan Mohammad, *Sir Syed Ahmad Khan* (Meerut, 1969), p. 82. The author refers to the College prospectus.
32. M. Mujeeb, *op. cit.*, p. 451.
33. Hali in his *Hayat-e-Jawaid*, devotes a chapter on "The Opposition to the Reformation" : Sir Syed had been branded 'Kafir' (unbeliever) by many.

    The main opponents of the establishment of Aligarh College and its educational programme were Maulvi Imdad Ali, Maulvi Mohammad Ali and Maulvi Ali Baksh. They procured "fatwas" from *Ulema* of various Indian cities and also from Mecca and Medina, declaring Sir Syed Ahmed Khan, among other things, "the Khalifah of the Devil", see Troll, *op. cit.*, pp. 20-21.
34. In reply to Muhsin-ul-Mulk's criticism of his exegetical methods, Sir Syed laid down fifteen principles of interpretation.

    The former had also accused Sir Syed of stopping short of adopting all the ideas of the contemporary European nationalists.

    Nazir Ahmed also could not go in for Sir Syed completely.
35. Chirag Ali (d. 1895) authored the following books in English : *Critical Exposition of the Popular Jehad, Reforms Under Muslim Rule* and *Mohammad—The True Prophet*. In addition, there are six books in Urdu.
36. Troll, *op. cit.*, p. 229.

16

Vivekanand's Hinduism

M.M. Shankhdhar

"The infinite library of the universe is in your mind—all knowledge secular or spiritual is in the human mind. In many cases it is not discovered, but remains covered and when the cover is slowly taken off we are learning. As the veil of ignorance is lifted men move towards ominiscience".

Reflection on Swami Vivekanand evokes pious and positive response, for in him one finds the quintessence of what is best in the country's tradition of theology and philosophy. He sought to present the uniqueness of the sublime Hindu thought in its contemporaneous relevance. As a brilliant disciple of Ramakrishna, Vivekanand exposed the Vedanta for commonman's comprehension. His speeches and writings had the extraordinary quality of appealing to the most knowledgeable and the most ignorant. Especially, his address to the Parliament of Religions in Chicago, a hundred years ago, is an illustrious case of reaching the hearts and minds of everyone regardless of one's level of consciousness. It touched everybody.

What strikes me most is that while Vivekanand had respect for all religions, he found Hinduism as the basis of all religions. In propounding Hindu culture and promoting traditional values, he was beyond comparison. When he talked of operative ideals and the potentiality of man for attaining divinity, he was the most impressive and powerful speaker at the World Parliament. He was not opposed to materialism *per se*, as he is sometimes made out to be, he was opposed to the materialistic attitude when it obstructed spiritual growth. Renunciation and spirituality need to be preached to the rich, for in the Swami's framework, the poor have nothing to renounce except their poverty. Removal of poverty is desirable but the worship of *Daridranarayan* is abominable. Poverty is hateful; the poor should not be objects of pity or compassion. To Vivekanand, the poor are the failures of society and they have to be restored to the status of self-respecting citizens useful to society.

To the ears of rigid fundamentalists and religious fanatics, Vivekanand's teachings of universality, divinity and tolerance sound utterly blasphemous. Unless *Dharma* replaces religion, conflicts over gods, books, faiths would continue. *Dharma* is like an ocean, not a wave; but religion is a muddy stream that can be purified by falling into the ocean. When he addressed all kinds of religionists assembled in Chicago as "brothers and sisters", he, at once, demonstrated the hallmark of Hinduism as *Dharma* that rises above *panth,* faith and community. To equate *Dharma* with religion has been one of the most retarding and sinister errors committed by populist secularists with a view to bring down Hindu Dharma from its high pedestal to the level of religion. That impedes proper comprehension, for Hinduism is unique because, unlike religions, Hinduism is not mere social ethics, it is also a metaphysic, a philosophy, a mode of spiritual realization and a personal code, all rolled into one. Its excellence lies in operating both at the cosmic and the mundane levels.

In spite of the simplicity and elegance of Vivekanand's thought, the difficulty arises with the English educated intellectual elites—a tribe alienated from the common consciousness of the common man—brought up in the Maccaulayian system who purposefully distort the letter and spirit of the ancient heritage as interpreted by saints like Vivekanand. The Indian Marxists who condemned religion as the opium of the people, after the battering communism received in the erstwhile Soviet Union leading to its collapse, have suddenly reverted to Vivekanand as their prophet. Vivekanand must be, I am sure, beating his chest in his heavenly abode over this phenomenon. Karl Marx, on the other hand, would be no less bitterly weeping in his grave over what his disciples have done unto him by committing this *harakiri*. Vedant of Ramakrishan as preached by Vivekanand, is beyond the understanding of the elite class though it is grasped easily by the illiterate, poor and backward denizen of a remote village.

The Vedantic vision of the *adwait*, non-dualism, one-ness of truth or reality, synthesis of matter and spirit comes easy to the ordinary man. And the man who subscribes to this glorious philosophy and is devoted to *karma, dharma* while striving for *moksha* is spiritual, patriotic and *rashtriya*. Vivekanand, as the apostle of Vedant and Brahm, was proud of being a Hindu to the core. He preached the sovereignty of spirit, soul or conscience over material attachment. The basic of Hindu metaphysics is "experience", for truth cannot be realized by the mind or the intellect. As emphasised by Adi Shankaracharya, everyman has the spark of divinity in him and the potential of enlarging his *atma* to the status of Brahm—*Aham Brahmasmi*. Vivekanand exhorted the people to expand their 'self' to a higher 'Self' by eroding the influence of the powerful ego on their personalities. The Self is to be heard, talked to, reasoned about and meditated upon. In the search for the Self, one finds answer to the perennial question, Who am I? The awakening experience of the Self in the process of human evolution is like an upward surge of the *Kundilini*.

Vivekanand warned that mind and language are very inadequate for self-realization, but they can be useful in preparing the ground for the achievement of the highest goal. Negatively used, both mind and language distort reality and alienate one from the right direction. Wrongly called "mysticism", meaning something beyond comprehension and reach, I think those who practice meditation and concentration find it an empirical, factual, actual and achievable phenomenon. The distinction between the visible and the invisible disappears for the *Yogi* who seeks everything within himself.

Viewed in this perspective, Hinduism and religious fundamentalism seem antithetical concepts. The Hindu can accept a non-believer or atheist with as much ease as a religious bigot. He can multiply his catalogue of gods with remarkable felicity and accommodate diverse creeds in a natural way. A Hindu can worship hundred gods at the same time; he is flexible, elastic and accommodative. He can accept Christ and Mohammad as his gods in the same manner that Buddha, Mahaveer and Nanak belong to his pantheon. He stands for universalising the religious spirit which denominational religions, *panths* and *sampradayas* have failed to do. In fact, religions have divided the people so deeply that the world has witnessed wars over creeds, books and priests and faiths. A Hindu by his nature, upbringing and temperament is neither communal nor fanatic or fundamentalist. He does, indeed, react, against fundamentalisms of all sorts when his own tolerance is pushed to the wall. Otherwise, given the normal conditions, he is tolerant to a fault. He militates against forcible conversions, use of sword, *jehad* and the concept of *kufr*.

When motivated intellectuals and crafty politicians preach him secularism, brotherhood, catholicity and broadmindedness, the Hindu feels provoked and even reacts because he is hit below the belt. He can observe Buddha's non-violence and Mahaveer's compassion, but on occasions he can also show his *Kshatr dharma* of fighting the evil by ruthless physical might. He has no moral compunction when it comes to defeat the inimical forces out to destroy the *Rashtra* with which his whole way of life is inextricably linked. *Dharma yudh* is what *Mahabharat, Ramayan, Dharmshastr* and *Arthsastr* have sanctioned. A Hindu would be a coward if he does not defend the honour of the motherland with all the might. *Janani janmbhumishch swargadapi gariyasi,* meaning that the love for the motherland is superior to love for heaven. A Hindu has not to remain passive when his geo-cultural entity is challenged and threatened and his whole Vedantic system faces a siege. Vivekanand was firm in conviction of the *Brahma-Kshatr* correlationship in the dominant Hindu mainsteam.

Looked in this perspective, Hinduism welcomes the coexistence of diverse religious creeds. The Vedant has no quarrel with the Buddhist tenets or the Christian creed. It has no hostility to personal god, be it Christ or Mohammad. It nurtures no illwill towards *Shias* or *Sunnis*, Catholics or Protestants, theists or atheists, Jews or Arabs. But Vivekanand made it amply clear that religions having exclusivity or particularism, implying a single god, one book and an official hierarchy—while they all would deserve respect—cannot be treated at par with *Dharm*. The difficulty in accepting a personal-god religion is that a personal god can neither be demonstrated nor proved. The whole idea is that since the self cannot be objectified, the impersonal, on the rational plane, is real.

"If as an Oriental", proclaimed Vivekanand, "I have to worship Christ, there is only one way left to me, to worship him as a god" who preached a code of ethics, such as, love, compassion, charity—the virtues taught by Hindu *dharm* as well. But if Christianity says, "My name is the only name, my form is the only form, my Godmen are the only Godmen", it becomes "a modem shopkeeping religion". Or, if a religious community claims that its religion is above *Rashtra*, he would see in it the seeds of theocracy.

In this country's theological-theosophical tradition emanating from the dominant *Dharmshastr* school of thought, Vivekanand perceived the profundity and beauty of finding answers to all questions of life and death, time and place, reality and illusion, truth and falsehood and what you have. In the wisdom of the ages is embedded the experience where Charvak, *Lokayat* and *Arthsastr* are as relevant as the Upanishads the *Geeta* and the *Manusmriti*. Amazingly, there are no contradictions in the scriptures produced at different points of time, place and condition. The output of the total scriptural authority is a big system of synthesis of experience, metaphysic and methodology. Science and faith are blended in a unique conformity, not to be found anywhere else. No wonder the eternal *sanskriti* has survived the vicissitudes of history and evolution and cast a remarkable influence on the Greek mind, which, in turn, influenced the Western civilization. The ancient *Rishi* had the exemplary genius of envisioning the phenomenal world as nescience, discovering truth by *neti-neti* and the dialectics involved in the interplay of forces of creation, preservation and destruction in a time-cycle of the *Yugas*.

It is the compulsion of our times, the imperative need, Vivekanand felt that the people should feel proud of the rich legacy if future of mankind is to be brightened. He insisted on the right kind of education, an education in man-making and character-building, an education that removes bestiality and animality in men and rids humanity of all bigotry and dogma.

Accordingly, teachings of denominational religions is not a free education though it has its uses in the inculcation of moral values in men. It, however, falls short of the goal of emancipating the mind by the temper of spirituality. Also, the education which fills the mind with facts is incomplete. The searching mind, mind prone to concentration, that receives true education. Faith in oneself has to be inculcated, for faith in self is the faith in god.

Hindu spirituality, metaphysics, philosophy, theology, science and ethics, besides *dandniti* as statecraft—all inspired by Vedas and Upanishads—provide the foundations for a world religion to benefit future mankind. This vision of *sarv-dharm* postulates human freedom's reconciliation with supreme knowledge, i.e. freedom from all bondage, *Mukti* after completing one's task in the world and society in an environment of freedom to be succeeded by freedom from the cycle of birth and death. One freedom leads to the other, the end being *Moksha.* We can disown these concepts at our own peril.

Vivekananda highlighted the multifaceted richness of our most ancient culture and inheritance, which has survived by the dint of its own virtues. Those who have read the Hindu classics either in orginal Sanskrit or through Western Indologists like Max Mueller and Sir William Jones or their Indian counterparts, such as, Radhakrishnan and Aurbindo know its excellence, sublimity and depth. If this country can take pride in exporting something to the world, it is its vital and dynamic understanding of the spiritual phenomenon which can provide the base for the structures of religion and the superstructures of ethics, economics and politics. A world system can be constructed on the edifice of Hindu culture. Swami Vivekanand drew up the tentative outline of a universal ideology. Maharishi

Arvind and Maharishi Mahesh Yogi in our times have formulated the guidelines of what can commonly be described as *Ram Rajya*.

But, ironically, the Hindus have fallen on evil days. They are still in a state of forgetfulness, and worse, vulnerable to the propaganda of self-condemnation and ridicule. Under the perversion of foreign and Marxist progressivism, they tend to detest what is best for their present and future. The wide framework of Hinduism allows them freedom to reject their glorious past. Paradoxically, such freedom is at once a point of strength and weakness of this system. It is here that Hindus' self-defeatism and superiority go side by side. Vivekanand warned the Hindus of their degeneration while at the same time lauded the supremacy of the Hindus in his Chicago address. And even his worst critics abroad admired the felicity of his reasoning and the logical appeal of his supra-rational convictions flowing directly from his heart and soul.

The useful lesson that I feel can be drawn from Vivekanand's life and thought is that the tide of obnoxious propaganda against Hinduism needs to be stemmed before disaster overtakes this subcontinent. The whole mischievous vocabulary of the country's political discourse has to be rehashed for conceptual clarity of our mission and goals, i.e. to make the *Rashtra* take a place of pride on the world map. Calling Bharat as India, *Dharm* as religion, *Rashtra* as nation are symbolic of our intellectual slavery and bankruptcy. Let the coming hundred years evolve a Vivekanand paradigmatics to shape the future and avert an impending human crisis.

17

Aurobindo from Revolutionary Nationalism to Spiritual Internationalism

R.T. Jangam

This analysis does not claim to be comprehensive enough to examine in depth all the dimensions or facets of Aurobindo's political philosophy. Aurobindo's own writings are diverse and numerous and a researcher would certainly require a great deal of time to study them in depth. In addition, there are secondary works produced by his disciples and others which are also numerous. The Pondicherry Ashram and the disciples have run a number of periodicals in different languages. This voluminous body of literature and the continuing discussions and studies going on at the Pondicherry Ashram and elsewhere are not easy to study in depth or comment upon. What is attempted here, therefore, is a brief critical study of the essentials of Aurobindo's political philosophy.

The study of Aurobindo's life and work naturally falls into two parts. The first part relates to his revolutionary nationalism. Before he entered upon the nationalist phase he acquired his education in England and became a professor of English at Baroda. However, a climacteric point was reached in his career when, in the Alipore jail, he saw visions of Krishna and was commanded to go forth into the world (so to say), and preach to the people here and abroad the glories of the Sanatana *Dharma*. Accordingly, Aurobindo concluded more or less this phase of revolutionary nationalism and moved on to the second phase of spiritual internationalism at the Ashram at Pondicherry. The intense intellectual life at the Ashram may be compared to the life at Plato's academy and the sustained rounds of research activities to those of his disciple, Aristotle.

Our analysis brings together the broad features of Aurobindo's philosophy and attempts a brief criticism of his mystic ideas. The analysis and criticism proceed side by side. Comparative references are also made to highlight Aurobindo's strong points and the limitations of his ideas and mission.

The Early Phase of Nationalism

Aurobindo, as he is popularly called, has been one of the earliest and greatest thinkers of modern India. Like several political thinkers of modern India who had to fight for India's freedom from the British, Aurobindo's thought bore the inevitable impress of his practical experience of his participation in the freedom struggle and his revolutionary activities.

With more than a decade's education in England, Aurobindo wanted to come back to India as a civil servant. His career as a professor and radical intellectual hastened his journey to Pondicherry. Thus his transition from the life of red-hot revolutionary to the sage of Pondicherry was accelerated by a rather strange combination of revolutionary urges and spiritual yearnings.

The Main Ideas and Limitations

The main basis of Aurobindo's later life at Pondicherry was the belief that humanity was moving progressively in the moral evolution and in this process conflict or hostility had no place. The psychological and spiritual consciousness had to be improved progressively and continuously. This was something akin to Bernard Shaw's realisation and instence that the socialist ideas should be practised through continuous education and improvement of people's outlook everywhere. Shaw insisted that there should be a rain of socialist ideas and influences.

Aurobindo's insistence was similar. Humanity as a whole was in the process of moral evolution and our job was to assist and quicken this evolution. Once such an evolution was proceeding satisfactorily, the problems of contradictions and conflicts, including those between the colonisers and the colonies, would become irrelevant and disappear. In pleading for such a universal and progressive change Aurobindo's philosophy compares in significant details with that of Hegel. The sweep and comprehensiveness of Hegel's philosophy, as those of Aurobindo, are compelling. Further, while Hegel's philosophy is complicated and flawed to an extent by the features of the dialectical march (of the absolute) etc., Aurobindo's philosophy is noticeably free from these burdensome features. Incidentally, the troublesome legacy of the dialectical march was passed on by Hegel to Karl Marx who burdened his own philosophy, in his own way, with the liability feature.

Like a good teacher and leader, Aurobindo did not stop with the preaching of his new philosophy and new vision. He set up the durable and phenomenal experiment at Pondicherry. In this respect, Aurobindo stands in the direct line of great men like Mahatma Gandhi and Vinoba Bhave who started their experiments to translate their ideas or visions at Sabarmati and Wardha. In the history of political thought, we find great parallels like the "New Harmony" project of Robert Owen. The Pondicherry experiment has been truly grand and to say that it was in all India experiment is to limit its scope and grandeur. It was truly universal. Eager seekers of spiritual light were attracted to Pondicherry not only from the different parts of India but also of the world.

The Western Influence

Pondicherry was a French enclave and it was therefore fitting that some of the best seekers were French. The most prominent of these was the mother who was greatly instrumental in disseminating Aurobindo's message far and wide and who acted as his spiritual successor and the inheritor of the Aurobindo tradition.

One may observe here that the association of the Europeans in general and the French in particular invested the Pondicherry experiment with an international aura and orientation. In a way, the Pondicherry model became less Indian (traditionally speaking) and more western.[1] One could easily observe that the life and living at Pondicherry was marked by discipline and methodical operations. Aurobindo's message and ideas came to have an international currency owing to the press and publications of the Ashram at Pondicherry. Of course, the education or uplifting of the Indians in general and seekers in particular was not neglected. Numerous independent books and translations and lecture series have been brought out in the various Indian languages for the spiritual education and guidance of the Indians.

The Pondicherry Model : The Elite Thrust

A related feature to be noted in this regard is that the Pondicherry model was mostly cherished by the educated, Westernised Indians. Professors, lawyers, and doctors, elites of other types marked the successful working of the Pondicherry model. Indian saints like Tukaram and Basaveshwara, in their search for spirituality and progress of the common people, routinely courted the cause of the poor and the illiterate. To some extent, this was also true of the experiments of Mahatma Gandhi and Vinoba Bhave. In case of Aurobindo, however, the appeal was effective specially with intellectuals or the elites whose degree of vagueness on social reconstruction may be said to be remarkable.[2] Like the several rationalist philosophers of the past, Aurobindo is deterministic in his orientation. He has divided human development or man's evolution in three main stages. The first was the pre-rational stage. We may be said to be living in the rational stage. Aurobindo says that mankind is poised to enter upon the supra-rational stage. So we shall be in future in the supra-rational stage.[3] It is obvious that, like the rational philosophers we have spoken of, Aurobindo lays himself open to several criticisms. The first question is: Why should we have only three stages of human development? Why not two or more than three, and so on? What happens after the third stage, the supra-rational stage? If there is no further stage, why not? Sooner or later, Aurobindo has to come face to face with the infinite regress. This has happened in case of Hegel and Marx too.

Aurobindo, like Hegel, has adopted the criterion of reason for indicating the richness and progress of the human race. One may ask, why reason only? Why not reason and the physiology of man? Indeed, why not only physiology as was done by Charles Darwin in course of his theory of the evolution of the species? To such questions there is no perfect or absolute answer. Some explanation or justification may be offered, as has been done by Aurobindo himself. But beyond such explanation, Aurobindo's view cannot be defended. It has to be pointed out as a patent weakness of his philosophy.

The Constraints of Thought and Style Arising from Mysticism

Another shortcoming of Aurobindo's philosophy is its presentation and style.[4] They are both wordy and opaque. In this respect, he resembles Hegel rather than Locke or Hume. But Aurobindo may be more defensible than Hegel. Hegel was a rationlist and of course an eminent professor of philosophy. He had no reason to be involved and difficult to understand. But he was. One side-effect of this incomprehensibility was that he was given the credit for being deep. Incomprehensibility tended to be taken for profundity. Aurobindo's presentation does carry the stamp of profundity although it (profundity) is less forbidding than Hegel's. But, as we have said, Aurobindo is more defensible. The chief reason is that Aurobindo was a mystic which Hegel was not. Aurobindo's numerous disciples called him Yogi Aurobindo. As Yogis go, they are seldom clear or analytical in their utterances or writings. Some of our ancient *Rishis* have used the expression *Neti, Neti* (not this, not this) (while trying to describe God). The exposition of the Yogic philosophy, specially by the *Yogis* themselves, is likely to be profound and mystifying. The *Yogic* exposition may be linguistically rich and captivating, but it may be less helpful as a piece of logical analysis. This is an inevitable attribute of Aurobindo's philosophy.[5]

Aurobindo's Prognosis *vis-à-vis* the Current One-World Situation

How should we view the current psychological and informmation revolution going on in the world *vis-à-vis* the supra-rational environment (of the future) predicted by Aurobindo? Well, Aurobindo may be credited with having glimpses the revolution. Aurobindo had a tremendous perceptive mind. He could easily see the shape of things to come. Further he was just a half-century away. He died in 1950. The Second World War had ended and the computer and satellite age was beginning to be born. (It was about ten years away). On the wings of such modern technologies, multinationals have been travelling far and wide and are found in practically all countries today. The collapse of cummunism as a socio-economic and political system has meant that even the remaining bastions have fallen and the capitalist forces can roam about at will across the world. At the close of the Second World War, intellectuals felt the need to prepare the people of various countries for the coming of the one world. Now people seem to feel that the one world is here and the time for speculation is long gone. The satellite TV, tele-conferences and the video-phone have left people no option but to feel that they are a part of one community, whether they like it or not. Now is this the world that Aurobindo pictured? To some extent, yes. But not wholly. People of the different lands are coming together and feeling together. Information-wise, this seems to be a growing reality. However, this is not the supra-rational world, not even a sufficiently rational one, with so much violence, hatred, terrorism, bloodshed and deep-seated ill feelings all-round. So some coming together due to the technologies has occurred and the process is continuing. However, the irrational forces and forces of hatred and violence which are inimical to human life and moral and spiritual development have grown strong and there is no sign of their weakening yet. It would appear, therefore, that we are still far away from Aurobindo's vision and maybe we may continue like this for quite some time in the foreseeable future before the supra-rational age dawns on us at some distant date.

The Aurobindo Model : Disinclination to Action

One more difficulty with Aurobindo seems to be the fact that his *Yogic* background led him to think about the world and the people in it in terms of the moral and spiritual development. He emphasised education and moral development of man but seems to have paid insufficient attention to the creation of viable socio-economic show-cases. This has been done by some of our thinkers. Mahatma Gandhi was the prime example. He called himself a practical idealist. And that was indeed what he was. He initiated and set up numerous projects of socio-economic nature and while a few of them have become less relevant after a lapse of so much of time, the others seem relevant and continue to inspire and sustain idealist workers in their efforts to build men and their societies socio-economically (and also intellectually indirectly). Even (comparatively) less important a figure like Vinoba Bhave could do something significant because he was intent on building socio-economic forces and projects. Vinoba's Bhoodan (land gift) project has given a tremendous meaning to the concept of equality and sharing and the lifting up of the marginalised sections of the Indian society. The revolutionary leader, M.N. Roy, tried to operationalise his model of radical humanism and party-less democracy. He of course failed.[6] The Aurobindo model, while unparallelled in the moral and spiritual realm, on the socio-economic front, was not even as good as M.N. Roy's. Because Aurobindo remained a visionary, a mystic, an intellectual. Vivekananda, who was also an intellectual and spiritual leader primarily, proved to be an inspirer of generations of workers and institution builders in India and abroad. Aurobindo could not launch this kind of movement or phenomenon because he was too mystical or contemplative. On the socio-economic side, his Pondicherry experiment was rather limited.

A Critical Estimate

Aurobindo Ghosh was undoubtedly a great philosopher of modern India. A special feature of his life and mission was that he was not only a great philosopher and mystic who led a contemplative life at Pondicherry, he was also a revolutionary in the early part of his career. He was highly educated and took to revolutionary activities early in his life. And like other revolutionaries, he had no patience, he wanted quick action. He was not quite happy with the sustained and patient round of activities initiated by leaders like Mahatma Gandhi. He was for striking major decisive blows against the British power in India. Aurobindo's revolutionary activities and achievements have been great and his place in the Indian freedom struggle is unique. However, his conversion to spiritual internationalism and the high-profile mystic life he led at Pondicherry was not easy to predict in the early years. But it did come and the period at Pondicherry revealed the mighty spiritual and mystic dimensions of his great personality and the model at Pondicherry that he set up as an international endeavour in the transformation of the human society into a rational and moral society has been phenomenal. However, as we have pointed out, the Pondicherry experiment was obviously an elite experiment and it did not imply any country-wide mass mobilisation as in case of Mahatma Gandhi. It should also be noted that, as a wholetime philosopher and fully absorbed mystic, Aurobindo took only a limited interest in the mainstream politics of India and his involvement in that sphere was now less than significant. However, the Pondicherry experiment stood for a tremendous disseminaion of his ideas and influence and this has deeply touched the lives of many intellectuals and (other) educated people generally for the last several generations in India and abroad.

REFERENCES

1. We must say that this is all to the good. Generally, the Indian religious or spiritual establishement has lacked discipline, cleanliness and orderliness. Several visitors, Indian as well as Western, specially the latter, have been (rightly) appalled by the unclean and chaotic situations at our temples or shrines and the holy places with *Sadhus* and *Swamis*. A brief (suitable) association of the Western individuals (or teams) is desirable as it can introduce a degree of organisation and methodical performance of the various tasks at such establishments.

   Our military men seem to have appreciated the strength of the Western traits long back. Mahadaji Scindia, in the north, who became a king maker of the (Mogul) rulers of Delhi, and Tipu Sultan, in the south, who had to keep at bay his various adversaries (the English, the Marathas, the Nizam, in turn or in concert) remarkably succeeded in their objectives because both of them took care to employ the French experts of their times to train their troops. (As to the training of Tipu Sultan's soldiers, the matter was verified by the author with Mr. P.A. Majeed, an English language expert in Dharwad, whose forefathers have served in Tipu's army.)

   In the end, we should be aware that the Aurobindo Ashram was a lofty spiritual establishment, unique in several ways, and one should not compare it (because of its Western influence) even remotely with the commercial outfits of the several self-styled godmen or *Swamis,* who set up shop these days in India or West, with a sprinkling of Westerners, with the main aim of glamour, publicity and fast buck.
2. The Aurobindo disciples and followers were essentially elites of various types. They were not mass leaders or organisaton builders. The Aurobindo plan of the supra-rational world was too wide and general. It contained India but only in the universal perspective. Therefore, like the followers of Mahatma Gandhi who had definite comprehensive plans and organisational perspectives for building a new India, the Aurobindo disciples were not explicit or concrete, in terms of programme and strategies, on social questions, say,like Harijan uplift, Swadeshi, youth volunteer body or Seva Dal, women participation, trade unions or workers' associations, peasant bodies and so on; as in case of the Gandhian workers, there was no plan of getting into the streets, of demonstrations, picketing, fasting, non-cooperation with the government and so on. Therefore, the Aurobindo followers were naturally less ready with any plans of mass mobilisation or immediate large-scale social reconstruction.

3. We are not taken into confidence about what lies beyond or what happens after the supra-rational stage. If Aurobindo is assuming a linear model of human development, then he must indicate the next stage, the next and the next, and so on, or face the wall of infinite regress. In the alternative, he must go in for a cyclical view of human development or evolution. This indeed is the case and Dr. Verma provides a cogent analysis of how Aurobindo takes recourse to the cyclical model of evolution which involves advance and retreat, construction and destruction, rise and fall, in the process of human progress. In following this model, Aurobindo is in the good company of the authors of the ancient Hindu Puranas and some German thinkers.

   For details see Dr. V.P. Varma, *The Political Philosophy of Sri Aurobindo* (second revised edition; Delhi : Motilal Banarasidass, 1976), pp. 135-40.

4. Aurobindo was not one of those philosophers who adopt a deliberate policy of employing long sentences and packing them with thundering sound so that the length and the sound impress or confuse the reader and make him struggle to grasp the philosophers' message or meaning. Like some, he was not short on substance and long on sentences. He had plenty to say and perhaps it would be right to say that his words could not bear the burden of all that he wanted to say. Aurobindo, like several other writers of his times, usually uses longish sentences. They can also be involved (as in case of Hegel). Consider, tentatively, the following sentence :

   "That change would be the growth of the living idea or religion of humanity; for only so could there come the psychological modification of life and feeling and outlook which would accustom both individual and group to live in their common humanity first and most, subduing their individual and group-egoism, yet losing nothing of their individual or group-power to develop and express in its own way the divinity in man which, once the race was assured of its material existence, would emerge as the true object of human existence." [Sir Aurbindo, *The Ideal of Human Unity* (second revised edition; Pondicherry : Sri Aurobindo Ashram, 1959), p. 340.]

   One may say that the above sentence is a fairly common and representative sentence. This may be natural for Aurobindo. But it may be difficult for his readers. Here again, the education, age and experience, and motivation of the readers can make a difference in tackling such sentences. One may say that, other things being equal, such sentences are difficult. One's approach and style can make a difference to the clarity of one's composition. It may be noted here that Lokmanya Tilak, whose philosophy was held in high regard by Aurobindo, did not hesitate to employ longish sentences, as can be seen in his writings like *Arctic Home of the Vedas, Being Also A New Key to the Interpretation of the Many Vedic Texts and Legends* (Poona : Tilak Brothers, 1956). But Tilak's style is (generally) legal and argumentative and the length does not seem to come in the way of the readers' grasp. Here again one must say that such arguments and illustrations are relative or tentative, varying as they do from writer to writer and reader to reader. The point of presentation and style is made here as a piece of brief analysis (of Aurobindo's writings).

5. There is a peculiar difficulty with regard to a Yogi's writing or treatment. A Yogi or mystic who has a direct experience of reality or God states his experience in his own way. He does not feel obliged to conform to the canons of clarity or communicability. The reality of his experience carries its own credentials and justification. The Yogi is not other-dependent. To help others out he may provide elucidations and clarifications. But he may still be incomprehensible. What is more, some mystics believe that to express or analyse is to destroy. The mystic experience is in a way unspeakable. To speak about it is to affect it, modify it or distort it. Therefore, a mystic's expression is cramped specially if he is required to demonstrate the truth or validity of his experience or knowledge for public consumption. Some such limitations seem to characterise the writings and ideas of Aurobindo.
6. Of course, in a way, who should become a visionary and who should also try to translate his vision in practice is not for others to say. Theoretically, to remain a visionary (only) is not necessarily a limitation. A person may think that he can best be a visionary and not an activist also because his efforts to put into practice his vision may end in a miserable failure. A few of the thinkers are so keen on trying out their theories and demonstrate their validity or workability in our day-to-day life that they do not mind working ceaselessly all the way and even facing all kinds of criticism and (sarcastic) jokes etc. and undeniable failures. Aurobindo confined his activities more or less to the intellectual and spiritual realm and left the business of mass mobilisation and street fighting (so to say) to those who found themselves fit for the job. From the viewpoint of social reform and reconstruction, however, we tend to think that thinkers and doers are generally better than only thinkers. Continuing in this strain, we should think that M.N. Roy's plan was somewhat better than Aurobindo's. M.N. Roy had the intensity of a practical philosopher; he had the rich experience of working in the international communist movement and of working with the different political leaders in India. He (like Socrates)

thought that if an idea is valid, it had better succeed. His exprience had confirmed that political parties, no matter which particular ones, publish manifestos and undertake programmes which land them in election rivalry and political hatred and the manifestos and programmes do not receive their central attention. Therefore, he argued, right-thinking, rational scientific individuals should not rely on the problematic instrument of a party and proceed to practise their democracy on their own. His model was theoretically sound but it was not supported by people. He tried his ideas in the Uttar Pradesh but he did not succeed. His failure seems to prove that, in the atomised form, individuals do not function viably and to function ably and successfully individuals need a fighting force, a rallying point, a machinery, to bring their energies into a focus, an organisation to shape their designs and activities in particular way. The organisers or machineries may have moral and political limitations. But they do seem to work in some ways. People think that this will do. After all, something is better than nothing! From this viewpoint, M.N. Roy's experiments merit our appreciation.

18

Subhas Chandra Bose
A Pilgrim of Revolution

Ranjan Kumar Ray

It is very difficult to go through the enormous documents, pamphlets, books for the last one hundred years regarding Indian nationalism, religion, culture and politics along with the personalities whose relentless efforts have provided for a proper shape to all these. Several research workers have been engaged in finding out the real story behind incidents, but to have a panoramic view is not too easy for any scholar. As a result, attempts are being made to look at things from different angles. But, sectarian outlook only breeds sectarian thinking and very often the total picture escapes vision. The legendary personalities like Subhas Chandra and others are at the same time creators of history and actors in history of India. Their utterances and writings have also historical values. Each of them is guided by some philosophy or ideology. Even there had been heroworship regarding their personalities. This heroworship is an important part of the ideological dimension of Indian history.

On the other hand, many neo-historiographers regard this ideological dimension as superficial. They think that in fact any type of ideological unity or basis of nationalism was missing in the subcontinent. They regard that Indian society, culture, religion and politics have been changing from time to time depending on the interests of millions of people. Ideologies sometimes emerge out of local, regional interests, personal frustration, class interess and again these disappear in the sea of interests. Even the analysis made by so-called Marxists who followed the line of class struggle ultimately played down the role of ideology and patriotic motivation. Thus, they also succumbed to sectarian outlook and unduly negative estimates of national leadership.

It is necessary to comprehend the different developments in Indian nationalist experiment and how the different courses were effective on the part of the Indians. But, the warning remains that we should not miss the entire forest while looking at the trees, our total approach must be on alert. Generally, we are so carried away by the uncanny and stuffy dinginess of the environment surrounding us, that the greater canvas remains out of sight. However, there has been a contradiction between these two outlooks, philosophical and grassroots. But, the total approach is always playing the major role in creating the unified picture of Indian culture, religion and politics in comparison to the grassroots one. Sectarian, personal or other class-interests, however, powerful they may be, can't change the course of history anti-clockwise. However, is India moving to an aimless situation? The ideas which crystallise our unity among diversity are championed by philosophers and statesmen like Subhas Chandra Bose, M.K. Gandhi, C.R. Das, Rabindranath and others. These people have attempted to chalk out new way of life even amidst situations most trying.

II

Subhas Chandra Bose's career, performance, and achievements, both in the positive and negative sense are more or less known to the scholars as well as the people. He had some definite ideas as well as planning for future India. He wished to give a new political orientation to the existing situation supported by the Congress against British imperialism. Subhas Chandra was himself prepared to sacrifice anything for self-rule. He was very much influenced by the writings of Swami Vivekananda and also believed that the future progress or development of India were essentially intertwined with the upliftment of the Indian people. By Indian people, he meant to say the people struggling against foreign rule. He wanted a result-oriented political programme against the imperialist domination. That is why, quite naturally he wished that the speed of political programme should be bewildering rapid, revolutionary and not a gradual time-consuming slow type.

The Congress session at Lahore in 1929 passed the resolution of complete independence (*Purna-swaraj* pledge). Subhas Chandra categorically highlighted and recommended mass organisation for the attainment of "*Swaraj*". He said that a new awakening of the pulsation of a new life in the whole naion was to be achieved. Then all sorts of artificial social inequalities must be done away with and a radical change, a total revolution should be brought in Indian socio-economic system.

Subhas Chandra believed that the main weapon in the hands of Indian people was mass organization. As a student in his young age, he saw the failure of the revolutionary terrorists who believed in individual attack on government officials, the police and so on. But, Subhas Chandra was in favour of concerted efforts achieved through mass mobilization and extensive and incessant propaganda.

Subhas Chandra had a definite concept of independent India's economic development and state structure. A National Planning Committee was set up by him in 1938 when he was President of Congress, with Jawaharlal Nehru its Chairman. The main aim of the Committee was to formulate a plan which would ensure country's self-sufficiency and high standard of living within the next decade. In the Indian Struggle Bose had visualized the formation of a left wing party which would seek to set up a strong central government with dictatorial powers. Military discipline would be essential for the party as well as to the State. Because to him discipline and order were both indispensable for the Indian nation as a whole which was subdued by British imperialism. The maladies which affected India could be cured only when people are organised under a strong leadership dedicated towards achieving its end even by ruthless measures. The organisational structure of parties in

Soviet Union, Nazi Germany amd Fascist Italy influenced his mind.

Subhas Chandra Bose was quite confident of Indian people especially the youth force of our country. He regarded them as the living embodiment of national hope, aspirations and prestige. Their innate idealism would foster among them a fraternal bond which would definitely act as a source of inspiration in the struggles against imperialist domination. Like Vivekananda and Chittaranjan Das, Subhas Chandra felt the need of self-preparation of the people, spiritually, morally and materially. Organisation should aim at providing physical, intellectual and moral training so that they may, individually and collectively turn out to be ideal citizens of future India. In his *"Taruner Swapna"* (Dream of the youth) he reiterated his feelings towards the country's improvement.

III

Bose's theory of ideal state was not a single idea. The immense improvement achieved by Nazi Germany, Fascist Italy and Communist Russia did not escape his notice. He wrote that both communism and fascism believed in supremacy of state over people, planned industrial development and reorganisation. All these common traits could form the basis of a new synthesis which he branded as *"Samyavad"* or Equality. He strongly opined that India's task to work out this synthesis, should be of topmost priority.

In this context, a question may naturally be raised regarding differences between Bose's concept of *'Samyavad'* and the concept of equality which forms one of the supporting pillars of democracy. Was Bose not a supporter of democracy? Was he a supporter of fascism?

In order to answer this question, one must not judge these two terms in the remote sense of the term. Bose perhaps, was a perfectionist. He was not against democracy. He was conscious of the innate defects of democracy as slow progress, majority decisions, too much deliberations. Now, one has to keep in mind that S.C. Bose had been thinking of emancipated India. For a nation, subdued politically, economically and culturally by foreign imperialism for more than a century regimentation in the initial stage of reconstruction was indispensable. Subhas opted for socialism but at the same time he wanted India to evolve her own brand of socialism subject to the changing needs of the time. The quesiton of national reconstruction after independence was visualised by him. The irony of fate was that he, even as President of Congress could not revolutionise the political and economic programmes of Congress though there was no doubt in his sincerity to do so.

S.C. Bose realised that India's major national problems relating to the eradication of poverty, illiteracy and disease and to scientific production and distribution could be effectively tackled only along socialist lines.

The immediate objective would be to prepare the people for self-sacrifice, to unify the country and to give scope for cultural autonomy. This should be precipitated by the establishment of a strong central government which would look after a radical reform of our land system, liquidation of agricultural indebtedness. Besides, a comprehensive scheme of industrial development under state ownership and state-control was needed for national prosperity. The entire agricultural and industrial system in the sphere of production and appropriation should be socialised.

Subhas Chandra had profound faith and respect for Indian religion and culture. But, this he did not follow blindly or dogmatically. His religion was patriotism and his culture was nationalism. In the ultimate analysis Subhas Chandra had been an ardent nationalist revolutionary, both in thinking and in deeds. His renunciation of coveted government service (I.C.S.) and of all personal comforts definitely placed him on a high altar. He sacrificed his life to the cause of freedom of his motherland. From 1920 onwards he relentlessly tried—sometimes succeeded and sometimes failed due to unfavourable circumstances.

Subhas Chandra hailed from a particular class (highly educated Bengalee aristocrat) of which patriotism emerged not from Xenophobia. So, the anti-British feeling was limited to political enmity and did not become racial enmity. This class though was very much desirous of freedom but did not adopt anti-Western feeling so far as different aspects of social life were concerned. This class imbibed revolutionary spirit from the history of national struggle of America, Ireland, Italy, Poland and Hungary. So, the high ideals of freedom struggle were not unknown to them. Subhas Chandra also visualised a revolutionary upheaval in and outside India against the British imperialism. He believed that freedom comes to those who dare and act.

His foundation of the I.N.A., its organization in the foreign land, its programme for complete independence—all speak of his leadership capability during the Second World War.

Lastly, Subhas Chandra Bose can't be treated as an individual. The Indian subcontinent had witnessed different types of developments, upheavals—movement—their reactions and counter-reactions. But, the general trend—the fountain of struggle flowed incessantly—with number of personalities and different types of leadership emerging and strengthening the movement. Subhas Chandra Bose, the great crusader was a symbol of the ideals, aspirations of the nationalist movement in the real sense of the term. His philosophy, his patriotism, his renunciation and life-long struggle remains and would remain glorious in the history of Indian freedom movement.

REFERENCES

1. *Subhas Chandra Bose, An Indian Pilgrim*, p. 142.
2. *Subhas Chandra Bose, The Indian Struggle.*
3. Important speeches and writings of Subhas Bose.
4. P. Sitaramayyia : *The History of the I.N.C.*, Vol. I.
5. Tara Chand, *History of the Freedom Movement in India*, Vol. 4.
6. N.G. Ganpuley; Netaji in Germany, 1964.
7. Hugh Toye, *The Springing Tiger : A Study of a Revolutionary*, London, 1959.
8. Selected speeches of S.C. Bose.
9. *Crossroads : The works of Subhas Chandra Bose.*
10. *The Indian Annual Register*, 1931, Vol. II.

11. Suniti Kumar Chatterjee, "India and the Fascist Ideal", *The Modern Review.*
12. Congress Presidential Speeches, 1938 and 1939.
13. Abul Kalam Azad, *India Win Freedom.*
14. V.S. Patil; *Subhas Chandra Bose : His Contribution to Indian Nationalism.*
15. *Shah Nawaz Khan INA and Its Netaji,* 1946.
16. Hari Hara Das, *Subhas Chandra Bose and the Indian National Movement;* New Delhi, 1983.
17. Durlab Singh; *Formation and growth of Indian National Army,* Lahore, 1946.
18. *The Amrita Bazar Patrika,* March 1938.
19. *The Tribune,* 26th and 29th December, 1929.

19

Political Philosophy of Gandhi and Subhas

A Comparative Study

Janardan Pandey

Since the beginning of the Indian Freedom Movement, there were two sets of people who were equally thriving hard to win freedom for the Mother India. Lokmanya Tilak was an extremist who had acclaimed that "Freedom is our birth right and we shall have it". On the other hand, there were Moderates headed by Gopal Krishna Gokhale, who were also wedded to have freedom but with peaceful means. Netajee Subhas Chandra Bose was in the line of Lokmanya Tilak and had acclaimed that "Give me blood, I will give you independence". This was the type of Netajee, who became more popular among the youth than anyone else during the Freedom Movement. At no stage, Gandhi's creed of non-violence attracked him, though he was full of praise for Mahatma. Similarly, Gandhi never supported Subhas in his mode of achieving independence, though he had abundance of love and affection for Subhas, who was very lovingly called Netajee. Subhas was so popular among the youth, the Gandhi's candidate for the Congress Presidentship, Mr. Pattabhi Sitaramiyya was defeated by Subhas by over 2000 votes. Ultimately, Gandhi crippled Subhas by asking thirteen out of fifteen members of the Executive Committee to resign and did not compromise with Subhas. Similarly Subhas did not compromise with Gandhi and left the country after resigning from the Congress Presidentship and formed the Indian National Army on foreign soil to fight out the Britishers with the help of the axis Powers. Subhas created a situation when Gandhi was compelled to give slogan of "Quit India Movement" which ultimately became the real Mass Movement and crippled the British Government to hand over the reign of administration to the Indian people.

Thus, for understanding the political philosophy of Gandhi and Subhas, we must discuss the following ideas threadbare.

Nationalism

Three concepts of nationalism prevailed in India from before :

(i) That the British rule was instrumental in bringing together the different races, regions, religions and languages together. It was the unitary British administration that brought unity among the Indian people and ultimately evolved the political concept of Indian Nationalism.

(ii) Secondly, the Marxist ideology was responsible to bring the sense of national unity and this view was supported by Jawaharlal Nehru also in his book "Discovery of India" which was highly impressed by the Marxist ideology.

(iii) Thirdly, two-nation theory was advocated by the Muslim League.

Gandhi and Subhas never agreed to anyone of the views of the Indian Nationalism as mentioned above. The above views were not justifiable—historically, sociologically or philosophically. Both of them were firm believer that a common feeling of unity and oneness had developed among the people of Bharat even in ancient times. Subhas believed that the sense of unity of the Indian peple was not the by-product of the unitary British rule over them, but it was the gift of the ancient history and culture of India. That unity transcended the innumerable diversities of different kinds but in no way, the ethnic diversity of India has ever been a problem as ultimately everyone absorbed into a common culture and tradition. Both believed that the most important factor has been the Hindu religion because all-over the country, we find the same religious ideas, the culture and the tradition and each Hindu feels that India is his Motherland and hence India is a holy land like the Gita and the Ganges.

Unlike the arch Hindu nationalism, Gandhi and Subhas emphasised that nowhere before the demand of Pakistan, Mohammedans were arch enemy of the Hindus. Both believed that the synthesis of religions, cultural and social values of the Hindu and the Muslims and other religious communities of India had abundantly contributed in the growth of Indian nationalism. They were arch opponent of the British concept of the growth of Indian unity and Indian nationalism. Our common culture and civilization had contributed in the healthy growth of the Indian nationalism as we have had feelings of oneness and Indianness from ancient times.

Indian nationalism was the growth of cultural heritage of the Indian civilization and it had nothing to do with the political compulsion. Though India remained politically fragmented many a times, yet its heritage did not allow its real division and cultural line and this is not found anywhere else in the world.

Gandhi and Subhas were thriving hard for political freedom but always cautioned the countrymen not to forget their own cultural heritage as the Indian nationalism has always been a cultural concept as it has always been the binding force.

Both of them have opined as follows :

1. Though Hindu constituted the biggest number of the Indian population, the concept of its nationalism never meant Hindu community or Hindu religion.
2. Because of the various religions, the concept of one nation never ceases. All merge in a nation and become one entity for all time to come. Hindustan belongs to all those who live in it, irrespective of caste and creed.
3. In the Gandhi's Ashram and in the Indian National Army of Subhas, men of all religions lived together and

carried their mission for the independence of the Mother India.

4. No other theory of nationalism was acceptable to them and hence multinational nationality was not acceptable to them.
5. They always looked upon their country as "divine motherland". They were true Indians and Indian nationalism was a kind of political religion for them. Hence, both of them decried about the proposed division of the sacred motherland.
6. On account of the abiding faith in the leadership of these two great nationalists, towering personalities of the Islamic faith also favoured their concept of nationalism and always denounced the division of India. Among them were Khan Abdul Gaffar Khan of Khudaikhidmatgar and Maulana Azad who was an internationally recognised Islamic Theologist. They were the towering pillars of the Indian National Congress. Similarly, Shah Nawaz and others were the pillars of the Indian National Army who fought so bravely for the freedom of the sacred Motherland from foreign land.
7. Gandhi and Subhas were emphatic for Hindu-Muslim unity but Subhas never agreed with "All Party" and he always put emphasis on the agreement between nationalist Hindus and nationalist Muslims. Much before Gandhi and Nehru, Subhas has declared about the dirty design of the British Government to divide India. At Haripura Congress, Subhas had declared, "I have no doubt that British ingenuity will seek some constitutional device for partitioning India and thereby neutralising the transfer of power". In 1942 also, Subhas warned from Berlin in similar fashion. His ideas were:

(i) India was one geographical and historical unit.
(ii) Hindus and Muslims are so mixed up in many parts that it was not possible to separate them.

(iii) If, India is divided, new minority problems with new difficulties would be created.

(iv) Only in a free and undivided India, unity of Hindu and Muslim is possible.

Gandhi always believed like Subhas that Pakistan was an impossibility and Gandhi had declared that "Pakistan would be created only on my dead body".

8. First concrete proposal of Pakistan came from the Wavell offer in September 1944, Netajee from Azad Hind Radio at Rangoon denounced it in his impassionate speech and told to his countrymen—"We have resolved to create a united and free India. Therefore, we shall oppose all attempts to divide her and cut her up into bits. Ireland and Palestine have taught us a lesson." While warning the Congressmen, he said "If India is divided, she will be ruined economically, politically and culturally". To the millions of Muslims youth, he said "What will be your status in divided India? My friends, if you want freedom, you must fight for it and kick the British out... Our divine motherland shall not be cut up".

Similarly Gandhi met Governor General Mr. Wavell and rejected his Plan. Gandhi was closer to Subhas's ideas when he was fighting along the Imphal front. There is least doubt that 1942 movement was widely influenced by Subhas's fighting for national liberation along the eastern fronts of India and hence a non-violent Gandhi had given slogan of 'open rebellion' in the shape of Quit India Movement of 1942.

Concept of Freedom

Freedom was dear to both and they tried in their humble way to free the Mother India. Generally speaking, Gandhi is supposed to be the apostle of Nonviolence and this was his means to achieve freedom and Subhas wanted freedom through violent means.

Subhas broadly followed the Gandhian means of non-violent mass movement till 1941 but had no faith in the success of the technique of Gandhi. Gandhi through his Constructive Programme and *Satyagraha* wanted to accelerate the freedom movement. Though Subhas called Gandhi's method 'a new method' to fight for India's freedom, but was opposed to accept nonviolence as an obsolute creed. At Haripura Congress (1938) Subhas said, "*Satyagrah*, as I understand it, is not merely passive resistance but active resistance as well". This new phrase *'active resistance'* is a new political strategy which ultimately culminated in the armed rebellion against British rule from foreign soil. Here, Subhas was Pole's apart from Gandhi, who believed in nonviolent peaceful transfer of power but Subhas wanted freedom with the help of 'armed rebellion' which was contradictory from Gandhi's technique. Subhas has written in his book "The Indian Struggle" as follows : "Inordinate belief in fate and supernatural" of the Indian people and "the peaceful contentment engendered by the later day philosophy and adherence to *ahimsa* carried to the most absurd length "was the cause of" India's downfall in the material and political sphere".

Subhas was eagerly waiting for world sympathy for Indian Freedom Movement and hence he was a step forward than Gandhi and the Congress. He wrote in "The Indian Struggle": "If we desire to win our freedom through nonviolence, diplomacy and international propaganda are essential". It is an accomplished fact that till 1942, the Congress, Gandhi or Nehru never made any positive effort to welcome and cultivate international attention for the cause of Indian Freedom and it was the exclusive task to be undertaken by Subhas himself.

Gandhi wanted to achieve freedom in phases through peaceful means, whereas Subhas wanted full freedom at a single stroke and he was very near to Lokmanya Tilak. Subhas would not have accepted any idea of a dominian status for India within the British Commonwealth and this idea was totally repugnant to him. As we know, Subhas wanted full freedom. He never believed in the negotiated settlement with the British Government as it would never take us to our goal. Hence, he borrowed the idea of "parallel government" from Irish revolutionaries and in this venture, he was wholeheartedly supported by C.R. Das and Tagore.

Unlike Gandhi, Subhas was very clear in his mind that in the final phase of the non-cooperation-*cum*-civil disobedience movement, without the active support of the army and the police, administrative vacuum would never arise. Mahatma Gandhi never called or planned for the participation of the army and the police, in his struggle and hence according to Subhas, Gandhi could not achieve freedom. In the Nagpur session of the Congress, Subhas pleaded for forming parallel government in the last phase of the final struggle for freedom but Gandhi differed and hence Subhas had to plan for leaving the country to wage an armed attack to achieve freedom for the country.

"Seizure of power" was the theory of achieving freedom from the British Government and this theory of Subhas was based on the fact that only then, they would not "divide and rule" over the Indian people and ultimately the 'Partition of India' could prove that Subhas was cent-per-cent correct in his approach towards getting freedom because the British Government could get sufficient time to divide the people and achieve their goal.

Though Subhas always differed with Gandhi as his techniques were not conducive to him, yet Subhas had appreciated the supreme sacrifice of the patriots who were engaged in Satyagrah but his exit from India was the "Parting of the Ways" and he never looked back in supporting Gandhi's *Satyagrah* for Indian Freedom. Thereafter, he became violent revolutionary and believed in the revolutionary seizure of power. He formed Azad Hind Fauz and became the father of the Azad Hind Revolution and emerged as the Netajee of the Indian national revolution for all time to come. Thus, his concept of Freedom differed from Gandhi. However, Subhas had an abundance of regard for Gandhi. On 75th Birth Anniversary of Gandhi, from Bangkok broadcast on 2.10.1943, Subhah said, "The service which Mahatma Gandhi has rendered to India and to the cause of India's freedom is so unique and unparallel that his name will be written in letters of gold in our national history for all time". While comparing Gandhi with Kamal

Pasha, Subhas said, "The nearest historical parallel to Mahatma Gandhi is perhaps Mustafa Kamal Pasha who saved Turkey after the defeat in last World War I and who was acclaimed by the Turks as the Gazi". On 6th July, 1944 in another broadcast, Subhas said, "Father of our Nation". In this holy way of India's liberation, we ask for your blessings and good wishes."

Gandhi had paid unreserved tributes to the sacrifices made by Subhas and his men of Indian National Army and he hailed Subhas as "Netajee". While addressing the INA men, Gandhi observed, "Netajee was like a son to me. I came to know him as a lieutenant full of promise under the late Deshbandhu Das. His last message to the INA was that whilst on foreign soil, they had fought with arms, on their return to India, they would have to serve the country as soldiers of nonviolence under the guidance and leadership of the Congress. Though the INA failed in its immediate objective, it has a lot to its credit of which it might well be proud. The greatest among its achievements was to gather together, under one banner, men from all religions and races of India, and to infuse in them the spirit of solidarity and oneness, to the utter exclusion of all communal and parochial sentiment. It is an example which we should all emulate."

Political Ideology

Gandhi stood for *"Sarvodaya"* and Subhas for *"Samyavad"*. Gandhi called his political ideology as "nonviolent socialism", whereas Subhas termed his socialist ideas as 'Indian socialism'. Constructive programme of Gandhi has been praised by his one of the most ardent and eminent analyst Acharya Kripalani as 'practical reforms' in his book "The Gandhian Way". Subhas along with Nehru and J.P., Narendra Dev and other socialists were not wholly satisfied with his reformist profile. They were one when they categorically said that kind of a mission of a revolutionary ideology, that was needed to galvanize the younger elements in the country was missing in the thinking of Gandhi and they formed Congress Socialist Party in 1934. In his book "The Indian Struggle" (1935), Subhas became critical of Gandhi. Subhas remarked that it is erroneous to call Gandhism as an alternative to communism. Subhas calls Gandhi as a reformist and not a revolutionary. Subhas felt that Gandhi's reformist movement should be replaced by Indian Socialism or Bhartiya Samyavad and for this, he formed a party known as Bhartiya Samyavadi Sangh and ultimately in 1939, he had to form a party for promising India's final struggle for national liberation and named his party as Forward Block.

Gandhi and Subhas had abiding faith in Indian heritage. Therefore, Gandhi called his political ideology as 'non-violent socialism' or Sarvodaya and Subhas called it as '*Samyavad*'. Both of them aspired to reconstruct the national life of India in an Indian way and on the basis of Indian principles and, as such, they urged the Indian people to evolve their national ideology essentially as an Indian concept. These ideas are based on the values of equality and social justice as the cardinal principles. For both, the value of Indian spiritual humanism was the kind of a fundamental faith and it was in fact, the inspirational genesis of their ideas of *Sarvodaya* and *Samyavad*.

It was in the fitness of things that both accepted the mission of serving *Daridra Narain* as the primary impulse to fulfil their ideals of *Sarvodaya* and *Samyavad*. About Indian socialism, Subhas says that his socialism did not derive its birth from the books of Marx, rather its origin is in the thoughts and culture of India. He was influenced by Vivekanand and M.N. Roy. He clearly advocated that he wanted to establish Indian Socialism and not Marxian Communism. Similarly, nonviolent socialism was the ideology of Gandhi and this was based on his spiritual concept of Indian humanism. His socialism was nothing but Swaraj which he significantly said : "Swaraj of my dream is the poor man's Swaraj" (*Young India*, 1931). His socialism like Subhas is rooted to his faith in the spiritual evaluation of Indian humanism. Thus we find that in the evaluation of essential ideas of socialism, the perceptions of Gandhi and Subhas were unmistakably identical.

Gandhi and Subhas had similar opinion about the Communist Russia. Neither of them could agree with the basic tenets of the philosophy of Communism, nor did they consider it patriotically honourable to display a mentality of subservience to Russian politics like many Congress leaders who were emotionally charmed by the call of Communism. Gandhi observed in unmistakable words : "It is my implicit faith that India will not be able to imbibe communism and Lenin's cult will not take root in this soil." He further said : "In so far as it is based on violence and denial of God, it repels me". Similarly, Subhas writes in his "The Indian Struggle": "While many of the economic ideas of communism would make a strong appeal to Indians, there are other ideas which will have a contrary effect... communism in USSR has grown to be anti-religions and atheistic... In India... there is no feeling against religion... Materialistic interpretation of history which seems to be the cardinal point in Communist theory will not find unqualified acceptance in India even among those who would be disposed to accept the economic contents of Communism."

About planning for employment, Gandhi was opposed to industrialisation. However, in 1946, he changed his stand but wanted that (i) *khadi* and village industries should not be destroyed, (ii) moral and human values of the workers should not be made the vagaries of industrialism, and (iii) the power of capitalism should not be increased. On the other hand, though Subhas had firm faith in planning, yet he always highlighted the task of the removal of unemployment and poverty, like Gandhi, as the principal objectives of national planning.

Both of them wanted to leave medium and cottage industries outside the scope of large scale and centralised production so that the maximum scope for mass production by the masses and for the masses could be ensured for opening opportunities of greater employment under conditions of decentralization. However, they differed on planning concerning the area of large scale industries. Problems of Indian peasantry should receive greater attention by the Indian planning.

Either in Sarvodaya of Gandhi or Samyavad of Subhas, capitalism was not expected to have any place like Gandhi, who spearheaded Champaran, Kheda, Bardoli and Ahmedabad movements; Subhas also spearheaded the Tata strike, Assam-Bengal railway strike, Kisan movement in Bihar with Swami Sahjanand etc. They pleaded for the rights of the workers but both were averse with the theory of the class war of the communism.

Gandhi believed in the theory of Trusteeship for the conversion of capitalism to social ownership of the means of industrial production, whereas Subhas said in his Tokyo speech : "Class conflict is something that is quite unnecessary in India. If the government of Free India begins to work as the organ of the masses, then there is no need for a class conflict. We can solve our problems by making the state the servant of the masses."

Thus, the two great revolutionaries, Gandhi and Subhas were adamant in abolition of capitalism and feudalism. Gandhi and Subhas had given warning to the Capitalists and the feudal lords to mend their ways, lest a violent and bloody revolution is a certainty one day unless there is a voluntary abdication of riches give and sharing them for the common masses.

Development of the Hindustani language as the national language of India was their objective but Subhas wanted Roman Script. None of them wanted to abolish English altogether.

Gandhi wanted Ramrajya or Gramrajya or Panchayat Raj as his concept of the state in free India. He wanted India to be a democratic country based on "disciplined individual freedom", but he desired to build its edifice on the village 'panch' as its principal plinth. Subhas also advocated democracy and he called it a political and social democracy in India. He wanted to ensure that leaders are not thrust upon the people from above but are elected from below. As he believed in freedom, democracy and socialism, he wanted all powers to the Indian people as the power base of the state in free India. However, he wanted strong central government with dictatorial powers for some years to come in order to put India on her feet and holding India together and preventing chaos when Indians are free and are thrown entirely on her resources. However, he wanted that dictatorial power was expected to be given morally, voluntarily and democratically to the party which fought for and won the freedom of the country as the patriotic organ of the people. He wanted a balance of dictatorial power at the centre and the people's power at the bottom through the system of Panchayat Raj.

As regards decentralisation of power, both differed abundantly. Gandhi wanted total decentralisation but Subhas did not favour this idea. Subhas stood for a central authority at the apex of the Indian polity, based on the Panchayat system.

Gandhi and Subhas believed in the Indian heritage. They were true Indians and true Indian nationalists. They were opposed to the exploitative system of decadent capitalism. Both of them said that communism was wholly alien to the concepts of Indian values, Indian heritage and the Indian way of life.

Gandhi and Subhas had conceptualized an ideology of Indian socialism—which was often called Sarvodaya by Gandhi and Bhartiya Samyavad by Subhas—on spiritual outlook of Indian humanism.

Gandhi and Netajee wanted national ideology on the basis of the acceptance of the Indian philosophy of synthesis and emphasised the necessity for a harmonious fusion of the values of spiritualism. They wanted to consolidate Indian freedom and reinvigorate the spirit of national integration of the Indian people on the recognition of the principle of responsive harmony of the various values, cultures and aspirations of the Indian people belonging to various regions, religions, races, communities and linguistic fraternities. However, they were opposed in building the foundation of the national polity of India by initiating the political system of Fascism or Communism or British system of parliamentary democracy. They wanted the national institution of Indian polity as a Panchayat Raj, based on the age old Indian system of the rule of the Panch. They wanted the power of the people at the bottom and as such both of them urged for the gradual develuation of political and economic power. For the economic development of the country, they stressed the necessity of drawing up a programme of national planning by giving primary importance to the task of speedy removal of unemployment and poverty of the common masses of India.

Gandhi and Subhas wanted an ideologically oriented political party and said that it was unavoidable like Gandhi who wanted to dissolve the Congress and build up a new political party to rule the country, Subhas also wanted a party with people's power and thus wanted to build up an Indian party. He wanted people's party to build up the people's power at the bottom of the power of a people's state.

As the national polity is facing a gigantic problem, it is but imperative to understand the following points of Sri Samar Guha of his book, *"The Mahatma and the Netaji"* (p. 222) :

> "Will the new generation in India pledge to work out the integrated ideological missions of Mahatma Gandhi and Subhas Chandra Bose, two men of destiny of modern India, to rebuild the life of the Indian people in an Indian way and in accordance with the heritage of India? Will they move to build up an egalitarian humanist society of the Indian people on the basis of harmonious integration of the principles of Sarvodaya of the Mahatma and Samyavad of the Netaji? It is now time to realize that Gandhi and Subhas, in synthesis, is the answer to the ideological quest of the present-day India for galvanizing the Indian people into the spirit of a new clan of a new mission for the speedy national reconstruction of India, giving primacy to the essential needs of the masses, and the lowly masses in particular."

REFERENCES

1. *The Mahatma and the Netajee* by Sri Samar Guha.
2. *Subhas Chandra Bose as I Knew Him*—Kitty Kurti.
3. *Netaji the Great Resistance Leader*—Girija K. Mukherjee.
4. *Netaji Subhas Chandra*—I.N. Ghosh.
5. *Netaji : Dead or Alive?*—Samar Guha.
6. *Beacon Across Asia*—Orient Longman.
7. *The Indian National Army*—K.K. Ghosh.
8. *My Memories of the I.N.A. and its Netaji*—Shah Nawaz Khan.
9. *India Wins Freedom*—Maulana Abul Kalam Azad.
10. *Netaji : His Life and Word*—edited by Ram Sharma.

11. *India's Struggle for Freedom*—A.C. Chatterjee.
12. *Netaji in Germany*—N.G. Ganguley.
13. *Writing and Speeches of Netaji*—J.S. Bright.
14. *Netaji : The Man*—Dilip Kumar Roy.
15. *An Autobiography*—Mahatma Gandhi.
16. *Constructive Programme : Its meaning and place*—M.K. Gandhi.
17. *Sarvodaya*—M.K. Gandhi; N.P.H.
18. *Towards Non-Violent Socialism*—M.K. Gandhi; N.P.H.
19. *Gandhian Constitution for Free India*—Shriman Narayan Delhi Diary; N.P.H.
20. *Towards the Gandhian Plan*—Shriman Narayan.
21. *Life of Mohandas Karamchand Gandhi*—D.G. Tendulkar.
22. *Mahatma Gandhi* : (i) *The Early Phase*—Pyarelal, (ii) *The Last Phase*—Pyarelal, N.P.H.
23. *History of Freedom Movement of India*—R.C. Majumdar.
24. *Autobiography of An Indian Pilgrim*—Subhas Chandra Bose.
25. *Gandhi : His Relevance for Our Times*—G. Ramchandran and T.K. Mahadevan.
26. *The Indian Struggle : 1920-1934*—Subhas Chandra Bose.
27. *The Indian Struggle : 1935-1942*—Subhas Chandra Bose.
28. *Selected Speeches of Subhas Chandra Bose*; Publications Division (Government of India).
29. *Speeches and Writings of Mahatma Gandhi* : G.A. Natesan & Co.
30. *Rebuilding Our Villages*—M.K. Gandhi; Navajivan Publishing House (N.P.H.).
31. *Diary of Mahadev Desai*; N.P.H.
32. *Young India*—edited by Mahatma Gandhi before 1933.
33. *Harijan*—edited by Mahatma Gandhi since 1933.

20

Gandhi
Religion, *Dharma* and the Concept of Politics

M.S. John

Gandhi, it should be noted, was not a political philosopher in the sense of being concerned with the epistemological requirements of philosophy. Most of his ideas available to us in written form are responses to specific situations that arose while he was engaged in his peripatetic mission. Yet there cannot be any doubt that consistency, which is perhaps more of a moral than logical kind, is discernible in his speeches and writings. His being not very systematic, however, suggests an indirect questioning of an epistemology which used reason in an instrumental way. To a student of politics brought up in the liberal Western tradition, which is the dominant one in the discipline, Gandhi's ideas of politics would appear, at first sight, aberrant. From a Machiavellian or realpolitik point of view the resources employed by Gandhi in politics would be seen as liabilities rather than sources of strength. But closer examination, accompanied by an ability to think beyond the ethnocentric confines of liberal politics, would reveal the far-reaching implications of Gandhi's political discourse for political life. The failure of some of the early political commentators to appreciate this aspect lay in their inability to think beyond the liberal paradigm. Morris Jones had reservations about Gandhi's status as a political thinker except for his contributions in the narrow realm of resistance politics as he understood it.[1] But even resistance politics is seen in terms of power politics—the struggle to subvert existing institutions and seize power. This is perhaps not appropriate in categorizing Gandhi's case. Gandhi himself was aware of his being dismissed as non-political. He said: "My intelligence is not recognized in the field of politics. Those who are deeply involved in politics laugh at me. They wonder if this is politics. I acquired some status in politics because I had been a fighter, not because of my intelligence."[2]

True, Gandhian ideas on resistance politics are capable of being accommodated within the liberal paradigm while his other pronouncements are not. While Gandhian methods of nonviolent resistance have gained popularity and familiarity in the West, his critique of modern civilization and the technical and material rationality which engenders it, and upon which notions of politics are based, are relegated or dismissed as irrelevant. In fact it is a critique of liberalism in its social, political and economic dimensions. It is also a critique of all philosophies which privilege material progress or see such progress necessary for political and social progress. It is axiomatic to say that nonviolence has an intrinsic as well as a strategic value. The latter is often hailed by many in the West as it can satisfy tests based on rational choice, the reigning principle which governs decision-making in liberal regimes. This suggests the need to understand Gandhi within a total framework rather than in a piecemeal form.

It should be borne in mind that parrallels with Western political theorists cannot be neatly made due to the fact that the problems that Gandhi confronted or diagnosed were totally different from those of most political theorists. Writers who have influenced him most were not first order political theorists familiar with the requirements of epistemic enterprises. They were visionaries whose agenda were not strictly political. If at all elements of similarity can be struck, it is with anarchists, certain feminist groups wedded to environmentalism and need-based models of development, certain grassroots movements and some moderate post-modern thinkers. Here again, one has to guard oneself against sweeping comparisons.

Before we proceed further, it is necessary to remind ourselves that Gandhi struck at two levels in his thinking, a fight aganist British imperialism, on the one hand and a critique of modern civilisation with a view to creating a normal one on the other. The latter enterprise is relegated by Western scholars like Morris Jones and Indian scholars like Kothari (particularly in his early writings). Kothari's comment was that the Gandhian approach to politics has a negative legacy and his moralization was "at odds with the reality of democratic politics" and also far removed from the "essence of democratic politics",[3] a categorization which assumes the privileging of the liberal 'model of democracy as the standard form. Gandhi's task of confronting an extant order and the compromises that he would be required to make in his ideal order in the context of independent India that inherited a structure of politics from the British resulted in some ambivalences. Unlike other political theorists who hardly have an activist experience, Gandhi was mainly a man of action and he had not cared for academic consistency.

Dennis Dalton delineates three strands in the conceptualization of politics in the normative sense. The first is a notion of politics as an all-embracing activity in the Aristotelian and Hegelian fashion with a moral tag attached to the political order. Further, power, as long as it is exercised rightly, has no limits. In this view politics and power are apotheosized. The second is the individualist or liberal perception of politics as an indispensable activity although not a desirable one at that. According to this view, politics can only concern the public realm of an individual's life leaving the private realm untouched. They concede primacy to the latter realm. The third is built around a rejection of state and politics as a constraining factor on human freedom and moral behaviour. According to this view, voluntary cooperation among individuals should replace politics and state. Dalton considers Gandhi as an exponent of this tradition which is commonly known as anarchist, a trend which was already set by Vivekananda, Aurobindo and Tagore. That this trend of distrust of state continued even after Gandhi through his interpreters like Vinoba and JP only shows that it had come to assume a generic form.[3a]

The problem that ancient Indian polity faced was the dichotomy between power and authority. The king had power but its successful exercise required authority which laid with the Brahmin who was always watchful of playing into the hands of the king for fear of being accused of corruption. Traditional Indian polity was governed by the principle of *Dharma* which made the immanent order subservient to the transcendental one."[4] *Dharma* concerned the society and not the state. It never had a compulsive character. According to Aurobindo state arose at "an advanced stage of corruption of *Dharma* marked by the necessity of the appearance of the legislator and the formal government of the whole of life by external or written law and code or rule."[5] Hence, confrontation with the West especially Western imperialism only led modern Indian thinkers like Gandhi to the traditions. The notion of *Dharma* is supposed to harmonise the relationship between freedom and order, one of the perennial problems of political theory.

To a great extent this model is reflected in his notion of politics. The Brahmin, in ancient India had been the upholder of the Dharmic order. So also, while there will be seekers of power, there will be people who would not seek power but erect a parallel power centre based on the goodwill and self-less service that they generate through their constructive activities. They would also generate sufficient people's power so as to challenge political power particularly when it is abused. Gandhi obviously wanted the Congress organization to become a Lok Sevak Sangh. When it was found that seekers of power were there, he held that they should not be members of the Sangh simultaneously. The Lok Sevak Sangh "was to the state what the Brahmins were to the Kshatrias in a traditional Hindu polity: cooperative, respectful, willing to advise and help, but also fiercely independent and ready to give a call for disobedience should the occasion so require."[6] While Gandhi is not averse to constitutional liberal politics, he had a suspicion of it given its utilitarian and egoistic underpinnings. The notion of power elites was anathematic in his thinking. But he failed to create a set of parallel elite bestowed with the power of the people to challenge political power when abused. A mechanical interpretation of the principle of *Dharma* can also send wrong signals because in the Hindu tradition the social order reflected in the hierarchical dominance of the Brahmins enabled them to preserve their social position unchallenged. This explains the lack of development of ancient Indian political theory as Parekh says.[7] In cantrast Gandhi's notion of *Dharma* was different. He said : "To a person whose life is dedicated to *dharma*, politics, economics, etc., are all aspects of *dharma*, and he cannot leave out any one of them. According to me, a person who regards *dharma* as one of the many activities of life does not know what *dharma* is. It is, therefore, inconceivable to me that I might some day give up politics, social reform and other similar activities. I have entered the fields of politics, social service, etc., for the sake of *dharma*."[8] This is a far cry from the largely *status quoist* notion of *dharma*. This is a dynamic notion of *dharma*, as one involving performance of duties towards society including struggle for social change and the welfare of the entire humanity. What we see is a broadening of the very meaning of politics and an erasing of boundaries of the concept making all concepts interrelated.

Implicit in such a notion is a radical departure from the reigning notions of power which is top-down and is intimately linked with such terms as coercion, domination, control, hierarchy and sanctions for noncompliance. Power has a material and quantitative connotation. There is also an attempt towards uniform semantics in power which is not correct as different cultures view power differently. Nobody talks about the qualitative dimension of power. Gandhi sees power as derivative of self-less service. His notion of power is synonymous with the moral power of the *karmayogi*. Like his notion of politics, he says that power should be checked with power, but not of the same kind. The basis of one type of power is fear of punishment. that of the other is acts of love. It is here that he strikes a departure from the realists and even the revolutionaries. Marxists who see violence and oppression in the existing power structure seek to subvert it in their favour through violence, a quality which has been legitimately the sole possession of the state. In Gandhi's view, power will be generated not in the cities, not in the parliament houses, not in the ministries, the bureaucracies and so on. It will be generated in the umpteen villages of India. As Galtung says "Gandhi's approach to power, to put it at its simplest, was through power-over-oneself rather than through building up new types of power-over-others."[9] The fear, submissiveness and dependence associated commonly with power should vanish. All power has some class base and the advantage with Gandhi's power is its universal embrace inasmuch as it seeks to empower the people who are not categorized in terms of classes. Obviously Gandhi was critical of liberal democracy because of its embeddedness in dual notion of sovereignty, the people in theory but the representatives in practice. For him, there is only a popular and undivided sovereignty in which the community is self-regulating and political power is dissolved into the collective moral will.[10] One of the ways in which Gandhi sought to weaken political power with a view to eliminating it was to make a plea for decentralization. His theory of decentralization is crucial because none of his predecessors were emphatic and unambiguous about it. This was intimately linked to the parallel politics he was advocating. As Sethi says: "Briefly Gandhian decentralization means the creation of parallel politics in which people's power is institutionalised to counter the centralising and alienating forces of the modern state and then, through a long-drawn struggle over a long period, to overtake the state itself. Thus the Gandhian decentralization policy has a built in process of the withering away of the state."[11] Gandhian notion of power actually seeks to demonstrate the fragile nature of political power. According to Gandhi, if the sources of power, namely the people, to whom the power holders are continually indebted for replenishment, withdraw their consent, the whole structure of government collapses. Consent can be withdrawn mechanically as in periodic elections. It can also be undermined by refusing to take recourse to the state structure for human needs and welfare. Gandhi advocates the latter strategy and sees political power diminished proportionate to the capacity of people to cultivate the quality of self-sufficiency. This, however, does not mean disengagement from politics. Instead it means only disengagement from that type of politics which only seeks to replace the power holders. Ultimately, the purpose is to create a new form of power whose hallmark is not domination and self-aggrandisement but love and service. Gandhi's resistance politics is in essence a struggle against all forms of power which is oppressive by harnessing this innate power of the people to love and serve their fellow beings.

Like any political philosopher Gandhi was engrossed in unravelling the ingredients of his view of human nature. Different notions of politics are also rooted in different notions of the self, human nature and the world—all mutually interrelated. A concept of human nature may be doubted for its epistemological validity given its speculative tenor, but is nonetheless "central in political theory". A view of human nature reveals what people actually potentially and ideally are. Views of human nature also are intimately linked to conceptions of history with the conservative among them always turning to the past for guidance.[12] Gandhi rejected history as a guide for determining the nature and potential of human beings. He also rejected atomistic views of the self and the centrality of self-interest in determining human nature. The Western notion of the self, which is mainly a possessive and egoistic entity, does not preclude concerns for an ordered social life. But the basis remains self-interest as ever. In other words, what is social interest is the aggregation of the self-interest of individuals rather than an ethical entity. Politics in this view is nothing but closely associated with notions such as interest articulation and aggregation and Gandhi's ideas would, therefore, appear as aberrations. For Gandhi, politics was the main sphere of action in the modern age. Gandhi sought to introduce moral principles into politics. He acknowledged Gokhale as his political guru mainly because his motives for entering politics were pure. Approving Gokhale, Gandhi held that politics should be a full time occupation engrossing the attention of some of the best in the country guided by truth, fearlessness, nonviolence and selflessness.[13] He saw engagement in politics as a part of his religious duty. Gandhi identified the absence of morality as the bane of modern politics and he did not hesitate to dub modern civilization as the culprit. Gandhi said: "For me there is no distinction between politics and religion. Politics are a sham without a religious backing; and if I am today immersed in the political life of the country it is because politics, i.e. the political conditions of the country are the predominant part of national life. No advance is possible without touching the political life at one point or other."[14]

Gandhi's view of politics is in concordance with his views on non-violence which denies the existence of an adversary. Outwitting the adversary in politics is seen like a game. Game theory in politics would imply a non-zero sum scenario although cases of variable sum are also possible. Conflict and cooperation are inevitable aspects of liberal politics. Even when cooperation takes place, the guiding principles are based on rational calculations rather than questions of morality.[15] Gandhi said: "The British people apply the same laws to the game of politics that they apply to the game of football which I believe is their intention. They give no quarter to the opponent and ask for none."[16] Further he said : "A believer in non-violence cannot be anybody's opponent. He would wish to build up the science of non-violence with the help of everyone. His is not the politics of opposing or vanquishing anyone.."[17]

Western notions of politics are based on anthropocentricism which privileges man's ontological status *vis-à-vis* the non-human world. In this view man belonged to a superior species, superior to and endowed with the power to dominate the rest of the universe. Such a notion of man as abstracted from the rest of the universe was not what Gandhi envisaged. He saw tendencies like imperialism and oppression as the result of this anthropocentric view. Gandhi believed in the indivisibility of the cosmos, the interdependence of the entire universe. What sustains that order is the spirit of mutual service, mutual performance of duties. The notion of self-interest which dominates the anthropocentric view of man has no place there. Because of the interdependence existing in the cosmos, what appears to be self-concerning for an individual is also other-concerning.

Gandhi questions at once the role of a professional politician and a political scientist. For him, knowledge has to be understood by everybody. His language which became often controversial given its occasional use of religious symbolism, was nonetheless couched in words which were known to all people. In other words, Gandhi could not think about anyone claiming a right to be an expert. His approach to epistemology was directed towards creating an idiom which will be understood by everybody.

More than any other political thinker or practitioner, it was Gandhi who showed to the world the uses of the body in the realm of politics. One of the major planks of his resistance politics is the employment of the full potentiality of the body to creative purposes. In doing so he breaks the notion of the body as a tool to be used by the mind. As Roby Rajan says:

> "For Gandhi, 'politics' is emphatically not a matter of formulating tactics and strategies for gaining the power to control and distribute resources, as it is for the Marxist; it is rather the living out of day-to-day suffering of the exploited other within the embodied self, and of continually applying the experimental lessons of this suffering to the process of ordering our collective lives. The role of the body is crucial here because of the Gandhian conviction that more can arise out of the body than whatever order society programmes into it, that there can be a morality that comes from the sensibilities of the body rather than from the imperatives of the super ego, and that it is by no means inevitable that our perception of social and political reality be channelled exclusively through the socially constituted ego. This runs counter to all the theories since Marx and Freud that have assumed there can be no feedback from the human organism except disorganised and dyspeptic resistance. Such theories can deny the body a critical capacity of its own only be reducing the body's organization to being either biologically programmed or to being completely

formed by social domination, by thus, denying the body's capacity to contribute to political processes, these discourses can then justify macro-socio-engineering; because change cannot come from individual bodies, it must be imposed on them—as market, as socialised means of production, or as some combination of the two."[18]

One of the strengths of Gandhi's political philosophy and for which he has anticipated many moderate post-modern thinkers is his refusal to think along Cartesian or Manichaean lines. He could not, for example, think of the private as contradistinguished from the public, body from mind and man from woman due to his faith in the doctrine of *Advaita*.

Roby Rajan continues:

".... Gandhi's central demonstration is that political claims can arise from the body's capacity at the crossroads of power to feel pain, experience suffering and sense unfulfilled needs. The speech that comes from this suffering motivates a correspondingly critical analysis of culture and a critical social praxis. There is no purely "inner" realm here that is not connected to social, political, economic and cultural conditions, just as there is no purely "outer realm" that is not connected with bodily experiencing. To effect a fissure between body and mind, between public and private, as the conventional discourses have done, is to betray the body's capacity to engage in political discourse, and to neglect changes in the self that call for and are in turn responsive to change in the larger society."[19]

Gandhi sought to spiritualise politics by depriving it of its strong egoistic moorings. Earlier those who belonged to the realm of spirituality best avoided politics. They were guided by the principle of individual salvation, which, they thought could be achieved by contemplation implying social disengagement. When Gandhi uses the word religion, spirituality and morality, they all mean the same. Earlier to Gandhi political theory, dominated as it was with principles of expediency and success in politics, paid less importance to the question of moral means. By insisting on the centrality of means in political theory, Gandhi struck a blow to mainstream political science by asking us to develop a normative science of politics that is non-violent. Why was Gandhi so obsessed with politics. He saw his salvation tied with improvement of the selves of others. He said: "Politics cannot be divorced from religion. Politics divorced from religion becomes debasing. Modern culture and modern civilization are such politics."[20] Also, "My bent is not political but religious and I take part in politics because I feel that there is no department of life which can be divorced from religion and because politics touch the vital being of India almost at every point."[21] Gandhi obviously considered the ends of politics and religion as same.

Gandhi often called the activities of the constructive workers true politics. True politics can come only when people lessen their dependence on the state; it took place outside state power. By making politics almost synonymous with social service, Gandhi makes the political subservient to the social.

In this respect, we see Gandhi heavily at odds with the Machiavellian/Augustinian/Hobbesian tradition in politics especially international politics represented in the tradition of political realism. Political realists think of the problem of politics as a purely technical one. St. Augustine finds no political obligation for the Christian to drive out his oppressors. Wicked kings will have to be endured and one can at best pray for them. Augustine had only pessimistic hopes of reforming the temporal order. Saintly men are to forsake the temporal in search of the spiritual or transcendental one, a purely private enterprise. In other words Augustine would recommend passivity for virtuous men.[22] Although modern political scientists interpret passivity as a mode of political protest, there is always the charge that a passive man is an escapist who is reneging on his responsibilities as a citizen. In Gandhi we see an attempt to wedge the gap between the spiritual and the temporal by seeing the temporal as the means for attaining the spiritual, of course through dispassionate self-less service. Politics thus becomes a pathway to achieve virtue. Tilak had used religious sentiments in his nationalist agenda. However, its thrust was more symbolic and realpolitik rather than moral. Political realists dichotomise the operation of morality by literally making it inapplicable in the public sphere. This is done by making the statement that politics is an autonomous activity governed by its own rules. The autonomy of politics or economics for that matter is challenged by Gandhi. Politics particularly in liberal democracies has come to assume an autonomy thanks to the "technocratization of politics" as Pantham calls.[23] The alternative Gandhi proposed to the notion of autonomy is the principle of *Dharma*. As Roy says : "To deny autonomy to politics is to argue for its subordination to some higher values which, for Gandhi, resides in *Dharma*. Without the support of *Dharma*, without the sustenance of a moral authority, a political order, even while it is a constitutional, representative democracy, has to rely on violence and coercion to uphold its authority. The increase in state violence is symptomatic of the erosion of *Dharma* at the individual level."[24] Technocratization is also a kind of mechanization as I see it inasmuch as a machine is simply run; it has never a chance to reflect upon what is going on. This is not to say that there is immorality in liberal politics. But they apply mechanistic notions of legitimacy, equilibrium, stability etc., to justify practices. They have reverence for existing structures. The dichotomy between private and public morality is rejected by Gandhi. He says,"I think political life must be an echo of private life and that there cannot be any divorce between the two."[25]

At a time when politics appeared ubiquitous Gandhi saw the political arena as the best place to serve his fellow beings. His model of a religious person, therefore, forced him to see politics as an arena of moral action and a means for self-realization. In other words, a truly spiritual person who is interested in self-realization should engage in politics. As Parekh says "Gandhi was one of the first to define morality in political terms, and politics in terms of active struggle against injustice and oppression."[26]

Political leadership as understood by Gandhi was nothing but moral leadership, not their oratory or their glamour but their capacity to undergo self-suffering and truthful *satyagraha*. The importance of suffering and abnegation in politics has been unheard of. In fact Gandhi does not see any contradiction between true democracy and morality. In order to work democracies, popular support and glamour alone are not enough. Only morally inspired leaders who are not enamoured with power alone can lead people. In contemporaray politics, the basis for political leadership is never a moral claim. A political leader is a person who can use oratory, lobbying skills, manoeuvring, propaganda and recently also glamour to carry forward his team and agenda. He should be a person who is capable of engaging in processes of adjustment among different groups. The channels of political recruitment are varied. According to Gandhi none of these qualify a person to become a public servant. In fact Gandhian ideas change the notion of political development and political socialization considerably. Political development consists of efforts aimed at reducing dependence on power politics and a weakening of the central apparatus. It also entails increasing capacity to become self-sufficient in every sense so as to make the intervening role of state and politics redundant. Political leadership should be thrust upon by the people and not sought after. Here Gandhi was all too conscious of his own leadership in the national movement. What will be the nature of such a leadership is difficult to say except that it has to arise not from the main field of politics but from the field of constructive programme, where leaders are expected to be closer to the people. We know that there is no evidence to privilege the power-seekers as the best people to run the affairs of the state. Although the masses and the leaders are said to act in confluence, a hiatus very often develops leading to the seeing of people as mere instruments rather than ends. Gandhi was aware of the increasing gap between the leaders and the masses. He appealed over their heads to the masses directly to find people who would dedicate themselves to the constructive programme and the development of a new political ethic.[27] This he called true politics. Hence the meaning and channels of political recruitment gets diverted from the field of power politics to one of social service and reform. Further, the importance of the role of conscience in social and political field is emphasised by Gandhi. He believed that even very small groups fired with zeal can make dramatic effect upon society. Voluntary poverty was suggested by Gandhi for politicians.

Now, the techniques that Gandhi would employ in politics need some consideration. The dominant mode of reasoning in politics is a rational one. Although *Satyagraha* is also rational, ultimately change is sought to be affected through change of heart thanks to suffering by the *satyagrahi*. While bargaining is seen as the very stuff of politics wherein moral principles are sought to be combined with the principle of expediency, Gandhi considered politics as a matter of principle compromise on which is possible only in matters related to details and incidentals but not on essentials.[28] In other words, Gandhi sought to create a new political ethic by emphasising moral persuasion as the main means of social change. It may be noted here that ancient Greeks considered political rule as government by pure persuasion and they spoke of force in governing as a pre-political phenomenon.[29] However, moral persuasion does not rule out the use of moral force or soul force. The employment of soul force can assume heights of intransigence for an external spectator. But for the participants, their involvement is not based on the publicity their movement might gain but a belief in the justness of the cause.

Suffering is a means of communicating with people as long as it is done for a just cause and is disinterestedly done. Gandhi said: "It has been said to me, 'Surely it is not necessary to impose this suffering upon ourselves? Why cannot the object be obtained by way of negotiation?' I reply, 'Argument has never convinced any man, but, on the contrary, conviction precedes argument.' If that were not so, all books would appeal to all men alike. I have been touched by books which made no appeal to millions, because I already had the conviction within me."[30] Moral persuasion has also a rational component. Rational communication is honest unlike manipulative communication, which is not honest. However, moral persuasion of Gandhi is not confined only to striking the rational faculty but also the heart or conscience of the opposing party. In this way Gandhi makes rationality subservient to conscience.

While assessing Gandhi's political philosophy one could either take a consequentialist/teleological approach or deontological approach. Partha Chatterjee has taken a former approach and has called Gandhi's arrival on the national scene as the "moment of manoeuvre in the passive revolution of capital in India."[31] His criticism that Gandhian ideology could not identify a social base and the net beneficiaries were the bourgeois is well taken. It is true that the peasants who participated in the national movement in gusto were distanced from the state of affairs after freedom. Judging everything in terms of its consequences is a typical liberal strategy. Gandhi was more for the intentions. If the intentions were pure, moral and self-less, one need not be obsessed with what came of an act for Gandhi had a hidden belief that the results cannot fail. In this way Gandhi demonstrated his cultural revulsion to the utilitarian Philistinism embedded in liberal politics. Events in the latter part of this century demonstrate that liberal politics is in crisis due to the feeling of alienation and loss of community that people experience. Popular participation in elections have declined. Further, new social movements are able to challenge the monopoly of political parties quite successfully. It may be noted that Gandhi had addressed this problem of alienation by providing us an alternative notion of politics, one based on a communitarian basic-needs model of democracy.

The monastic ideal of non-materialism is also reflected in Gandhi. Marxist approach to politics is to see it as derivative of economic development. Hence political development is to be measured by growth and change in the same material forces. A political system built around an agrarian or peasant order represents a less developed political system and social consciousness according to them.

Gandhi did not think that the liberal remedy of building suitable political institutions as a sign of political development. Institution-building has been of a late considered crucial by a number of political sociologists influenced by the behavioural persuasion. It is held that creation of legal and political institutions will take care of human caprices. Such a view has been quite strong in the West. In other words, predominant reliance is placed on external restraints to the exercise of power, i.e. institutional rather than ethical limits. The founding fathers of the US Constitution had this mechanical view, that once you have something like a clock in momentum, it will work in a Newtonian fashion uninterrupted by minor turbulences. Huntington was a strong advocate of institutionalisation for political development and political stability.[32] However when Gandhi says that private morality has public consequences, he is calling for an ethic of individual restraint rather than institutional restraint.[33]

The implications of Gandhi's approach to politics are clear. We have to develop a poltics which is nonviolent, so also a science of politics. In this view politics ultimately becomes a cooperative enterprise rather than a competitive enterprise. Cooperative because there is nobody who gets defeated in it. No political resistance agenda have talked about emancipation as one involving the agents of emancipation, the oppressors and the oppressed. This type of politics, based as it is on a notion of power as derivative of self-less service, is expected to bridge the hiatus between the leaders and the masses and make democracy more meaningful.

While looking at Gandhi's political philosophy, one notices points of criticism. One may question his excessive abhorrence of the state. This could be due to the experience of an oppressive state under British imperialism. The very same state can be used for moral freedom and human welfare, the possibility of making a present state a moral state has been almost out of consideration by Gandhi. The nature of each state should have been examined by Gandhi. A political scientist may notice elements of danger in Gandhi's strategies aimed at abolishing power politics. We know from history that when politics was abolished, it was replaced by administration by bureaucrats who had absolutely no knowledge of the pulse of the people. In democratic theory attempts to replace politics is seen as attempts towards totalitarian tendencies. It is only when we read Gandhi's ideas in their totality that it becomes clear that there is no space for totalitarianism in his thinking in view of the societization of politics that would follow rather than the politicisation of the social.

All said and done, Gandhi was sidelined in the post-independence phase, which suggests that he found solace only at the personal level. He did not thrust upon his followers ideas which they would not accept. Perhaps his anathema of power politics was responsible for his long survival. Judith M. Brown, in retrospect, says: "He (Gandhi) was used by India's politicians, followed for his skills and potential, and at times tactfully ignored by them when his priorities and practices seemed unproductive or divisive. He recognised this with a cheerful realism, and was content to be put on the shelf in ordinary political terms, provided that he was permitted to get on with what he perceived as his life's work—the construction of a new Indian polity and society infused with nonviolence and godliness—by other means. Ironically it was precisely because he was not a career politician that he had such a long career in politics, survived what to others would have been political retirement or even suicide, and was able to come back again and again to play a formidable political role when events made him a valuable resource to a significant number of his compatriots. He did indeed have charismatic effect on individuals and on vast crowds; but it was utility rather than charisma or mass conversion to his ideals which gave him at times such influence in national politics. Once this is understood it becomes clear why his influence in independent India was so limited. He himself sensed this would be so in the closing months of his life: that there would be no place for his ideals of self-denial and service when power was within the politician's grasp, that there would be more scope for his modes of action once Congress was the government rather than opposing the established regime."[34]

REFERENCES

1. Morris Jones, 1978. *Politics Mainly Indian*, Madras: Orient Longman, p. 89.

2. Raghavan Iyer (ed.) 1986. *Moral and Political Writings of Mahatma Gandhi,* Oxford : Clarendon Press, Vol. 1, p. 422 (hereafter referred to as Moral and Political Writings).
3. Rajni Kothari, 1972. *Politics in India,* New Delhi: Orient Longman, 1982 reprint, p. 57.

3a. Dennis Dalton, 1982. "The Concept of Politics and Power in India's Ideological Tradition" in Jeyaratnam Wilson and Dennis Dalton eds. *The States of South Asia : Problems of National Integration,* New Delhi: Vikas, pp. 176-77.

4. Dalton, 1979. "The Theory of Anarchism in Modern India—An Analysis of the Political Thought of Vivekananda, Aurobindo and Gandhi" in R. J. Moore (ed.) *Tradition and Politics in South Asia,* New Delhi: Vikas, p. 216.
5. Quoted in Dalton, *op. cit.,* 1982, p. 175.
6. Bhikhu Parekh, 1989. *Gandhi's Political Philosophy : A Critical Examination,* London: Macmillam, p. 122.
7. Bhikhu Parekh, 1986. "Some Reflections on the Hindu Tradition of Political Thought", in Thomas Pantham and Kenneth Deutsch (eds.) *Political Thought in Modern India,* New Delhi: Sage, pp. 17-31.
8. *Collected Works of Mahatma Gandhi,* New Delhi: Publications Division, Vol. 51, pp. 22-23 (hereafter referred to as Collected Works).
9. Johan Galtung, 1985, "A Gandhian Theory of Conflict", in David Selbourane (ed.) *In Theory and Practice: Essays on the Politics of Jayaprakash Narain,* New Delhi: Oxford University Press, p. 100.
10. Partha Chatterjee, 1986. *Nationalist Thought and the Colonial World : A Derivative Discourse,* New Delhi: Oxford University Press, pp. 90-92.
11. J.D. Sethi, 1986. "Centralisation, Decentralisation or Parallel Politics", In Ramashray Roy (ed.) *Contemporary Crisis and Gandhi,* New Delhi: Discovery, p. 230.
12. Graeme Duncan, 1983. "Political Theory and Human Nature" in Ian Forbes and Steve Smith (eds.) *Politics and Human Nature,* London: Frances Pinter, pp. 5-6.
13. *Collected Works.* Vol. 35, p. 297.
14. *Ibid.,* Vol. 22, p. 404.
15. For an excellent amplification of this position, see, Robert Axelrod, 1984. *The Evolution of Cooperation,* New York: Basic Books.
16. *Collected Works.,* Vol. 65, p. 250.
17. *Moral and Political Writings,* Vol. 1, p. 422.
18. Roby Rajan, 1990. "The Discourse of Exploitation and the Exploitation of Discourse", *Alternatives,* Vol. 15, pp. 47-48.
19. *Ibid.,* p. 48.

20. *Moral and Political Writings*, Vol. 1, p. 374.
21. *Ibid.*, p. 376.
22. William T. Bluhm. 1981. *Theories of the Political System*, New Delhi: Prentice Hall, p. 138.
23. Thomas Pantham. 1986. "Beyond Liberal Democracy: Thinking with Mahatma Gandhi", in Pantham and Deutsch (eds.) *op. cit.*, p. 333.
24. Ramashray Roy, 1984. *Soundings in Political Philosophy*, New Delhi: Chanakya, p. 78.
25. *Moral and Political Writings*, Vol. 1, p. 375.
26. Bhikhu Parekh. 1989. *op. cit.*, p. 104.
27. Raghavan Iyer, 1978. *Moral and Political Thought of Mahatma Gandhi*, Oxford: Clarendon Press, p. 369.
28. *Ibid.*, p. 309.
29. See Hanna Arendt, 1959. *The Human Condition*, Garden City: Double Day, pp. 29-30.
30. *Moral and Political Writings*, Vol. 1, p. 327.
31. Partha Chatterjee, *op. cit.*, p. 113.
32. See Samuel, P. Huntington. 1965. "Political Development and Political Decay", *World Politics*, 17, 3.
33. Susanne Hober Rudolph and Lloyd I. Rudolph, 1987. *Gandhi: The Traditional Roots of Charisma*, New Delhi: Orient Longman, p. 40.
34. Judith M. Brown, 1990. *Gandhi: Prisoner of Hope*, Delhi: Oxford University Press, p. 389.

21

Manavadharma and Pt. Nehru's Concept of Secularism

S.H. Patil

The concept of *Dharma* constitutes the central thinking of Indian people from the ancient period to the modern period. Etymologically, the Sanskrit word, *Dharma* is derived from the root, *dhar*, which means to hold or to maintain. But the philosophical meaning of *Dharma* is interpreted differently by different sages through *Srutis* and *Smritis*. However, it has generally come to mean observance of principles and prescriptions as laid down in the holy books. The word, *Dharma*, has some prefixes like *Rajdharma*, *Manavadharma*, etc. *Manavadharma* covers certain cardinal virtues like respect and concern for humanity.

Though Pt. Jawaharlal Nehru did not believe in any religion, yet he believed in and practised *Manavadharma* on secular basis. He had the greatest concern for humanity and wanted to lift it from poverty, ignorance, superstition, communal passions, etc. and planned to make men and women prosperous, rational, scientific, humane, secular, etc. The means that he adopted for these goals in India were democracy, socialism and secularism. The last one runs through the former two means. His concepts of democracy and socialism were coloured by secularism.

The present chapter intends to explain how Pt. Jawaharlal Nehru's concern for *Manavadharma* shaped his concept of secularism. Pt. Nehru's concept of secularism is rooted in his ideological foundations and practices which were developed/cultivated from his early days.

Nehru's Ideological Sources of Secularism

Pt. Nehru had faith in indivisibility of humanity and was known for his concern for human dignity, equality and freedom. He was an international humanist and used to react to every wrong in any part of the world. His concept of *Manavadharma* transcended all barriers of nations, nationalities, races, religions, castes, etc. Though he did not believe in any religion, yet he had greatest regard for innate spirituality of human beings. Thus his concept of secularism springs from his belief in indivisibility of humanity.

As Pt. Nehru had developed rational and scientific mind, his general outlook was not coloured by religious beliefs and practices and he was totally opposed to superstitions and dogmas. As a rationalist, he looked at problems from secular angle rather than from communal angle. His was objective approach to the problems of the country. He was critical of those who looked at politics through religion and he was more concerned about human life on earth rather than life after death. As Indian society was bound by tradition, orthodoxy, communalism and scientific backwardness, he wanted to build a new India on the basis of modernity, secularism and scientific spirit. Thus his concept of secularism is the outcome of his rational and scientific outlook.

Pt. Nehru was totally opposed to oppressive tendencies of organised religion but believed in moral and ethical development of individuals and society even without reference to religion. His concept of social religion is one which leads to inner change and development of individuals which in turn influences outer environment.[1] Though he was opposed to religion, yet he had belief in the innate spirituality of human beings.[2] He did not attack religion for the sake of criticism. His concept of secularism was not directed against the internal contents of religion but was directed against purposeless and outmoded external manifestations of religion. He wanted both man and state to be free from such religion which puts restrictions on change and progress which are inherent in both individual and society. In this respect he was very much influenced by Kemal Pasha of Turkey who was non-religious, abolished the sultanate and Khilafat and built a secular state. Pt. Nehru thus admired Kemal : "This very policy, however, made him more popular among the younger generation of both Hindus and Muslims."[3] Thus Pt. Nehru welcomed and appreciated the progressive forces/movements in any part of the world. As an opposition to the oppressive nature of organised religion and as a believer in scientific training and spirit, he developed liberal and progressive concept of secularism.

Pt. Jawaharlal Nehru was very much influenced by scientific socialism of Karl Marx. Though he modified scientific socialism in his own way at both ideological and operational levels, yet he continued to be under the influence of scientific spirit of socialism. He declared himself as a socialist at the Lahore session of the Indian National Congress (1929) in his presidential address and believed in all pervading philosophy of socialism : "I must frankly confess that I am a socialist and a republican. ... But we must realise that the philosophy of socialism has gradually permeated the entire structure of society the world over ... India will have to go that way too."[4] Scientific socialism had profoundly influenced Pt. Nehru's concept of secularism. Scientific socialism and communalism do not go together because they are diametrically opposed to each other.

As a socialist, Pt. Nehru considered both the Hindu Mahasabha and the Muslim League as reactionary forces which stood for vested interests. Addressing the students of the Banares Hindu University, Pt. Nehru said, "Under the cover of seeming nationalism, the (Hindu) Mahasabha not only hides the rankest and narrowest communalism but also desires to preserve the vested interests of a group of Hindu landlords and princes."[5] On some other occasion, Pt. Nehru said that the Muslim League was a reactionary organisation and stood for vested interests as against the general and national interests.[6] He opined that the communal forces were not only anti-secular but also reactionary. Thus, he believed that such communal and reactionary forces could be eliminated only through secularism and socialism.

Communal unity, tolerance and peace which are some of the elements of secularism had tremendous influence on Pt. Nehru's outlook towards communal harmony. In this connection, he was influenced by Buddha, Asoka and Gandhi. In his broadcast to the nation at Delhi on 26th March, 1964, he emphasised tolerance and communal harmony : "Ever since the distant past, it has been the proud privilege of the people of India to live in harmony with one another. That has been the basis of India's culture. Long ago, the Buddha taught us this lesson. From the days of Asoka, 2300 years ago, this aspect of our thought has been repeatedly declared and practised. In our own day, Mahatma Gandhi laid great stress on it and indeed lost his life because he laid great stress on communal goodwill and harmony. We have, therefore, a precious heritage to keep up, and we cannot allow ourselves to act contrary to it."[7] Thus, Pt. Nehru's concept of secularism has been influenced by India's legacy of social harmony.

Nehru's Two Concepts of Secularism

Pt. Jawaharlal Nehru's concept of secularism can be explained at two levels—ideal and practical.

Ideal concept of secularism of Pt. Nehru which exists at his free thinking level is free from existing conditions and compulsions and is based on the highest concept of *Manavadharma* and scientific spirit. As Pt. Nehru was influenced by scientific rationality and socialism, his concept of secularism was totally free from the control of religions. Religion is personal and private. State has nothing to do with religion and religion has nothing to do with state. Under such free conditions the individuals are free thinkers and grow with their creative abilities. They interact with one another as fellow human beings and are held together by common secular ideas. They are humane and are guided by concept of *Manavadharma* in their social interactions and in the pursuit of common goals.

Pt. Nehru's another concept of secularism is a compromised concept which is a mixture of his free thinking and compulsions of existing conditions in India. This second best concept of secularism is influenced by concern for unity of India. He believed that territorial unity of India should be based on a unity of mind and heart.[8]

The following are the features of Pt. Nehru's operational secularism (secondbest concept of secularism) : (i) In his concept of secular state all religions have equal status. "India will be a land, as in the past, of many faiths equally honoured and respected"[9], said Pt. Nehru. (ii) All religions shall have freedom to perform religious ceremonies. (iii) No religion shall have any special privilege. (iv) No community shall be deprived of its legitimate rights on the basis of religion. (v) There shall be equal opportunities for followers of all religions. Pt. Nehru proclaimed : "We have laid down in our Constitution that India is a secular state. That does not mean irreligious. It means equal respect for all faiths and equal opportunities for those who profess any faith."[10] (vi) Pt. Nehru had respect for composite culture of India which is a multi-religious country and has been home to all those who have come and settled here. In such composite society majority and minority communities should learn to believe in peaceful co-existence. However, the majority religion has a major role in maintaining communal harmony and secularism. Pt. Nehru as the president of the Indian National Congress used to write letters to the presidents of the Pradesh Congress Committees about need for communal harmony and responsibility of major community in preserving and promoting secularism. In one of his letters he emphasised that the Hindus must always remember that the interests and the well-being of the minorities were their sacred trust. (vii) Every citizen has the same rights, duties and privileges and has full freedom to profess and practise his religion. No citizen is subject to any social inequalities imposed by religious sanctions. (viii) The state shall follow the policy of neutrality in religious matter and the government shall not directly associate itself with any religion. Pt. Nehru's concept of national state is not a theocratic state but a secular state in which citizens of different religions live peacefully. In his address to the students of Aligarh Muslim University in 1948, Pt. Nehru opposed the concept of theocratic state and opined that such state was outdated. The modern state should be essentially a secular system. (ix) As a modern state is a secular institution, it has nothing to do with religion. Pt. Nehru did not accept the relevance of religion to national identity.

Nehru : Symbol of Secularism

Pt. Nehru's early association with Muslims, cosmopolitan atmosphere in the home, early exposure to Western influence in England, his love for science, etc., shaped his concept of secularism.

Pt. Nehru set an example of secular spirit and practice. He has been described as an Englishman by training and education, Muslim by culture and Hindu by accident of birth. Though description is satirical, yet it represents secular and universal character of Pt. Nehru. As he was brought up in such composite environment, his views and practices were secular and universal.

As a visionary and revolutionary, Pt. Nehru preached and practised secularism which was an article of faith with him. Secularism was a part of his inner self. Even if one studies Pt. Nehru from psychological angle, one finds secular dimensions of his inner self. This part of his inner self was projected through his writings, speeches and actions. Thus there was no gap between his private life and public life with regard to secularism. He set an example in this regard and wanted his countrymen to be secular in thought and action. As a charismatic leader, he had an emotional hold over the people of India. He was able to convince the masses about potentialities of secularism from various angles.

Two Models of Secularism

Secularism was developed by the Indian National Congress during the freedom movement as a means to bring about unity and harmony among the various religious groups in India. Among the Congress leaders, Mahatma Gandhi and Pt. Nehru immensely contributed to the concept and practice of Indian secularism.

Gandhian secularism is based on oneness of God, one mankind, religious tolerance and mutual respect. It has religious touch and is in tune with the traditional Indian ideal of *Sarvadharma Sambhava*.

Pt. Nehru's concept of secularism is influenced by humanism, rationalism, scientific spirit and socialism. It comes nearer to the Western liberal concept of secularism.

In course of time these two models of secularism (Gandhian and Nehruvian) came to be developed informally. Indian secularists are influenced by either of these two models depending upon their upbringing and ideals. The Constitution of India has tried to provide synthesis of Gandhian and Nehruvian models of secularism to some extent.

Challenges to Secularism

Pt. Jawaharlal Nehru considered the religious passions, organised religions, communalism, alliance between religion and politics, etc., as serious challenges to the Indian secularism.

He was totally opposed to religious passions which blunt reason. He said, "But religious passions have little to do with reason or consideration or adjustments."[11] Such irrational passions are hurdles to bring about tolerance and adjustment among different religious groups.

Pt. Nehru was against organised religion which develops vested interest in course of time and becomes reactionary force opposing progress and change. He saw a continuous and unending war between religion and science. Religion imposes restrictions on mind while science encourages open mind. Secularism flourishes only in open and rational societies. Thus organised religion which is a closed religion cannot sustain and encourage scientific secularism.

Communalism not only divides the people but also puts back the state to the medieval period. It exploits and encourages hatredness against another religious group in the name of religion. According to Pt. Nehru, the conflict is not between the Hindus and the Muslims in India but it is between communalism and secularism and between reactionary forces and progressive forces. Thus he condemns communalism : "Communalism is the badge of a backward nation, not of the modern age."[12]

According to Pt. Nehru, "Alliance between religion and politics is unholy. Such alliance leads to disintegration of plural societies and such politicised communal groups are always at war with one another and are enemies of India. Such communal forces have, therefore, taken advantage of the cloak of religion to cover up their reactionary policies, have exploited the name of religion in politics and have excited people's passions in that name."[13] Speaking in the Constituent Assembly on 3rd April, 1948, Pt. Nehru condemned alliance between politics and religion : "We must have it clearly in our minds and in the minds of the country that the alliance of religion and politics in the shape of communalism is a most dangerous aliance, and it yields the most abnormal kind of illegitimate brood."[14]

Nehru's Measures to Secularise India

Pt. Nehru suggested among others two important measures to establish secularism in India. These are secular social life and secular education.

Though Pt. Nehru was fully aware of hold of religions in India on social codes, social rules, marriage, inheritance, civil and criminal law, social organisation, etc., he wanted to secularise all walks of life of Indian people. He introduced many social legislations to secularise the life of people. He was not merely interested in a secular state but was very keen in establishing a secular society. According to him, it is only secular society which can sustain and promote secular state.

As education is a means to bring about predetermined socio-economic and political changes in society, Pt. Nehru emphasised scientific, rational and secular education with concern for society and individuals. He believed that such modern education alone could create secular citizens who in turn could build a secular state. On several occasions, he laid greater stress on modern and secular education and made attempts to restructure educational system in that direction.

Relevance of Nehru's Concept of Secularism

Pt. Nehru's concept of secularism is not only relevant to India but also to the whole world because it is progressive and is in tune with evolution of human civilisation and scientific development.

If India has to come out from the clutches of communalism, ethnicism, casteism, etc., it has to adopt Pt. Nehru's concept of scientific secularism. Communal conflicts, communal hatred and communal violence which have assumed structural dimensions and have become autonomous in recent years can be removed by implementing Pt. Nehru's measures meant for establishing secularism based on *Manavadharma*.

Though the framers of Constitution of India had given secular state structure to great extent, in recent years attempts have been made by the various political parties and pressure groups to restructure Indian political system and subsystems on communal/caste basis in order to win over votes. It is Nehruvian secularism which can provide antidote to these attempts to communalise Indian politics and can keep Indian political structure and Indian citizens secular. It is only secular citizens who can create secular political process.

When Nehruvian secularism is relevant today, its contents should form a part of syllabi of textbooks in schools and colleges.

Mass media like T.V., Radio and newspapers should periodically carry features on Nehruvian concept of secularism.

Mass movements should be carried on in the various parts of India to convey the message of Pt. Nehru's concept of secularism to the people.

Pt. Nehru's secular practices should be model to the leaders and the masses of India.

Pt. Nehru firmly believed that the Indian nationalism is to be built on secularism rather than on communalism. As a student of Indian and world history, he was convinced that

Indian nationalism is to be built on secularism. He was totally opposed to the concept of Hindu nationalism, Muslim nationalism and Sikh nationalism. He was in favour of secular nationalism. Today Nehruvian concept of secular nationalism is to be developed vigorously to meet the communal challenges from the various parts of the country to the unity of India.

Secularism based on *Manavadharma*, socialism and scientific temper is one of the greatest contributions made by Pt. Nehru to the nation-building process in India.

Pt. Nehru maintained and promoted secular nature of sub-system like the party system. Under his leadership, the Congress never lost its secular character and outlook. It had become a vehicle for secular expression and a secular agent for political socialisation.

As Pt. Nehru was an internationalist, he believed in peaceful co-existence of different nations based on different religious, social and economic ideologies. According to him, India should be a model in peaceful co-existence and should demonstrate it from its own experience of peaceful co-existence on secular basis. He was very confident that India would be a model in this respect and would become a part of one world order in future. Thus he expressed his hope : "As far as India is concerned, I can speak with some certainty. We shall proceed on secular and national lines in keeping with the powerful trends towards internationalism. Whatever confusion the present may contain, in the future, India will be a land, as in the past, of many faiths equally honoured and respected, but of one national outlook, not, I hope, a narrow nationalism living in its own shell, but rather the tolerant creative nationalism which, belief in itself and the genius of its people, takes full part in the establishment of an international order. The only ultimate aim we can have is that of one world."[15] Thus, Pt. Nehru's concept of secularism which is based on enlightened *Manavadharma* and rationality is not only relevant to India but also to the whole world. Essentially it is a unifying ideology and force for the whole mankind. In Nehruvian concept of one world, peace, prosperity, freedom and secularism are indivisible.

REFERENCES

1. Nehru, Jawaharlal, *An Autobiography* (Bombay : Allied Publishers Private Limited, 1962), p. 379.
2. *The Hindu*, March 28, 1960, quoted by Neeraj, *Nehru and Democracy in India* (Delhi : Metropolitian Book Co. Pvt. Ltd., 1972), p. 74.
3. Nehru, Jawaharlal, *The Discovery of India* (Delhi : Oxford University Press, 1989), p. 350.
4. Nehru, Jawaharlal, *India's Freedom* (London : Unwin Books, 1962), p. 14.
5. Nehru, Jawaharlal, *Recent Essays and Writings* (Allahabad : Kitabistan, 1937), pp. 45-46.
6. *Ibid.*, pp. 49-51.
7. Nehru, Jawaharlal, *Jawaharlal Nehru's Speeches*, Vol. V, March 1963—May 1964 (New Delhi : Publications Division, Ministry of Information and Broadcasting, Government of India, 1968), p. 12.
8. Nehru, Jawaharlal, *Jawaharlal Nehru's Speeches*, Vol. II (Delhi : Publication Division, Ministry of Information and Broadcasting, Government of India, 1967), p. 93.
9. Sen, N.B. (ed.), *Glorious Thoughts of Nehru* (New Delhi : New Book Society of India, 1964), p. 62.
10. Saxena, A.P. (ed.), *Jawaharlal Nehru and Indian Administration* (New Delhi : Uppal Publishing House, 1991), p. 171.
11. Nehru, Jawaharlal, *An Autobiography* (Bombay : Allied Publishers Private Limited, 1962), p. 135.
12. Nehru, Jawaharlal, *Jawaharlal Nehru's Speeches*, Vol. IV, September 1957-1963 (New Delhi : Publication Division, Ministry of Information and Broadcasting, Government of India, 1964), p. 12.
13. Nehru, Jawaharlal, *Jawaharlal Nehru's Speeches*, Vol. II, (Delhi : Publication Division, Ministry of Information and Broadcasting, Government of India, 1954), p. 351.
14. Nehru, Jawaharlal, *Independence and After* (A Collection of the More Important Speeches of Jawaharlal Nehru from September 1946 to May 1949) (Delhi : Publications Division, Ministry of Information and Broadcasting, Government of India, 1949), p. 47.
15. Sen, N.B. (ed.), *Glorious Thoughts of Nehru* (New Delhi : New Book Society of India, 1964), p. 262.

22

Rajendra Prasad and Religion, *Dharma* and Politics

D.N. Mallik

A religion is a set of beliefs. It may involve a certain philosophy, a framework of life values, forms of worship and concomitant rituals—all based on certain teachings, precepts and scriptures—to which people organised in a sect for certain range of time, numerically limited and small or demographically and territorially widespread, may be committed as followers. But *dharma,* quite often taken or mistaken as the Hindi versions of religion, has a different connotation. Whereas religion concerns only human beings, *dharma* bears not only on human beings but also on all other animate or inanimate objects, so much so that it may well be attributed to the tiger, the crow, the rose, fire or water apart from human beings. Among human beings the *dharma* of the father may not be the same as the *dharma* of the mother. It may have diverse callings on diverse individuals in diverse situations. It has to do with the intrinsic nature of a person or an object, may be with reference to its kind or its particularities along with its resultant functional dispensation. Linked inseparably with the question of legitimacy, which has its reference to volition beyond brute force in collectivity, politics concerns only human beings and does so in a specific social context of theirs—the context of governance—which, however, is of utmost importance to their social existence. That context may involve several levels.

The three—religion, *dharma* and politics—may well be perceived as linked in the human context and that perception has prevailed in the Indian political thinking right from its deeply ancient origins. In recent modern Indian thinking, largely like Gandhi, though not always identically like him, Rajendra Prasad appears personifying the linkage with a striking purity intellectually as also behaviourally.

I

He may be viewed to have been concerned with religion (i) as a factor of his own growth as a human person, (ii) as a practitioner of it, (iii) as a front-rank political leader of India's national movement and its sequel, and (iv) as a patriot caring for the country's interest.

(1) In his growth as a human person he deeply bore the influence of the *sanatan* Hindu religion as a stimulant to living life in a family and a society rather than as a sect. That is why he also amply bore the influence of inter-religion social harmony or fraternity in which he grew. He detested and deeply regretted inter-religion misunderstandings and conflicts which, however, he tried to comprehend dispassionately, analyse constructively and allay with utmost sincerity of thought and action. The social life which he had lived had imparted to him a dispensation to respect all other religions while adhering firmly to his own. Yet religion does not appear to have concerned him as a thought or life preoccupation.

Religiosity occurred to him as a necessity and was not transmitted. As a dawn-riser from his very early childhood he used to "coax" his mother to recite *bhajans* and narrate stories from the *Ramayana,* waiting for the morning to come, and in that process he felt "stirred by interest" and "deeply" influenced. He grew in the midst of group recitals from the *Ramayana* and the *Bhagwat* in the village, the *kathas,* the *Ramlila* parties, etc., which presented to him a social atmosphere which he liked and loved. But, at the same time, his first tutor-teacher was a *maulavi* of deeply religious temperament and habits whom he endearingly respected. While religion permeated his vllage society which was characterised by a "perfect harmony between Hindus and Muslims", each community joining in religious festivity of the other as a matter of course and life habit. Although, as he recapitulates in his autobiography, the Hindus, who accepted sweets from the Muslims, would not accept water from their hands, the latter understood the sentiments of the former and did not mind.[1]

(2) As a habitual practitioner of *sanatan* Hinduism, he adhered not only to its essence but, generally, to its forms also. For instance, even on attaining adulthood he would not accept meals cooked by non-high caste Hindus and would not co-dine with them[2] and would observe worships, occasions and rituals demanded by that religion. Whereas that was normal for him, he would not hesitate in giving up orthodoxies and, in that, his family liberally encouraged him. For example, he and his family members decided to have a community dining with one of his castemen who had returned from abroad on completing his studies and patiently faced the wrath of the bulk of his caste community in his locality which sought, practically in vain, to excommunicate and boycott that gentleman and those who had had community dinner with him. Prasad had no regrets on that account.[3] Another minor instance of departure from the orthodox practices may be had from the fact that whereas in every *pitripaksha* he would not shave, in one *pitripaksha* he shaved and, on being questioned, he made the matter light by taking the position that his personal convenience had sway over religious observance.[4] Otherwise, he had also a strong tendency even to bank on *ayurvedic* treatment.[5] He believed in the Hindu deities just as any devout Hindu would do, but, perhaps, without much ado.

(3) As a front-rank political leader of the national movement and free India he could not escape having his concern for religion which, in India's traditional and colonial society, necessarily impinged on politics directly or, *via* social structures, indirectly.

Right since his entry to the legal profession and politics (of the state or national) he remained inescapably concerned with communal situations of major and minor character. For quite some time in the beginning he went on noting with delight how the wave of nationalism appeared frustrating the imperialist game of 'divide and rule' indulged in by the British *raj* and, particularly, by its scheming bureaucrats.[6] In his own state he relished the availability of leaders like Mazharul Haque whom he revered for his dedication to the cause of Hindu-Muslim unity.[7] It was a matter of great satisfaction to him that up to the pursuit of the Khilafat movement in right earnest, the national scenario of inter-community harmony presented an encouragingly happy state of affairs. But, with the advent of 1920s, which witnessed the waning of the Khilafat Movement zeal of the Muslims as the very cause of it was lost and ushered in the politics of elections for Council Entry under the Government of India Act, 1919, he began to note with deep regrets, that vitiation set in and the Muslims began to distrust and doubt the intentions of the majority Hindu community and went on getting alienated from the latter.[8] He was very much a party to the national struggle to ward off that unhealthy trend and continued to play his role at times with delighting success—more particularly in Bihar, his own state.[9]

The Indian National Congress stood in a state of division and confusion in relation to the question of Council Entry and, in that kind of pathetic situation, its grip over communal harmony went on loosening, the advantage gradually passing to the Muslim League which, by sectorally championing the Muslim interest, began to generate a new Muslim psyche in Indian politics and went on successfully enlisting larger and larger Muslim loyalty and support.[10] Although in the context of protest against the visit of the Simon Commission Prasad felt happy with the instances of some kind of revival of Hindu-Muslim cooperation, he felt frustrated with the realisation that the national endeavour to project right kind of constitutional reforms failed to carry the Muslims with it.[11] The two Round Table Conferences brought that fear to the fore as a glaring multi-pronged communal schism by playing on the scheme of Communal Awards not only for the Muslims but also for the Sikhs (whom Prasad viewed as largely an offshoot of Hinduism) and the Scheduled Caste Hindus (who continued to belong clearly to the fold of Hinduism).[12]

The dirty imperialist game had its cherished victims and national politics went on getting plagued. Rajendra Prasad, as a front-rank Congress leader, at times as its President, fought against the trends and prayfully associated himself with Gandhi's life-costing (fasting) strifes full of pangs and sacrifices in that struggle. He took those pangs to an intellectual level by authoring *India Divided* in which he forcefully and vividly exposed the nasty logic and pernicious obstinacies of the Muslim League without being bitter.[13] It was a great relief of him to find that the Sikhs and, particularly, the Scheduled Caste leaders like B.R. Ambedkar could get persuaded out of the pitfall.[14] In fact, the efforts to do away with untouchability with a view to demolishing a highly undesirable Hindu "social structure", heralded and crusaded bravely by Gandhi, inspired, convinced and stirred Prasad to go into a wholehearted action on a nationwide scale although he never failed to realise that such a demolition would naturally take a considerably long time because of the petrification that the structure had gained for millenia.[15] At this point, even as a *sanatani* Hindu, Prasad had no hesitation in kicking off what is today being despised by neo-Ambedkarites as a deplorably *manuvadi* dispensation or disposition. Politics of elections ensuing under the Government of India Act, 1919 and, subsequently, under the Government of India Act, 1935 had brought to the fore not only communal but also casteist and regional tendencies as fall-outs of the age-old Hindu practices of discrimination and social repression and Prasad never failed to underline such unfortunate developments which had to be viewed as highly undesirable and had to be contained.[16]

In so far as the working up of the Muslim psyche in Indian politics was concerned, Prasad's interaction with it had a few more interesting features. In the early 1920s, when Gandhi's impact on Prasad was not as deep as it developed to be later, Prasad passed through a phase in which his position approximated to B.G. Tilak's. In the late 1890s and the first decade of this century Tilak had advocated and worked for unity among the Hindus in order to contain the vitiation of the Muslim psyche under 'divide and rule' machinations of the imperialist bureaucrats. In the early 1920s Lala Lajpat Rai and Madan Mohan Malviya began to take a similar line in politics. Rajendra Prasad supported and encouraged Malaviya in the pursuit of that drive of his in Bihar. Recapitulating that phase much later Prasad owned what he had done, stating that since the Hindu Mahasabha did not cut across the Indian National Congress at that stage and its action, at that stage, did not smack of communalism he had no regrets for what he had then done.[17] The fact of the matter appears to be that while doing what he did, he did not have any anti-Muslim bias and all he had intended was to correct the Muslim mindset undesirably so developing in its early phase.

The other feature of Prasad's interaction could be seen in his reaction of apprehension at the realisation in the late 1920s and 1930s that the Muslim migrants from Bengal had started upsetting the demographic contours of sparsely inhabited Assam and other north-eastern parts of India. In fact, he moved to counteract that trend by inducing the people in Bihar to purchase land in those parts and settle there both for prosperity and for containing the demographic imbalances in a situation in which Biharis were much more welcome to the Assamese and others as compared with the Bengalis whom they viewed as somewhat imperious. Prasad admitted that the counteraction, though tried, could not go far in view of the bad physical climate in those parts.[18]

Yet another feature of Prasad's interaction could be seen in the context of pre- and post-parition communal riots, consequent problem of rehabilitation and the nature of emigrations which took place from India to Pakistan and *vice versa*. Prasad, with all his genuine secularism, had no hesitation in pinning down the greater onus on the Muslims and particularly their League leadership for the riots.[19] He portrays the multi-dimensional pangs of rehabilitation as a tragedy of contemporary Indian history with utmost humanistic and patriotic concern[20], and shows no inhibition in frankly expressing his fear that though a large number of Muslims did migrate also from India to Pakistan (quite a few of them voluntarily), the Hindus in West Pakistan and largely also in

East Pakistan faced virtual extirpation. He found such developments dismayingly unfair.[21] This feeling of his had more a patriotic hue than a political leaderly one.

II

Ingredients of the perception of *dharma* in Rajendra Prasad bear on the individual human person's relation to his family, society in its village, community, locality, provincial, national and international manifestations, Nature and the Cosmic Force or God and, naturally in view of such conditioned relations, they bear vitally on his perception of politics also.

(1) For Prasad, who grew as an individual in a joint Hindu family, was cheered up, hailed and esteemed socially for his brilliant academic performances and rose, first, as a student leader and soon as an endeared and esteemed political leader in his province and from that plinth as a front-rank national political leader reaching the national apex as the President of the Indian republic, the individual's *dharma* had all these social manifestations. But, as it appears, the individual might have to resolve dilemmas when faced with the conflicts of duties beween levels. Which was prior—the individual's duty first or more to his family or to larger levels of society? For Prasad, whereas the individual owed his duty, services and sacrifice to all social levels, his *dharma* lay in attaching priority to the level of society which was higher. Prasad was aware that the individual, with his higher, deeper and more enlightened understanding of things, might be faced with much lower, much more shallow and much less enlightened members of society and yet, according to him, he had to indulge with them as a spiritual exercise which demanded compassion, patience, sincerity and humanity.[22] Prasad, as it appears, viewed all kinds of egotism and ostentation—individual, ethnic or national—as misplaced, uncalled for, futile and even injurious to the health of the sociality of human existence. He had abhorrence for pride of any kind.[23]

(2) He would like human beings to be inasmuch harmony with nature as they could and had a kind of aversion to what

often appeared to him as an excessive exploitation of nature by man. In fact, he viewed it as man's capriciousness and held that it essentially injured human interests as also the universe.[24] Prasad often reflected on the ruins of the great national memorials (such as Egyptian pyramids) developed in the past at colossal human costs and regretted their ultimate futility.[25] He often had reservations on what continue to be hailed as feats of science and technology.[26]

(3) Prasad was a *pucca* believer. What guided him as a believer was the message of the *Gita* which would like a human person to pursue his duties from the station of his life with utmost humility and without any attachment to their results which depended not on his own will but on the will of the Cosmic Force. Such a detachment of the *sthitprajna* explained in that classic, Prasad believed, might be very, very difficult to attain, but had to be cultivated by the individual to the extent he could with his given weaknesses as a living creature, for only in that kind of struggle lay his redemption and deliverance as also the much larger well-being of the mankind in all its collectivities.[27]

(4) The spirituality, of which *dharma*, as perceived by Rajendra Prasad, was a coefficient, was no bar against some of his proclivities like his inclination not to dismiss astrological readings and calculations[28], some meditational or yogic exercises[29], some miraculous happenings, and some supernatural practices like the planchet playing.[30] In all such things he contrasted with Jawaharlal Nehru.

III

Rajendra Prasad felt drawn to politics not owing to any high ambition for power or for self-aggrandisement but because of the ideal of service to society for which it appeared to offer opportunities even though entailing sacrifices and sufferings. Not that he got drawn to it in any kind of flamboyant zeal; in fact, he felt tortured and torn in abandoning three of his primary loyalties which did weigh very heavily with him—loyalty to his joint family which had brought him up with high hopes as it was fast declining financially, devotion to his studies in which he had been shining and making great many others proud of himself and love for the legal profession in which he had started doing reckonably well because of the competence which he had soon acquired.[31] But, going by his *dharma* as a person in his given social situation (the newly emerging, neglected, province of Bihar where he was born and brought up and its educated youth who had to be woken up, stirred and mobilised as a force to take the province out of its backwardness on the one hand and the nation of India under the imperialist yoke struggling to achieve self-government on the other), he found politics as a higher or the highest calling.

(1) Apart from the nobleness of society-serving embedded in it, politics for Prasad was essentially a kind of interaction in which its practitioner, in being guided by certain objectives which he pursued, had to act in a collectivity constituted by many, many others like him. Some of them might also radically differ from him and his like-minded politicians or even adversely opposed to them. He expected fairness, decency and, as far as possible, amiability in such dealings and conducted himself accordingly.[32] If he knew that he and his like-minded colleagues did not command a majority following, he would like the majority-holders to carry. But, since the course or courses of action being followed would be the latters', he and his colleagues would maintain a position which would, in all fairness, keep away the onus from them.[33] If the differences would be minor or of procedure rather than of substance, they might cooperate also.[34] But on certain basic essentials Prasad would not compromise. Whatever the character of differences, Prasad would successfully shun bitterness in interactions and had a tremendous capacity to continue admiring and endearing his opponents, adversaries and rivals also for whom he maintained friendly disposition.[35] It may be contended that the behavioural essence of his politics was of a constructively liberal-democratic high order—free from dirty machinations or politicking. He was a realist rather than an idealist and yet his realism had little to do with realpolitik. His realism seldom entertained any kind of romanticism or utopianism and it was

such timbers in his political making as distinguished him not only from his peers but also from his political preceptor, i.e., Gandhi and made him a highly respected and, essentially, popular national leader.

(2) No doubt, there were some early influences on his induction to politics—intellectual, youth-activity-oriented and of great men and women like Gopal Krishna Gokhale, Annie Besant and St. Andrews, etc. But the deepest and lasting influence on his political making was that of Gandhi. That influence did not pass to him abruptly or as a matter of spell. He got drawn to Gandhi only after two or three first contacts in which, though aware of his South African feats, he was not deeply and greatly impressed.[36] The influence began to be catchy only in course of the Champaran *satyagrah* in which he worked with him and it went on deepening as he gradually grasped the mind, the ways, the principles and the techniques of that great man[37] and tended to accept him as his spiritual-political master to such an extent that, short of turning into a blind follower of his, he began to act in politics and calamities as his alter ego. He began to subscribe to his exalted principles of truth and non-violence along with the techniques like *satyagrah*, non-cooperation, civil disobedience, peaceful *hartals* and demonstrations and courting imprisonment, etc. He fully subscribed also to the Gandhian dictum on means-and-end equations. In Prasad's case, it was not merely subscribing to those principles. In fact, he became an exponent of those principles—often excelling the master in intellectually interpreting and communicating them.[38] There were several occasions when he highly successfully conducted big mass agitations in terms of those principles often suffering and even sustaining minor or major injuries notwithstanding a delicate physique and even more delicate health as a chronic patient of asthma. On quite a few of such occasions the remarkably peaceful passage of the agitation thrilled him and he often wondered the understanding shown by the English officers for his steersmanship, for, otherwise, they were awfully repressive.[39] In the pursuit of Gandhian politics of the national movement he was second to none among its political generals—

Jawaharlal Nehru, Ballabhbhai Patel, Abul Kalam Azad and Chakravarti Rajgopalachari. The fact of the matter was that none among them was essentially as faithful to the master and as self-affacing in being faithful as was Prasad and it was not at all surprising that only he among them gave no occasion to the master to feel constrained or correcting. He followed the master with utmost sincerity and effectiveness in matters like organising, propagating and developing the *Khadi* industry as a noble national cause, in seeking to do away with untouchability and in promoting the Gandhi Seva Sangh institutionally. Yet, sometimes, he had initial reservations on Gandhi's moves and in a few things, though they were very few, his stands, differed from those of the latter. For examples, he would not go whole hog with Gandhi in projecting free India as a non-violent state[40], and was much more categorically anti-fascist in the dilemma which arose in the Indian national movement with the coming of the Second World War because of the British intransigency and the menace of Japanese invasion of India.[41] He had won the hearts of the master and peers with the way he led the people of Bihar in facing the calamitous earthquake of 1934.[42]

(3) Although Rajendra Prasad had no systematic political thinking with any steady ideological basis for it except the Gandhian principles and Gandhi's leadership and guidance, the political values to which he subscribed and the kind of politics he would approve may be overviewed with reference to two phases—the national movement and its aftermath.

During the national movement, beside the values upheld and followed by him, as stated earlier and above, he, as a youth, was opposed to the move for partitioning Bengal.[43] He did not have any admiration for the violent freedom-fighting activities of Bhagat Singh and others even as he respected their patriotic sentiments.[44] Although he was a firm No-Changer with regard to the question of Council Entry in the sequel to the Government of India Act, 1919 and regretted the division and confusion because of the No-Changers *versus* Pro-Changers controversy, he stood for maximum accommodation of Pro-Changers' views. But he was very clear in his disapproval of the Pro-Changers' stand that they, on entering the Council, would work for disrupting the government process as that kind of stand smacked of an unbecoming duplicity.[45] In and around the endeavour of the national movement to project the track of right kind of constitutional reforms by by-passing the visit of the Simon Commission and, subsequently, in and around the two Round Table Conferences Rajendra Prasad was a votary of India looking for the Dominion Status rather than Complete Independence as being voiced by Jawaharlal Nehru, Subhas Chandra Bose, the socialists and others.[46] The simple reason for the stand which he had taken was his conviction that the people of India had yet to be prepared for Complete Independence and that Dominion Status would bring to India respectable self-government and yet enable it to remain connected with Great Britain and its Dominions. Later, as the trend developed towards the demand for Complete Independence, he accepted the same. The politics of elections at diverse levels in the 1920s and more so in the 1930s caused him, as an eminent member of the Congress Parliamentary Board with only Patel and Azad to share its decisions with him, some serious worries on account of the trails of disaffections and jealousies and trends of indiscipline they surfaced.[47] During that phase whereas many stalwarts of the Congress, other than those who professed socialism and communism, felt attracted to Marxist principles and outlook, Prasad did not. In fact, he disapproved of such ideas and activities of the socialists and communists and, subsequently, of Subhas and his followers as appeared upsetting Gandhian politics.[48] That, however, did never mean that he did not approve of progressive ideas and measures. In fact, he was all praise for the consciouness being projected in the late 1930s by Jawaharlal Nehru and others for economic planning.[49] He associated himself in right earnest and in major ways for the betterment of *Kisans* although he had no hesitation in welcoming any initiatives coming from the *zamindars* towards that end.[50] He had occasions to go into the problems of industrial workers and he sincerely tried to help solve them in ways which would not leave employer-employee relationship essentially embittered.[51] Although Prasad, like all other bigs in the Indian National Congress, did not develop any specialised concern with international developments leaving the matter to Jawaharlal Nehru as their specialist, he did move in Europe, getting an opportunity, to voice India's national anti-war stands.[52] He subscribed to liberal-democratic values and had a great deal of respect for the British political institutions. As stated earlier, he was dead opposed to Nazism and Fascism as an opponent of imperialism and, in fact, he was opposed to all kinds of totalitarianism and authoritarianism. Of some interest here may be of note that Prasad made a special mark for himself in course of the national movement with his ardent advocacy for Hindi as India's national language. He did a lot for promoting Hindi.[53] Even Gandhi had a modified version in that respect as he advocated Hindustani, a mix of Hindi and Urdu. Prasad was for Hindi which he would like to avoid banking heavily on Sanskrit words. He as well disliked Urdu being made to bank more and more on Persian words. Prasad's stand on Hindi was based on his deep conviction that making it national language would help national unity and integration as it had the widest demographic and cultural base and it was not very difficult in being followed by non-Hindi people. It may be noted in this context that Prasad learnt his first education in Persian from a *maulavi* and began to be interested in Hindi only after his graduation.

(4) As India moved towards self-government, constitution-making, independence and post-independence consolidation and nation-building, Rajendra Prasad, beside continuing to have his general apexual stature, worked as a member of the Interim Government cabinet having the portfolio of Food at a juncture of its national crisis and, concurrently, as the Chairman of the Constituent Assembly and later as the President of the Republic from 1950 to 1962 (the office coming to him and staying as long in view of the esteem in which he was held in the Congress and outside at a national scale). He remained engrossed in his responsibilities and, on becoming President, also reserved and reticent. That prevented him from freely articulating his views publicly. His idea of coming up with his reminiscences and views on retiring from Presidentship, intercepted by India's

major clash with China, his shattered health and death, could not materialise. In fact, his letters written to Gyanwati Darbar "in the nature of a diary or daily jottings", in which "he regularly chronicled and recounted" for her "contemporary events and the procession of ideas which passed his mind",[54] constitute the only most authentic and reliable source of his post-Independence political thinking, as his public speeches, etc., were generally guarded in view of his official responsibilities to which he was highly sensitive. In the above jottings also his political thinking has come as beads of casual 'reflections' or 'concerns' amidst diverse topics dealt with and does not offer a convenient basis for being brought out. Nevertheless, it may be brought out in a nutshell with the help of some other additional sources.

Unlike Gandhi, who often tended to be anti-statist in his political outlook, Rajendra Prasad believed in the welfare of state with some reservations on excessive legislation.[55] He was a votary of democracy but, at times, he wished that there were some ways to ensure an enlightened and well-informed electrorate against the sweep of universal adulthood suffrage so that democracy would work with greater efficacy and much more meaningfully.[56] He did believe in the parliamentary system of government but often felt weary of the proceedings on the floor.[57] He often felt attracted to the cross-party management in American law-making.[58] He gradually began to feel sick with the trends developing in the Indian Party System. He felt concerned with the declining public standards in the Congress Party and the increasing disaffection of the people at large in view of its functioning. There were occasions when he felt that Gandhi was right in asking the Congress to disband itself for becoming a Public Service forum rather than remaining a political party. He would have been happy to see some other political party emerging as an equal alternative of the Congress.[59] But, instead, he felt dismayed with the types of unprincipled and unstable coalitions which were likely to be formed in the future. He dreaded that kind of possibility.[60] He felt deeply concerned with the increasing corruption in public life. Whereas the Constitution of India had been discussed and drafted under his Chairmanship and he knew well that it was intended to work dominantly with the spirit which made the British political system work, by the end of 1950s and the beginning of 1960s he had started getting somewhat disillusioned as, in his opinion, trends developing in India were not in tune with the conventions being followed in Great Britain. He felt that some re-thinking was needed. Whereas only a little earlier he appeared gauging certain ministerial resignations and post-resignation stands in terms of cabinet responsibility (as practised in Britain), now he would like it to be examined if the President of the Republic had to be as titular a constitutional head as a British monarch was.[61] In law-making he would like serious attention being paid to the readiness of the people to accept it and, accordingly, stood to discourage the Hindu Code Bill.[62] He doubted if the bureaucrats and government officers could be allowed to indulge in trade union activities and yet he could not dismiss their right to do so altogether.[63] Whereas he believed in welfare measures and progressive economic policies, he did not like hasty and ambitious populistic steps as also moves to launch new development projects without ensuring the completion of such projects as were already at hand and were languishing for availability of adequate funds.[64] He often wished that the performance—achievements, shortcomings and failures—of the regime at work in India be reviewed for its better working and for allaying diverse kinds of disaffections among the people in general and in some sectors, conceding that some amount and certain types of resentment could not be helped.[65] He felt deeply concerned with the complications and difficulties generated by the basically linguistic re-organisation of states because of certain deviations which could not be avoided and noted the fall-outs of the same in the elections which followed.[66] He continued to regret that Hindi was not getting its due position as India's national language.[67]

His views on international politics remained largely confined to his concern over India-Pakistan relations and international developments bearing on them, the Kashmir problem and, at times, the international situation bearing on world peace.[68] He regretted the trends toward war and deplored the highly dangerous defence preparations of great powers as a kind of sad and, ultimately, thoughtless state of affairs. He, however, had a kind of patriotic outburst of emotionalism when India encountered humiliating military reverses at China's hands late in 1962. But he had retired by that time.

In all his political reflections he was generally guided by the considerations of *dharma*. But such considerations appeared taking him to dilemmas. He would often fret over virtually a captive-like situation in which, for security reasons, he had to live as the President of the republic.[69] He regretted that the functionaries like the President and the Prime Minister had practically no leisure, no holiday, no leave.[70] He felt concerned with heavy staffing at points of administration.[71] He was conscious that the expenditure incurred on the upkeep of the President's office and the Rashtrapati Bhawan and the salaries, allowances, etc., given to the President often irked many especially because of the Gandhian background he had. But he was not sure if they were altogether unjustified.[72] Similarly, Prasad had been President in an *ad hoc* tenure for the first two years as the Constitution was put into force and then was elected for a full term. On the eve of the next term the situation was hazy and uncertain regarding he being the choice again. It was in that phase that he appeared struggling to exercise a kind of detachment in the matter, leaving his own desire to the course of developments.[73] But, finally, he became the choice and accepted the choice so made. *Dharma* thus put him to queer situations and that had been so right from the prime of his youth. He was nevertheless candid about that aspect of his personality and character which, as he admitted, he could not help.[74]

IV

In summing up it may be held that in Prasad's political thinking and behaviour *dharma* was the cardinal concept with which he conducted himself behaviourally as well as intellectually as an individual in relation to society within or without the ambit of politics and in relation to religion with or without reference to politics.[75]

REFERENCES

1. Rajendra Prasad, *Autobiography* (National Book Trust, India, New Delhi, 1957, First Reprint, 1994), pp. 4-14.
2. *Ibid.*, pp. 57-58.
3. *Ibid.*, pp. 35-39.
4. *Portrait of a President* (Being letters of Dr. Rajendra Prasad written to Mrs. Gyanwati Darbar, Vikas, Delhi, 1974), pp. 36-37.
5. *Ibid.*, pp. 102-03.
6. *Autobiography*, Note 1, pp. 106-40.
7. *Ibid.*, pp. 248, 301.
8. *Ibid.*, pp. 141-43, 146-47, 180-83, 247-48.
9. *Ibid.*, pp. 248, 518-19.
10. *Ibid.*, pp. 220-26.
11. *Ibid.*, pp. 248-52, 262-64, 265-67, 335-37.
12. *Ibid.*, pp. 339-42, 391-402.
13. *Ibid.*, pp. 349-57, 556-59.
14. *Ibid.*, pp. 351, 356.
15. *Ibid.*, pp. 351-55.
16. *Ibid.*, pp. 429-30, 431-32.
17. *Ibid.*, pp. 182.
18. *Ibid.*, pp. 259-60.
19. *Ibid.*, pp. 589-91. Prasad never is as strong as he appears to be in giving his view of the Calcutta riots of autumn 1946. "This", in his words, "was perhaps the bloodiest carnage witnessed in India since the sacking of Delhi by Nadir Shah, although I am not sure that his armies could really have massacred so many people."
20. *Portrait*, Note 4, pp. 16-17, 158-59.
21. *Ibid.*, pp. 15-19.
22. *Ibid.*, as quoted in Gyanwati Darbar's 'Introduction' to it, pp. x-xi.
23. As he puts it, "Pride is a sin which remains hidden even in the purest of hearts and like a serpent concealed within the folds of one's clothes bites him at the crucial moment when it is touched even unwittingly." *Ibid.*, pp. 221.
24. *Ibid.*, pp. 264-66.
25. Rajendra Prasad, Note 1, p. 272.
26. See Note 24.
27. *Portrait*, pp. 76-77, 226-28, 242, 245-46, 267-68, 284, 293.
28. *Autobiography*, Note 1, pp. 53-54.
29. *Portrait*, Note 4, p. 75.
30. *Ibid.*, pp. 116-17.
31. *Autobiography*, Note 1, pp. 40-47, 64-67, 82-86, 382-86.
32. *Ibid.*, pp. 189-90, 212, 248-51, 285, 485-90.
33. *Ibid.*, pp. 479-85.

34. *Ibid.*, pp. 417-20.
35. All through his autobiography and elsewhere Rajendra Prasad refers to Jawaharlal Nehru, notwithstanding some serious differences of opinion and attitude between them on occasions more than once, with deep regard. He was very much a factor of the decision to expel Subhas Chandra Bose from the Congress and, yet, while giving the account thereof, he speaks so highly of his qualities and his personal relationship with Bose. He was deeply anguished over C. Rajagopalachari's changed stand on Hindi and yet maintained his regard intact for him. These are only a few instances of his disposition which had a remarkable constancy about it.
36. *Autobiography*, p. 86.
37. *Ibid*. In fact, he got published *Champaran Men Mahatma Gandhi.*
38. A. Appadorai writes: "Rajendra Prasad in his *At the Feet of Mahatma Gandhi* (1961) brought out the connection between satyagrah and non-violence, perhaps, more clearly than Gandhi himself..." See A. Appadorai, *Indian Political Thinking in the Twentieth Century* (Second Edition, Oxford University Press, Calcutta, 1987), p. 67.
39. Autobiography, Note 1, pp. 308-10.
40. *Ibid.*, pp. 494, 511-13.
41. *Ibid.*, pp. 532-34.
42. *Ibid.*, pp. 364-72, 386.
43. *Ibid.*, pp. 42-43.
44. *Ibid.*, pp. 294, 333. While mentioning Bhagat Singh's and others' (Lahore Conspiracy) case and some developments related thereto he maintains a kind of emotional non-involvement regarding their role in the national movement.
45. *Ibid.*, pp. 192-98, 243-46.
46. *Ibid.*, pp. 288-90.
47. *Ibid.*, pp. 429-32.
48. *Ibid.*, pp. 479-92.
49. *Ibid.*, pp. 474.
50. *Ibid.*, pp. 455-61.
51. *Ibid.*, pp. 462, 464-66, 508-09.
52. *Ibid.*, pp. 278-80.
53. *Ibid.*, pp. 76-77, 103, 256, 421-24.
54. *Portrait,* Note 4, pp. (Introduction) vii.
55. *Ibid.*, pp. 26-27, 181.
56. *Ibid.*, pp. 118-19, 131, 203.
57. *Ibid.*, pp. 90-92.
58. *Ibid.*, pp. 176-77.
59. *Ibid.*, pp. 188-90, 149-50, 151, 199-201.
60. *Ibid.*, pp. 171-72, 188-90.

61. Anup Chand Kapur, *Select Constitutions* (Ninth Edition, S. Chand, New Delhi, 1975), p. 771; D.C. Gupta, *Indian Government and Politics* (Fourth Enlarged and Revised Edition, Vikas, 1978), p. 377.
62. Gupta, Note 61, p. 96.
63. *Portrait*, Note 4, pp. 162-64.
64. *Ibid.*, pp. 174-75.
65. *Ibid.*, pp. 137-38, 158-59, 160-61, 165-66, 179-80.
66. *Ibid.*, pp. 134-35, 146, 160-61.
67. *Ibid.*, pp. 180, 184-86, 196.
68. *Ibid.*, pp. 3-28.
69. *Ibid.*, pp. 34-36.
70. *Ibid.*, p. 202.
71. *Ibid.*, p. 197.
72. *Ibid.*, pp. 45-46.
73. *Ibid.*, pp. 131-32, 133-34, 153-55.
74. *Ibid.*, pp. 251-52, 266-67, 267-68, 268-69.
75. As he puts it, "I take it all religions of a theistic nature must aim at true knowledge of God and love for Him. But in fact in course of time religions have lost the significance of love which means nothing more or less than giving one's all—complete surrender—to God and have come to signify that to love God is only a business transaction in which one has to offer empty love and get in the bargain all that is good and grand in this world and in the next...implies selfishness of the extreme and worst type. I believe there is no religion higher or better than giving one's best to the service of God which is the same thing as service of others". *Portrait*, Note 4, pp. 109-10.

23

Acharya Narendra Deva's Ethical Dimension of Socialism

T.R. Sharma

Ironically enough, the movement for democratic socialism has been only a fringe movement in India both before and after independence. Trying to steer clear of Congress variety of socialism on the one hand and the communist variety on the other, it got sandwitched between the two. While the democratic component was appropriated by the Congress, the socialist component was captured by the communists. Consequently, on the ideological-philosophical plane as well as on the power-political plane the movement for democratic socialism could never become a force to reckon with on the Indian political canvas. An indication of this frailty and fragility may be had from the fact that a recent celebrated work edited by Thomas Pantham and Kenneth L. Deutsch on *Political Thought in Modern India,* which has twenty chapters, has not assigned a single chapter to any of the social democrats : Acharya Narendra Deva who was the main idealogue of Democratic socialism or to any of its other key exponents—Achyut Patwardhan, Acharya Kriplani, Ashok Mehta, S.M. Joshi and N.G. Gorey *et al.* only three of its early sympathisers and exponents, Jawaharlal Nehru, Jaya Prakash Narayan and Ram Manohar Lohia, have caught the eye of the scholars and that too for reasons other than their early infatuation with democratic-socialist ideology. Nehru, for example, is better known for his commitment to liberal democracy, planned economy, secularism and scientific temper; JP for his early stint with Marxism and his concepts of Sarvodaya, partyless democracy and total revolution; and Lohia for his anarcho-syndicalism.

One finds this lopsidedness depite the fact that Acharya Narendra Deva is one of the very few ideologues of democratic socialism in India who never abandoned, or compromised his essential position. Even when the Congress Socialist Party decided to part ways with its parent organisation—the Indian National Congress—in 1948-49, the Acharya continued to adhere wholeheartedly to the key ideals of democratic socialism. He fully realised its ecletic character and understood it as a hybrid born out of marriage of parliamentary democracy and cooperative economy with historical materialism and socialisation of means of production. Democratic socialism, for him, was a blend or concoction of elements of liberalism and Marxism yet distinct from the both. It had its own cutting edge, or at least so the Acharya thought.

His doctrine of democratic socialism was shaped in the 1930s more by design than by chance. It was borne out of his intense concern for the success of national liberation movement—a movement which was being spearheaded by the Indian National Congress. In his calculation for the success of liberation movement it was imperative to link it with the infant Kisan movements which were gaining momentum in the rural side particularly in United Province. Such roping-in of the peasant movements was possible only if the problems of the rural poor were appended to the broader tasks of the freedom struggle. He was convinced that answer to the problems of exploitation and oppression of the rural poor lay in socialism alone and organisation of a socialist party within the fold of Indian National Congress was the most appropriate vehicle to do so. It was this conviction which led him to the founding of Congress Socialist Party (CSP). However, this could not be done by rolling back or blunting the thrust of national liberation movement. There had to be some sort of simultaneity in undertaking and carrying out these twin tasks. It would thus seem that the early ideas of Narendra Deva represented a blend of militant nationalism and scientific socialism. This comes out clearly in his draft proposal for the formation of the Congress Socialist Party as a distinct group within the Congress Party. The twin objectives delineated in the draft were achievement of complete independence (which was reassertion of Congress' demand for *Puran Swaraj*) and establishment of a socialist society in India after independence. In a way Narendra Deva's strategy during the early phase of his political career bears some family resemblance to Maoist strategy of mobilising support for socialism by invoking the nationalist sentiment of the masses. It is, of course, a different mater that while Mao succeeded, Narendra Deva failed. It seems highly probable that, among other things, the main reason of this failure was that the Congress Socialist Party continued to play second fiddle to the Congress party during the national movement which stands in sharp contrast to the Maoist strategy of distancing himself from the Kuo-Min-tang. In other words, while Mao was able to give an autonomous status to his movement for liberation of China and to his socialist vision, Narendra Deva failed to do so.

Of course, there is more to this assertion than meets the eye. Irrespective of what it might mean, it needs to remembered that Narendra Deva's very notion of democratic socialism was borne out of its ideological counterpart in the West. This received ideological position was indeed rearranged by Narendra Deva in a new hierarchy of significance and new ordering of priorities. However, notwithstanding such reordering, the anti-imperialist thrust of Western socialists (which the Congress Party had successfully inherited and Indianised) remained the core of Narendra Deva's doctrine till about the time of Indian independence. Soon after independence when the Congress Party took up the task of national reconstruction its socialist stance got considerably diluted. So much so, that Narendra Deva and his Congress Socialist Party decided to part ways with the ruling party. Nay, it would be more appropriate to say that they were pushed out. From then Narendra Deva fought simultaneously on two fronts—denigrading the ideological-strategical stance of Indian communists and the Indian National Congress almost in a single breath.

To have a clearer idea of this tight-rope-walking it would probably be useful to examine more closely Narendra Deva's ideas during the two phases—before and after independence, with a view to highlighting the shift that occurred in his ideological baggage as he moved from one to the other. In ideological terms these ideas centre around such fundamental questions as : the nature and class character of the Indian bourgeoisie, the principal and minor contradictions of the given period, the prioritisation of these contradictions and the strategy and tactics in terms of class alliances for resolving them. In practical-political terms this necessitated a critical evaluation of the Indian National Congress on the one hand and the Indian Communists on the other.

Before independence Narendra Deva by and large struck to the view that contradiction between British imperialism and the Indian people was the principal contradiction. Till about early 1940s, the Indian National Congress appeared to him to be the main bulwark of Indian people which could resolve this contradiction. He argued that the Indian National Congress not only represented the whole Indian society, it also stood for parliamentary democracy. Hence, it needed to be strengthened. Along with it, he also discerned the contradiction between the Indian bourgeoisie and the Indian working class. While he fully endorsed the anti-imperialist struggle of the Congress; he was critical of its indifference towards the prevailing exploitation and oppression of the masses, i.e. the peasantry and the proletariat. He warned the Congress leadership that the national movement could accomplish its anti-imperialist goal only if the national liberation struggle was linked with the economic demands of the masses. He was fully convinced that adopting the agenda of radical social change wold lend support to the national movement. It is interesting to note that the Gandhian leadership did not agree with this view. In fact, Gandhiji held quite the opposite view. Gandhian calculation was that raising the class (and caste) question at a time when the national movement had entered a decisive phase would blunt the thrust of anti-imperialist struggle by pitching the Indian people along class (and caste) lines. Narendra Deva believed that in order to achieve the twin tasks of national liberation and social justice the Congress Party must transform itself into a radical force. However, he did not totally rule out the possibility that Congress might go astray and fail to take up the task of socialist transformation. In that event it would have exhausted the possibility of radical social transformation and a new organ to take up this task will have to be created. The CSP began to be shaped and nurtured by him as such as alternative-in-the making. As soon as Narendra Deva realised that Congress had exhausted its radical potential his party, the CSP began distancing itself from the Congress. Narendra Deva bittlerly criticised the Congress leadership for its acceptance of Cabinet Mission and Mountbattan Plans leading to the partition of the country which entailed unprecedented death and destruction. In 1948 when the socialists began to be hounded out of the Congress, Narendra Deva asserted that right since 1934 the CSP has been maintaining that Congress could not be an instrument of socialism and it has been proved right. However, this assertion of Narendra Deva must be taken with a grain of salt, for if the CSP actually believed that Congress was a reactionary force why did its members continue to remain in the latter's fold till they were forced to quit historical evidence to support my contention in quite weighty. After all, even in 1948, it was not the CSP which broke away from the Congress because of its failure to radicalise it, rather it was Congress which forced the members of the CSP to leave. It may be recalled that initially the Congress President with a view to getting rid of socialists asked the CSP to drop the prefix 'Congress' from its name and demanded that the 'Socialist Party' must open its doors to non-Congressmen. Even though the CSP at its fifth annual Conference at Kanpur on March 1, 1947 meekly complied with these demands, yet the Congress was in no mood to accommodate the CSP in its ranks any more. This witch-hunting of the socialists must have left Narendra Deva totally disillusioned and disenchanted. In 1949, when the CSP finally broke away from the Congress he criticised the leadership of the Congress Party for curbing inner-party democracy. He criticised the growing authoritarianism in the party. He charged the party leadership of resting on its oars and for giving up its progressive stance altogether. He also disapproved the Congress Party's policy of opening its doors to all sorts of people including anti-national and anti-social elements and for branding the true patriots as traitors. He also contested the Congress Party's claim of being anti-communal because one could find several hard-core communalists in its ranks. "By one door the Congress expels the socialists and through another it admits the capitalists and the communalists. God alone can save the Congress". Around this time Narendra Deva started hoping that the Socialist Party would emerge as the main opposition party. However, his hopes were dashed soon when the socialists splintered into umpteen groups.

Interestingly, Narendra Deva was not critical of Congress Party only, he was equally (or perhaps more) critical of the Communist Party of India. In fact, one significant feature of the CSP before as well as after independence has been the lack of any *modus vivendi* with the Indian communists or any segment of them. As early as 1935 in his Presidential address at the Ahmedabad Conference of the Gujarat Congress Socialists, he criticised the CPI for its failure to recognize that the Indian National Congress alone represented the broad platform of anti-imperialist struggle in India. He was particularly criticial of the 1928 Comintern line which directed the communist parties of the colonial countries to de-link themselves from the bourgeois-led liberation movements—a thesis which was expounded by M.N. Roy at the second Comintern Congress in 1920. Such a strategic line in his view was not only isolationist but also suicidal. He branded the Indian Communists as 'agents of imperialism' for their failure to join the mainstream of national movement. This criticism became more bitter after the Soviet Union joined the Second World War which the communists designated as the 'people's war'. He was of the view that the Comintern line since 1928 has been aimed at serving the interests of the Soviet Union alone.

He chided the CPI for supporting the war in the name of defence of father-land instead of treating it as an inter-imperialist conflict for colonies. He also criticised the European communist parties for supporting the war effort in the name of defending democracy against Fascism but at the same time failing to fight for democratic socialism. In their own countries. As Indian independence drew near Narendra Deva began to advocate that the CSP's strategic line should be one of equi-distance from the Congress and the communists, for the former's failure to prevent partition of the country and for latter's extraterritorial loyalties. Strangely enough, this strategical posture of Narendra Deva was not much different from M.N. Roy's assessment of the Congress and CPI. Needless to say that on almost every other question he sharply differed with Roy. He was particularly harsh on Roy for the latter's view that India must support the allies against the Nazi aggression. He also contested Roy's view that Congress was ideologically and organisationally a party of the Indian bourgeoisie only.

After independence there was a shift in Narendra Deva's ideological stance. While he became increasingly critical of the Congress for preaching one thing (socialism) and practicing another (capitalism); he was critical of the CPI for its anti-democratic and anti-humanist stance and for its lack of faith in the parliamentary democracy. Moreover, the communists, in his view, cared only for the ends not for the purity of means. He started arguing that given the Congress Party's pro-capitalist bias and given the CPI's anti-democratic stance neither of them could fully satisfy the people's aspirations. It was only the Socialist Party which was the most genuine party of the left, and not the CPI. Morever, it was only the Socialist Party which was genuinely committed to radical changes in the economic structure of society and not the Congress. It was only the Socialist Party which believed in parliamentary as well as extra-parliamentary methods of struggles.

Narendra Deva contested the notion that socialism and democracy are incompatible. He approvingly quoted Rosa Luxemberg that totalitarianism scuttles the development of individual personality. Narendra Deva was convinced that the future belonged neither to capitalism nor to totalitarianism but to democratic socialism. Man was bound to affirm his essence which lies in freedom rather than the authoritarian rule. To support his contention he pointed out that even the totalitarian countries have to speak in the language of democracy.

In a policy statement presented at the Second Annual Conference of Praja Socialist Party at Gaya he criticised the anti-democratic tradition and way of life in India. In order to counter this tradition it was necessary for the socialists to permeate the socialist ideology among the masses. Initially, even the Congress Party subscibed to this view but gradually it diluted its socialist stance. Therefore, it was left only to the socialists to fight for fullest economic and political democracy.

There is a clear peasant bias in Narendra Deva's vision of socialism. Unlike Marx, he emphasised the role of peasantry in the socialist movement in a developing country like India. He criticised the usuarious practices of landlords and *mahajans*. To rid the peasantry of its impoverishment and exploitation, Narendra Deva advocated the setting up of cooperative commonwealths. He stood for linking the peasant struggles with the freedom movement. Thus, he visualised the possibility of intertwining the bourogeois-democratic and proletariat-socialist stage of revolution. He argued that socialist-revolution has every chance of breaking out first in a country which has been ruined by economic exploitation even though it may not be industrially developed. He asserted that India satisfied these conditions and hence the possibility of inter-linking the two revolution existed here.

For him true socialism meant full employment, greater role to the cooperatives including cooperative farming, promotion of cottage and small scale industry, state ownership of big industries, workers' participation in management, right to work as a fundamental right and denial of absolute and inalienable right to property. Struggle for establishments of such a socialist society must be linked to day-to-day struggles of peasants against oppression and exploitation. Large inequalities of ownership of land must be abolished. He also stood for greater role to the village panchayats. He visualised a new world order based on freedom, equality, social justice and peace. While placing these tasks on the agenda of the Indian socialists Narendra Deva came under the strong influence of Gandhiji, particularly his position on ends and means. Consequently, he appreciated the Gandhian technique of *Satyagraha* and disapproved the technique of violent insurrection. For him the Socialist Party was not a platform of left unity. It was different from the communists as well as from the Congress. It has its own distinct ideology, programme of action and approach. His plea for socialism is based on scientific attitude and draws it inspiration from human urge for freedom, equality and brotherhood. For him socialism alone was full democracy. He extensively quoted Marx's article of 1847 published in the *Communist League* which said that "We are not among those communists who are out to destroy personal liberty, who wish to turn the world into a gigantic work house. We have no desire to exchange freedom for equality. We are convinced that in no other social order will complete freedom be assured as in a socialist society based on common ownership of property." He stands for freedom and democracy and does not undermine the liberal tradition altogether.

In sum, Narendra Deva's philosophy is a unique blend of democracy, socialism and Gandhism. He attempted to incorporate in his doctrine of socialism all that is best in all the three. He was quick to realise and emphasize that true democracy was possible only if accompanied by economic and social equality. Therefore, the true goal of the freedom movement could be achieved only if economic and social questions were woven into the national liberation movement itself. In some sense, he wanted to reach the Marxist goal of socialist society *via* the Gandhian techniques of non-violence. In fact, Narendra Deva always stressed the ethical dimension of socialism as an end and nonviolent struggle as the means. He realised that real problem in India was that democracy was being introduced here in the midst of an undemocratic economic system and a hierarchical social structure.

It seems surprising that in spite of his incisive analysis of Indian society till about the end of his political career, Narendra Deva did not show sufficient concern for oppression and indigniy which operated on caste lines. It was only at the Second National Conference of Praja Socialist Party at Gaya that he squarely criticised the institution of caste. In this view caste system could have no place either in democracy or in socialism because it hinders social mobility and perpetuates vocational rigidity. It upholds the feudal order and degrades the dignity of labour. True freedom for the masses must mean release from the humiliation and pain of social inferiority. But he saw a total caste-class overlap. To ensure caste and communal harmony, peace and amity he emphasized the importance of economic issues. Thus, caste for him had a economic dimension. A classless society would *ipso facto* be a casteless society as well, and such a society was a necessary condition for the success of democracy as also for the success of socialism.

In short, Narendra Deva's ideology of democratic socialism has elements of strong nationalism and strong anti-imperialism coupled with emphasis on class struggle, commitment to genuine democracy and decisive role to the Indian state in the socialist construction. His economic ideal is rooted in communism; while his political ideal is rooted in liberal democracy. His focus has always been on immediate questions of economic and political interests rather than on abstractions. By taking a non-sectarian position on the question of caste and communal divisions he tried to adopt a scientific and rationalist outlook. He continuously endeavoured to tailor his ideological-strategical posture so as to make it a perfect fit to his understanding of the Indian specificity. It is, of course, a different matter that this understanding could not grasp the complexity of Indian social reality in its totality.

24

The Notion of *Dharma*, Society and Polity

A Lohian Perspective

Prakash C. Shastri

Before an attempt would be made to discover why Hinduism has so far been unable to work this conflict between the fanatical and liberal out of its system, it is necessary to recall the broad differences of view that has always prevailed. On four major and concrete issues, thereof caste, women, property and tolerance, Hinduism has suffered from a perpetual suring between the liberal and fanatical attitudes.[1]

"The Hindu has therefore acquired a split personality. At his best, a Hindu accepts appearance without losing insight in to the ultimate and over striving to enrich his insight, at his worst, his hypocrisy is matchless. His split mind between appearance and reality often encourages him to do so until the Hindu learns to accept the fact of the scientific and secular spirit, fact relating to work machine output... is there any hope to overcome his split personality."[2] "The liberal alone can unite the country. India is too ancient and vast country. Hence no force can unite it except the voluntary human will. Fanatical Hinduism cannot try its nature mould such a will, while liberal Hinduism can do it, as it has often done in the past. Hinduism of course is not a political religion in the narrow sense, a religion of doctrines or organization. But it has been the eminent medium and inspiration for the great impulsion of the Indian political history towards the unity of the country. The great war between Liberal and Fanatical Hinduism may well be called a conflict between the two processes of unification and disintegration of the country."[3] "Today the religious and the human problem is eminently a political problem. The Hindu if faced with the serious choice of accomplishing a complete mental revolution or else of going under. He must be Muslim and Christian and feel like one. I am not talking of Hindu-Muslim unity for that is a political, institutional or at best a cultural problem. I am talking of the emotional identification of the Hindu with the Muslim or Christian, not in religious faith and practices, but in the feeling that I am he... The Hindu faith of emotive oneness of all life and things is also the political necessity of the Indian State that Hindu shall feel one with the Muslim. On the path may yet lie setbacks and defeats, but the direction that the Hindu mind should take is clear."[4]

There is no denying the fact that Dr. Rammanhoar Lohia (19-10-1967) was one of those 'rare' socialists who used to take keen interest in understanding the intricacies of the Hindu psyche. He was always eager to know that why a great civilization of hoary past meekly surrendered before alien civilization without putting any kind of resistance. Being a keen student of history, philosophy and economics of India, i.e. 'Bharat' that its ancient sages and *'Pundits'* did a commendable job while imagining the heights of freedom or *'Swaraj'* (It is notable that ancient *Vedic-Upnishadic* literature is full of references of *'Swaraj'* which ultimately provided a philosophical basis for launching freedom movement in modern India) but when the time arrived for its implementation they simply failed to materialize it in practice. Ultimately that gave birth to split personality and double thinking among Hindus. Rammanohar Lohia used to say that while *'Dharma'* is a kind of long-term politics' or *'rajniti'*, the politics or *'rajniti'* is a kind of short-term *'Dharam'*. Hence he tried to establish a link between *'Dharma'* and *'Rajniti'*. And in this context he tried to draw our attention towards an ongoing conflict between forces of *status-quo-ante* and of radical change since the Vedic times. That is why Lohia concluded with clarity and perceptivity that if India is 'Bharat' has to survive as a strong and integrated nation-state than the movement led by the 'liberal Hindu' must emerge victorious, otherwise the fate of this great country is doomed. And every Indian nationalist must be careful and vigilant regarding the outcome of this ongoing conflict between liberal and fanatical force of Hinduism. Moreover, he must try to know his position in this historical conflict and must chalk-out his role and performance. That is also the objective for writing this article.

It is the considered opinion of veteran political scientist Prof. K. Seshadri that nobody can claim to know India, i.e. *Bharat* until and unless he develops an insight into the ancient Sanskrit Vedic and classical literature, because that provides us a glimpse of perennial conflict between pro- and anti-changes in India. Further he said that every social/political scientist must strive to know in detail the commentaries written by Badarayana, Adi Sankaracharya, Mandana Misra, Ramanujacharya, Madhavacharya and Saint Gyaneshwar and so on to understand the Hindu psyche and mind of India.[5] Another student of literature and the cultural history of India, Dr. Rangya Raghava held this view that as and when India, that is Bharat, developed great maritime tracks with Rome and other countries then there was spurt of 'progressive humanism' in every walk of life. While in the days of economic and political hardships India switched back to the quagmire or morass of fanaticism and exploitation. And it is obvious that slowly and slowly the Hindu civilization lost its age old dynamism, process of assimilation and ideal of tolerance.[6] Thus we find a co-relationship between era of economic progress and movement of liberalism in India.

'Dharma' always guided, motivated and mobilized the people of this country. It will not be out of context to asses that besides Lokmanya Bal Gangadhar Tilak, Mahatma Mohandass Gandhi was one of those pioneers who grasped the powers or process of *Dharma* in vast segments of the Hindu masses. In a way Mahatma Gandhi did belong to the reformist saintly *'Vaishnava'* tradition of the ancient India which always strived to rejuvenate the great values of humanism, i.e. *'Manavvad'* through its religious idiom. He used to assert that if all the

ancient scriptures or *'Sashtras'* support the abhorring untouchability system of India, then he will like to throw them into Indian ocean or Bay of Bengal. Further he said that untouchability is a curse or a bloat on our civilization, hence he will try to do away it with all the force at his command. That is why scripture bound classicist 'Hindu pundits' never liked the preaching and practices of Mahatma Gandhi. Yet it is also a matter of fact that Mahatma Gandhi always used to act through religious 'idiom' as and when he fought with his British masters in the days of the freedom struggle in India. And his declared 'successor' Pandit Jawaharlal Nehru and his fellow comrades simply failed to understand the message of Mahatma Gandhi. Thus a communication gap and hiatus was created between them. The irony of the fate is that even today this hiatus is still prevalent between believers of *'Dharma'* and upholders of westbound modernization in India. How it will be bridged nobody knows its answer?

In this context Rammanohar Lohia used to call himself as 'conscientious Gandhian' as well as 'conscientious Marxist'. Moreover he used to say that he is a 'philosophical liberal' and also a 'programmatic extremist'. If one goes through his writings then he finds a genuine concern for well-being and prosperity of his country, i.e. India. Lohia wrote that right from his Berlin (Germany) study days he was always bothered by this question as why a great like India, i.e. Bharat remained under foreign domination for more than 1500 years? He used to ask this question to his both Hegelian and Marxist friends that why she remained under alien rule for such a long time?[7] Since he was always nagged by this query hence he tried to delve deep into the politico-cultural history of his motherland. Being a true nationalist he was in favour of countary's dignity and honour, and fought for her integrity as and when it was attacked by communist China and Pakistan. He also raised his voice when communist China devoured and digested Tibet. Lohia was well versed with the ancient *Vedic-Upnishadic* literature. When he wrote his book "India, China & Northern Fornties" then he began to define India by citing this *'sloka'*, i.e. "यक्ष्य उत्तर दिशायां नगाधिराज हिमालया......" Later on, he used to quote the famous

'Yama and Nachiketa *Samvad*' (dialogue) in support of socialist tradition of India. Further while writing on the malpractices of '*Jati Pratha*' (caste system) he used to cite the examples of ancient Vedic '*rishi*' who used to act as sculpture and traditions of 'Satyakam Jabali'. It is a famous episode as when this fellow went to his '*guru*' (teacher) to seek knowledge then he asked him who is his father ? He went back to his mother to know the reality. His mother replied that she does not know about antecedent of his father. Further she said that you must reply he is a son of his mother 'Jabali'. The teacher was highly impressed by his courage of conviction and gave him this name, i.e. 'Satyakam Jabali'. Besides this there is a '*sloka*' in which it is said that the absolute '*Brahman*' gave birth to four '*varna*' and that *Brahman* was created from his mouth, *Kshatriya* was born from his shoulders, *Vaishya* was formed from his stomach and *Shudra* was made from his toes. Ultimately this dynamic and interchangeable '*Varna* system' got converted into rigid, orthodox and forbidding '*Jati Vyavastha*' caste system accompanied by notorious or famous '*Jijmani Vyavastha*', i.e. clientele system. Still the million dollar question is open ended. Dynamic and liberal Hindu social system was metamorphosised into closed door, exploitative and fanatical caste system in India. Is something to do with the emergence and fortification of the '*purohit varga*' that is priestly class in India. Is it something to do with continuous pauperization and dehumanization of India? Is it something to do with the declining and ultimately closing of foreign maritime trade of India with other countries? These questions demand immediate solutions otherwise the country will be further disintegrated and divided.

The peculiarity of India and Hinduism is that as and when the need arose in the society for reform, it always began from within. And its 'idiom' was always 'religious'. That is why saints, sages and religious reformers did play the dominant role, because they did not confine themselves to the strict societal code of conduct prescribed by the priestly class (*Purohit Varga*) in the form of four *varna* systems. According to Dr. Rangeya Raghava there is continuous religious thread of reformism right from the days of Narada say up to the Gandhian era. In this context the million dollar question is that who is a saint or in other words, who is a *vaishnava* ? In this context one will also like to refer to the views of the famous Russian academician Dr. V. Brodov who propounded this thesis that if you want to grasp the intricacies of the thinkers of Modern India e.g. Raja Rammohan Roy, Aurobindo Ghosh, Vivekanand and Mahatma Mohandass K. Gandhi and others, then one must go back to their ancient *Vedic-upnishadic* roots.[8] Obviously everyone tried to reinterpret the basic 'Vedantic' philosophy to find the solutions of the problems of modern India. It is also a matter of fact that every religious reformer has had to face lot of opposition even humiliation at the hands of religious fanatics—who always cited the proofs or '*pramanas*' of the ancient scriptures (*shastras*) in favour of their religious dictates. Ultimately Mahatma Gandhi has also to become martyr in the hands of a fanatic called Nathu Ram Godse.

It is also distressing that except few exceptions like Professor K. Seshadri and Professor Yogendra Singh, no social scientist has undertaken a whirlwind tour or comprehensive survey to gauge the massive impact of '*Bhakti*' and Saintly movement of medieval India. This '*Bhakti*' period encompasses a period of one thousand years. Besides this, the medieval India was not at all backward as the then Europe. In other words there was no 'dark age' in India. Dr. Rangeya Raghav also contradicts the two prevailing myths, they are : (1) That Sufism accompanied the Islamic brotherhood did initiate the egalitarian movement among Hindus through religious reformers. (2) That *Bhakti* or Saintly movement began in India say after 7-8th century, i.e. after the advent of Islam. Dr. Raghava further holds this opinion that this movement began in southern part of India in 2nd and 3rd century. When Alwars, Nayanars, Lingayats and Saiva saints and religious reformers worked for liberal, human and progressive ideas among masses. And Ramanuja Acharya was the first saint who gave the name '*Kulantar*', i.e. '*Harijan*' to the then untouchables. And he caused a stir or a flutter when he invited the downtrodden and he gave them the needed religious 'initiation' by reciting the secret '*Mantra*' of '*Nirvana*' loudly.

The beauty of the *'Bhakti'* and saintly movement of India lies in this fact that each one of them drew their inspirations from ancient scriptures—which used to be considered as the fountainhead of obscurantism. For example Saint Gyaneshwar of Maharashtra cited the authority of 'Srimad Bhagvad Gita' in favour of his egalitarian movement launched in an orthodox society. He quoted the famous saying of Lord Krishna that all *varnas* including *'shudras'* merge into me, i.e. *Brahman* as all the rivers ultimately merges themselves into great ocean. Another saints like Samartha Guru Ramdass and Saint Namdeo also worked earnestly for spreading the message of progressive humanism among the masses. Saint Namdeo even went to region of the Rajputana and Punjab also. Another great saint was Guru Nanak of Punjab who left an indelible mark on society, polity and religion of his times. That gave birth to a unique kind of 'saint *cum* solider' phenomenon like Guru Govind Singh—who not only established egality and equity in the Punjab and brought dignity to the downtrodden sections, but he also fought against exploitative alien rules like Aurangzeb and others.

From the above analysis one may conclude that though Dr. Rammanohar Lohia was a busy political leader, he did not have ample time to articulate his thesis, yet he has provided us with a 'perspective' of ongoing conflict say between 'liberal' and 'fanatical' section of the Hindu society. Through this 'perspective' of Dr. Lohia, one may proceed further to undertake a comprehensive survey of the vast cultural and intellectual history of India and arrive at a conclusion that a 'mental revolution' is the need of the hour.

Conclusion

Our earnest suggestion is that the time has arrived when Indian social scientists must try to look at their 'roots', if they want to find the solution of the present day conflicts that are afflicting the 'body-politik' of India. In this regard one must proceed to take help from the pioneering efforts of both 'Mahatma' Mohandass Gandhi and his 'conscientious' follower Dr.

Rammanohar Lohia who provided us their 'perspectives' to develop 'empathy' and critical appreciation regarding the basic tenets of the 'Hindu' culture of India. Amen, Amen and Amen.

REFERENCES

1. Dr. Rammanohar Lohia, 'Hindu V/s Hindu,' *Mankind*, Vol. XIII, No. 5, June-July 1969.
2. *Ibid.*
3. Dr. Rammanohar Lohia, Hindu V/s Hindu, *Ibid.*
4. *Ibid.*
5. Seshadri K., *Social Ethos of South India*, Arihant, Jaipur, 1997.
6. Raghava Rangeya, *Maha Yatra Gatha* (two volumes), Kitab Mahal, Allahbad, 1961 and 1963.
7. Lohia Rammanohar, *Wheel of History*, Now Hind, Hyderabad, 1961.
8. Brodov, V., *Indian Philosophy in Modern Times*, Progress Publishers, Moscow, 1986.

25

Vinoba's Concept of Religion, *Dharma* and Politics

Rakesh Kumar Jha

Saint Vinoba Bhave, was a revolutionary thinker and leader of Modern-age who, through his Bhoodan-Gramdan Movement as well as idealistic thought inspired the Indian masses and intellectuals. He also laid a profound imprint upon the mind of all those who champion the causes of a sustainable world civilization. As a true revolutionary, he denounced the evils of religion, morality and politics, but at the same time, with similar sincerity, he also announced the new model for them to reorient the new world civilization. Bhave, enriched by the power of different languages specially Sanskrit and having a deep study of devotional literature of the eminent saints of India as well as ancient Indian thinker, religion and culture, equipped with the mathematical intelligence inherited from his father Sri Narahari Bhave and immensely religious temperament from his mother Rukmini Devi. All this occasioned Vinoba in shaping his ideas on different subjects like philosophy, religion, morality, politics and others, leading him to be a thinker par-excellence.

Before any discussion on the subject chosen, I wish to take this opportunity to divert the attention of the readers to the event which, it seems to me, has direct bearing on the subject for discussion.

While camping at Pusa Road in Bihar in connection with Bihar-Dan in August 1967, Vinoba in course of his usual discourse after prayer said, "I give first importance to faith in

God, second to mathematics and third to self-restraint". These three priorities may be reconstructed as spirituality, science and morality respectively. In these priorities, religion and politics stand nowhere. Elsewhere, he made it clear that religion and politics have outlived their utility. This is the age of science and spirituality. Going a step further, he remarked, "If Science and spirituality join hands together, surely the heaven can discend on this earth". What it means by narrating all this, is to say that Vinoba is critical to the roles played by religion and power politics and wants to reconstruct them on the principles of spirituality, science and morality. It implies that religions and politics in present forms are not tenable. If they are to survive, they will have to become spiritual, scientific as well as moral. The goal of religion without spirituality is soul-less and unscientific in application, is worse than useless. Similarly politics without spirituality (service and sense of equality) is irrelevant and untenable and without morality, it is demonic. Both religion and politics have to undergo radical changes. Religions must perfect them by proceeding towards oneness and Politics renouncing its power sharer must become *lokaniti*—people's religion, having *lok-shakti*—people's power at its base. With these preclusive, we shall analyse the Vinoba's concept of religion in the present chapter.

'Religion' in the West, means—belief in God, this belief amounts to the satisfaction of emotional needs by establishing some sort of relationship with him and this relationship can be best expressed through some acts of veneration. In this sense, Hinduism, Islam, Christianity– all are religions. Buddhism and Jainism, however, may be called a system of sect more than a religion. The equivalent term of Religion in Sanskrit is 'Dharma'. It may be noted here that 'religion' and 'dharma' are not identical terms. The Sanskrit term 'dharma' is very comprehensive and is used in many senses, i.e. 'religion', 'duty', 'quality', 'property', 'nature', 'virtue', 'sect' etc. Vinoba uses the term mostly in three different senses—in the sense of religion, sect and duty or righteousness. His concept of '*Swadharma*' and '*Sarvajanik dharma*' or '*nitidharma*' is the concept dealing with different kinds of duties prescribed for certain groups or irrespective of any group affiliation. These concepts are the concepts of morality and not religion. The terms like 'Hindu-Dharma', 'Islam', 'Christianity', 'Jainism' and 'Buddhism' *et cetera* are indicative of different paths of the realisation of the supreme and are the examples of sects. But the concept of '*Manvadharma*'—'The religion of Man' actually is the concept of *Dharma*. When Vinoba opines that *dharma* and *rajniti* have outlived their utility, he uses the term '*dharma*' in the sense of 'sect'. But, when he recommends for the '*Manavadharma*', his intention is to follow true religion (*Dharma*) which is one and universal.

The Goal of Religion : Spirituality

There are many religions on this earth; the aim of all religions is one and the same. This is called spiritual realization. However, the spirituality is conceived by them differently. According to mystical religions spirituality consists of self-realization while the theistic religions aspire for God realization. Both self realization and God realization are understood as the state of *Moksha* or Liberation, where all sorts of miseries are banished and one realizes perfect equanimity, peace and happiness. According to Vinoba there is no qualitative difference between the self realization and God realization. They differ only in degree. *Jiva*, Soul, God and *Brahma* all are metaphysical foundations of spirituality, and therefore, of the same category, but to understand them from the point of view of realization, one will have to make distinction between them.

According to Vinoba, *Brahma* is the ultimate reality, God and Soul are its different manifestation.[1] In other words, soul different from the body is body-based consciousness which recognizes the body similarly God different from creation is reality, which indwells in the creation and recognizes it. But the *Brahma* transcends both. Thus from the point of view of extension, *Brahma* is the widest of all. God is wider than the soul. But all are of the same nature that is consciousness. *Jiva* is nothing but the soul mixed with impurities. *Brahma* is *nirguna*—unqualified, God *saguna*—qualified, but the soul is both qualified and unqualified. However, all of them are same in the sense that they are spiritual, one and the same reality—*Brahma* is inherent in them. Qualitatively they are the same, but quantitatively they differ. All have the same quality of removing the vices—*"Papnivaran Shakti"* but they differ in the power of removing the miseries—*"Tapanivarak Shakti"*. *Jiva* is like muddy water of the river Ganges put in a pot, soul is the pure water put in the pot. God is like water of the river Ganges and *Brahma* is like the vast ocean. The realizations of *Brahma*, God and Soul are the one but in different context. To make it more clear Vinoba said that, we can understand the realization of *advaita* in the four great statements of *Vedanta*, when it is said, *"Pragyanam Brahma"*, it reflects advaitic knowledge. *"Ayamatma Brahma"* indicates God realization. *"Aham Brahmasmi"* shows self realization and *"Tat-tvam-asi anubhuti"* is essential for the emancipation of universe.[2] Thus, *"Advaita-Gyan"*, *"Ishwar-Sakshatkara"*, *"Atmanubhava"* and *"Vishvoddhara"* are the different contexts of the same spiritual realization. With this distinction we shall now proceed to the different stages of the spiritual realizations.

According to Vinoba, the religious journey begins with the state of *Jiva*, where the soul, due to ignorance identifies itself with the body. He refutes the contention that *Adhyatma vidya*—science of spirit has no relevance for youth or those who live ordinary life. On the contrary he holds that religious and spiritual training from the very beginning of life is very essential for the proper growth of human kind. The first aim of religion should be to make people aware that man is not only body but soul also. Body is the tool with which the field of soul or God is cultivated. In other words, body is not an end in itself but means for higher purpose of life. If this realization occurs in the devotee, at least fifty per cent of his miseries will go for ever. *Jiva* which identifies with the body easily becomes the victim of attachment with it and also excess indulgence. Excess indulgence and attachment to body, cause physical, psychic and intellectual disorders in the forms of diseases, tensions, pride, selfishness, loss of memory, faulty judgments and alienation from the soul consciousness which result in moral

The Foundation of Religion: *Manavadharma*

No doubt faith in God is the foundation of every religion in every society of the world; however, the superstructure has yet to be erected accordingly. According to Vinoba, the superstructure of religion should be made according to the principles of *Manavadharma*. The principles of religion of man are as follows :

(1) The chief function of religion of man would be "to promote virtue, piety and devotion, to give an indestructible foundation to morality, to encourage fellow-feeling and love among different communities and to establish peace in the world."[10]

(2) Religion of man should be guided by the principle of synthesis. Vinoba, in his self-composed prayer, tried to synthesize most of the values cherished by the deities of different religions and also wished to organize all the essential features of different religions—like servicing attitude of christianity[11], Penance of Jainism[12], feeling of fraternity[13] of Islam and synthetic and *advaitic* temperament of Hinduism into one organic whole. This would lead to the highest religion of man.

(3) The religion of man enthuse objective rational and scientific temper among its believers. There would be no room for subjective and mystifying elements.[14] Vinoba remarked that no religions so far had become religion, for they suffered from subjectivity. They are in fact sects—different roads to reach at religion—religion of man. The realization of religion of man can be made only when the believers of it worship all religions together.[15] This means that they would try their best to actualize all the important contributions of all religious scriptures in their own life. If this stage comes, the religion of man becomes a reality and all the believers would fight together against violence and atheism prevailing in society.

(4) Religion of man is one[16], but not indescribable. It can be conceived in a definite framework, constituting humanity and spiritual experience—the essence of all religions. Vinoba believed that humanity and spirituality combined together alone can lead us to *Moksha* or liberation.[17]

(5) Vinoba believed that no modern religion can hence forward be founded on the concept of rewards and punishment in life—after death.[18] They must be grounded on the consideration of noble life on this earth. Inequalities of all forms—social and economic—must not be tolerated by the new religion of man. It must recognize the due importance of dignity and value of bread labour.[19]

(6) Integrality is the other very important principle of religion of man. Vinoba did not approve the lopsided or partial implication of religious truth. For example, if stealing is disapproved from a religious point of view and held as sin, the accumulation of wealth—its counter part should also be treated like that.[20] No religious judgment can be made on the basis of partial truth.

(7) Last but not the least, the religion of man is grounded on the universal recognition of the fact that religion is not only individual's personal affair but it is also societal[21] in nature. If a true religion is practiced in one's personal life, it would change the shape of present society. Thus integrality and universality are the essence of religion of man.

Prior to Vinoba, Swami Vivekananda, Rabindra Nath Tagore and Mahatma Gandhi also thought of the concepts of "universal religion", "religion of man" and "ethical religion" respectively. They are the same in spirit, but Vinoba's concept of *Manava-dharma*, is certainly an improvement upon them. Vinoba shares their ideas regarding the aim and foundation of religion, but Vinoba's speciality lies in erecting a structure for them. While the approaches of the Swami and Tagore were individualistic in a sense, Vinoba's approach is socialistic, objective, scientific and more realistic. His synthesis of all religions is very appealing. He is very clear on this point that humanity and spiritual experience are the common points of all religions and hearse can be the real path of self-realization or *Moksha*.

The Path of Realization: *Samya Yoga*

We have said that the goal of religion is spiritual experience—Self realization, God realization, *Brahma* realization, *Moksha* or Supreme equanimity. In order to achieve it, one has to go a definite way—called path of realization. *Gita* talks about the four paths of realization—path of knowledge, path of action, path of devotion and the path of meditation. However, the commentators of *Gita* like Shankar, Lokamanya Tilak, Ramanuja, give exclusive emphasis on knowledge action and devotion respectively. Gandhi laid stress on this detached action called "*Anashakti Yoga*". To Saint Vinoba all these theories are negative (*Vyavartaka*) in a sense which can only protect us but cannot lead to—what is desirable and desired.[22] But a scientific path of realization must be negative and positive both simultaneously. Keeping this view in mind, he invented a new concept called "*Samya Yoga*"[23]—the path of equanimity.

The term '*samya*' means—'balance', 'equanimity', 'equality', 'identity', steadfastness, harmony, etc. Therefore, *Samya Yoga* means the path of realizing spiritual goal through the realization and practice of equanimity of mind, equality in social and political, and economic justice, inner and outer harmony leading to the balanced growth of life towards the realization of oneness with the whole universe. Thus, *Samya Yoga* is both means and end in itself and acceptable to all the dimensions of our life making religious practice an integral whole.

Vinoba strongly believed that religion is not an isolated phenomenon. It is holistic and therefore, only after attaining the lower harmony (*Aparsamya*) like social and economic equality, moral and psychological harmony and scientific equality, one can realize the supreme identity called "*Param Samya*" or "*Brahma Samya*."[24] He concedes that the processes of obtaining equality, equanimity and identity may vary but all of this in meet on only one point that is *'Samya'*. Knowledge, selfless action, devotion, meditation all are the different processes reaching at one goal—identification with the whole or God or *Brahman* which is called *"Parama Samya."*[25]

As religion cannot be isolated from the other activities of life, similarly it cannot be separated from the masses. Vinoba believed in mass salvation. Individual salvation to him was contradiction in term; this concept of mass salvation led him to invent two more concepts—concept of mass equanimity *"Samuhik Samadhi"* and mass action *"Samuhik Karma"*. By the concepts of mass equanimity and mass action, Vinoba intends to say that the equanimity and liberation is not the subject of a few elites but the subject of the all masses and hence only individual's effort is not enough but there should be mass efforts towards this goal is required. In other words, everyone should not try for his or her own salvation only but for the salvation of all without any reservation. By *'Samadhi'*, Vinoba means 'equipoise mind'—the scientific mind free from frivolity, 'I-ness' and 'my-ness' and all other narrowness.[26] In mass equanimity, the masses elevate themselves from the mental consciousness and keep themselves above from the barriers of individuality, communality, rascality and narrow nationalism. The whole society is guided by the independent thinking and dispassionate judgment.[27] The aim and objective of mass equanimity is to serve the masses both in the realm of material welfare and moral as well as spiritual uplift. Thus, in the practice of mass equanimity, welfare of all takes the place of self-interest. According to Vinoba, in mass equanimity, there is complete homogeneity, for what is deemed to be good in personal life, is also practiced in public life. Self-knowledge or spirituality is not a secret thing for the seekers of mass equanimity. It is practiced in public. Vinoba advises that after giving cool consideration over the Wisdom of the Saints, we should modify a new and widely implement it in society.[28] As a scientist first experiments in the laboratory and then implements its result in various field, so spirituality realized in personal life should also be implemented and experienced in the wider field of society.[29] Mass equanimity is a stage of *jivan-mukti*—living in permanent unchangeable, indestructible and infinite state of being, still serving the neighbour with love contemplating the dictum "love my neighbour" continuously and progressing towards complete identity with them.[30] The feeling of I-ness and my-ness are wiped out. Our experience is gradually widened and the world undergoes towards gradual change.[31] There remains no ill-will and conflicts in society, everybody gets his due and solution of the problem. We realize both individual and social equanimity simultaneously.

Synthesis is the basic principle of *Samya Yoga*.[32] Vinoba believes that it is synthesis on which the individual and social life can be erected. Therefore, he tried to synthesize the demands of soul and body both, individual and society and life here in this world and life after. He made a synthesis between knowledge and action on the one hand and knowledge action and devotion on the other. He also made a synthesis between unqualified and qualified God and meditation and productive manual labour. Thus he tried to unite the divergent views of metaphysic morality and religions in his concept of *Samya Yoga*.

The process of *Samya Yoga* begins with the realization of what Vinoba calls *"Apar Samya"* the lower stage of equality and equanimity. These are the realization of physical, mental, social, economic and moral equilibrium. But Vinoba warns that these cannot be realized by any artificial method but in a natural way with the use of discriminative wisdom[33] (*Viveka Buddhi*). The purpose of *Samya Yoga* is not to eliminate the beauty of diversity but to realize unity in diversity. Equality of *Samya Yoga* is not mathematical equality but the equality that has solution for all—*"Samyam Samadhanam"* and which we see in a family life. Vinoba wanted to establish such a social and economic egalitarian society which would make easy the realization of supreme equanimity. *"Param Samya"*—already found in the universe in the form of *"Brahma Samya"*. The lower equalities are established by the effort of each one and everyone. The spiritual equanimity is attained only when we are free from the ignorance.

How can we attain social and economic equality without maintaining the equilibrium of body and mind of the individuals? Therefore, Vinoba suggests that the equilibrium of body and mind can be maintained with the help of the process of sublimation—"*Guna—Vikash—Kriya*". He believes in *Sankhya* theory of three attributes of *Prakriti—Sattvaguna, Rajoguna* and *Tamoguna*. Our body is nothing else but *Prakriti* and material ground for the working of the soul. The three *gunas* take the form of impulses in our spiritual life and under-lie every action of the body. The *Sattvaguna* is marked by knowledge, *ragas* by motion and *tamas* by rest, inertia, dullness and indifference. All the *gunas* have due importance in our life provided they are pure and at right position. The position of *Sattva* or knowledge is like that of rail which shows the direction of *ragas* or motion like that of engine which moves and the position of *tamas* or inertia is like that of railway compartments which are drawn by the engine.[34] Therefore, all actions of life should be directed by knowledge and sense of duty. However, the impurities of the three *gunas* have to be refined for keeping physical and mental balances. Knowledge is vitiated by pride and it can be sublimed by the practice of politeness and devotion to God. Motion takes the form of action and causes all physical and mental activities. But this also should not be left unrestrained. It has to be controlled by strictly observing to *Svadharma*—duty to one's station and according to one's temperament—"*Vegasya Samnam Swadharma*". In other words the action can be purified if it is altruistic and performed with a sense of duty or *dharma*. The blemishes of the lamas can be overcome by the perspiration resulting from manual labour. For this, Vinoba gives two aphorisms—"*Shram Sangata Varna*" and "*Yanti Pramadam Atandra*", which mean that hard manual labour causes perspiration resulting good sleep at night which ultimately makes us cheerful and happy. All miseries are vanished in the state of happiness and we attain steadfastness of Wisdom—says the *Gita*. Thus in order to have a balanced personality, sublimation of knowledge, action and habits are very essential. A balanced personality alone can proceed towards the highest equanimity.

The path of *Samya Yoga* involves all the ways of realization described in the *Gita*. Vinoba has his own explanation and comment on them. Therefore, it is desirable to dwell upon them.

Way of Knowledge

The way of knowledge according to Vinoba, consists in the incessant contemplation of the great dictums of *Vedanta*—"*Aham Brahmasmi*" and "*Tat tvam asi*" which mean, "I am different from body and you are not weak but endowed with the tremendous power of the soul or the cosmos."[35] The continuous recollection of these dictums awakens the power of the soul which is matrix of all the physical and mental powers. Vinoba expresses this idea in his aphorism—"*Atmashakter bhanat*"—realization of the soul force. The moment soul power arises; we become free from all kinds of slavery—mental, social, biological and slavery of other persons and animals and attain equanimity. The way of knowledge is mistakenly identified with the way of renunciation of actions and the world. According to Vinoba renunciation described by the *Gita* does not mean giving up of actions and worldly life. The *Gita* simply hints at giving up of the all selfish actions or actions performed with selfish motives. Therefore, the way of knowledge is not inconsistent with selfless action. He argues that renouncing of action is impossible because renunciation itself amounts to an act.[36] Further, to take to renunciation has really no meaning, for renunciation itself means to give up.[37] Vinoba is very much animate to the fact that in the name of renunciation and spiritual quest, inaction, idleness, hypocrisy and so many complexes crop up in the seekers and among the masses. Worldly life is looked down upon by the spiritual leaders. Even today, there are sects which promote the culture of inaction in the name of religion and univocally declare that "*moksha dharm*". Works of the householders are held to be responsible for bondage and at the same time the propagators of this religion who do not produce but thrive upon the recalled sinful acts of the householders. Vinoba does not commend such way of knowledge and renunciation. He was a born ascetic yet remained actively engaged in productive work throughout his life. Therefore, it can safely be said that Vinoba's way of knowledge is not devoid of way of action.

However, Vinoba concedes that the way of knowledge can be easy for great souls like Shankar and others only, but the common people cannot go through that way.[38] Worship of the abstract is beyond their power of understanding. It involves high degree of asceticism, which is not possible for an ordinary people. It necessitates complete reliance on intellect alone and there is no room for love, sentiment and devotion. Last but not the least, the way of knowledge is inadequate for the *Moksha*. Narrating his experience Vinoba said, "there was a time when I had placed complete reliance on the way of knowledge. But experience has taught me that mere knowledge does not deliver the goods knowledge does reduce to ashes the grosser impurities of the mind, but it has no power in it to wash away the subtle blemishes."[39] Therefore, the way of knowledge needs the help of way to devotion to root out the blemishes left so far.

Like way of knowledge, the way of meditation according to Vinoba, is also not suitable for laymen. It is esoteric and hence requires the services of experienced and honest teachers. It has danger of falling out in the way due to achievement of supernatural powers. The common people, who are engaged in productive and other responsible work, cannot preserve their valuable times for meditation. Only a few old and economically well off can sit for meditation regularly. The poor masses cannot opt for it. The process of meditation is artificial and unnatural. Therefore, Vinoba while giving due importance of the way of meditation, prefers the way of action or productive work. He gives more emphasis on productive work (*Udyoga*) and cooperation (*Sahyoga*) than the work of meditation (*Yoga*).[40]

From the above discussion it appears that for Vinoba way of selfless action and productive work and the way of devotion are more important than the above two. Therefore, let us see them separately here.

Way of *Karma*

Karma or action according to *Gita* means work skilled or unskilled which is prescribed for a person in accordance with his nature, ability or ancestral profession. According to Vinoba, action is the fuel of knowledge, if it is performed without a selfish desire for its fruits, but in the spirit of service to the community and as an offering to God, it does not lead to bondage. On the contrary, it helps in purifying the mind and realizing the state of *Akarma*—as if we were not doing *Karma*—a state of equanimity, way of action, according to Vinoba is two fold—way of gross action and subtle action. In the way of gross action we perform the allotted work without selfish motive. But in the way of subtle action—*"Sukshma Karma Yoga"*, the seeker remains more interested in purification of heart than the gross outward action. On account of the purity of heart even less action generates tremendous of powers. Here, the importance is given more on speech, feeling and thinking than mere action.[41] Consequently, our external sympathy and feelings assume the form of internal sympathy and feeling.[42]At this stage, the seeker becomes free from all desires, passions and pride and attain the stage of *Jivanmukta*. It does not mean that he becomes apathetic to the world. He observes the whole world as manifestation of God. These processes are actually the internalization process in which we gradually reduce the gross actions and proceed towards subtle, subtler and the subtlest and ultimately reduce ourselves to zero. This process is also applicable in the way of knowledge, devotion and meditation, when one enters into subtle path of action, knowledge, devotion and meditation, without any active participation, inspires the whole world into the path of action and does great service to them in the similar way as the sun activates the whole world but itself remains static.

Vinoba finds no contradiction between the way of knowledge and the way of action. Both are one and the same—*"Sukgama karyoharekeh punthah"*. The *Karmayogi* is overtly active and inertly inactive and similarly the *Gyana Yogi* is overtly inactive but inertly active. Both enjoy the same state of equanimity. None can realize the state of *"Akarma"* equanimity without going through the path of *"Karma"*—action. For action is the cause of equanimity—*"Akarma matrikam karma"*. According to Vinoba attainment of highest equanimity is the goal of our life. The *Karma Yogi* attains, by doing action as a part of duty or moral obligation while the *Gyan Yogi* realizes it by inspiring others in action keeping himself busy in contemplative and meditative work.

No doubt *Karma Yoga* is universally acceptable and very much practicable way of realization, however, like *Gyan Yoga* it cannot claim to reduce the blemishes to zero. The flow of *Karma* and *Gyan Yoga* can be removed only by the *bhakti yoga* path of devotion acceptable to even laymen and women.

Path of Devotion

To Vinoba, God is love, in the path of devotion, one becomes completely selfless and long for union with God. This means the love of the *bhakti yogi* remains no longer centred on particular person, place, time or period but becomes universal which is called a gape in the *Bible.* The devotee feels the presence of God everywhere around him. He looks upon every good and bad events as the expression of God and therefore, he welcomes all the diversities as the act of God.

Vinoba said, "Such is the attitude of a devotee, if a son is born to him he considers it as God's favour. If his son dies, it is equally because of God's grace. The position of a devotee is that whether in happiness or misery, in the pleasurable consequences of good actions or in the even consequences of bad actions, he sees, in both, God's kindness alone. He believes that not a blade of grass moves but by His will. That is why the peace and composure of a devotee's mind is never disturbed. He attains to this composure in a very natural way, while the *Yogi* finds it difficult to acquire."[43]

The path of devotion assigns great importance of reciting *Ramnam* of the name of God. This performs double tasks—(1) it increases the virtues in the devotee if he is good—*Namna Sadgunyam,* (2) it extinguishes the vices—*tadahi papaphari* if altered with devotion, both help in realizing supreme equanimity.

Thus all the paths—knowledge, action, meditation and devotion—lead to the same goal of attaining the highest equanimity. However, our body has certain limitations. Therefore, the perfect equanimity will be achieved only when we are permanently free from the shackles of body, this is called *Videhamukti*.

Conclusion

Vinoba's concept of religion is a good improvement upon both the theistic and mystic religions of the world. While retaining all the good aspects of them, he transcends them forming an original whole like Gandhi, Vinoba's religion is not an isolated phenomenon, but a complete way of life founded on the basis of science and spirituality. Consequently, his thought of religion is a fine conglomeration of humanism, theism and mysticism. His approach to religion is more realistic, universal and natural than esoteric, elitist and artificial exercises in abstraction. It is culturally adequate for the type of thought, speech and action that could lead to higher levels of existence. **The basic sense of word religion—religio meaning thereby reunion, finds good expression in Vinoba's concept of religion as it helps in the re-linking of human personality, individuals, nature, different societies, nations, different sects and finally human beings with higher spiritual realities. If this is strictly followed, the human beings would be enlightened, society would develop, nature balance religious harmony and world peace would be established and most of the violence would stand nowhere.**

REFERENCES

1. Vinoba, *Purnapravaha*, p. 110.
2. Singh, Dashrath, *Gandhivad Ko Vinoba Ki Den* (Patna; Bihar Hindi Grantha Academy, 1975), p. 178.
3. Bhave, Vinoba; *Talks on the Gita*, p. 204.
4. *Ibid.*, p. 205.
5. *Ibid.*, p. 207.
6. *Ibid.*, p. 207.
7. *Ibid.*, p. 210.
8. *Ibid.*, p. 210.

9. *Ibid.*, p. 210.
10. Nargokar, Vasant; *The Creed of Saint Vinoba* (Bombay; Bhartiya Vidya Bhavan, 1963), pp. 73-74.
11. *Vinoba Chintana*, Number 16, p. 179.
12. *Ibid.*, p. 180.
13. *Ibid.*, p. 180.
14. *Ibid.*, Number 55, p. 247.
15. *Ibid.*, Number 16, p. 173.
16. Bhave, Vinoba; *Atmagyan Aur Vigyana*, p. 192.
17. *Ibid.*, p. 392.
18. Nargolkar, *Vasanta*, Ref no. 10, p. 73.
19. *Ibid.*, p. 73.
20. *Ibid.*, p. 73.
21. *Ibid.*, p. 73.
22. Bhave, Vinoba, *Samya Sutra*, p. 9.
23. *Ibid.*, p. 9.
24. *Ibid.*, p. 12.
25. *Vinoba Chintana*, Ref no. 11, Number 4, p. 91.
26. *Ibid.*, Numbers 26-27, pp. 89-90.
27. *Ibid.*, p. 91.
28. *Vinoba Chintana*; Number 14, p. 90.
29. *Ibid.*, p. 87.
30. Bhave, Vinoba; *Atmagyan Aur Vigyan*, p. 28.
31. *Ibid.*, pp. 25-26.
32. *Vinoba Chintan*, Ref. 11, p. 37.
33. *Atmagyan Aur Vigyan*, p. 6.
34. *Samya Sutra*, p. 45.
35. *Ibid.*, pp. 13-14.
36. Nargolkar, *Vasanta*; Ref. no. 10. p. 74.
37. *Ibid.*, p. 84.
38. *Ibid.*, p. 88.
39. *Ibid.*, p. 89.
40. *Ibid.*, p. 90.
41. *Vinoba Chintan*, number 14, p. 20.
42. *Ibid.*, p. 11.
43. *Ref. no. 10*, p. 96.

26

Jayaprakash Narayan
Life, Thought and Action

Bijay Dhari Singh

Jayaprakash Narayan (1902-1979) was born in Sitabdiara, a village now in Uttar Pradesh, on October 11, 1902. His father was a subordinate official in the Bihar irrigation department. The young Jayaprakash was studious and earnest and rather reserved with other children. But he was fond of birds and animals. Though there were few comforts at home, the family, which belonged to the enlightened Kayastha caste, subscribed to magazines and newspapers and regularly bought books on a variety of subjects. By the time he was ten, Jayaprakash had begun to read historical novels glorifying the kings and heroes of ancient India. He also read about national heroes abroad like Garibaldi and de Valera.

It was only when he was sent to Patna Collegiate School at the age of 12 that he was first exposed to the wave of nationalist feeling inspired by Gandhiji's civil resistance movement in South Africa. His friends in the boy's hostel argued fervently that if *Satyagraha* could succeed in South Africa, why could it not achieve at home? Some of them later achieved eminence in Bihar's public life.

Mr. Narayan was drawn close to the world of politics when he married Prabhavati, the daughter of Mr. Brajkishore, one of the leading lawyers of the day and a close friend of Dr. Rajendra Prasad. Both were Congressmen of repute. Shortly after his marriage, Jayaprakash passed his matriculation, obtained a government scholarship, and entered the Science College in Patna. This was the time when the country was convulsed by the infamous Rowlatt Act and even more by the Jallianwala Bagh tragedy. Gandhiji launched his non-cooperation movement in 1920. He could not resist the Mahatma's appeal to students to drop out of schools and colleges to protest against a system of education which was designed only to produce clerks to man the British administration.

In August 1922, Jayaprakash went to America to pursue higher studies. He supported himself by working at a variety of low-paid jobs. He first found work as an agricultural labourer—on a large grape farm where he spent ten hours a day. The savings from his meagre income—four dollars a day at the rate of forty cents an hour—took care of the fees. He enrolled himself in the science faculty of the University of California where he studied mathematics, chemical engineering and biology. But a sharp increase in the fees forced Jayaprakash to leave California. He moved to Iowa and entered the University there. Here is where he came to be known by his initials. In Iowa J.P. continued to pay his way through college by washing dishes in a restaurant, varnishing furniture and shovelling snow in winter. A year later he went to Chicago in search of a better paid job. What he found instead was a politically alive and congenial atmosphere in the University of Wisconsin.

It was during his three-year stay in Chicago that Mr. Narayan got interested in Marxism. How far this interest was related to his first-hand experience of the working conditions on American farms and factories is not easy to say. But there is little doubt that he was influenced by a young Jewish intellectual, Prof. Avron Landy, who was a card carrying member of the Communist Party of America. Jayaprakash began to attend secret meetings at the cell the Professor ran on the campus. Later he came into contact with another Communist, Mr. Samuel Gomez, who was in-charge of the party's eastern zone.

These two mentors not only influenced Jayaprakash to the classics of Marxism and to the writings of M.N. Roy but they also persuaded him to pay a visit to the land of the October revolution. But lack of funds obliged him to give up the pilgrimage to Soviet Russia. He went on to obtain his master's degree in Sociology from Ohio University and returned to India in 1929 "bursting with socialist doctrines and hopes".

A Profile in Changing Convictions and Courage

Turning down the past of Professorship of Sociology in Banaras Hindu University he plunged headlong into the nationalist movement. Although a confirmed Marxist he did not join the Communist Party which at the time was keeping away from the freedom struggle on orders from the Comintern. He joined the Congress instead. During his stay abroad, his wife Prabhavati had become a disciple of Gandhiji and was living at his *ashram* at Wardha. Mr. Narayan was sceptical of Gandhiji's politics, though Gandhiji, ever a shrewd judge of character, prophesied: "One day this man will speak my language."

Within a couple of years of joining the Congress, Mr. Narayan became one of the secretaries of the All-India Congress Committee. Soon after he was arrested and sent to Nasik jail where, along with several others young leftist Congressmen, he laid the foundations of the Congress Socialist Party, a lobby within the parent organisation to convert the Congress to a more socialistic ideology.

Mr. Narayan was arrested several times during the years that followed, but it was his daring escape from Hazaribagh prison during the "Quit India Movement" and his subsequent exploits that made his name a house-hold word allover the country. Thereafter, for 11 months in an attempt to revive the sagging guerilla raids that harried the British war effort, he directed the campaign of cutting telephone wires and ripping up railway tracks. He became one of the most hunted men in the country and the British offered a reward of Rs. 10,000 for information leading to his capture. He was finally caught in September 1943 and released on April 10, 1946 long after all the nationalist leaders were freed.

Jayaprakash was openly critical of the constitutionalist and parliamentary approach adopted by the party's leaders. He wanted them to launch a mass struggle to prevent partition and to achieve independence. This the leaders refused to do. They decided instead to accept the British Cabinet Mission's plan to set up a Constituent Assembly.

In the now-famous letter explaining his stand Mr. Narayan wrote : "If the present Congress leadership persists in its attempt to transform the Congress into a mere parliamentary body with no constructive programme, relying entirely on governmental machinery to serve or rule over the people, turning more and more bureaucratic, keeping its hold over the Congress organisation by the distribution of patronage and largesse, we shall no doubt be unavoidably drawn into conflict with it."

The final break came at Nasik in March, 1948. In his historic report Mr. Narayan not only explained his disillusionment with the ruling party ("The British have gone; the I.C.S. have come") but also with Marxism. "The experience of totalitarian countries, whether fascist or communist, has shown that if the state is looked upon as the sole agent of social reconstruction, we get nothing but a regimented society in which the state is all powerful and popular initiative is extinct and the individual is made a cog in a vast unhuman machine.... Democracy requires that people should depend as little as possible on the state."

The new socialist party was, however, quickly weighed down by differences, especially between Mr. Narayan and Dr. Ram Manohar Lohia. Some of these differences were personal; others related to matters of tactics and even policies.

Late in 1952, Mr. Nehru sought close ties with the Praja Socialist Party to counterbalance the conservatives in the Congress. Discussions were held with Mr. Narayan, Acharya Kriplani and Acharya Narendra Dev to explore the chances of including them and some of their colleagues in the Union Cabinet and in some state governments. The talks proved abortive largely because the socialists did not wish to join the government merely to become ministers. They wanted the Congress to launch a "bold, joint venture of national reconstruction."

But the very fact that talks had been held at all created suspicions in sections of the PSP led by Dr. Ram Manohar Lohia.

The differences were patched up after a while but the electoral fortunes of the PSP proved to be disappointing and this disappointment in turn created so many further dissensions that Mr. Narayan resigned from the primary membership of the party and indeed gave up party politics altogether in 1957.

He was attracted by Vinoba Bhave's Sarvodaya Movement. Mr. Narayan also felt that Westminster style democracy with political parties competing for power was not suited to India. Nor could rapid industrialisation on Soviet lines eradicate poverty. The answer lay in the Gandhian vision of a rural-based society of small, self-governing, self-sufficient village republics where political power was decentralised and where decisions were taken according to the *panchayat* tradition of consensus. His repudiation of Marxism had become total by then. He rejected dialectical materialism because, in his own words, it "did not offer me an answer to the question why should man be good?"

Dacoit Menace

For the next two decades, Mr. Narayan campaigned long and tirelessly for the Bhoodan and Gramdan movements. But he did not cut himself off from national and international issues. Some of his activities included the peace mission in Nagaland, campaign for the release of Sheikh Abdullah, relief work during the great Bihar drought of 1966-67 and the 16-nation tour during the Bangladesh crisis to explain India's stand. He resigned from Nagaland Peace Mission in February 1966 because he thought that he had lost the confidence of the underground Naga leaders. But in the long run his effort did not go waste.

In 1972, Mr. Narayan performed a near miracle when he persuaded the Chambal dacoits to surrender with their stenguns and rifles.

Foreign Affairs

In foreign affairs, J.P. wanted India to continue with its policy of non-alignment in spite of his anti-communist predilections.

He, however, expected New Delhi to come closer to Islamabad, especially in the face of the Chinese threat in the late 'fifties' and the 'sixties'. For this purpose, J.P. advocated the conclusion of a joint defence pact with Pakistan and if possible, the formation of a confederation between the two countries. For the solution of Indo-Pakistan tangle, J.P. urged upon India to accord the people of Kashmir the right of self-determination to choose their destiny, a stand which earned him widespread unpopularity at home.

Link with Trade Unions

Mr. Narayan was active in the labour movement for long and was President of the All-India Railwaymen's Federation, All-India Posts and Telegraphs Employees Union and the All-India Ordinance Employees Federation.

Gujarat Movement

In Gujarat, the movement began in the form of a protest against hostel bills at a college and there was no evidence to show that it grew out of Narayan's appeal. Narayan visited Ahmedabad for four days and talked to student leaders and within weeks the movement snowballed into a general protest against price rise and corruption at high places and engulfed the whole state.

Re-emergence from Political Asceticism

Though he repeatedly claimed that he was no longer in politics, JP all too often got embroiled in sharp political controversy. By 1974, he was spearheading the mass campaign for the dissolution of the Bihar Vidhan Sabha. When this agitation failed to achieve the desired result, he broadened its scope and carried it to the national plane, with a view to bring about "total revolution". This brought him into headlong confrontation with government. The Allahabad High Court judgement against Mrs. Gandhi on the election petition by Mr. Raj Narain further complicated an already complex situation.

On June 25, together with other opposition leaders, JP announced a "time-bound programme" of agitation. He also gave a call to the armed forces and the police to refuse to obey the "unconstitutional" orders of the government. The next morning he and other leaders of the proposed agitation were arrested as part of a countrywide swoop.

He was released on parole on November 12, 1975. Though physically a wreck, he resumed his opposition to Mrs. Gandhi and his efforts to unite the major opposition parties—the Congress (O), Jana Sangh, Socialist Party and Bhartiya Lok Dal were outstanding. These efforts, which had been frustrated in the past, finally bore fruit with the formation of the Janata Party in January 1977. The historic success of the new party in the March 1977 poll was the crowning achievement of his extraordinarily versatile career. It vindicated his abiding faith in the Indian people's commitment of freedom and dignity.

Magsaysay Award

On many occasions, J.P. stood as the champion of truth and justice in international affairs. His forthright advocacy of the Tibetan right of self-determination and his denunciation of the Soviet suppression of Hungarian revolt in 1956 were widely acclaimed in the country. He received the Ramon Magsaysay Award in 1965 for "outstanding public service toward the constructive articulation of a public conscience for modern India."

Rare Gesture by U.N.

In a rare gesture, the U.N. General Assembly paid homage to the memory of Jayaprakash Narayan. The Assembly President, Mr. Salim A. Salim of Tanzania, interrupted the general debate to inform the House of the sudden passing away of "one of the most revered Indian leaders, Sri Jayaprakash Narayan". The Secretary-General, Dr. Kurt Waldheim, also expressed his condolences to India at the passing away of its "elder statesman."

Thought

The intellectual and revolutionary activity of JP from his early youth to his death represents one of the great creative upsurges of Indian history. It was unique in that his restless intellectual exploration went hand in hand with political action. In his lifetime, JP was like a navigator of the ship of history moving in troubled and uncharted waters. He watched every current and cross-current, altering the course where necessary.

While it may be said that JP's thought was definitively formulated long back, recent political developments in the country presented a challenge to his theory of society and polity. His theory was put to practical test and numerous lacunae of a serious nature came to the surface.

It is true that conscience or the inner voice conceived in strictly private and personal terms can never be an entirely reliable and safe guide to social conduct and that it may create impossible situations for the State. The sting of the gadfly may be felt to be a nuisance but it can be the only means of keeping the steed awake. As Socrates said, "It is literally true, even if it sounds rather comical, that God has appointed me to this city, as though it were a large thoroughbred horse which because of its great size is inclined to be lazy and needs the stimulation of some stinging fly." JP's thought as "stinging fly" revolves round the "rediscovery and redefinition" of the roots of community.[1]

Intellectual Orientation

As his Secretary Mr. Brahmanand has noted in the Introduction to the four volume compilation of J.P.'s writings, "Towards Total Revolution", J.P. was from early days interested in social change.[2] His thesis for the M.A. degree, judged the best thesis of the year by Ohio University, U.S.A., in 1929, sought to establish the fact that cultural variations (changes in cultural traits of a group) are mainly responsible for social change, and not race and geography. It was, however, at Wisconsin University, U.S.A., that a Jewish intellectual, Avron Landy introduced J.P. to Marxism. He read Marx's three volumes on

Capital as well as Engels and Lenin. "As I embraced Marxism, I naturally came to regard the American state of those days as reactionary." However, J.P. adds, "Freedom still remained the unchanging goal, but the Marxian science of revolution seemed to offer a surer and quicker road to it, than Gandhiji's technique of civil disobedience and non-cooperation."[3] However, as J.P. got more exposed to the brutal methods of Marxist states and he came to realise that in practice, in the so-called socialist states the individual had lost all freedom to a highly organised and centralised state, J.P. began to turn away from the basic postulates of Marxism. J.P. says, "The ideal polity is built neither on power nor on material prosperity. Rather, it is built to the spiritual re-generation of man."[4]

The whole journey of J.P.'s ideology has been dedicated to a perpetual quest for reality—the field of his research being always the social world. In "Incentives to Goodness" published in September 1952 issue of Freedom First, J.P. enumerates how he at last jettisoned Marxism. He says, "For many years, I have worshipped at the shrine of the Goddess dialectical materialism—which seemed to be intellectually more satisfying than any other philosophy. But while the main quest of philosophy remains unsatisfied, it has become patent to me that materialism of any sort robs man of the means to become truly human. In a material civilisation man has no rational incentive to be good. It may be that in the kingdom of dialectical materialism, fear makes men conform and the party takes the place of God. I feel convinced, therefore, that man must go beyond the material to find the incentives to goodness. As a corollary, I feel further that the task of social reconstruction cannot succeed under the inspiration of a materialist philosophy."[5] Jayaprakash was convinced that in the state of dictatorship of the proletariat the state swells but the individual shrinks and the Marxism and dialecticism has no answer to the question "why should man be good, or why should anyone be good?" Dwelling upon the varying nature of the ideological and value commitments, J.P. says, "I am concerned only with the type of men I should like to live within society."[6]

Sources and Development of J.P.'s Speculations

If there is any political creed or doctrine named after J.P. it is certainly a body of ideas taken from different sources and put together to meet the exigencies of the situations. While in his revolutionary orientation J.P. has been profoundly influenced by Marx, Engels, Avron Landy and Samuel Gomez, he has not in any respect been less influenced by Gandhi, Vinoba, Bakunin, Peter Kropotkin, Immanuel Kant and Trotsky in his socio-political activism. Again, J.P.'s proposed political order has on it the indelible impact of Ramond Aron and the Spanish political philosopher, Salvador de Madariaga while his proposed economic order has been influenced by George Goyder, Folkert Wilken and the British economist, E.F. Schumacher.

Jayaprakash proposes to reconstruct the Indian polity on the lines proposed by Western federal anarchists.[7] The social structure is to rise "storey by storey from the foundations", from the village panchayat to the Lok Sabha. The primary unit will be the family. But since the family is too small a unit to live by itself, a number of families come together to cooperate and satisfy their common needs. Thus comes into being the village or local community. J.P.'s ideal polity will be a decentralised polity in which power and functions are shared by other organisations of society.[8] Ramond Aron in his book, *"In Defence of a Decadent Europe"* expresses views similar to J.P.'s. He makes the interesting observation that decadence may not prove such a bad thing for Western Europe since it may induce it to evolve a system where the exercise of political, economic and social power is effectively decentralised.[9]

Borrowing a phrase from the Spanish political philosopher, Salvador de Madariaga, J.P. calls the Village, Regional, District, Provincial and National Panchayats as "organic" since they are the outcome of a natural and voluntary evolution.[10] J.P. does not prefer nationalisation of large industries since nationalisation only brings industry under "social control" in a formal and legalistic sense. At one place, J.P. approvingly refers to George Goyder's book, *"The Responsible Company"* which advocates a firm which is responsible not only to its proprietors and share-holders but also to its producers, workers and employees, as well to the consumers who buy its products so that they do not sell shoddy goods or overprice them.[11]

Elsewhere J.P. recommends Folkert Wilken's suggestion "to neutralise the power of capital by setting up an independent association for the administration of capital which will have the right to own profit capital as a trustee and would decide its disposal to enterpreneurs for productive use or for consumption to such persons as educators, teachers and researchers."[12] In the Foreword to Wilken's book J.P. urges those having the "requisite emotional identification and intellectual convinction to provide the drive towards a trusteeship economy.[13] In "*Prison Diary*", J.P. pleads for regrouping of villages as per a predetermined Optimum size and for establishing "radial towns" from where roads, power and other services radiate to the countryside.[14] It is all a question of deciding appropriate technology says J.P. who fully endorses the view of the British economist E.F. Schumacher expressed in his well-known work, "*Small is Beautiful*" that industrialisation on a large scale is just colonisation by the big metropolitan areas.[15]

So far as the development of J.P.'s political speculations is concerned, his transition from socialism to *sarvodaya* has a different story. Allan and Wendy Scarfe in their biography of J.P., put forth an additional reason for J.P. joining Vinoba. They opine that J.P. joined Vinoba largely because of the adverse impact of the fast he had undertaken in July 1952. The fast, the Scarfes claim left J.P. in a state of 'extreme emotinal vulnerability'. "In this position of humility he reached after his fast, J.P. was prepared to submerge his ideas and his vitality in Vinoba's personality."[16] The early 1970s witnessed the beginning of another crucial phase when J.P. disillusioned with Vinoba's method and technique of gentle persuasion, deliberately opted for the Gandhian techniques of mass action (*Satyagraha* and Civil Disobedience) to achieve social change. In the pamphlet "*Face to Face*" published in 1970, J.P. confesses that the *Bhoodan-Gramdan* movement has failed to achieve its revolutionary objective of *Gram-Swarajya.*

The Basic Postulates of J.P.'s Political Thought

Jayaprakash's political thought is a creative compact of his ideas of stateless society, futility of constitutional checks on state-power, negation of majority-rule, partyless and participative democracy, negation of westminster-type parliamentary government, opposition to monistic concept of sovereignty, individual freedom, local government, internationalism, priority of the means over the ends and *satyagraha* and non-violence. His political thought is a curious amalgam of all that he considers good in any ideology. His Westernised idiom and distinct leaning towards classical anarchism are far removed from Vinoba Bhave's traditional Hindu idiom and what many consider to be antiquated ideas.

J.P.'s Total Revolution—Background Meaning and Concept

Perhaps no name in recent Indian history has evoked so much praise as well as hostile criticism as that of Jayaprakash Narayan. The greatest event in J.P.'s life was undoubtedly the Bihar Movement which the fast ageing leader chose to lead and guide in 1974 and which aimed at removing a corrupt state government.

Jayaprakash clarifies that "Total Revolution" means that 'the system and the people change together, not one after the other, but both simultaneously'. To Narain Desai, "The word 'total' is not to indicate completeness or accomplishment as some conceive it to be. Many a time J.P. has explained that the revolution is not complete or over. In fact he has often said that it is a continuing revolution. The word 'total' to J.P. is more akin to comprehensiveness...by 'total' he wants to indicate a revolution that covers the totality of life and that which encompasses the multifarious aspects of life."[17]

In the "*Prison Diary*" J.P. observes that 'Total Revolution' is a combination of seven revolutions, i.e. social, economic, political, cultural, ideological or intellectual, educational and spiritual.[18] "This number may be increased or decreased. For instance, the cultural revolution may include educational or ideological revolution. And if culture is used in an anthropological sense, it can embrace all other revolutions. Likewise social revolution in the Marxian context covers economic and political revolutions and even more than that. This is how we can reduce the number to less than seven. And we can add to this number by breaking up each of the seven revolutions into different categories. Economic revolution may be split up into industrial, agricultural, technological revolutions etc. Similarly intellectual revolution may be split up into scientific and philosophical. Even spiritual revolution can be viewed as made up of moral and spiritual, or it can be looked upon as part of the cultural."[19]

Trotskyite-Neo-Kantian-Revisionism in J.P.—An Analysis

Jayaprakash's 'Total Revolution' among its myriad counterparts (social, socialist, bourgeois, permanent etc.) seems to be an intellectual descendant of Leon Trotsky's 'Permanent Revolution'. The element of permanence in J.P.'s concept of revolution comes to the surface when he says that his model of revolution is neither 'complete nor over', it is a 'continuing revolution'. Hence J.P.'s concept of 'total revolution' reappears in the garb of Trotsky's 'permanent revolution'.

The title, 'permanent revolution' was adopted from a slogan 'the revolution in permanence' that Marx proposed to the Communist League in 1850 when he anticipated that a revolution was about to break out in Germany. Trotsky first published the theory as a chapter of his account of Patersburg Soviet, written while he was in prison after its failure. The theory was elaborated in *"The Permanent Revolution"* (1930); English translation, New York (1931). It is summarised in Isaac Deutscher's *"The Prophet Armed"*, Trotsky : 1879-1921. Thus in 1850 Marx supplied the concept of 'Permanent Revolution' which Trotsky adopted and developed in 1906, and which laid down substantially the policy that Lenin followed in 1917 relative to the middle-class revolution in Russia. Thus Permanent Revolution became Trotskyism."[20] J.P.'s concept of 'toal revolution' is 'comprehensive' in its purpose and 'permanent' in its nature. Hence, this hypothesis.

The appelation of J.P. as being neo-Kantian revisionist simultaneously leads one to find in his thought a unique blend of ethical socialism, revolutionary romanticism and religious anarchism. J.P. appears to be close to Bernstein's neo-Kantian revisionism characterised by anarchist and voluntarist conceptions. Declaring that socialist views are independent of philosophical views, the left revisionists tried to combine scientific socialism with Kant's moral philosophy. Neo-Kantianism was utilised by revisionism in its struggle against Marxism. Further, J.P. is an ethical socialist because he considers that socialism should be regarded chiefly as a totality of moral and ethical principles and norms. The revolutionary romanticism is reflected in J.P. because he has a progressive revolutionary direction with a tinge of utopia. Lastly, J.P. is a religious anarchist because he believes in Tolstoy's dictum, i.e. nonviolence and non-cooperation.

The J.P. Movement : Genesis, Objectives and Strategy

The Indira Gandhi government, shortly after the proclamation of the emergency in June 1975, published a booklet, "*Why Emergency*?", in which it sought to explain the genesis of the J.P. movement. In its second chapter the booklet claimed that the inspiration for the Bihar movement came from the student agitation in Gujarat which succeeded in compelling the central government to dismiss the state government and order fresh elections. The booklet quotes J.P. as saying, "For years I was groping to find the way out....Then I saw the students in Gujarat bring about a political change with the backing of the people...and I knew that this was the way out". The chapter concludes: "The events in Gujarat leading to the dissolution of the Assembly had undoubtedly their own lessons. The opposition parties who participated actively derived satisfaction that violence by exploitation of the youth could be productive of the results which they could not achieve through normal constitutional means. Here then was the inspiration."[21]

During the course of the movement J.P. made it clear that the dissolution of the Bihar Assembly was not on the original agenda of the movement. J.P. observes, "It was only after the complete collapse of the administration on 18th March, and the way the government handled the Gaya firings in April that I realised that the Government was totally inept and had no right to continue."[22] J.P. looked on the dissolution as "barely a first step". He observed, "I told them (the Nav Nirmal Samiti) if they wanted the movement to succeed they had to look beyond the dissolution...I want society to be transformed politically, culturally, economically. That is why I refer to this as a movement for total revolution from which a completely new society will emerge."[23] There is ample evidence to show that right from early 1970s, J.P. was beginning to get disillusioned with Vinoba's teachings and the technique of gentle persuasion, and was consciously planning mass action along Gandhian lines of mass *satyagraha* and civil disobedience. Subsequent developments after 1970 such as the Twenty-fourth amendment of the Constitution of India, growing weakness of the opposition parties, Supreme Court's judgment in the *Golaknath case* etc. strengthened J.P.'s belief in the need to organise a mass movement.

The insignia of major objectives of the movement can be traced back to its ontological-historical evolution. The charter of demands presented to the government by the students and later on another such charter presented to the Speaker of the Lok Sabha and the Chairman of the Rajya Sabha by J.P. orchestrate the avowed objectives of the movement which is woven round an all comprehensive and all pervasive social revolution. J.P.'s was a multi-dimensional approach so far as the gamut of strategy and tactics is concerned. It is reflected in acts of launching different programmes of action and simultaneously setting up of committees to look into matters of public concern.

To lead the revolution J.P. preferred to rely more on students and youth than on workers and peasants. In reply to M.R. Masani's question as to why he concentrated on youth, J.P. observed, "You and I have gone through that socialist phase....and we believed in the leadership of the industrial working classes in revolution. Now the Indian industrial working class is more or less a petit bourgeois class. Their standard of living is higher than the living standards of the lower middle class for instance. If you compare their wages with the wages of agricultural labour, they (industrial workers) are much better off. So I don't think they are a revolutionary force at all."[24]

J.P. and His Critics

Besides numerous important concepts of the foremost Indian thinkers of modern times, the critics of Jayaprakash Narayan have focused their attention on his concepts of stateless society, partyless democracy, majority rule and election, alternative political and economic orders, *satyagraha* and nonviolence, total revolution and last but not least the 1974 movement led by him.

The critics may have their rationale and predilections, prejudices and objectivity. J.P.'s concept of stateless society comes as a prelude to myriad criticisms that have been levelled against him. J.P. shares with Gandhi the belief that the state is one of the "noblest goals of social endeavour." They are of the view that powers and functions of the state are to be reduced as far as possible. This in turn presupposes that men acting in small primary groups can fulfil their primary and secondary needs by self-endeavour. It was this theoretical assumption that made Marx speak of the "withering away of the state." The same assumption constitutes the base of continental socialist utopian thought, viz. the thought of Owen, Fourier and many others. But nowhere, neither in Soviet Russia nor in the experimental Communes in France—has this assumption proved true. If anything, history has proved the contrary. Man's ever increasing desire for comfort and conveniences has led him to found bigger organisations which could serve his needs more efficiently than the primary groups.

Jayaprakash equates parliamentary government with brute force because it is based on majority rule. What is overlooked here is that Government based on majority rule is the "least evil" of the various forms of government. The party as Lowell in "*Public Opinion and Popular Government*" has observed, acts as a "brokerof ideas" and helps the citizen obtain "vision of the whole nation, otherwise distant in history, territory and futurity." F.S. Oliver aptly observes in his book *"The Endless Adventure"*, "The nation that we can save ourselves without their help is an illusion; for politics is not one of those crafts that can be learned by the light of the nature without an apprenticeship."

Jayaprakash claims that his new polity will be built neither on power nor material prosperity but on the "spiritual regeneration of man." Like all other utopia builders JP refuses to accept the lesson of social history that such a man has not yet evolved. JP argues that to seek more than the essential needs, which he has spelt out as sufficient food, clothing and a decent house to live in, is to seek material progress at the cost of moral achievement. But according to Bertrand Russell, "Nothing improves the moral level of a community as much as an increase of wealth and nothing lowers it so much as a diminution of wealth."[24]

Even the weapon of *satyagraha,* which JP commends, is not free of the charge of being coercive. Its persuasive value is at best doubtful. However, the really important criticism about Gandhian (or J.P.) means is not that they are coercive, but that their application would produce disastrous consequences. *Satyagraha* and civil disobedience may not only destroy the democratic fibre of society they could as well usher in ananarchy in which all else could also be lost.

With regard to J.P.'s concept of 'total revolution' it is best to realise that democratic (constitutional) means and revolution cannot go together. To be committed to both democracy and revolution is a patent self-contradiction. As Karl Popper in his classic "Open Society and its Enemies" has noted, "a revolution requires a totalist approach to social change, whereas democratic social reconstruction is always piecemeal. Democratic social change implies compromise between opposed or conflicting value system."

Ghanshyam Shah in his study, "Protest Movement in Two Indian States", contends that judged by the criteria of what constitutes a revolution, J.P.'s movement was not a revolution.

Shah opines, "J.P. gave no blueprint of that (alternative) society nor outlined the various stages of the revolution. Instead he gave a long list of proposals; agricultural development, equitable land ownership, appropriate technology, rural and small industries etc. He did not spell out how the land was to be so distributed, nor how the social and economic hierarchy was to be abolished."[25] R.K. Barik, another critic of J.P., supports the contention that J.P. had no ideology, by citing J.P.'s view as reported in the *Calcutta* daily, *Statesman* of the 16th June, 1974. J.P. is reported to have said, "I do not think ideology helps clarity. I think all ideologies have become old. It is not ideology but science that can answer all the questions. Let scientists and economists sit and chalk out a programme."[26]

As Mr. W.H. Morris-Jones noted almost some decades ago, Indian political life has been conducted in broadly three languages which may be described as 'modern', 'traditional' and 'saintly'. "Of these the last has gone more or less out of vogue or it seems that many of those who continue to use the first do so with decreasing convinction regarding its relevance. In a sense the 'saintly' language has been a perpetual phenomenon. If it had struck some roots in pre-independent India under Gandhiji's influence, these withered away quickly in independent India. Acharya Vinoba sought to give a concrete content to the 'saintly' language when he launched the Bhoodan movement in the 'fifties'. Needless to say the movement proved a failure. J.P. made an attempt to revive the 'saintly language' in Indian politics in 1974 which he sought to build a popular movement on the issue of corruption in high places. But the effort was vitiated at the very start. As the 'saintly language' began to lose importance with the achievement of independence, the Indian political life came to be conducted in the 'modern' language—the language of the constitution."[27]

JP—The Reluctant Messiah

To most Congressmen, obsessed with acquiring the epaulettes of influence, Jayaprakash Narayan was an anachronism. Just as the Mahatma was. Several Congress governments, from

Jawaharlal Nehru to Indira Gandhi, courted him assiduously, offering him opulent sinecure and position which he rejected without a second glance. Severing his bond with politics in the fifties, J.P. seemed destined for an active role in obscurity like his friend Achyut Patwardhan. But depressed by the death of idealism and increasing malfeasance, he thundered back into public life in the mid-70s, instantly obtaining apotheosis. Completely devoted to recreating a nation with a strong value system, J.P. quickly became India's conscience. But this eagerness to spawn a resurgent society served as a catalyst for the emergency. The collapse of the Janata government fragmented his dream, and it was fortunate that he did not live to see it. But the optimism and value he made this country believe in still live on.

REFERENCES

1. G.N. Sarma in his Foreword to Adi H. Doctor's J.P.'s *Total Revolution—An Exercise in Utopia,* p. 7.
2. *Vide* Introduction (by Mr. Brahmanand), J.P. Narayan, *Towards Total Revolution : Search for an Ideology,* Vol. I, Popular Prakashan, Bombay, 1978.
3. J.P. Narayan, *A Picture of Sarvodaya Social Order,* Sarvodaya Prachuralayam, Tanjore, 1961, p. 95.
4. *Vide* J.P. Narayan, *Towards Total Revolution,* Vol. III, Popular Prakashan, Bombay, 1978, p. 344.
5. As quoted by M.R. Masani in his J.P. *Mission Partly Accomplished,* MacMillan Co. of India Ltd., New Delhi, pp. 14-15.
6. J.P. Narayan, *Towards Total Revolution,* Vol. I, pp. 96-97.
7. Michael Bakunin's *God and the State,* Boston, 1893; and same author's *Marxism, Freedom and the State,* London, 1950. Also Peter Kropotkin, *Modern Science and Anarchism,* London, 1912.
8. J.P. Narayan, *The Challenge of Nation Building,* Orient Paperback, New Delhi, p. 72.
9. Quoted by Adi H. Doctor in his *J.P.'s Total Revolution—An Exercise in Utopia,* Seema Publications, Delhi : 1987, p. 41.
10. *Ibid.,* p. 45.
11. *Vide* J.P. Narayan, *Towards Total Revolution,* Vol. IV, p 159. For an example of a Trusteeship Company, viz. "The Scott-Bader Commonwealth", see Dr. Schumacher's essay in *Sarvodaya* (Monthly Journal), Tanjore, September, 1972, pp. 105-113.

12. Folkert Wilkens, *New Forms of Ownership in Industry,* Sarva Sewa Sangh, Varanasi, 1969.
13. J.P.'s Foreword to Wilkens' book, pp. 12-15.
14. J.P. Narayan, *Prison Diary,* Popular Prakashan, Bombay, 1975, p. 62.
15. *Vide* Schumacher's book *"Small is Beautiful"* (Indian Edition published by Akhil Bhartiya Sarva Sewa Sangh) and the book *"Good Work"* Indian Edition published by B.L. Publications, Delhi.
16. Allan and Wendy Scarfe, *J.P. His Biography,* Orient Longmans, New Delhi, 1975, ch. 12, p. 285.
17. Narain Desai, 'Total Revolution and Non-violence' in *Total Revolution—a symposium* (ed.) S. Das Gupta, Noya Prakash, Calcutta, 1978, p. 42.
18. J.P. Narayan, *Prison Diary,* pp. 87-88.
19. Acharya Ram Murti, *Sampoorna Kranti : Kya Kyon Aur Kaise* (in Hindi), pp. 3-5.
20. George H. Sabine, *A History of Political Theory,* Oxford & IBH Publishing Co. Pvt. Ltd., New Delhi, Reprint 1973, Fourth Edition, pp. 720, 744 and 794.
21. Cited in Vasant Nargolkar, *J.P. Vindicated,* S. Chand & Co., New Delhi, 1977, p. 10.
22. "J.P. on his own movement in Bihar", *Radical Humanist* (English Monthly), Delhi, August 1974, p. 9.
23. *Ibid.,* p. 10.
24. Bertrand Russell, *Power : A New Social Analysis,* Unwin Books, London, 1960.
25. Ghanshyam Shah, *Protest Movement in Two Indian States,* Ajanta Publications, Delhi, June 1977, pp. 104-105.
26. R.K. Barik, *Politics of the J.P. Movement,* Radiant Publishers, Delhi, 1977, p. 57.
27. Girilal Jain, "Language of Indian Politics—Borrowed Idiom Giving Way", *The Times of India,* 31-3-1980.

27

Ambedkar's *Dharma* Upliftment of Oppressed Class

S. Sri Krishna

Born as a untouchable, Dr. B.R. Ambedkar had to face social ostracism and isolation and early in life he realised that a large section of his countrymen had denied their legitimate rights by the oppressive social customs. Equipped with an almost encyclopaedic knowledge of Hindu society in particular and human society in general, he began the task of reconstructing the Hindu society simultaneously by offering devastating criticism and suggesting possible ways for its reorganisation. A pragmatist to the core Dr. B.R. Ambedkar believed that the establishment of a democratic society in India would be possible only when the untouchables and other weaker sections of society would be given the opportunity to enjoy basic human rights.[1] He gives a graphic picture of the plight of the untouchables in the following words:

> "The Hindu society insists on segregation of the quarters of the untouchables. The Hindu will not live in the quarters of the untouchables and will not allow the untouchables to live inside Hindu quarters.This is a fundamental feature of untouchability as it is practised by the Hindus. It is not a case of social separation, a mere stoppage of intercourse for a temporary period. It is a case of territorial segregation and of a cordon sanitaire putting the impure inside a barbed wire, into a sort of cage. Every Hindu village has a ghetto.

The Hindus live in the village and the untouchables in the ghetto."[2]

Therefore, Dr. B.R. Ambedkar came to the conclusion that nowhere except in India there existed permanent segregation camps and there had never been a case of people, treating a section of their own people as permanent and hereditary slaves. Untouchability was a unique phenomenon unknown to humanity except the Hindus. Dr. B.R. Ambedkar proves this by citing the example of the condition of the untouchables during the period of the Peshwas.[3]

The definition of a 'slave' given by Plato was appropriately applicable to the untouchable. Plato has defined the slave as one who accepts from another the purpose which control his conduct. Therefore, Dr. B.R. Ambedkar pointed out that the untouchables were treated as slaves because (1) they were so socialised as never to complain of their low state; (2) they never dreamed of trying to improve their lot, by forcing the other classes to treat them with the common respect; (3) the idea that they had been born to their lot was so ingrained in their mind that it never occurred to them to think that their fate was anything so irrevocable; (4) nothing would ever persuade them that men are all made of the same clay, or that they have the right to insist on better treatment than that meted out to them."[4]

Dr. B.R. Ambedkar described the state of slavery of the untouchables and the denial of human rights at the time of giving evidence before the Reforms Committee (Franchise), (South-Borough Committee), on 27th January 1919. He said, "The exact description of the treatment cannot be attempted. The word 'untouchable' is an epitome of their ills and sufferings. Not only has untouchability arrested the growth of their personality but it comes in the way of their material well-being. It has also deprived them of certain civil rights. For instance, in Konkan the untouchables are prohibited from using the public road. If some high caste man happens to cross him he has to be out of the way and stand at such a distance that his shadow will not fall on the high caste man."[5]

His slogan, "Tell the slave that he is a slave and he will revolt against his slavery" had a telling effect in that it generated a consciousness in the untouchables and the downtrodden about their plight and the need to secure their human rights. For the steady and systematic upliftment of the downtrodden he started educational and social institutions and journals and also launched a movement of *Satyagraha* on 9th March, 1924 at Damodhar Hall, Bombay, he called a meeting of the Social workers both from the untouchables and others and he established the Bahiskrit Hitkarini Sabha.[6]

Dr. B.R. Ambedkar ceaselessly strove to make the untouchables conscious of their self-respect and the need for self-elevation. In one of his speeches, he said : "My heart breaks to see the pitiable sight of your faces and to hear your sad voices : You have been groaning from time immemorial and yet you are not ashamed to hug your helplessness as an inevitability. Why did you not perish in the prenatal stage instead? Why do you worsen and sadden the picture of the sorrows, poverty, slavery and burdens of the world with your deplorable, despicable, detestable and miserable life? You had better died and relieved this world if you could not rise to a new life and if you could not rejuvenate yourself. As a matter of fact, it is your birth right to get food, shelter and clothing in equal proportion with every individual, high or low. If you believe in living a respectable life you should believe in self-help which is the best help."[7]

It was in this manner that Dr. B.R. Ambedkar made the oppressed lot of the backward classes conscious of their rights, which as a part of humanity, were their legitimate dues but which were deliberately denied to them. Educating the down-trodden people, he thought, was a sure way to instill in them a sense of self-respect and dignity. This in turn would provide the necessary cultural basis for their progressive assimilation into the mainstream of an enlightened national life. He was bitterly opposed to every kind of oppression and unequality but, at the same time, it was his earnest desire to bring about changes through peaceful and constitutional means.[8]

Dr. B.R. Ambedkar sought to kindle a sense of dignity and self-respect in the meek and submissive minds of his followers through his *Satyagraha* Movement. The *Satyagraha* at Mahad was a historical event in as much as it was conducted for the purpose of securing to the downtrodden the right to drink water from the public tanks. This right, which the birds and animals enjoyed in full measures was senselessly denied to the untouchables. The *Satyagraha* received the wholehearted support of no less a person than Sri Nanasaheb Tipnis, the then President of the Mahad Municipality, Kolaba district. According to Shri Tipnis, several caste Hindus like Shri D.V. Pradhan, Shri Anantrao Chitre, Shri Joshi and Shri Sabnis and many members of the Samaj Samata Mandal joined this Satyagraha of the untouchables. In spite of virulent opposition from the orthodox section of the Hindus, the *Satyagraha* succeeded in attaining its objective.[9]

The movement launched by Dr. B.R. Ambedkar to inspire the Depressed Classes to fight for their rights gradually gained momentum and successfully brought about improvements in their economic and social conditions, political representation and educational and cultural achievements. The Mahad *Satyagraha* for the right of drinking water and the Nasik *Satyagraha* for entry into the temple were outstanding struggles of the untouchables to win equal social rights.

Dr. B.R. Ambedkar considered that, "Unless the Indian people secure political power and this political power concentrates in the hands of the socially suppressed section of the Indian society, it is not possible to completely wipe out all social legal and cultural disabilities, from which this section suffers."[10] He further said, "Nobody can remove these unless you get political power into your hands....we must have a government in which men in power will not be afraid to amend the social and economic code of life which the dictates of justice and expediency so urgently call for. This role the British Government will never be able to play. It is only a government which is of the people, for the people and by the people, in other words, it is only the Swaraj Government that will make it possible."[11]

The mission of Dr. B.R. Ambedkar's life was the establishment of human dignity, development of self-respect among the downtrodden classes, and attainment of self-salvation. In a word, it was man-making. Dr. B.R. Ambedkar was a great teacher who taught the common man to have belief in his potential power to rouse it up to develop it and to stand on his own feet. Man should not think that he was a mere nobody that he was good for nothing and that he was a helplers log. His advice to the downtrodden classes, and especially to youngmen, was exemplary. He asked them to rely on their self, on their own efforts, to trust and exercise their own intelligence and to seek refuse in reason. To him nothing was more sacred than learning. Nature made none a slave. No man was born a dullard.

His message to his people was that they should strive endlessly, sacrifice to present pleasures for a great future, and should go through the ordeal fire and sacrifice till they attain their goal. "You must have a firm belief in the sacredness of your goal. Noble is your aim and sublime and glorious is your mission. Blessed are those who were awakened to their duty to those among whom they are born. Glory to those who devote their time, talents and their all to the annihilation of slavery. Glory to those who would keep on their struggle for the liberations of the enslaved in spite of heavy odds, carping humiliations, storms, and dangers till the downtrodden secure their human rights."[12]

Dr. B.R. Ambedkar, therefore, did not like that his hungry men should envelop themselves in the coils of Bhakti, the cult of devotion, the opium of helplessness. He asked the common man not to resign himself to his fate and accept his position as a divine dispensation. The ignorant people believed that their fate was pre-appointed and irretrievable. Dr. B.R. Ambedkar wanted to root out this disease from their minds. Like Vivekananda, he told them that it was sentimental nonsense which made them impotent. For *Bhakti* made their nerves soft, delicate and yielding.[13]

By any standard, Dr. B.R. Ambedkar may be regarded as the shining star among all the revolutionaries of our time. Dr. Babasaheb Ambedkar was a great political thinker and social revolutionary that, modern India had produced. Being born as a member of the downtrodden community, he perpetually endeavoured to left his community from the age-old suppressed position. He had shown by his own example, that given the determination and proper direction in life, anyone can realise the highest goal in life. Apples may fall in the lap of some people's for others, they must climb the tree to get the fruit. Dr. B.R. Ambedkar, with courage and determination, with self-confidence in his heart and sincerity on his tongue, he climbed the life to success. Today he is the symbol of inspiration for millions in this country.

Dr. B.R. Ambedkar said that all people of the Scheduled Castes and other backward communities should be united under one banner so as to show their united strength. They must give up their political aloofness and unite with all progressive minded parties in order to hold the balance of power in the new democratic set up. He declared, "Political power is the key to all social progress and the Scheduled Castes can achieve their salvation if they captured this power by organising themselves into a third party and holding the balance of power between the rival political parties."[14]

When the country was passing through the darkness due to casteism and anarchy was prevailing on account of all the social evils and superiority and inferiority at this Juncture, the social reformer like Buddha who for the first time questioned the validity of casteism and revolted against it. After 2,500 years, another great social reformer was born in this country, he being no other than Dr. Babasaheb Ambedkar. Dr. B.R. Ambedkar is the Liberator of the Downtrodden Classes in India, Hero to the oppressed masses, Saviour of the suppressed souls and the maker of the Constitution of India. He was a social revolutionary who spent his life fighting against social evils, which have weakened India and made her a slave. Unfortunately many of his contemporaries have failed to recognise the real service he rendered to the entire country mistaking him as the leader of the downtrodden masses only.

Dr. B.R. Ambedkar developed his own political strategy in order to secure political rights for the depressed classes and to ensure proper distribution of political power in different elements of Indian society. He was dealing with a very complex situation as the country was in great ferment and defined simple solutions.

NOTES

1. Kokhande, G.S., *Bhimrao Ramji Ambedkar—A Study in Social Democracy,* Intellectual Publishing House, New Delhi, 1982, p. 156.
2. Ambedkar, B.R., *The Untouchables* Amrit Book Co., New Delhi, 1984, p. 22.
3. Gupta, C.B., *The Harijans in Rebellion, Case for Removal of Untouchability,* Sterling Publishing (P.) Ltd., New Delhi, 1964, pp. 11-12.
4. Ambedkar, B.R., *What Congress and Gandhi have done to the untouchables,* Thacker and Co. Ltd., Bombay, 1946, p. 194.
5. Lokhande, G.S., *Bhimrao Ramji Ambedkar—A Study in Social Democracy,* Intellectual Publishing House, New Delhi, 1982, p. 102.
6. *Ibid.*, p. 170.
7. Keer, Dhananjaya, *Dr. Ambedkar : Life and Mission,* Popular Prakashan, Bombay, 1950, pp. 60-61.
8. *Ibid.*, p. 63.
9. Lokhande, G.S., *Op. Cit.*, p. 175.
10. Bhagawan Das (Compiled by) *Thus Spoke Ambedkar,* Vol. I., The Bheem Patrika Publications, Jullunder, 1963, p. 67.
11. Keer Dhananjay, *Op. cit.*, p. 151.
12. *Ibid.*, p. 163.
13. *Ibid.*, p. 164.
14. Moti Lal Nim (Compiled by) *Thoughts on Dr. Ambedkar,* Phonix Publishing Agency, Agra, 1971, pp. 20-21.

Index

Abdul Razzaq Malihabadi, 59
Aberrations, 74, 78
Abhinav Bharat, 107
Absolute Truth, 85
Acharya Kripalani, 271, 366
Acharya Narendra Deva, 330-35
  ethical dimension of socialism, 327-35
  ideology of democratic socialism, 336
  philosophy of, 335
  political career, 335
  vision of socialism, 334
Adam Smith, 182
Adharma, 26, 126
Adhyatma Vidya, 348
Adi Puran, 115
Adi Sankaracharya, 339
Advaita philospopy, 149-50
Advaita Vedanta, 388
Advaitavadins, 146
Afghanistan, 74-75
Agnosticism, 79
Agricultural production, 183-84
Ajanta, 52
Akbar, 69
Akrasia, 46
Almighty Power, 56
All India Muslim League, 167, 208-09, 311-12
Allaho Akbar, 64
Ambedkar, B.R., 24-25, 120, 312, 383-88
  dharma of, 383-88
  life of, 386-87
  political power, 387
  political strategy of, 388-89
  satyagraha movement of, 385-88
American Methodists, 69
Amir Khusro, 70
Anashakti Yoga, 353
Anekantavada, 73
Anglo-Indian Bureaucrates, 180
Angosticism, 79
Animal sacrifice, 138
Annie Besant, 141, 317
Anthropocentricism, 285
Anti-national *dharma*, 126
Aphorism, 356
Arab traders, 69
Arabia-Persian-Islamia influence, 145
Arbitrariness, 230
Aristotle, 98
Artha, 9, 41-42, 49-50
Arthasastra, 55, 90, 97-98, 104
  position of, 105-06
  scope of, 98-99
Arya Samaj, 70, 134-35, 175, 228
  Hindu rivalist movement of, 157
  movement of, 16, 142-43
Aryan, 51-52, 69-70, 76
Aryan civilization, 62
Aryan and Non-Aryan cultures, 75-76
Aryavarta, 135
Ashoka, 52, 76
Aswaghosh, 116
Aśramadharma, 85
Atmiya Sabha, 150
Aurengzeb, 71

Aurobindo Ghosh, 20-21, 126, 187, 192, 243, 280-81, 342
  ideas and limitations, 246-47
  political philosophy of, 245-46, 249-50
  Pondicherry experiment, 247-48, 252
  prognosis *vis a vis* current one-world situation, 250-52
  revolutionary activities, 252
  western influence, 247-48
  yogic background, 251
Ayodhya tragedy, 75
Azad, Abul Kalam, 58-59, 318
Azad Hind Fauj, 270

Babarnama, 71
Babri Masjid agitation, 75
Badruddin Tyabji, 205
Bagh paintings, 52
Bahadur Shah, 213
Bahiskrit Hitkarini Sabha, 285
Banaras Hindu University, 299, 365
Banerjee, Surendra Nath, 162
Basava Puran, 115
Bentinck, William, 153
Bernard Shah, 246
Bhagat Singh, 318
Bhagwad Dharma, 172
Bhagwat Gita, 54-55, 188-89
Bhakti religion, 52
Bhakti movement, 70
Bhakti-yoga, 66
Bhakti yogi, 360
Bhandarkar, R.J., 171, 176
Bharat Sewak Samaj, 17, 168-69
Bhartiya Jan Sang Party, 129
Bhartiya Samyavadi Sangh, 272, 275
Bhatta Nilakantha, 92
Bhavishyapuran, 108
Bhisma Piṭamaha, 34
Bhoodan-Gramdan movement, 345, 373
Bhubaneshwar, 52
Bible, 53-54, 68, 227-28
Bihar movement, 376
Bihar Vidhan Sabha, 368
Blue Book, 151
Bombay University, 107
Bond of Common Blood (Racial Unity), 113-14
Bose, Subhash Chandra, 21, 270
Brahma, 347
Brahmacārin, 84
Brahamanas, 193
Brahmo Samaj, 173, 175
British Political system, 322
British Policy of Divide and Rule, 74
Buckingham, Silk, 147
Buddacarita, 33
Buddhism, 57, 61-65, 346-47
Burke, Edmund, 166

Cāndrayāna, 93
Capitalism, 23
Caste system, 61-62
Casteism, 388
Catholism, 72
Chaitanya, 65
Chaitanya Charitramrit, 116
Challenges, 10, 139-40
Chanakya, 97, 131
Chandragupta, 52, 97
Chaudhary, R.K., 99
Child marriage, 175
China, 34, 340
Christ, ethical teachings, 146
Christian missionaries, 69-70, 228
Christianity, 13, 25-26, 54-56, 68-70, 77-78, 81-82, 137-38, 146-50, 173
Civilization crisis, 49-50
Closeness between Islam and Christianity, 227
Committee of Orthodox Muslims, 232
Common Culture, 114-15

Common laws and rites, 118-19
Common literature, 115-16
Communal Awards, scheme of, 311
Communalism, 272-73
Conflict between individual well-being and collective well-being, 45-46
Confucianism, 173
Congress Socialist Party (CSP), 328, 330-32
Constraints, 249-50
Contradiction between British imperialism and Indian People, 330
Controversy between Christianity and Islam, 228-29
Corruption, 22, 281
Cosmic Force, 315
Crawford, J., 157
Criticism, 139, 146-47, 180, 228, 248, 292
Cultural synthesis, process of, 60-61
Cultural tradition, 51-56
Cupidity, 34

Daishik Shastra, 125
Dalton, Dennis, 280
Dandaniti, 87, 97-98, 104, 243
Daridranarayan, 238, 272
Das, C.R., 258
Das, Chittaranjan, 260
Deliverance Day, 207
Demarcation between *Dharma* and *Panth,* 10
Democratic Socialism, 23
  movement for, 237-28
Demonstration, 38
Deoband Dar-ul-Ulam, 233
Depress classes, 386
Desires, 43-44
  satisfaction of, 41-45, 48-49
Distinction between beneficial and harmful desires, 45
Devotional Cult, 70
Dharma, 13, 20-23, 25-27, 34-35, 84-88, 90-91, 98-100, 124-28, 160-65, 239-40, 289-90, 308-10, 314-18, 323, 338, 346-47
  categories of, 9-10
  corruption of, 22
  essentials of, 1-15
  objectives of, 9-10
  perception of, 281-82, 314-15
  protection of, 34
Dharma and Politics, 97-105
Dharmacharan, 127
Dharma-danda, 131
Dharma Rajya, 129-30, 132, 194-95
Dharmashastra, 14, 83-84, 90-91, 98-101, 104
Dharmasutras, 83
Dharma Tatva, 15, 127-28, 132
Dharma Yudh, 241
Dichotomy between private and public morality, 35, 289-90
Differences between Dharma and Religion, 121-22
Differences between *Hindutva* and Hinduism, 118-19
Differences between Islam and Buddhism, 62-63
Disciplines, 47-48
Distinguish between monoism and monotheism, 149
Distinguish between mundane and ultra-mundane, 10
Doctor, Adi H., 16, 145
Dogmatism, 199
Dominion States, 319
Dravidian, 52

East India Company, 178, 204
Economic nationalism, 161
Economic policies, 183
Education for All, 176
Election Commission, 80
Engineer, Asgar Ali, 19, 211

Encountering religion, 202
Enlightenment, 38-39
Eternal (*Sanatan*), 14
Ethical principle, 168
Evil customs, 176
Extremism, 74

Faraizi movement, 204
Fascism, political system of, 22
Fascist Grand Council, 209
Fascist Hindu Raj, 19, 207
Fatwa, 233
Forced conversions, 71, 75
Foreign policies, sin types of, 102
Freedom movement, 264
Fundamentalism, 68-70, 73-75

Ganas, 91
Gandhian decentralization policy, 283-84
Godse, Nathu Ram, 342
Gokhale, Gopal Krishan, 17, 171, 264
  abilities in art of political management, 163
  approach to contemporary problems, 164-65
  politics of, 168-69
  political ideas of, 17, 162-63
  spiritualization of politics, 160-70
Gramrajya, 274
Gram Swarajya, 373
Gujarat movement, 368
Guru Govind Singh, 110, 343
Guru Nanak, 66, 343
Guru Tegbahadur, 115
Gurukulas, 140
Gyana Yogi, 359-60

Hadiths, 230-32
Har Har Mahadeva, 64
Heimsath, Charles C., 142
Hindu *Bhakti*, 52
  movement of, 78
Hindu Code Bill, 322
Hindu devotional reform movement, 71
Hindu dharma, 20, 118-120, 239-40, 343-48
Hindu fundamentalism, 74-75
Hindu law of Inheritance, 154
Hindu Mahasabha, 78, 108, 299, 313
Hindu Mystic saints, 70
Hindu nationalism, 266, 306-07
Hindu religious orders, 62-63
Hindu Sanghatan Movement, 118
Hindu-Muslim communities, 61-64
  food, basic activities, 65
Hindu-Muslim Cooperation, 167-68, 266-67, 311-12, 338
Hindu-Muslim rivalry, 206
Hindu-Muslim Unity, 267-68, 338-39
Hinduism, 16, 20-22, 61-64, 66-68, 72-74, 77-79, 118-20, 137-39, 148-50, 173-74, 186-88, 208-09, 239-40, 242-44, 311-12, 337-40
Hindustani language, development of, 274
Hindutva, 14, 75, 109-117
  characteristics of, 111-12
  concept of, 107-10
  essential of, 118
  requisites of, 114-15
Hitler, 132
Hopkins, E.B., 68
Hume, A.O., 171

Idol worship, 138-39
Incarnations, 72
Indian economic development, 259
  policies, 183-84
Indian Freedom movement, 74, 269-70
Indian fundamentalsim, 68-70

Indian National Congress, 171-72, 216, 218, 299, 301, 311, 320, 328-30, 332
Indian nationalism, 107-110, 265-66
Indian polity, 294
Indian religious, quest for synthesis in, 51-56
Indira Gandhi, 368, 376
Industrial capitalism, 181
Industrialisation, 38, 42, 273-74
  process of, 40
Inheritance, 93-94
  Hindu Law of, 154
Interstate relations, 102
Islam, 19, 68-70
  against missionary criticism, 228
Islamic Personal Law, 69
Islamic sufism, 52

Jaeger, Warner, 33, 34, 35
Jain philosophy, 73-74
Jainism, 56-57, 64-65, 173-74, 346-48
Jallianwala Bagh tregedy, 364
Jamiyat-al-Ulema, 210
Janapada, 101
Janakas, 86
Janata Party, 369
Jangam, R.T., 20, 245
Jati dharma, 85
Jati Pratha, 341
Jayaprakash Narain, 24, 271-72, 363-380
  agitation, time-bound programme, 369-70
  appelation of, 376
  critics of, 378
  dacoit menace, 367-68
  foreign affairs, 367-68
  Gujarat movement, 368
  ideology of, 371
  intellectual and revolutionary activities of, 370-71
  link with trade union, 368
  movement of, 376-77
  political asceticism, 368-69, 372-74
    speculation, 373
    thought, 374
  prison dairy, 373-74
  rare gesture by U.N., 369-70
  reluctant missiah, 380-82
  revolution, 377-78
  speculations, sources and development, 372-73
  Total revolution, 374-75
Jayaswal, K.P., 88, 91, 94
Jessuit Mission, 69
Jesus Christ, 25
Jha, Rakesh Kumar, 24, 345
Jha, Rudranand, 17, 171
Jha, Sureshwar, 14, 83
Jijmani Vyavastha, 341
Jinnah, Mohammad Ali, 18-19, 120
  Pakistan movement, 204
    separatism, crusade of, 202-10
  two nation perception, 208-10
Jiva, 348-49
Jivan Mukti, 355
Jnana-yoga, 66
Job Charnak, 151
John, M.S., 22, 278
Joshi, M.M., 167
Judaism, 80, 173

Kabir, 65, 77
Kafir-i-Azam, 216
Kali, worship of, 16-17, 148
Kalidasa, 52, 73, 153
Kaliyuga, 17
Kama, 9, 13, 41-42, 49-50
Karl Marx, 239, 247, 299
Karl Popper, 379
Karma, 240, 359
  concept of, 188-90
Karmayoga, 66, 188, 190, 359-60

Karmayogi, 282, 359
Kashmir, 132, 150
Kaushik, Asha, 18, 202
Kaushik, P.D., 15, 97
Kaushik, S.N., 18, 202
Kautilya, 97-98
mandal theory of, 103-05
Kazimi, M.R., 18, 20, 186, 225
Khajuraho, 52
Khan Abdul Gaffar Khan, 267
Khan, Sir Syed Ahmed, 20, 204, 228-34
educational programme of, 225-235
growth of Ideas in education, 214-15
safarnama, 216
views on society and religion, 218-20
Khawaja, Fariduddin, 213
Khilafat, 130
battle of, 74
movement of, 18, 198, 205, 207, 311
Kisan movement, 328
Kingship, concept of, 99-100
Kshatr dharma, 241
Kumbh Mela, Haridwar, 135
Kundilini, 240
Kunzru, H.N., 167
Kuo-Min Tang, 329

Lady Hastings, 152
Lala Lajpat Rai, 187, 313
Languages, 51-52
Leon Trotsky's permanent revolution, 375
Liberal Hindu, 339
Liberalism, 70-72
Link between *Dharma* and *Rajniti*, 338
Lohia, Ram Manohar, 23, 340, 366
Lok Sevak Sangh, 281
Lord Buddha, 72
Lord Curzon, 187, 205
Lord Keynes, 41
Lord Krishna, 131
Lord Rama, 131

Machia Vellism, 162, 169, 278
MacIntyre, Alasdaire, 45
Maccaulayian system, 239
Madhavacharya, 339
Magsaysay Award, 369-70
Mahabharata, 34, 83, 86, 88, 91, 125, 141, 170, 193, 241
Maharaja Jaswant Singh, 137
Mahatma Gandhi, 23, 25, 49, 77-80, 140-42, 163, 174-75, 181, 247, 251-52, 267-72, 339-40, 342, 352
approach to power, 282
Champaran *Satyagraha*, 317
fight against British imperialism, 280
ideas of politics, 278
notion of *Dharma*, 282
political discourse, 278-79
political ideology, 271-72
political leadership, 290
political philosophy, 264-272, 287, 291-93
spiritualise politics, 287-88
true politics by, 288
trusteeship theory of, 274
views of politics, 284-86
Majumdar, A.K., 145
Mallik, D.N., 23, 308
Malviya, Madan Mohan, 313
Manavvad, 339
Manavadharma, 22-24, 27, 297-300, 305-06, 347
concept of, 345-46
principles of, 351-52
Manifestations, 38, 52
Manusmriti, 86, 141, 241-42
Manuvadi, dispensation, 312
Marriage system, 307
Martomea Christians, 69
Marxian communism, 272

Mathur, T.K., 19, 213
Matsyanyaya, 34, 99, 100
Max Muller, 187, 243
Mehta, Phirozshah, 161
Migration, 71
Mill, John Stuart, 16, 174
Milton Singer, 75
Mitākshara, 94
Mitra Mela, 107
Moderates, 179-80
Modern World, institutionalization of, 42
Mohammedenism, 173, 219-20
Moksha, 9, 13, 49-50, 149, 173-74, 240-43, 353
Moral education, 225-30
Morris Jones, 280
Mother Teresa, 69
Mountbattan Plan, 331
Muhamad-bin-Kasim, 69
Mujahideen, 204
Muslim communalism, 193, 198
Muslim Countries, 74-75
Muslim migrate from India to Pakistan, 313
Muslim nationalism, 208-10, 306-07
Muslim traders, 26
Muslim political rulers, 71
Muslim Saints, Sufis and Poets, 70
Mutiny of 1857, 226

Nagaland Peace Mission, 367
Naitic Viveka, 349
Namdeva, 65
Naoroji, Dada Bhai, 158, 161, 166, 171, 178-79, 182
Narendra Deva, 23
National langauge, 320
National Planning Committee, 259
Nationalism, 12-14, 18, 1064-65, 179-80, 192-93, 197-200, 265
  development of, 167-68
  early phase of, 246
  package of, 76
  wave of, 311-12
Nehru, Jawaharlal, 271, 318-20, 340
  concept of secularism, 297-300, 305-06
  ideological sources of secularism, 298-300
  measures to secularise India, 304-05
  operational secularims, 301
  secularism, symbol of, 302-03
Neo-Vendantism, 187
Niskama Karma Yoga, 190
Nitidharma, 346
Nitisastra, 83, 161
Nizamuddin Aulia, 70
Nivṛtti-dharma, 85
Non-absolutism, 79
  Jain philosophy of, 73-74
Non-Communal State, 128-29
Non-fundamentalism, 72, 78-79
Nyaya-shastra, 156

October Revolution, 365
Opposition between private and public, 35-36
Origin of State, 98-100
Organization of State, 100-11
Orthodox Hindus, 153
Orthodox nationalism, 188
Ortho-Prasix, 77

Pakistan, 19, 207, 266-68, 340
  revolution of, 208-09
  separate state of, 211
Pal, Bipin Chandra, 187
Panchayati Raj, 274-75
Pande, B.N., 13, 51
Pandey, Janardan, 21, 264
Panini, 105, 115
Parama Samya, 354
Paranjpye, R.P., 167

Parasar Smriti, 184-85
Paropkarni Sabha, 135-36
Partition of India, 270
Patel, Ballabhbhai, 318
Patil, S.H., 22, 299
Perfect harmony between Hindus and Muslims, 310
Phule, Jyotiba, 171, 175
Pitrapaksha, 310
Plato, 384
Politics, 308-10
 conceptualization of, 280-81
 spiritualization of, 168-69
Political development, 292-93
Political ideology, 202-10
Political order, 35-36
Political patriotism, 161
Political power, 283
Political revolutions, 61
Polytheism, 138
Pondicherry Model, 247-48
Poverty, 22
 removal of, 239-40
Prakrit languages, 108
Prarthana Samaj, 172, 174
Pravṛitti Dharma, 85
Prāyaścitta, 86
Prophet Muhammad, 53, 55
Protestant Reformation Movement, 149
Puranas, 84
Purna Swaraj, 259, 329
Purusharthas, 13-14, 33-38, 41-42, 49-50

Quaid-i-Azam, 210
Quazis, 69
Quit India movement, 141, 265, 268, 365
Quran, 55-58, 222-23, 230-33

Radha Krishan, 17, 160
Radhakrishnan, S., 141
Rajdharma, 14, 34, 87-89, 99, 104, 169, 297
Rajendra Prasad (former President), 308-10, 312-20, 363
 interaction in pre-and post-partition communal riots, 313-14
 perception of *Dharma*, 314
 political outlook, 321
 political relation, 323
 political thinking, 323-24
Rajgopalachari, Chakravarti, 318
Raj Narain, 368
Rajniti, 87, 168, 338, 347
Rajaniti-Ratnākara, 87
Ram-Rajya, 344, 374
Ramjee Singh, 68
Ramakrishna Mission, 76, 121
Ramayana, 83, 193, 241, 309
Ranade, Mahadev Govind, 17, 161, 171-80
 Indian economist, 181-85
 political thinkers, 177-81
 religious preacher, 172-73
 social reformer, 174-75
 Swadeshi movement, 175
Rathyatra, 116
Rationalism, 150
Rationality, 44-45
Ray, Ranjan Kumar, 21, 257
Realization, path of, 353-54
Reform Committee, 384
Relationship between man and nature, 42
Religions (*Panth*), 9, 13-15, 51-52, 68-69
 goal of, 347-48
 similarity of, 53-54
Religion and State, separation of, 70
Religious denomination, 124-30
Religious fanaticism, 25
Religious fundamentalism, 68, 240
Religious modernism, pioneer of, 145-46
Religious secularism, 128

Religious State, 129
Revival movement, 66
Revolutionary nationalism, 245-48
Revolutionary transformation, 38
Rig-Veda, 56, 97, 125
Rivers, 108
Robert Owen, 247
Roby Rajan, 287-88
Roman Catholic, 13, 54, 69
Romain Rolland, 121, 134
Romanticism, 44
Round Table Conference, 311, 319
Rowlatt Act, 364
Roy, M.N., 272, 332, 364
  assessment of the Congress and CPI, 333
Roy, Ramashray, 13, 33
Roy, Raja Rammohan, 145-50, 172-73, 179-80, 228, 342
  against *Sati* practice, 151-52
  condemnation of polygamy, 154
  criticism of Christianity, 146-47
  Indian Judicial system, 157
  political liberatism, 155-57
  religious liberalism, 16-17, 149-50
  social reform strategy, 150-52, 155-56
  vices of Hinduism, 147
Russell, Bertrand, 379
Russian politcs, 272-73

Sadhana, 76
Safarnama, 216
Saints and sufis, 66-67
Samadhi, 354
Sant Gyeneshwar, 339, 343
Samaj Samata Mandel, 386
Sam Veda, 97, 125
Samuhik Karma, 354
Samuel Gomez, 364
Samyavad, 260, 271-72
Samya yoga, 353-54, 357
  basic principle of, 355
Sanatana Dharma, 66, 119-20, 245
Sanatana Hindu religion, 309
Sandhya Upasana, 139
Saptang Theory, 100-102
Saptasindhus, 108, 110
  vedic application of, 109-10
Sarnath, monuments of, 52
Sarvajanik Dharma, 346
Sarvodaya, 183, 271-72
  movement of, 367
Sati, 147, 150-51
  abolition of, 154
  opponent of, 152-53
Sati-Pratha, 175
Satta Niti, 169
Satyug, 17
Satyagraha, 174, 181-82, 269, 289-91, 317, 334, 377-79, 385-86
Satyagrahi, 169
Savarkar, Vinayak Damodar, 14, 107-10, 112
Saxena, K.S., 15
Scriptures, 56-57, 66-67, 79-80, 148-50
Second World War, 207, 250, 318, 332
Secular State, 128-29
Secularism, 22-23, 74
  challenges to, 303-04
  concept of, 301
  ideological sources of, 298-300
  symbol of, 302-03
  two concepts of, 300-01
Self-aggrandizement, 34
Self-realisation, 39, 79
Seshadri, K., 339
Sewa Dharma, 17, 162
Shah, Ghanshyam, 379
Shah Waliullah, 204
Shankara, Monotheism of, 66
Shanakaracharya, 138, 146
Shankhdhar, M.M., 20, 238
Shariat Law, 230
Sharma, Mahesh Chandra, 15, 124

Sharma, T.R., 23, 327
Shastri, Prakash C., 23, 337
Shia political conference, 210
Shias and *Sunnis*, 241
Shitoism, 173
Shivaji Utsav, 192-93
Sikh nationalism, 306
Simon Commission, 311, 318
Singh, Bijay Dhari, 24, 363
Sir William Muir, 218
Smṛtis, 86
Smṛti Candrika, 85
Social equality and inequality, 150, 176
Social Synthesis, 61-62
Solanki, Ram Singh, 14
Spiritual creativism, 263
Spiritual discrimination, 349-50
Spiritual internationalism, 245-48
Spiritualism, 15
  values of, 22
Spiritualise politics, 287-88
Spirituality, 346-50
Srinivas, M.N., 76
Srinivas Sastri, V.S., 167
Sri Krishna, S., 24, 383
Sublimation, process of, 356
Sufism, 70
Sukshma Karma Yoga, 359
Surface between Islam and Hinduism, 62
Swadeshi, 140, 193-94
  movement, 176-77, 181
Swadharma, 140, 190, 346, 356
Swami Dayanand Saraswati, 134-140, 172-73, 177, 228
  conception of *Swarajya*, 141
  dynamic revolutionary reform movement, 139-40
  emphasized upon four factors, 140
  ideas on education, 140
  protection against external attacks, 139
  speaches of, 137
  teachings of, 15-16, 142-43
Swami Vivekananda, 76, 172-73, 177, 187, 260, 272, 280, 342, 352
  free education, 343
  humanism, 238-44
  life and thought of, 244
  teaching of universality, 239
Swarajya, 136, 140, 164-65, 193, 197-98, 259-60, 272, 338-40
  attainment of, 141
  concept of, 144-42, 194-95
Syadavada, 73
Syrian Christians, 69

Tagore, Rabindranath, 77, 258, 280, 352
Tasawwuf, 52
Technocratization, 289
Terrorism, 250
Tilak, Bal Gangadhar, 119, 171, 264, 312, 339, 353
  dharma, concept of, 190-91
  natural rights and freedom, 191
  on passive resistance, 195-96
  on individual happiness, 196-97
  orthodox nationalists, 188
  political thinking, 197
  political philosophy of, 186-200
  political remification, issues of, 188
  Swarajya, concept of, 194-95
Tippu Sultan, 71
Total Revolution, 374-75
Tarjuman-ul-Quran, 59
Theism, 173
Tri Murti, 66
Trusteeship economy, 373
Truth, 138
Tulsidas, 172, 177
Tukaram, 65, 172, 177, 248
Two cultures, amalgamation of, 64-66

Unified Humanism, 124
Unity against secessionism, 75
Universal religion, 65, 70
University of California, 364
Untouchability, 176, 383-85
Upadhayay, Deen Dayal, 15, 124-30, 132
Upanishads, 193
Utopian State, 128

Vaishnava, 339
Valmiki, 52
Valmiki *Ramayana*, 160
Varna Dharma, 85
Varna System, 341
Varnashrama dharma, 14, 85, 104
Varnashrama system, 17, 185
Varnavyavastha, 101, 139
Vedanta, monistic system, 33
Vedanta system, 48
Vedas, 52-53, 85-86, 125
Vedic dharma, 126
Verma, V.P., 90, 95, 121
Vibhajyavada, 73
Videhamukti, 361
Vidyaranga Swami, 131
Village Panchayats, 23
Vinoba Bhave, 24, 247, 251, 281, 348-52
  aphorisms, 356
  Bhoodan-Gramdan movements, 252, 345-46, 367
  concept of *Manavadharma*, 345-46
  concept of religion, 345-50
  path of education, 360-61
  sarvodaya movement, 367
  way of *karma*, 358-60
  way of knowledge, 357-58
Violent agitational method, 162
Vyasa, 52
Vyavaharika, 91-92

Wahabism, 227
War between liberal and fanatical Hindusim, 338-39
White Yajurveda, 86
Widow remarriage, 139, 176
Women education, 139-40
World religions, 68

Xenophobia, 261

Yajnāvalkya, 14, 86-87, 152
  political thinkers, 87-88
  political thought, 65-93
Yajnavalkasmriti, 86, 89-90, 91-92
Vyavahāra, 93
Yajurveda, 97, 125
Yama (God of death), 99, 341
Yoga, 358
Yogendra Singh, 76
Yugas, 184-95, 240, 242-43
Yogic Philosophy, 249
Yudhishthira, 39

Zakir Hussain, 77
Zamindars, 319
Zan-ul-Abdin, 150
Ziauddin Barni, 71
Zoroastrians, 13, 54, 57, 70, 80
  community, 25
Zorostrianism, 68, 173